CW01643414

BEYOND MATTER

The moving experiences of a scientist with the spiritual world and his afterlife research

Oliver Lazar

Information about the publisher and other books at
www.gigerverlag.ch

Edition 1.2 (2024)

8852 Altendorf, Switzerland
Phone 0041 55 442 68 48
www.gigerverlag.ch

Translated from German by Oliver Lazar
Cover photo by Stephan Langefeld
ISBN: 978-3-03933-034-8

I dedicate this book to all those courageous and honourable scientists who, without fear of personal consequences, allow themselves to be guided neither by world views nor by scientific dogmas.

Contents

Foreword

By **David Lorimer**, Editor, Paradigm Explorer, Programme Director, Scientific and Medical Network, Chair, Galileo Commission

Dr Oliver Lazar has written a landmark book combining his personal journey involving remarkable spiritual experiences and a subsequent research programme on the accuracy of mediumistic messages with a rigorous and informed critique of existing orthodoxies – usually critically unexamined - in physics, biology and neuroscience. Until his mid 40s, Oliver subscribed to orthodox scientific materialism that is hard-wired into the education system, especially with respect to biology, evolution, and the origins of life and consciousness.

Suddenly and quite unexpectedly, he finds himself catapulted into another dimension by the accidental death of one of his daughter's classmates, Joma. He experiences cosmic love and in two separate consultations, he receives subsequently verifiable information and the extraordinary message that he was Joma's father in a previous incarnation and had experienced a similar loss. If there were no truth in this insight, the bond experienced could surely not have felt so compelling. Oliver's concept of a 'main soul' in relation to the individual incarnations makes a lot of sense, especially in the light of his further research of the work of Dr Brian Weiss and others. Moreover, existential challenges and suffering seem to be necessary for growth and transformation, as argued by Dr Elisabeth Kübler-Ross.

An important leitmotif in the book and indeed in the work of the Scientific and Medical Network (https://scientificandmedical.net) and the Galileo Commission (https://galileocommission.org) is the contention that scientific materialism or scientism is in fact a belief system insofar as it marginalises and rejects evidence inconsistent with its foundational assumptions, almost like an intellectual immune response. This is true even in mainstream avenues of enquiry, and the consensus is reinforced by the peer (pressure) review system and the sociology of career success that is intolerant of deviations from the norm, as many pioneering scientists have discovered. These include Dr Pim van Lommel, cited in the book, whose work on NDEs has been attacked by dogmatic materialists. Etzel Cardeña's 2018 review article on parapsychology in the American Psychologist is another case in point, whether the so-called refutation cobbled together by well-known sceptics was published without right of reply, and argued that such phenomena are a priori impossible – hence there is no need to engage with the evidence! Materialistic peer pressure within academia and science is a serious limitation on the freedom to research spirituality and the further reaches of consciousness. However, as Jeff Kripal puts it: 'To dismiss is to miss.' And research results inconsistent with scientific materialism are rigorously excluded.

Readers will find themselves getting to grips with detailed arguments about the origins of life and the nature of chemical and molecular evolution, irreducible complexity in the light of Intelligent Design, the relationship between science – especially quantum theory - and spirituality, information theory, and the question of whether the brain gives rise to consciousness. In all of these areas, Oliver discovers that orthodox positions taken for granted and incorporated into the educational curriculum are in fact critically and empirically contested from within the disciplines themselves. Underpinning these positions is an implied defence of materialistic and reductionist approaches, which are in fact based on a series of philosophical presuppositions as demonstrated, for instance, in Collingwood's 1940 Essay on Metaphysics where he points out that 'the answer to any question presupposes whatever the question presupposes… And because all science begins with a question (for the question is logically prior to its own answer), all science begins with a presupposition.' Scientism is therefore by definition a philosophy underpinning science – it is not itself scientific, nor can it be validated by science.

Oliver proposes an expansion of the presuppositions of science while maintaining an empirical approach on a deeper evidence base, as also argued by the Galileo Report (https://galileocommission.org). To this end, he set up the EREAMS (Empirical Research into the Effectiveness and Authenticity of Messages from Spirit) research study involving two mediums and a questionnaire administered to 500 people to assess the accuracy of messages received, changes of attitude before and after the session, and the transformative effect on grief when such a loss is involved. The results are by any standard remarkable and convincing, especially as they also involve people sceptical before the session who are transformed by it. A series of charts shows results of 80 to 90% in positive response to questions about the accuracy of messages and, on the part of subjects, that they will once more meet the departed loved one. Of special interest is information unknown to and only subsequently verified by the sitter, of which many specific instances are given.

On the basis of my own decades of reading and reflection, I agree with Oliver's conclusion that we are multi-dimensional beings embedded in and shaped by a larger spiritual reality where consciousness is fundamental and love is a cosmic organising principle. In my book co-edited with Marjorie Woollacott, Spiritual Awakenings (https://spiritual-awakenings.net) featuring personal accounts of transformative experiences and processes from 57 scientists and academics, it is clear that personal transformative experience is the most powerful catalyst for a change in worldview, as is also Oliver's case. Brilliant and ground-breaking books like this one can also play a significant role for those whose minds are critically open; and for those whose opinions on these subjects are genuinely in the balance, its analytical rigour can potentially prove a tipping point towards a necessary expansion of science beyond its - sometimes stifling - materialistic limitations.

- David Lorimer -

Introduction

How does one begin to write a book that unites science and spirituality? In our enlightened, highly technological and advanced society the materialistic world view prevails as a matter of course, the view that claims that everything that exists, whether living or not, can be explained by material structures and processes. The natural sciences based on this are the cornerstones of our prosperity and progress. Without the scientific successes in medicine, industry and information technology we would no longer be able to maintain our idea of a functioning, orderly world worth living in.

But this world view is beginning to waver after many decades of scientific-materialist dominance and a social rethinking seems to be in the offing. In Chapter 2 below, *Science and* Spirituality, I will describe this change in detail. Nevertheless, anyone in our Western-orientated world who dares to mention the two terms *science* and *spirituality* in the same breath is treading on thin ice. Esotericists call you a materialist who questions everything spiritual a priori, and natural scientists call you a God-fearing creationist[1] who dogmatically follows the ideology of his faith. For many decades there has been an impassable gulf fixed between the spiritual and the scientific worlds and anyone who follows the discussions in literature, at congresses and on social networks will find irreconcilably hostile

[1] A person who believes in a literal interpretation of the biblical creation story of the origin of the universe and life.

camps that are extremely unobjective and highly emotional in their hostility. In this book I do not take anyone's side from the outset, I simply follow the factual path of the best arguments, the best evidence and the greatest probabilities, as a scientist should always do. I tread this exciting path with complete freedom, wherever it may lead me. I will not mince my words, especially when I critically question long-established structures and views. I see it as my duty as a scientist to publish my findings, no matter what worldviews I shake or tempers I raise. My findings are true and honest; I do not follow any religion or ideology and my own study of afterlife contacts has been conducted with the usual scientific seriousness and methodology. I am not writing this book to proselytise or to convince other scientists of a spirit world, although I would welcome their openness on the subject. I am writing this book out of a need to share my experiences and scientific findings in the hope of helping those who are willing to accept this help. In particular, I hope to give comfort and hope to people in the deepest grief.

If someone had told me a few years ago that I would one day write a book about death, soul love and the emergence of consciousness and life, and that I would research afterlife contacts, I would probably have been deliciously amused, because all these topics played no role at all in my life as the father of a family and a computer science professor. Yet here I sit writing this book, which is the result of a fundamental change in my life. What kind of event could have changed me in such a definite way, touch my soul in such an incredible way, and completely realign my life in a way that I hadn't planned? I think it is important that you first get to know me a little better so that you can properly assess my reasoning and experiences. Don't worry, I'll refrain from a detailed life story and avoid self-portrayal here and I'll keep it short.

In the first chapter I tell you about my personal family and professional-scientific development and how I experienced my spiritual awakening completely unexpectedly through the tragic accidental death of a child who seemed to be a stranger to me. Then I take you on a journey of discovery through science and spirituality, from the oldest teachings and philosophies to current research, in order to go some way towards answering the question of who we really are at our core.

Of course you will have certain expectations of me and my book. You may be hoping for answers to spiritual questions about life, love and death, or you may simply be curious as to whether these spiritual topics can actually be recorded and substantiated with empirical research. No matter what the expectations you read this book with are, I ask you not to be dogmatic in your worldview or beliefs but to open yourself to factual argumentation on every level.

Before we get started, here are a few formal explanations about the book. For the sake of better reading flow, I always use the masculine spelling (that is I use 'he' instead of 'he or she' and 'his' instead of 'his or her' and so on) but of course this refers to all female, male and diverse persons. Since this is in large parts a scientific book you will find many references in the text to endnotes which contain details about the respective source. If necessary, page numbers or, in the case of videos, timestamps (TS) are given in the endnotes. Many sources are in German; insofar as an English version of them is also available, I have noted this accordingly.

1 And suddenly everything was different

Original version in German

Heimat

Wir haben eine Heimat,
die wir gänzlich nie verlassen.
Der Vorhang des Vergessens
lässt Erinnerung verblassen.
Mit seidig zarten Fäden
dem Schicksal stets Geleit
sind wir tief verbunden
und lernen durch viel Leid.
Im Körper durch das Leben
kehr'n wir Stück für Stück
als wundervolle Seelen
in die Heimat bald zurück.
Und wenn uns dann die Liebe
ganz bedingungslos begrüßt,
hat uns unser Sterben
unser Leben noch versüßt.

Oliver Lazar

English translation by analogy

Home

We have a home
that we never leave altogether.
The curtain of forgetfulness
makes memory fade.
With silken threads
that always accompany fate
we are deeply connected
and learn through much suffering.
In the body through life
we return piece by piece
as wonderful souls
soon return home.
And when love then
greets us unconditionally
our dying
still sweetened our lives.

Oliver Lazar

1.1 43 years of life – a prologue

A child of the Ruhr area in Germany, I was born in 1974 in the town of Essen where I experienced a happy and sheltered childhood. I had a secular[I] upbringing and led a completely normal childhood and teenage life. Topics such as illness, religion, spirituality or death played no role in my life. After graduating from Grammar school in 1994, I did my 15-month civilian service in a hospital as preparation for my subsequent medical studies at the University of Essen. I worked as a nurse in a septic surgical ward, where I was confronted for the first time, as a 19-year-old, with a normal if hard professional life. I gained a lot of valuable experience there some of which kept me intensely occupied even when I was away from the workplace. I did not find it easy to accompany the patients and their relatives in their suffering - quite often neither treatments nor care could save them from dying - and I will never forget the moment when I saw my first corpse. That open mouth, the pale skin colour, the cold body and the absolute silence still distress me today. In my youth I did not yet think deeply about what death actually means and whether there is such a thing as the soul. However, I found it deeply impressive how empty and inhuman a dead body looks. Over time I developed a routine. After all, as part of my medical studies I had to be able to dissect and explain all (and I really mean ALL!) the details of the human body on a donor corpse in the anatomy dissection course, so I got to know the human body in its entirety. In addition to anatomy I also acquired a profound knowledge of many other subject areas such as chemistry, biology, biochemistry, physiology and psychology.

After my state examination I experienced everyday clinical life in all its intensity and the idea of having to work as a doctor every day for the rest of my life caused me great unease. I was still far from having a spiritual mindset but I had always listened to my gut feeling and knew that I had to take a different professional path in order to be happy. Since I was incredibly fond of the computers and software that occupy my free time I

[I] Not ecclesiastical; one based on a natural, materialistic world view

wanted to turn this hobby into my profession. So I started an apprenticeship as a programmer at the State Office for Data Processing and Statistics in Düsseldorf and then studied computer science at the Technical University in Dortmund. In 2005, with my diploma in my pocket, I moved with my wife and our daughters to Zell-am-See in Austria where I took over the management of the IT department of the general public hospital. After a little more than two years in the Alps we went back to Germany where I wrote a doctoral thesis and obtained a doctorate from the medical faculty of the University of Essen. My dissertation concerned the effects on the sympathetic nervous system of combination therapies in the treatment of patients with hypertension. My next professional post was the Fraunhofer Institute for Microelectronic Circuits and Systems (IMS) in Duisburg, where I was able to experience the effects of applied research first-hand as a scientist and project manager in various BMBF[I]-funded research projects. Since 2012, I have been a professor of computer science at the FOM in Düsseldorf, one of Germany's largest private universities.

So these have been the stages of my life. Until I was 43 I considered the life I had to be full and complete. Family-wise and professionally everything was going wonderfully. We were happy and there was nothing to suggest that this would ever change. Spirituality, as already mentioned, played no role in my life - it simply didn't matter to me. I never thought that I would find myself at the beginning of a completely new and unexpectedly exciting stage in my life.

1.2 The day when everything changed

We are all just visitors in this world and at this time. Our souls are only passing through. Our job here is to observe, learn, grow, love and then go home again.

Aboriginal wisdom

[I] Federal Ministry of Education and Research

We had started a small car-pool in our district to take our children to school in the morning. We were three families and we always took turns. It was my turn on that Monday morning in October 2017 and I got into my car to drive the children to school; I had no idea that this day would change my life to an extraordinary degree. Just before we got to the school I saw that a traffic jam had formed at the driveway to a farm. I came to a stop a few metres before this driveway where a big truck was blocking the entrance. A man was running up and down excitedly with his mobile phone and at that moment I heard a siren and saw an ambulance coming in the rear-view mirror. I quickly pulled over so that the ambulance could get past. I saw the emergency doctor get out and after a few seconds start running frantically to get equipment out of the ambulance. I realised that the situation must be serious, that there had obviously been an accident with the truck and that the emergency doctor was fighting for someone's life. Finally, with a queasy feeling, I drove on to the school where I dropped the children off. But on this day, unsurprisingly, lessons were cancelled. Later on that morning, when my daughter came home, she stormed into the house and shouted: 'That was Joma this morning!'

Joma was one of my daughter's classmates. She was hit by a turning lorry on her way to school on her bicycle. I didn't really know this girl, she was only known to me from a few fleeting glances. I can still remember that I was no longer aware of anything else around me that day. My thoughts revolved exclusively around the girl who was a complete stranger to me, as were her parents. I constantly updated my news pages to keep up with the latest reports until finally, in the afternoon, the news that the girl had died as a result of the accident was posted on the internet with a black symbolic cross. At that moment I felt that something happened to me. I knew immediately that this was a drastic experience in my life. A world collapsed inside me. My heart was torn apart. I could no longer think clearly and I felt grief for the girl to a depth that I had never experienced before in my life. And this state simply wouldn't let me go. At first I thought that it was a natural, normal reaction and if you say that this was just usual empathy then to a certain point I would agree. But what I felt went far beyond that to the point that my family didn't recognize me any more.

I became depressed, silent and withdrawn. The pain just wouldn't go away but I couldn't explain why I was reacting in such an extreme way. What I was going through went far beyond the normal level of empathy, and the grief did not diminish but on the contrary became greater and greater. Several days later, when I was talking to my father about Joma's funeral and memorial service, he told me about a colleague at work whose child had also died a few years ago. He said that you have to take a step back so that life can go on. Take a step back? That was out of the question for me, it would have made me even more unhappy. On the contrary, I felt an irrepressible need to be close to these people. I no longer understood myself - after all I knew neither the girl nor her parents. Joma was pretty much the only child in my daughter's class with whom I had never had any real contact. But again and again a brief moment came to the front of my mind, a moment where she had passed very close to me at a school event and where our eyes met for a split second. At the time I had not noticed this inconspicuous moment at all and I was not aware that I possessed a memory of it. But since the accident this image blossomed very intensely inside me and it came in full clarity. I could think of nothing else but Joma and her parents, and at some moments I was afraid that my empathically highly-sensitive nature and these intense feelings would pull me down and even destroy me.

My own family had to live with me for several weeks and months in a quiet and withdrawn state - a kind of depressive and disturbing mood; they reacted initially with incomprehension. My wife was even worried about my mental state. Only recently, now about five years after the accident, she told me that she believed at the time that our marriage would break up because of it. For her, my excessive suffering was incomprehensible. When I told her that I felt an insatiable need within me to contact the parents and visit them she expressed doubts as to whether this was a good idea. In her eyes the parents would not need someone like me visiting them at the worst time of their lives. After all, they were strangers to us. I replied, 'It doesn't feel like that to me!' I was torn inside and constantly in dispute with myself. Should I contact the girl's parents now, as my heart was telling me in no uncertain terms, or should I listen to my head, withdraw and leave the people alone in their grief? While I was giving free rein to my thoughts and trying to assess the situation empathically, I unexpectedly had by far the most impressive and greatest experience of my life. I will try to describe to you as accurately as possible the incredible feelings that flowed through me although I simply cannot find the words that would do justice to the experience. Even if I used all the wonderful adjectives from all the languages of the world I could only describe a fraction of what I really felt. This is how it went:

I suddenly got incredible and wonderful goose bumps on the left side of my body, first on my head, then on my neck, then down my back to my legs, things I had never felt before in my life. These goose bumps ran up and down my body and I began to vibrate on the inside. Then a gigantic wave of infinitely great, unconditional love flowed through me in a dimension that cannot be compared with anything in the world. There are no earthly words to describe this boundless bliss. You can't even begin to imagine so much love, a love that exploded within me with glistening light and radiated into every single cell of my body. This light had such unimaginable power that it felt as if the whole universe was shining. Even the brightest stars paled in comparison. It was unbelievable, of enormous clarity and without any doubt absolutely real. I didn't have to think for a second whether I really perceived what I was feeling or whether I was just imagining it - it was impressive beyond all doubt.

I was aware that this love was nothing earthly. Tears of joy and happiness ran down my cheeks. It was an indescribable feeling that shook me but also scared me a little. These intense feelings definitely did not come from me. They were rather brought to me from the outside; you can't imagine something like that. After these events I was understandably quite confused and I couldn't explain what was actually happening to me. Who could I talk to about it? No one would understand or be able to comprehend it. I had the feeling that I was the saddest but at the same time the happiest person in the world. This roller-coaster ride of emotions from the deepest sadness to the greatest love and back again manoeuvred me into a bittersweet loneliness. Who or what triggered these feelings in me was not really clear to me at that moment, but Joma certainly played a part in it. I wondered whether she was opening a door to a new world within me and since that time I have realised that I was indeed experiencing soul contact with Joma, as we will see. Such feelings cannot be controlled and I had not asked for them. I was aware that this experience would change my life in a drastic and incredible way.

Eventually I began to read up on spirituality. I virtually devoured books on the subject and read more of them within a few weeks than in the previous 43 years of my life combined. I found my first answers and parallels above all in the experience reports of people who had had a near-death experience (NDEs). They reported experiences exactly like my own: an indescribable love for which there are no words and the feeling of having been in the true home of one's own soul. Like me, they all completely changed their lives and lost their fear of death in the process. While I was reading this, I kept thinking, 'Yes, exactly! I don't believe it. This is just like me.'

I read, for instance, about Anita Moorjani who received a serious cancer diagnosis in 2002 and fell into a coma four years later, terminally ill. After a while, contrary to all medical assessments, her tumours regressed completely and she found her way back to life. While in a coma, she experienced an NDE which she recounted in her New York Times bestseller *Healing in the Light: How I Defeated Cancer and Was Reborn Through a Near-Death Experience*[1] and spoke about at the 'Spirit Summit' online conference organised by the Swiss online publisher PSI ONLINE in 2019. Her words echo exactly what I too had gone through: 'I felt enveloped in a feeling of unconditional love, there are no words in our human language to describe the things I felt on the other side.'[2] I just (fortunately) didn't have to die to have these experiences, a fact which, by the way, should put a stop to all the critical doctors who, for example, consider a lack of oxygen to be the cause of the NDEs: I was definitely not suffering from a lack of oxygen during my spiritual experience and was not under the influence of any drugs. Finally, I started meditating, although I had never done it before in my life.

At first it was strange and I didn't know if I was doing it right at all. Just sitting and going into silence is damned hard and, contrary to the general belief that meditation is for relaxation, I have found that it can be incredibly upsetting and exhausting. When you are confronted with your deepest inner feelings and issues meditation can quickly become an emotional roller-coaster. But over time I developed a certain routine. I meditated purely intuitively, got those goose bumps more and more often and had the vibrations and tingles combined with an incredible amount of love.

During this time it became clear that writing poetry was a good outlet for me (as it still is) and a very good way to express my feelings. I had never been interested in poetry before, let alone written a poem myself. But somehow these poems were just in my head and I couldn't help but write them down. You will find some of them in this book (with the originals in German). In the English translation the rhymes and the feelings naturally get a bit lost. I apologise for this.

Original version in German	*English translation by analogy*
Rainbirds	***Rainbirds***
Bin ein Vogel! Will nicht fliegen!	*I'm a bird! Don't want to fly!*
Muss mein Trübsal erst besiegen.	*Must conquer my gloom first.*
Schwarze Federn, Schnabel stumm.	*Black feathers, beak silent.*
Sitz' im Baum apathisch 'rum.	*Sitting apathetically in the tree.*
Hab' dir ein schönes Nest gebaut,	*I've built you a nice nest*
hast mir dein Leben anvertraut.	*You trusted me with your life.*
Bist jetzt einfach abgestürzt,	*Now you've just crashed,*
dein Leben tragisch abgekürzt.	*Your life tragically cut short.*
Sitz' auf meinem Ast allein.	*Sitting on my branch alone.*
Gewöhne mich ans Einsamsein.	*Getting used to being alone.*
Nichts im Leben hat mehr Sinn.	*Nothing in life makes sense anymore.*
Nehm' die Leere einfach hin.	*Just accept the emptiness.*
Sehr vertraut kommt eine Meise,	*Very familiar comes a titmouse,*
sitzt neben mir und flüstert leise:	*Sits beside me and whispers softly:*

'Ein Seelenpartner ist ein Segen, wir Vögel singen auch bei Regen.'	*'A soul mate is a blessing, We birds sing even when it rains.'*
Oliver Lazar	*Oliver Lazar*

A few months after Joma's accident I had booked an appointment for an aura reading with a reputable and renowned spiritual teacher called Nina Herzberg. As I was sitting in my car and driving south my heart was racing, I was terribly excited, so excited that I couldn't even eat. Nina had been a great comfort to me via many helpful YouTube videos during my difficult time. Nina was trained by Pascal Voggenhuber, one of Europe's best-known mediums from Switzerland, and she practices according to the tenets of British Spiritualism as is usual for a reputable medium. In that practice a strict distinction is made between sensitivity, mediumship and reading auras. In Chapter 7 below (*Is there evidence for a spirit world?*) I will explain in detail the concepts of sensitivity and mediumship in interaction with clairvoyants. An afterlife contact according to British Spiritualism works with evidentiary proof. This means that messages from the deceased are only of value if the deceased can clearly prove who he is, for example by mentioning circumstances that only he and his relatives can know. But I had not booked an afterlife contact, the appointment was only supposed to be about my aura.

The aura is an energy field that surrounds us and stores all our experiences and feelings, at least that is what is understood in spiritual circles. During the car journey conflicting thoughts kept coming up in me, some of which I laughed at, shaking my head. What am I doing? I wondered. How could a completely secular scientist with a doctorate in natural sciences throw everything he had learned about the world and life overboard to meet with a medium? Was I being taken in by a quack or was there really more to it than that? On the other hand I had experienced and felt some incredibly impressive things, things from another world, things that could not be explained by materialistic science. Deep inside myself I knew the truth and had known it for a long time, but my mind kept fighting against it. I did what I have always done in life when in such situations: I followed my intuition and my heart. I was able to re-ignite this attitude, and the excitement was suddenly joined by a feeling of radiant joy.

From my aura reading appointment I hoped to be able to learn more about myself and my incredible experiences in a direct conversation. As I sat in Nina's practice, I had no idea that this appointment would once again change my life in an incredible way. She started by exploring my aura and mentioned some rather insignificant things about my parental family, which I have to admit didn't really knock my socks off. I had the feeling for the first few minutes that this conversation would be of no use and that it was a mistake to consult her. But then something unusual happened. After about five minutes, Nina suddenly said that she was sorry, but she couldn't see anything anymore and she couldn't tell me anything. At first I was very disappointed and surprised, but on the other hand I thought to myself that she was being very honest. She could have told me some irrelevant stuff for sixty minutes, but she did not. So it was clear to me that there was no mumbo-jumbo going on here and that I could rely on what she said. It was strange, but somehow I was happy that the aura reading didn't work, because my heart was longing for something else. I just didn't know what exactly it was. I then got the answer from Nina. She opened up to the spirit world and said that with absolute clarity she was sensing a girl on the other side who had died in an accident with a bicycle and asked whether I could do something with it. I never expected that this appointment would so suddenly turn into an otherworldly contact. After all, I was a stranger to Joma and I didn't feel that I of all people was entitled to an afterlife contact. But it felt incredibly great.

'Oh yes, I can do that very well', I answered her expectantly and explained that the girl was one of my daughter's classmates although she was someone I did not actually know. Nina said that the girl was very happy about this contact. My heart began to glow and I realised unmistakably in that unique moment that I had probably come for exactly this connection. Joma proved herself as well as she could - since after all I didn't know much about her. She told me about her long blonde hair and about horse riding. Nina saw her on a horse. I could relate to that, I knew she was a passionate rider. Then Nina said that Joma would show her a number one and another number one, but that didn't mean anything to me. She made it unmistakably clear that it was not an eleven, but definitely two single number ones. But two single number ones made no sense to me at all. I first suspected a date and went through all the house and telephone numbers that could have played a role. But I couldn't match them with anything significant. So at that moment neither the medium nor I could do anything with this information. Nina said that such things are quite usual and they would usually resolve themselves afterwards. And indeed a few weeks later, in a conversation with Joma's mother, I was actually able to solve the riddle of the two number ones. I asked her about the two number ones and first she didn't know what they could mean either. But when I told her about Joma showing herself riding a horse just before it changed the situation. Joma's mother looked at me in amazement and explained that shortly before her accident Joma won first place twice in an equestrian tournament. I can't even describe how wonderful it feels when such things suddenly come together coherently. Now it all made sense. Nina had told me that she had seen Joma riding a horse, and right after that she mentioned the two number ones. It seemed that it was not meant for me to know this at the time and it would only be resolved in my later conversation with the mother.

Neither the medium nor I could originally do anything with this information, yet later everything turned out to be absolutely coherent, correct and therefore authentic. So the question was where this information could possibly have come from, if not from Joma herself? In my opinion, it is precisely these messages, which can only be verified afterwards, that have a particularly great emotional effect because they make it clear once again that they cannot come from oneself but are brought to the medium from the outside. A widespread criticism of the work of a medium is the accusation that they work with psycho-tricks and only use cold or hot reading to extract information from the client. Cold reading refers to techniques used to acquire information about a stranger unnoticed during a conversation with that person in order to give the impression that the information was obtained in a psychic way. Assessments of appearance, jewellery, clothing, age, gender and so on, but also non-verbal communications, are used for this purpose. Hot reading means that one already has information about the person or soul in question in the run-up to a sitting, for example by doing research via social networks. I think that the example with the two number ones clearly shows that the accusation of cold- and hot reading can no longer be sustained.

In Chapter 7 below I will report very similar evidence in the context of our EREAMS[1] study, which is the world's largest empirical and evidence-based study on post-mortem afterlife contacts with 500 participants. The medium shared that Joma was incredibly happy that I had been able to perceive her because she had difficulty in reaching anybody else. She was so happy that she had found a way to communicate with her parents through me. But this was not the only reason for our contact and our bond. Joma said that I should not be sad - after all I was the only person in the world who had not *lost* her but who had *found* her. Since I was not allowed to meet her in this life this statement made perfect sense, which was very comforting for me. But I was very sad that I was not allowed to get to know her properly. I would have liked to have a short conversation or at least a small conscious moment with her so that I would at least have a small memory. But it is what it is, and there is also something unique about this situation for me. Everyone who knew Joma has lost her, in a way, and it would never be like it was before the accident. With me it is different. Everything I now get from her and about her is completely new to me, heart-touching and much more than I ever had from her. I rather have the feeling that I am now allowed to get to know her and this is the opposite of losing her. Despite the great sadness, I am very grateful for that.

Then I received a message through the medium that really took my breath away. She looked as if through me and said, 'A father? It's unbelievable, but it doesn't surprise me. The spiritual world confirms that you are a father.' Joma shared through the medium that I had once been her

---

[1] EREAMS: Empirical Research of the Effectiveness and Authenticity of Messages from Spirit

father in a previous life, and I too had lost her in that life and had to experience her early death. I was totally surprised and overwhelmed. This news touched my heart in a wonderful way. At that moment I didn't think about it or question the information, I just felt it. On the one hand, I was somehow totally relieved and happy about it because finally my feelings made sense. On the other hand, I hardly dared to believe it. But my mind was in stand-by mode at that moment so the critical examination of it would have to wait a bit. So much incredible information was coming at me and I was just very moved. The fact that I had suffered the same fate as Joma's parents in a previous life made me feel an even greater connection. At that point there was no doubt in my mind and I did not question anything the medium told me as a matter of course. The doubter and critical scientist in me only emerged again later. Time at the session with Nina flew by, and when we were already twenty minutes over, she said that she had to send Joma away now because new clients were coming soon. As the session drew to a close, I received a final message. Joma let me know that I should do a past-life regression if I wanted to know more. For the critical reader who might now suspect that the medium only wanted to sell me a regression and that the statement was only a business model I would like to say that Nina does not offer past life regressions and does not cooperate with other mediums who make such offers.

Even after all these events I am still a down-to-earth natural scientist and I am not easily convinced by supernatural phenomena. How could my mind construct a conclusive and comprehensible picture out of all this information and these events? On the one hand, deep inside I felt that everything was true and consistent, but on the other hand my mind needed clear evidence so that I could really believe and accept it. Just because one woman conveyed these admittedly credible-sounding messages did not mean that I had to take it all at face value. I was torn. Should I now have a past-life regression or was it all just nonsense? The decision was more or less taken away from me because only two days after the appointment with the medium I became aware of an interesting event: 'Four-day seminar on reincarnation in Essen - Only two places still available'.

The seminar took place in my home town of Essen, just fifteen minutes away from where I live. It was conducted by a highly renowned medium known throughout Europe by the name of Bettina Suvi Rode (hereafter Bettina) who had been spiritually trained by James van Praagh and Gordon Smith, among others, two of the greatest mediums in the world. At this point I would like to explicitly mention that Bettina and Nina do not know each other and certainly do not work together. I can say this with absolute certainty because I have known Bettina for several years now; I meet her regularly and speak with her. Together we are the initiators of the EREAMS study. Bettina is my spiritual teacher and I did a mediumistic training with her. I am also in contact with Nina from time to time and I can guarantee that there is no collusion between these two mediums; they know each other by name but have never met or spoken. I attach great importance to this clarification because it is incredibly important for further events.

So I couldn't help it: I had to book this reincarnation seminar immediately and secure one of the last two remaining places. Three weeks later I was at this seminar and had no idea what to expect. Secretly, of course, I hoped to get more answers, maybe even messages, but I didn't have too many expectations because there were about twenty other participants besides me, and everyone brought their own fateful story. But the spirit world once again did well by me that day and I received exactly what I needed most. As luck would have it my seat was right next to the medium. Bettina is an incredibly loving woman with a warm, trusting and motherly presence. And I felt in good hands with her from the very beginning. We started with a short round of introductions, with me being the last to go. I gave my first name and told her very briefly that I had witnessed the accidental death of one of my daughter's classmates and that it had touched me so deeply. While I was talking about it, Bettina interrupted me and said, 'Yes, and the girl is here. She is standing right behind you and she says that in a previous life you were her father and that you too had lost her in that life. But it was not meant for you to happen again in this life.' At that point my jaw literally dropped. Within just three weeks two mediums who were complete strangers to me, whom I had never seen before in my life and who definitely did not know each other, were telling me exactly the same extraordinary story about my previous life. If the two mediums had just told me that I was once Joma‘s father in a previous life I think it could have been explained by association, according to the motto: 'Well, let‘s tell him that he was once the father of the child who died in the accident, then we will make him happy.' But it was different. Both mediums said, independently of each other, that I had also experienced the early death of my daughter in that life. And that is a very specific piece of information.

Bettina went on and told me about the accident in all its details, knowing absolutely nothing about me or the accident beforehand. Even if she had known my full name or email address, she would not have been able to find anything about a connection between me and the accident or the accident details in a presumptive search. Basically anything could have happened, but she gave such details as if she had been there herself. The information was so precise that it could not possibly have been explained by luck, coincidence or research. Since I didn't know all the details of the accident myself, I had it all confirmed later when I talked to Joma's parents. Not all the little details were 100 per cent correct, but about 90 per cent of the details Bettina mentioned were correct and coherent. She said that Joma had not consciously experienced the accident herself, she felt neither fear nor pain. Joma told me about it because she asked me to break the news to her parents. I can still remember my first reaction to this request very well. I thought to myself, I can't just go to her parents' house, knock on the door and say, 'Hey guys, I have a message here from your deceased daughter.' They'd think I was crazy. I first had to come to terms with it myself, accept it, understand it and believe it. For me, too, it was all new and exciting. And the sceptical scientist in me had not yet been silenced. In my first reaction I answered the medium and Joma: 'I'm sorry, I can't do that. Actually, it's none of my business. I think it would just be going too far.'

No sooner had I uttered this sentence than I realised that somehow my decision didn't feel right. Thought upon thought ran through my head. I could think of nothing else for the rest of the day and through an entire sleepless night. How much I would have loved to help the girl to whom I felt so incredibly attached! But I was afraid that I might hurt the parents even more than they were already hurt. Finally I did what I seem to do best. I listened to my heart, closed my eyes and just let myself fall into the arms of the spiritual world, a world which I now trusted more and more. I spoke to Joma and to all the other people in charge in the spiritual world and told them that I would trust them and asked them not to let me down. If I had the unique good fortune to have such a request from the spiritual world then I could not simply refuse it. If all this was really true, and so much spoke in favour of it, then I was something like Joma's last hope of getting in touch with her parents. After all, I had promised her and it was a matter of the heart to really do it. Out of a deep sense of connection I trusted and gathered all my courage. Normally one should never deliver a message from the spiritual world to someone without being asked. But in this case it seemed like the right thing to do. Nervousness, fear and awe were my companions, but my mind was made up: I couldn't disappoint the little girl after all, and even if I exposed myself to ridicule, my heart was stronger than the fear of embarrassment. Finally, I delivered Joma's message as I had promised her.

After all these events, there is no longer any doubt in my mind that Joma is indeed still there as a soul and that all my experiences and feelings are real. She still gets everything and can communicate with us. For me, this is a crystal clear proof that our consciousness cannot originate in the brain and that it must exist detached from and independent of everything material. How else could all this be explained? There is undoubtedly a bond of attachment between souls of one soul family. It isn't in every earthly life that this bond becomes visible, yet it is always present. Everyone who has ever been connected in love is separated neither by death nor by a life in which one was not allowed to get to know each other. Separation is a purely earthly experience that the soul does not know. I am completely convinced that the messages of the two mediums were absolutely authentic. I would be lying to myself if I simply ignored this clear evidence.

A very convincing fact, moreover, is that this infinite love that cannot be put into words, which flows through me in waves, and also the feeling of connectedness, *actively came to me*. I did not set out to find it myself. I did not ask for it, nor did I know that this kind of feeling even existed. When someone loses a loved one, for example when their life partner or child has died, things look completely different. For these suffering people it seems absolutely normal and also socially acceptable that in their search for love and consolation they seek refuge in faith and can find support in the idea that the soul of their dead loved-one is still with them. They often receive a deceptive encouragement from their friends out of compassion, but these same friends say behind closed doors 'it's clear that our friend is now seeking comfort in spirituality. What else can he do?' But for me, the conditions were quite different. I myself was not affected by the death. I had no occasion or psychological need for spiritual consolation and there was no reason for me to go in search of it. Nevertheless, this love from another world found me, and it was brought to me from outside. So I began my spiritual journey without having consciously sought it out. And that's what makes it so valuable to me, because I know that all of this was in my emotional world not just because I was longing for it but because it came into my life like a tornado without any desire for it and without any action on my part. I read a post on Instagram recently that describes this very aptly:

> *'Destiny is when you find something you were never looking for and then realise you never wanted anything else.'*

1.3 Thoughts on reincarnation

In the following I will not present a complete treatise on reincarnation but I think it is useful to share a few important insights with you. If you want to delve deeper into the topic of reincarnation, I can recommend the books *Spiritual Regression for Peace & Healing: Discover Your Life Mission Through Past Life Exploration*[3] by Ursula Demarmels and *The Many Lives of the Soul*[4] by Brian L. Weiss, as well as the research of Dr Jim B. Tucker (child psychiatrist and Professor of Psychiatry and Neurobehavioral Sciences at the University of Virginia School of Medicine), some of which can also be found in Leslie Kean's book *Surviving Death: A Journalist Investigates Evidence for an Afterlife*[5] which also was the inspiration for the Netflix series of the same name from 2021.

The message from Joma that I was once her father in a previous life did not let me go. I felt I had no choice other than making an intensive study of the subject of rebirth. After I experienced my spiritual awakening I also had no further doubt that we actually incarnate life after life again and again. There are many reports and much research on this subject that describe highly impressive occurrences that can ultimately only be explained by the possibility of reincarnation. One of the most famous and best documented cases is the incredible story of James Leininger, which has been published in many TV reports and in his parents' 2009 book entitled *Soul Survivor. The reincarnation of a world war II fighter pilot*[6]. The story is about a little boy in the USA who had recurring nightmares about a plane crash when he was two years old. When his parents asked him about it, he was able to give them incredible details. He said, for example, that he saw himself as the pilot of an American fighter plane and that he was attacked and shot down by Japanese planes. He could name technical details and type designations of the aircraft and his aircraft carrier (the *Natoma Bay*). He produced countless highly accurate technical drawings that a child of his age could not possibly have known about. He remembered his name and the names of his fellow fighter pilots. At first, his parents thought it was all a fantasy. They themselves were devout Catholics and the subject of reincarnation had no place in their world. To show their son that he was wrong and that it was all just a bad dream they began to investigate. Hoping to learn that all the names and details mentioned by James were products of his imagination they visited an aircraft museum with World War II fighter planes. James, to their amazement, was able to describe and explain all the technical details accurately. Finally, they visited a war veterans' meeting of the Natoma Bay aircraft carrier. James was four years old at the time. He recognised many of his former comrades who were still alive and addressed them by their names. He recounted common experiences, all of which were confirmed by the veterans. His own shooting down and death could also be verified. So the parents found answers, though not the ones they had wanted. Everything pointed to the fact that their son's soul was indeed this World War II fighter pilot. It was the only logical consequence and explanation. Encouraged by the veterans, the parents decided to publish their research and findings.[7] Finally, the Leiningers made their peace with reincarnation, which henceforth found a fully-accepted place in their Catholic faith.

Probably the best-known reincarnation therapist in the world is the psychiatrist Dr Brian L. Weiss. Over several decades he led countless patients into past lives, but interestingly also partly into future lives. In his book *Same Soul, Many Bodies*, he tells of an extraordinary phenomenon that occurred with some of his patients:

> *'Some had mastered languages in their past lives that they had neither studied nor learned in this life, yet they could speak them during the session - a phenomenon called xenoglossia and an amazing proof that their reports were true.'*[8]

I asked myself how the soul must be structured and whether the soul of a deceased person could possibly incarnate again into a new life when I wanted to contact him. This is a fear expressed by many bereaved parents, that their child's soul could possibly reincarnate over the years and become someone else so that once they themselves die they would no longer be able to meet their child's soul. I have always received the same answer from spiritual teachers, an answer which is very consistent for me: a person's soul is much bigger than what makes up their current individual existence. Basically, we all have a higher self, a kind of a main soul in the spiritual world, which contains all our aspects from previous and future lives. This main soul always remains in the spiritual world, and when we incarnate only parts of this main soul are extracted, combined and formed into a new individual human soul. This constellation of soul parts is unique and will only exist once in this form. However, this human soul of an individual is permanently in contact with its main soul rather in the way of a radio link. If one has lived one's life as this unique person, all one's soul parts will return to the main soul complete with one's new experiences after death. So when I die one day as Oliver the soul aspects that made me up will merge again with my main soul. There I am stored eternally as Oliver and will never incarnate again in this constellation. I would therefore always be available for my surviving relatives in a possible afterlife contact and can emerge from my main soul as the individual Oliver. In these circumstances no one needs to fear that the soul of a loved one has already reincarnated and can no longer be encountered. In a new incarnation new parts of my main soul would again be combined and a new individual would be formed. This new individual soul would then also carry the experiences and memories of me (Oliver).

So when Joma speaks of me having once been her father, these were not the identical individual soul parts that made up Joma, but they were other parts of her main soul. And the same is true of me. I was not the soul Oliver in this previous life, but another individual soul made up of parts of my main soul. In my present life as Oliver I have a permanent connection to all soul parts through the permanent link to my main soul and thus also to my previous life as the father of the girl; her soul is now also available in Joma. It is hard to understand this in our present human state when we all perceive ourselves so clearly as individuals on earth. I imagine it in such a way that when we return to our main soul we will become aware that as human beings we have actually only slipped into a role. We will perceive ourselves as a whole main soul, but we can slip back into the respective roles of our lives at any time.

1.4 My life 2.0

I have become a different person. To express this in the language of a computer scientist, I would say that I received an update to version – '2.0'. My spiritual awakening gave me the feeling of having been reborn. However, one must not forget that we not only carry wonderful things from other lives but also the worst feelings such as infinite pain, sadness and longing. My problem was to find someone with whom I could share my love and sorrow without jealousy, incomprehension or alienation. I believe that strangers can perhaps understand things like this better than immediate friends and family and even though I now receive an incredible amount of support, especially from my wife, I still have the feeling at times that no matter what I say, think or feel, I first have to check whether I could hurt anyone in my own or Joma's family. Understandably, hardly anyone has an idea of how I feel about it because it doesn't make any sense from the outside. I know it's incredibly difficult to understand and it seems absurd and beyond our human horizon of experience. So I have learned that I find security in solitude and silence when I am feeling bad because it is precisely in such moments that the presence of the spiritual world surrounds me full of understanding and love.

The changes in my world view and personality are also reflected amazingly accurately in the work on near-death experiences by the Dutch cardiologist Dr Pim van Lommel. In van Lommel's study people who have had a near-death experience state that their 'interest in spirituality, meditation, prayer and surrender to the will of God increased, while at the same time there was a marked decline in church attendance and a lower appreciation of institutionalised religious practice.'[9] For example, before their NDE, only 32 per cent of those affected believed they were guided by God; after the NDE, the figure was an incredible 86 per cent![10] Although I was not dead, I have had very similar experiences and I can confirm all the above points for myself.

However, I think it is important to differentiate the concept of God more precisely. When I speak of God, I mean neither an ecclesiastical or biblical God nor a Lord or an omniscient individual. For me, God means a spiritual world full of love and intellect, a union, a merging of souls into a great whole, the We. So my personal change has brought me much closer to God, but, like the NDE subjects, I have moved away from the institutional church and religions in general.

I have understood that here on earth in this physical life we are only passing through. The physical body is only a means of transport in the material world. When we are born we get in, when we die we get out. We incarnate to have experiences that we cannot have as a soul. We might well ask why we need to incarnate if the essence of our soul is perfect love and the spiritual world also consists only of love. But how could we understand, appreciate and perceive love if we knew nothing *but* love? Only in loss do we often recognise the truthfulness of love. Suffering and longing ultimately act as positive emotional amplifiers. Anne Frank expressed this insight:

> *'The dead get more flowers than the living because regret is stronger than gratitude.'*

I would like to illustrate this way of looking at things with a slightly less tragic example from our everyday lives. The football club FC Bayern Munich has won the German championship every year for the last ten years - since the 2012/13 season in fact. Imagine a twelve-year-old Bayern fan who, since he has been able to think consciously, has known nothing but winning and always being German champion. He would certainly perceive that with satisfaction and enjoy the situation. But if, in contrast, let's consider a fan of MSV Duisburg who has seen his club relegated several times, who has experienced all the lows and has had to fear for years that his club's licence will be revoked because the club is constantly on the verge of insolvency. If then MSV Duisburg won the championship he would look on the victory with completely different eyes and see it with a quite different intensity and quality; he would be able to recognise its true value in a way that was not at all like that of the twelve-year-old Bayern fan. He would be able to feel the club's triumph to the core and to experience it at a great emotional depth and with quivering aliveness. So, on this analogy, from a purely spiritual point of view, we see how every suffering is basically a gift, because with every suffering the ability to perceive love that awaits us all in the spiritual world increases.

Sometimes it is not necessarily about one's own experiences. There are also loving souls who sacrifice themselves more or less for others, for example, who agree to die early or have a disability, in order to help another beloved soul to have a certain experience and thus to grow. These are also destructive and painful lives full of agony and loss that we have to lead. It is precisely these lives that allow us to mature the most and give our soul growth. The medium Nina Herzberg describes it as follows:

> *'If there is no duality in the spiritual world, that is, if there is only light and love, then you will not be able to feel yourself as light and love, and therefore you come into a dual world where you perceive through pain what love means, where you feel through hatred what peace is, where you feel through physical limitations what freedom means. So, we choose this dual world on a soul level to perceive ourselves. (...) On a soul level, it's mega exciting to have suffering, even if that's terrible for you and for me from a purely human point of view and we don't understand why one should choose such a thing. (...) The spiritual world doesn't have this evaluation in it. (...) It doesn't distinguish whether something is a beautiful or a bad experience. Both are worth the same.'*[11]

Elisabeth Kübler-Ross also writes something wonderful about this in her book *On Life after Death*:

> *'Most people see all their difficult living conditions, their being tested, their tribulations, their horrors and all losses as a curse, as God's punishment, as something negative. If only one could understand that nothing that one encounters is negative, I emphasise, nothing at all! All strokes of fate, experiences of suffering and even the greatest losses one has to go through (...) are all gifts. (...) It is an opportunity given to one to grow spiritually. This is the sole reason for our existence on earth. You cannot grow spiritually when you sit in a wonderful flower garden and have someone serve you the greatest food on a silver platter. But you do grow when you are sick, when you are in pain, when you have to accept a painful loss.'*[12]

It sounds so easy when you are not affected yourself. It's not so bad, it's just for the growth of your soul (I hope you can see the irony). But tell this to parents who have lost their child. They will say that they don't care at all and that it doesn't change their pain and endless longing in the slightest. This is true and should evoke our compassion, of course, but we can reflect that we are not only human beings, we are above all souls. As souls, we have probably even chosen these strokes of fate for ourselves and written them on our soul plan. I am empathic enough to know that this way of looking at things with soul growth is not necessarily comforting - it takes away neither the pain nor the longing. Nevertheless it is true. We have to realise that as pure souls we have a very different view of things. But we still have to experience human pain and suffering because if these feelings were not real we would not learn anything.

This insight into soul growth is also conveyed to us by Catherine who, as a patient of psychiatrist Dr Brian Weiss, was in a trance during her therapy sessions and gained unexpected access to her past lives and her spiritual team of spirit guides and teachers. Weiss published these profound conversations in his book *Many Lives, Many Masters.* During one session, one of the spirit teachers spoke through Catherine. When asked why we always have to come back to earth to learn and why we can't learn this as spirit beings, Weiss received the following answer:

> *'There are other levels of learning and we have to learn some of them in the incarnation. We have to feel the pain. If you are a spirit being, you don't feel pain. It is a time of renewal. Your soul is being renewed. When you are in the physical state in your body, you can suffer. In the spiritual form you feel nothing ... There is only happiness and well-being.'*[13]

It is important to accept and endure the pain and suffering because this is the most important reason for our incarnation and our greatest learning task. However, what I have some difficulties with in this way of looking at things is the maintenance of the concept of morality. If positive and negative experiences suddenly acquire an equivalence, how can one still define a concept like morality? Is it still reprehensible to inflict suffering on another human being when it helps them grow spiritually? I must admit that this is absolutely incomprehensible to me and that I am reaching a limit with my unexpanded human understanding. Nevertheless, I am still firmly convinced that it is right to help other people and animals because it is my inner drive, my desire and what makes me fulfilled and happy. It makes my heart shine and brings me a little closer to the spiritual dimensions full of love. In the Bhagavad-Gita (see Chapter 4.3: *Involution and Vedic Mystery Knowledge*) my perception is confirmed by Krishna, who represents divinity:

> *'I am the subtle force in good deeds that brings them into harmony with the good of humanity. I am the innate urge to help others.'*[14]

In my meditations, but also in some everyday situations, for example when walking in the forest, driving in a car or listening to music, I always come back to the connection and notice a tingling, an inner vibration as well as goose bumps and touches, sometimes more and sometimes less. When it is intense I feel how indescribably wonderful it is to be in touch with the home of our souls. I definitely and without a doubt perceive it as my true home and a part of me wants nothing more than to finally be allowed to return. I find it so wonderful to live in the knowledge that no matter what may happen to me in this world I can never fall lower than into the arms of the spiritual world, my true home. I have lost the fear of death. The fear of dying is still there, of course; everyone is probably afraid of dying slowly and agonisingly from a disease or in great pain, or of having to leave their loved ones behind in mourning. But when the day of my death comes, I will greet it with a smile because I know what awaits me. As I have perceived it, there is nothing more wonderful than returning to the unconditional infinite love of the spiritual world. And whoever has felt this love, which is not of this world, only once, will feel an almost unbearable longing for it all his life. However, this is not meant to be a call to suicide; one must live one's life with all its ups and downs.

A few years ago I happened to see a report on television about people who had had near-death experiences. In an interview, a mother of two small children said that she had experienced such great love and bliss during a near-death experience in the spirit world that she did not want to go back. She had children of her own in this life and still did not want to go back. At that time I thought this woman was crazy and I could not imagine that there could be a love greater than the love for one's own children. Anyone would want to return to their children; in my eyes this woman was mentally disturbed. In this life there is surely no greater love for me than the love for my children. Yet today I can understand the woman.

Only when you have experienced it yourself can you understand it which is why I don't hold it against anyone if they don't believe these experiences a priori or can't understand them. However, I would like to emphasise, expressly, that there is no competition between earthly and heavenly love, as I will call it. It is not a competition. Rather, earthly love is a part of heavenly love. The woman who wanted to choose to remain in the spiritual world would have done so in the knowledge that she would have continued to be connected with her children. She had the certainty that there was no separation. One only feels a separation as a human being on earth, but never as a disembodied soul. That is why all the deceased are fine, because they are always connected to us, even if we cannot perceive it.

I have become aware that deep love cannot only be felt for one's own earthly family. Loving souls find each other quite independently, they recognise each other by their feelings and in their eyes. They draw each other into their lives like magnets. Sometimes they walk a long path together, and sometimes a small inconspicuous moment of meeting is enough to change your whole world (as it was with Joma and me). I have become courageous and active, as is evident in this book, among other things. For me it has become a matter of the heart to give hope and comfort to all those people who have lost their faith and, in deep mourning for loved ones, are looking into an empty, black, desolate world. Most people in our western world always need proof in order to believe something. I can understand that well and I don't want to abandon the idea of proof; but I can trust quite well in the meantime. Together with two professional, serious mediums and a psychotherapist I have empirically investigated the immortality of the soul with a scientific methodology within the scope of our EREAMS study and have achieved impressive, completely transparent and verifiable results that can no longer be ignored even by a materialistic classical natural science. Nevertheless, I am sure that the majority of rationalists and scientists will not believe our research because, in their eyes, what *must* not be *cannot* be. Christian Morgenstern's Palström holds up a mirror to all these people so wonderfully when he muses on *the impossible fact* after being run over by a motor vehicle:[15]

Original version in German	*English translation by analogy*
Die unmögliche Tatsache	***The impossible fact***
Eingehüllt in feuchte Tücher,	*Wrapped in damp cloths,*
prüft er die Gesetzesbücher	*he examines the law books*
und ist alsobald im Klaren:	*and it is immediately clear:*
Wagen durften dort nicht fahren!	*Cars were not allowed to drive there!*
Und er kommt zu dem Ergebnis:	*And he comes to the conclusion:*
Nur ein Traum war das Erlebnis.	*The experience was only a dream.*
Weil, so schließt er messerscharf,	*Because, he concludes razor-sharp,*
nicht sein kann, was nicht sein darf.	*what must not be cannot be.*

2 Science and spirituality

'In my opinion, the scientifically honourable person is the one who writes down what he has found out and also explains how he reached his conclusion. I would have to be fully distrusted and almost accused of prostitution if I were to publish only what pleases the general opinion. I am not thinking of convincing or even converting people. I see my work mainly in passing on what I have researched. Those who are ready for it will believe me. And those who are not will want to argue with the most unbelievable rationalities and know-it-alls.'[1]

Elisabeth Kübler-Ross

Why is there a separation between science and spirituality? If one is in search of truth and knowledge, one must not allow oneself to be dogmatically limited either by world views or by religions. Those who allow this confinement cannot really be in search of truth. Those who move behind rigid boundaries lose their holistic neutral view and rather find themselves forced to defend their own opinions. In discussions, I experience time and again that spiritual or extrasensory skills are denied authenticity and scientificity. In the eyes of materialists, everything that cannot be scientifically proven does not exist. This view is not only grossly negligent, but simply wrong. Is it important whether something is scientific in order for it to be real? No - materialistic science cannot have any claim to an all-encompassing understanding of reality. I know that my definition of a holistic science is certainly not that of the die-hard materialists. In my eyes good arguments, probabilities, logical conclusions and subjective experience should complement empirical science at every level. The only thing that matters is whether something is true. We do not necessarily need classical, materialistic science to determine this. Such science does not have a monopoly on knowledge and truth. The best example to justify this is love. Is love scientifically tangible, definable? Can love be scientifically proven? Of course there are attempts to do so, but these scientific findings always build on endocrinological causes and brain activity to ultimately justify the sexual attraction between man and woman with procreation. However, as I will show in Chapter 5.2 (*Love*), research into true, deep heartfelt love (for example between parents and their children) is almost non-existent. Even though brain research has made great progress, no one has yet been able to localise or even begin to fathom the origin of this kind of love. Love cannot be explained scientifically! But surely we all agree that it exists nonetheless. If a materialistic scientist were consistent he would stop loving his family because this love cannot be explained scientifically and thus, according to him, does not exist. But I have not yet met such a consistent scientist.

Original version in German

quod erat demonstrandum

'So einen Quatsch hab' ich noch nie gehört!',
schimpfte der Zweifler auf mich ganz empört.
'Und ob, kannst mir glauben, deine Seele stirbt nie.'
'Du Freak bist verrückt, beweis mir doch wie?'
Musst du ein solches Gespräch mal ertragen,
solltest du folgende Taktik dann wagen.
Frag doch den Zweifler, ob's jemanden gibt,

den er von Herzen unendlich tief liebt.
'Ich lieb' meine Frau, meine Kinder, den Hund.'
Der Zweifler, er liebt. Jetzt läuft's für mich rund.
'Wenn du sie liebst, dann beweis es mir doch!'
Er rieb sich das Kinn, überlegte dann noch:
'Die Liebe ist anders, man kann sie nicht messen.'
Das war für mich ein gefundenes Fressen.
'Nicht messbar, nicht sichtbar und trotzdem vorhanden?'
Ich glaube, er hat es jetzt langsam verstanden.

Oliver Lazar

English translation by analogy

quod erat demonstrandum

'I've never heard such nonsense!',
the doubter scolded me indignantly.
'You know, believe me, your soul never dies.'
'You freak are crazy, prove to me how?'
If you ever have to endure a conversation like that,
you should try the following tactic.
Why don't you ask the doubter if there's someone,
whom he loves with all his heart.
'I love my wife, my children, my dog.'
The doubter, he loves. Now I'm getting the hang of it.
'If you love them, then prove it to me!'
He rubbed his chin, then thought some more:
'Love is different, you can't measure it.'
This was a dead giveaway for me.
'Can't be measured, can't be seen, and yet it's there'
I think he was starting to get it now.

Oliver Lazar

How often have I seen discussions in which materialistic scientists reach the red zone of their adrenaline level while listening to the explanations of spiritual people about their experiences with the spiritual world. If you want to get some idea of this you are welcome to do so: on 16th November 2010 *Das Erste* broadcast an episode of *Maischberger* with the topic *Supernatural Abilities: Mystery or Rubbish?*[2]. You can find the link to the online video of this programme in the endnotes. Guests included the medium Kim-Anne Jannes, the doctor and psychotherapist Dr Ruediger Dahlke and two hard-nosed materialists, the psychologist Dr Colin Goldner and the physicist Prof. Dr Heinz Oberhummer. When Kim-Anne Jannes reported on her mediumistic work, she met with sheer rejection from the scientists. According to Goldner and Oberhummer the experiences being reported were nothing but hocus-pocus and charlatanry. For Oberhummer, all supernatural phenomena are a product of fantasy that do not exist in reality:

> *'I am amazed at the things that people from the esoteric scene come up with in their imagination.'*[3]

He is supported by Goldner and his remarks:

> *'There are two categories of providers in the esoteric scene. Some are really convinced that they are in possession of supernatural abilities (...) The others know exactly that they can't do anything, but make money out of the worries of others (...) Some are cases for psychiatry, others for the public prosecutor.'*[4]

Goldner rightly raises a critical point here; because there are, of course, black sheep in this industry (as in every other trade by the way) who actually have no psychic abilities, cheat their clients and take their money out of their pockets. I deeply condemn these people and their trickery, especially because they drag the work of genuine mediumistic people through the mud and make it doubly difficult for us to present authentic mediumistic work in the right light. However, Goldner classifies all others who do not deliberately cheat as crazy people, because in his eyes such supernatural abilities cannot exist. I think he has forgotten two other groups of esotericists, as he calls them. The first - and I believe the largest - group of people I would add here are those who actually possess some psychic abilities but who often do not recognise their limits and overestimate themselves. It is not uncommon for these people to have read a few esoteric books, perhaps attended a weekend seminar on mediumship and then believe they can call themselves mediums. However, when these untrained people start practising with real clients their work is irresponsible. With their actions they often only aggravate the suffering of the grieving people who come to them full of hope. There is no deliberate fraud here, but the overestimation of one's own abilities and a pathological over-motivation ultimately lead to failure and this plays into the hands of all critics of spirituality.

But then there is another, very small group of people who actually possess absolutely genuine and extremely highly-developed psychic abilities. These mediums have trained their abilities over many years and are usually trained according to the tenets of British spiritualism. These highly talented and well-trained mediums are not found on every street corner, they have been proven to deliver authentic messages from the spirit world, as I explain in chapter 7 (*Is there evidence for a spirit world?*) within the context of our EREAMS study.

Goldner's accusation that all mediums are only trying to pull money out of their clients' pockets becomes untenable if we take into account all four of these categories. For instance: all renowned mediums I have met offer a money-back guarantee. If, in an afterlife contact, no reliable evidence of the deceased person could be provided or one had the impression that it was not an authentic contact, then one does not have to pay anything. I see nothing wrong with charging for this service if it is authentic. In my opinion, to claim across the board that the aforementioned groups of people do not possess psychic abilities, but rather a psychological disorder, is only proof that one has not studied the subject intensively enough, because in my extensive research, in my own experiences and in our EREAMS study on afterlife contacts, I have had completely different findings, which I also present in this book and can scientifically prove with a high degree of probability. I cordially invite all sceptics such as Goldner, Oberhummer and many others, to take a close look at my arguments and results. Anyone who has really read these with an open mind and discovers weaknesses or contradictions or who has counter-arguments and wishes to offer criticism, is very welcome to offer corrections. But anyone who makes condescending statements about psychic abilities a priori without a profound examination of the subject matter is an opponent of science. Anyone who has watched the Maischberger discussion will have noticed that a constructive and productive exchange with emotionally-charged materialistic scientists is unfortunately not possible as a rule. In fairness, however, one must also state that there are also religious fanatics who are in no way inferior to the dogmatic scientists in their closed and rigorous manner. Unfortunately, mutual listening and respect as well as openness to factual arguments do not often stand a chance.

How did it come to this that spirituality and science went their separate ways and developed straight into opposites? The first stone was probably set rolling by the English politician and lawyer Francis Bacon (1561-1626). With considerable wisdom he saw a great potential for human development in the technical mastery of nature. Those who possessed knowledge about nature could influence world events. Bacon hoped to promote science through government funding and investor money. He also saw this aspiration to dominate nature as justified by the Bible and referred to passages in Genesis that legitimated his vision of an all-encompassing natural science as a return to the power given to man by God.[5] He coined the phrase that is still often quoted today: 'Knowledge is power.'[6] Subsequently, from the beginning of mechanistic science in the 17th century, spiritual aspects were successively and increasingly banished from the understanding of life and the world. Scientists such as Johannes Kepler, Galileo Galilei and Isaac Newton laid the foundation for an increasingly dominant materialistic view of the world. While they themselves all still believed in a creative intelligent God as the primordial creator of their discovered phenomena, from the end of the 19th century creationism was no longer able to withstand an increasingly atheistic, enlightened population, and the belief system accepted in society flipped from one extreme to the other with the widespread acceptance of materialism. After centuries of the Inquisition, witch hunts and indulgences, it was time to put the church, which was wavering in its power and credibility, in its place. Scientific findings from geology, palaeontology, biology, chemistry and physics clearly spoke against a 6,000-year-old world inhabited by Adam and Eve. The greatest contribution to the move away from a spiritual world view was probably made by the British natural scientist Charles Darwin with his theory of evolution. Even today, his theory of the origin of species, which has since been further developed, is taught as the status quo at schools and universities. I consider precisely this theory of evolution to be a central point in the discussion of science versus spirituality. I even believe that the theory of evolution is the main reason for a predominantly secular society. Why should pupils and students ever have any doubts about what is taught, because life, its origin and further development are quite naturally explained with a deceptive matter-of-factness so that everyone believes that all questions about it have been answered and all knowledge has been proven. There are no doubts, and anyone who does have doubts must inevitably be a crank or a religious fanatic. Evolution is taught and accepted as a proven fact. I wonder how our children and students would form their view of the world if Darwin's theory of evolution was not taught as an absolute incontestable truth but with all its weaknesses presented along with its strengths, with all the probabilities and improbabilities for certain scenarios and with room for objective argumentative criticism. What would be objectionable about also teaching the scientific findings that contradict Darwin's theory? What exactly these findings are, I will explain in detail in Chapter 4.1 (*Materialistic/naturalistic origins*). May I say in advance that in the end one has to expend considerably more faith for the theory of evolution than for its alternatives. I would like to see a fair and honest presentation of findings, but once again there is a large public investment in defending the materialistic world view which is sold to people as factual and rational science and the only truth. What many scientists of our time do not know or consciously suppress is that materialistic science, like any other worldview, is based only on faith, on certain principles of belief that are not questioned. Thus, objectivity, causality (cause-effect relationships), time and space are taken for granted. Quantum mechanics (see Chapter 6, *Quantum Mechanics and Spirituality*) has demonstrated very impressively that each and every one of these mentioned assumptions must be questioned.[7] Basically, through the findings of quantum mechanics, classical science has got rid of its own principles of faith, but hardly anyone seems to want to draw the right conclusions from this.

When I meet people who have lost a loved one, parents who have had to accept the death of a child, then I see how a world collapses for these people, and it makes no difference at all at first whether these people are spiritual or atheistic. They all go through the same unimaginable suffering. But as soon as it comes to the subject of comfort and healing, that changes. The materialist has already learned in school that all life is the result of purely chemical, biological and physical processes and that materialistic processes and brain activity explain our being. For such a person, the death of a loved one means the end. Natural science basically tells him, 'That's it. End, over, forever and ever! Dead is dead. You will never meet your loved one again it's absolutely certain.' What a terrible idea that is, especially since there is so much to suggest that it is not true. How sad it must be for the bereaved to look into that black empty nothingness. In view of the fact that the theory of evolution stands on such shaky ground I find it irresponsible, indecent and dishonest to sell this theory as proven fact. We humans are far more than our physical bodies, and this has been proven many times over in evidence-based studies produced during what is now a hundred years of research in this field. One of the main aims of this book is to reconcile science and spirituality, because in my view they are not mutually exclusive disciplines but equally valid and complementary aspects of reality.

2.1 Perception and reality

'The non-perception of something does not prove its non-existence.'

Dalai Lama

This quote from His Holiness the 14th Dalai Lama, political and spiritual leader of the Tibetans, simply and logically shows that our world has more to offer than what we can perceive. The wonderful thing about this sentence is that it can be easily understood with trivial examples from our everyday life and eventually transferred to so-called supernatural phenomena. When I want to teach my students the first steps in programming as part of their computer science studies, I like to show small entry-level projects for the Arduino microcontroller[I]. In the following, I would like to back up the Dalai Lama's statement with a practical example before we take a look at the deeper meaning behind it.

Suppose a scientist constructs himself a small weather station with such a microcontroller, a temperature sensor and a digital display. The system is plugged together and programmed in such a way that the measured voltage at the temperature sensor is converted into the appropriate temperature and shown on the display. From the point of view of a classical natural scientist in this constructed scenario, there would only be room in this experiment for that which can be objectively measured in a repeatable manner. Accordingly, in the reality of this scientist with the small weather station, only the temperature would be a real existing value. If someone were to critically remark that there is also air pressure, and that the weather station could therefore only capture a part of reality, then one would have to agree with this criticism without a doubt. If no air pressure sensor is installed air pressure cannot be measured. Nevertheless, air pressure exists. Now, we are all aware of the existence of air pressure, but we cannot rule

[I] Microcomputer, usually for use in embedded systems (e.g. in programmable coffee machines or in control units for cars).

out the possibility that there may also be parameters unknown to us. On the contrary, I am even convinced that our world contains much more than we can perceive or our technology can measure. The German philosopher Immanuel Kant holds a very similar view. As one of the founders of modern philosophy he explains in the *Critique of Pure Reason*[8] that we can never know reality as it truly is because our reality is the product of our subjective perception of reality. We should be aware of this and aware that it does not only concern mental aspects. It can be seen in the simplest things in our everyday world. A dog with its highly developed sense of smell perceives the world quite differently from the way we do. A bee sees the world in ultraviolet light. A bat perceives the world by sending and receiving ultrasound. With a human, a dog, a bee and a bat we already have four different perceptions of reality. Which one corresponds to 'true' reality? I think we get closer to reality if we add up all the perceptions, but we should always accept that we can never know which senses and perceptions are even possible in the universe.

Few people have understood as well as the renowned quantum physicist, former director of the Max Planck Institute for Physics in Munich and peace researcher Hans-Peter Dürr how to reconcile the spiritual primordial knowledge of humanity with the modern findings of physics. As a recipient of the Right Livelihood Award (an alternative Nobel Peace Prize) and long-time companion of the German physicist and Nobel laureate Werner Heisenberg he may be called a bridge builder between world views. The following quotation from him specifically emphasises the limitations of scientific knowledge:

> *'It is grossly inadmissible and wrong to equate our perception of reality with reality per se. However, this is exactly what happens when we consider scientific knowledge to be all-encompassing.'*[9]

The German-born internationally-renowned physician and philosopher Karl Jaspers also shares this view:

'The disaster of human existence begins when what is scientifically known is taken for being itself and when everything that is not scientifically knowable is considered non-existent.'[10]

With the Dalai Lama, Immanuel Kant, Hans-Peter Dürr and Karl Jaspers, a Buddhist, a philosopher, a quantum physicist and a physician ultimately come to the same conclusion. They specifically point out that on the way to realising who we actually are and where we come from we must not rely solely on our superficial gross material perception. In other words, our perception obviously determines our reality, and our perception is through our senses. But our perception is far from being reduced to hearing, smelling, tasting, seeing, touching, the sense of balance, the sense of temperature and bodily sensation, for we humans are sensitive and mediumistically capable of far more. We should allow the idea that there are people who possess certain sensors with which so-called parapsychological phenomena (*psi*) can be detected via the clairvoyant senses (see chapter 7.1, The *EREAMS Study on the Effectiveness and Authenticity of Messages from the Spiritual World*). Scientific research that looks beyond materialistic natural science is mostly classified as pseudo-science and thus as allegedly unverifiable. This includes research into telepathic abilities, clairvoyance, near-death experiences and soul contacts. These concepts currently find no place in the academic world and are rejected a priori by faith-loyal materialists even though the findings on them have been collected according to the usual scientific standards. For me as an independent researcher this behaviour is incomprehensible because most of them, scientists whose public criticism is often hard to beat in terms of polemics, have not taken the trouble to deal seriously with the content of these studies. This view is also shared by the American neurosurgeon Dr Eben Alexander about whose near-death experience I will report in more detail in chapter 2.4.1 (*Our society is one step ahead of science*). He says of himself before he had his near-death experience:

'Like many other scientific sceptics, I refused even to look closely at the data relevant to questions about these (psychic) phenomena. I made

> *rash judgements about this data and those who provided it because my limited view did not allow me to have even a vague idea of how such things could actually happen.'*[11]

No halfway intelligent person would dare to criticise a publication on black holes in the centre of disc galaxies if they had no idea about it. But when it comes to the subject of psi, every materialistic natural scientist without the slightest idea of these topics seems to feel called upon to defame all findings on the subject. If certain people have not lived through their own spiritual experiences and have no other idea about this subject it is simply not their place to criticise. With their behaviour they abuse the universal conception of true science – true science being what claim only for themselves in their rigidly confined world of materialism. This arrogance is reflected in a statement by the physicist and philosopher Dr Lars Jaeger in his book *Science and Spirituality*:

> *'For the most part, the proponents of this thesis (of a higher intelligence for the origin of life) are not prepared to face the critical methods and reflections of the sciences.'*[12]

This is simply not true: many of these proponents are very willing to do so. Their studies and arguments are freely accessible and can be discussed publicly. But such discussion only happens rarely. Hardly any scientist takes the trouble to read these findings seriously or to try to understand them. Without any counter-arguments provided these topics are usually dismissed as crankery or creationism without any substantive discussion. I would be *very happy* if classical scientists would finally start subjecting psi studies to critical scientific debate instead of incessantly grumbling about them in a condescending manner. But because it is considered absurd from the outset this unfortunately does not happen. Therefore, I don't think it is a correct assessment to accuse psi-scientists of not facing up to a scientific discussion. Strictly speaking, it is quite obviously the materialistic scientists who do not allow this. As a true scientist one should always work with good arguments and not judge hastily and polemically.

But even the scientists who are open to these psi phenomena often do not dare to completely free themselves from the shackles of materialism. Thus, even Dr Reto Eberhard Rast, doctor and president of SWISS IANDS (Swiss Association for Near-Death Studies), is obviously unable to overcome the scientific limits imposed on him, probably also for his own protection, as his following statement shows:

> *'The review of spiritual experiences in an afterlife naturally eludes verification, since this world must be otherworldly, i.e. beyond our senses.'*[13]

I think this is a misconception, especially as the use of the word *naturally* here makes it clear that in the minds of many scientists there is an already-preconceived definition of what they consider as natural. We definitely possess more than our materialistic senses and highly sensitive and mediumistically-gifted people have access to many subtle perceptions. But it would seem that each one of us possesses these senses and we should accept that for some people it is absolutely *natural* to perceive the world through the clairvoyant senses. We need to broaden the concept of science and not just restrict research within a materialistic methodology. The view that only what can be proven materialistically is real conveys a very limited understanding of reality.

The physicist and philosopher of science Thomas Kuhn pointed out in the 1960s that there is something wrong with the majority of our scientists. He is of the opinion that conventional scientists only base their research activities on existing findings and theories, as if they were wearing blinkers, so that their results do not trigger any avalanches and fit nicely into the universally accepted materialistic paradigm.[14] I am absolutely of the same opinion here as the Dutch cardiologist and near-death researcher Pim van Lommel, that it is precisely the inexplicable phenomena - things that cannot be explained with previous scientific knowledge - that represent the greatest potential for the development of new knowledge.[15] If one were to describe all inexplicable observations sweepingly as false, manipulated or even insane the world of quantum mechanics would remain closed to us.

If one considers the processes involved in publishing a scientific paper, enormous weaknesses in the system are revealed. As a rule, a paper has to undergo a so-called peer review, which means that a small committee of scientists from the respective field reviews the submitted work. What do you think these scientists will accept and declare good? Only papers that fit the paradigm are funded. This system only promotes scientists who follow in the footsteps of their reviewers. Unconventional thinkers are weeded out without a chance, but it is precisely these revolutionaries who research at the frontiers of science who have the greatest potential for new knowledge. This review system does not promote progress and instead merely reinforces existing knowledge. Prof. Dr Eckhard Kruse confirms this assessment in his book *Der Geist in der Materie (Spirit in matter)*:

> *'No matter whether it's about funding or scientific publications, there are always reviews by a small group of colleagues from the same discipline. What the colleagues don't like is sifted out. It is a principle that promotes equality of opinion, suppresses lateral thinking and, on top of that, harbours the danger of nepotism.'*[16]

The materialistic worldview is the status quo in our society and is generally accepted as uncompromising, obviously because it is inculcated in us from childhood in school without any alternative. I ask myself why and with what right we dogmatically persist in a materialistic world view? Psi-sciences, after all, can quite easily be verified. In our EREAMS study, for example, we were able to obtain scientific evidence through objective verification of evidence. In addition to which, I consider personal experiences and reports of experiences to be legitimate sources of scientific knowledge as well. The Swiss afterlife researcher Franz Dschulnigg aptly refers to the near-death experiences of the people he interviewed as *journeys* and their accounts of them as travelogues.[17] Why should we not believe the many travelogues of people with near-death experiences? Every scientific methodology should allow for subjective verification in addition to objective verification; only in this way can we obtain a holistic picture of our reality.

Man is a subjective being. If we want to conduct research into man we must not banish subjectivity. The German philosopher and psychology pioneer Prof. Dr Johann Friedrich Herbart (1776-1841) correctly recognised 'that it is worthwhile for good reasons to think about human beings in a way other than on the basis of measurements.'[18]

Especially when it comes to researching the essence of human existence, the origin of life, consciousness and love, as well as the question of the infinity of the soul and a life before birth or after physical death, scientific knowledge quickly reaches its limits. This limitation fatally leads to the generally accepted misinterpretation that all this does not exist. The British biologist, biochemist, philosopher and best-selling author Prof. Dr Rupert Sheldrake describes today's natural science and its view of consciousness very aptly and at the same time reproachfully:

'Today's natural science rests on the assumption that reality is fundamentally material or physical in nature. There is material reality and nothing else. Consciousness is a by-product of physical brain activity. Matter is without consciousness. Evolution is not based on a plan. God exists only as an idea in the human mind, that is, in human heads.'[19]

2.2 There is more than materialism and creationism

On the cover of the German version of his book *The God Delusion*, evolutionary biologist Prof. Dr Richard Dawkins quotes himself as saying: 'I am an opponent of religion. It teaches us to be content that we do not understand the world.'[20] He also sides supportively with Eric Rothschild, the lead attorney for the plaintiffs in the 2005 Kitzmiller versus Dover Area School District lawsuit over whether Intelligent Design may be considered as an alternative theory of evolution in schools. Intelligent Design is a term first used by biochemist Prof. Dr Michael J. Behe in his book *Darwin's Black Box*. He was able to provide many conclusive arguments that certain structures and processes in biological evolution could not possibly have been implemented without intelligent planning.[21] His argumentation is purely scientific and deeply founded but, incomprehensibly, he and many other proponents are accused of creationism without any foundation. However, anyone who has actually studied Intelligent Design knows very well that creationism and Intelligent Design do not necessarily have anything to do with each other. In Chapter 4 below (*Origin and Evolution of Life*) I will go into the topics of evolution and Intelligent Design in more detail.

Rothschild praised the honourable materialistic scientists who, with the greatest effort, find ways and means to treat and cure serious illnesses and that they toil in secret without receiving royalties and lecture fees for it. On the other hand he accused those people who are concerned with spirituality, God or spiritual worlds of not doing anything that would advance scientific or medical knowledge. Moreover, they would be a bad example for future generations of scientists because they were too lazy to do proper research work and welcomed every gap in knowledge in order to justify it with God.[22] I would now like to put this praise for the scientists who were honourable in his eyes into perspective a little, because many of these scientists praised here usually do not act out of pure charity or pure passion (though there may be some here and there), but first and foremost they have their own career and reputation in mind. I am also very grateful for the scientific findings and successes of these people, from which we all benefit. These scientists do unbelievably great work and they deserve all our recognition. But anyone who has ever experienced adult scientists arguing about whose name should appear in which order on the publication also knows that the individual ego plays a very large role in this. A scientist researching psi phenomena or spirituality, on the other hand, will never do so for his ego or reputation. On the contrary, most such scientists run the risk of losing their reputation, career and job because of this kind of science (see Chapter 2.3 below, *Freedom in Research*).

All research in this field is usually done voluntarily, without payment and without any public recognition. In most cases, researchers are even ridiculed or insulted for their work, although the quality of the study design in the field of parapsychology has been proven to be particularly high. This is probably due to the fact that one knows in advance how excessively meticulous attention is paid to discrepancies and how harshly criticism is made in this marginal area of research. One quality criterion, for example, is the use of double-blind studies. The aim here is to avoid the experimenter effect, because it can happen that one's own expectations and beliefs influence the study. Double-blind studies are the tool to avoid this. This study design is widely used in clinical research. Neither the experimenter nor the participant knows who will receive which treatment. Increasingly in parapsychology double-blind and even triple-blind trials are taking place, the latter being trials where even the experimenter and evaluator do not know what outcome to expect or fear.[23] Rupert Sheldrake conducted a study over two years to examine publications in over 1,500 leading scientific journals for the use of such blind procedures.[24] In 2004, Caroline Watt and Marleen Nagtegaal repeated this study.[25] Table 2-1 shows the clear results of these two independently collected studies. The proportion of scientific studies using a blind methodology design is highest in parapsychology by a significant margin, at 85.2 per cent and 79.1 per cent respectively, compared to the other disciplines.

Table 2-1: *Proportion of blind method design in scientific studies in the various disciplines according to Rupert Sheldrake*[26]

Discipline	Sheldrake	Watt/ Nagtegaal
Physics	0 %	0.5 %
Biology	0.8 %	2.4 %
Psychology	7.0 %	22.5 %
Medicine	24.2 %	36.8%
Parapsychology	85.2 %	79.1 %

I do not consider the division made by Dawkins and Rothschild between the good and well-behaved scientists on the one hand and all the others, who must necessarily be deluded creationists, to be appropriate. I definitely don't want to take up the cudgels for the creationists here because I think it is dangerous to look for suitable arguments on the basis of religious convictions. And when Dawkins writes several times that creationists bend the scientific world and gaps in knowledge to fit their image of God, he is not always wrong. On the other hand, the question must be allowed whether materialistic scientists are not doing the same thing at some point, only that they are guided by a materialistic world view instead of God. I think there are other categories of scientists here who do serious, excellent work far from materialism and creationism, but these holistic free scientists find no place in the Dawkins universe. Perhaps it seems too dangerous to his own world view to allow such scientists to appear, so he creates this restricted two-category world for himself.

Many of these scientists, whose driving force is not creationism but the scientific desire for knowledge, have in turn asked valuable scientific questions that materialism is less able to answer than other theories. Dawkins, in my view, underestimates the fact that he is facing proven scientists here who are anything but lazy. They are brave enough to question even those things that materialists take for granted as proven long ago (for example macroevolution and the origin of species formulated in the synthetic theory of evolution). He also makes fun of the fact that there are scientists (creationists in his eyes) who question certain things on the basis of enormous improbabilities (for instance the emergence of life from dead matter). If comprehensible probabilities are no longer allowed to influence scientific knowledge, then what? A large part of scientific knowledge is gained by setting up and falsifying hypotheses. These hypothesis tests only work because they are based on probabilities. The entire scientific statistical evaluation for determining significance is based on probability principles. As long as the probabilities support one's materialistic world view, everything is obviously okay. As soon as the probabilities contradict this, they are apparently a meaningless tool of the creationists without significance for him because in his opinion great improbabilities completely dissolve again through long periods of time and the division into many small individual steps. To this end, he formulates his parabola of the *improbability mountain,* which one must not climb by ascending the steep side like the creationists, but which one must approach from the other side where there is a long 'flat' ascent.[27] However, a long flat ascent is of no use because it would have to be longer than the universe is large. Moreover, there are impassably deep ravines on this path, but Dawkins apparently looks past that.

I have the impression that it makes no difference here whether we are dealing with creationists or materialists. In the manner of Pippi Longstocking both camps make up the world as they please. Dawkins quotes in his book the geneticist Jerry Coyne, who made the following statement about science and God: 'If the history of science teaches us anything, it is this: Calling our lack of knowledge God leads nowhere.'[28] I think that a true scientist would not think of calling our Unknowing God either, but he would never banish from the gift table of all possible explanations the option that there are higher levels of reality that might also be called God. In my view, it is grossly unscientific to do this from the outset because of a materialistic worldview. I think Dawkins, Rothschild and Coyne would greatly benefit from taking a holistic view. Typically, these three gentlemen anchor all medical scientific knowledge for the good of man in a materialistic world, without exception. They thus consider all illnesses to be materialistically treatable because the causes (like everything else) can only be materialistic. But there is so much suffering in our world that has nothing to do with the body and the matter we are made of. How many people are there on earth who suffer in endless grief because they have lost loved ones? Unlike a disease, sooner or later every single person in this world will be confronted with it without exception, either through their own dying or the loss of loved ones and friends. Therefore, in my opinion, this topic should be one of the most important questions of our research, but exactly the opposite is the case. How can conventional medicine help with grief? It has only a very limited potential in this respect. In my view, it is comparable to symptomatic treatment for diseases whose cause is not known. Grief management strategies, professional grief counselling and psychotropic drugs are certainly a good support and can help those affected to find their way back into life. But they will never be able to provide comfort and healing. How much suffering could be cured if scientists who investigated supernatural phenomena and experiences with the spiritual world in a serious and methodical way would find significant positive findings and evidence in this field (which has already happened many times)? This kind of work is not laziness, it is at least as laborious and honourable as the work of materialistic scientists. Our EREAMS study showed that over 96 per cent of the 500 participants found their afterlife contact with a renowned medium to be comforting. This level of comfort cannot be achieved with a tablet or with talks about accepting and letting go in grief management with a psychotherapist. The question arises as to what the psychic medium in the case told the mourners that had this incredibly positive effect. A few kind words, pep talks and encouragement alone cannot have been enough. Anyone who has ever met parents who have lost their child knows that there is basically nothing in the world, really nothing at all, that could comfort the parents. The only thing these people want is to hold their child in their arms again. And these suffering people don't suddenly become stupid and naive and believe every comforting phrase, such as 'Your child is always with you and loves you.'

A bereaved parent would certainly not answer 'Oh yes. Thank you. Now I have found comfort.' It is only if a good afterlife medium can testify to the existence of the deceased through clear authentic evidence, only then that the messages are worth anything and only then that at least a little healing and comfort may take place. I am convinced that for mourning people a serious afterlife contact according to British spiritualism is the only way to experience comfort. But it would not stop at consolation alone. What would an evidence for the spiritual world with its immortal souls be able to do for our world, for togetherness and peace? It would mean that the value of all our actions and also non-actions would matter beyond death.

In my view, it is very likely that our human intellect and consciousness are not capable of certain higher realities. It would be arrogant to claim that we humans are capable of discovering and explaining everything and that it is only a matter of effort and time until the riddles of the world are solved. With the following simple example, I would like to show that there must also be a lack of knowledge for us humans that is to be accepted. Let us imagine the most intelligent dog in the world. Even with the greatest effort, even with the greatest patience, one would never be able to make Albert Einstein's special theory of relativity understandable to this dog. (Well, there will certainly be enough humans who would have problems with it too, but that is not the point here). Although the dog alone is not able to understand the theory due to its limited intellect, what this brilliant theory describes is obviously nevertheless true and existent (at least as long as we do not enter the quantum world, more on this in Chapter 6 below, *Quantum Mechanics and Spirituality*). Since we humans, just like dogs, are living beings on planet Earth, I ask myself how it is that dogs behave in a way that is different from ours. In short there certainly are realities that we cannot comprehend with our human intellect just as there certainly are realities that we can comprehend but the dogs cannot. There is no reason to believe that we are at the end of the intellectual rope, that would be highly arrogant and a testimony to a lack of humility. Elisabeth Kübler-Ross describes the situation in a very similar way:

> *'Humility is required of us scientists. We must humbly accept that there are many millions of things that we cannot yet understand. But that doesn't mean that just because we don't understand them, they can't exist and be realities.'*[29]

Of course, these things are not necessarily proof of God or of spiritual levels, but they do show that we have to fit into a much larger world than the one we think we know. But then to dismiss these things as unserious, nonsense or theocratic infiltration just in order to protect the material world view, and not infrequently to force the evidence into a materialistic straitjacket at all costs with extremely flimsy justifications, does not correspond to my understanding of a holistic science. In my opinion, Goethe sums it up perfectly:

> *'The most beautiful happiness of the thinking man is to have explored the explorable and to revere the inscrutable.'*[30]

In order to come closer to the true reality of our existence we should overcome these opposites of creationism and materialism. This is what Armin Risi calls for in his book *Der radikale Mittelweg (The radical middle way)*[31] which asks us to return, among other things, to the primordial human knowledge of multidimensional coexistence on both a gross physical and a subtle metaphysical plane.[32] It is astonishing and equally convincing that there are so many parallels between gross and subtle matter in the spiritual traditions of ancient civilisations across the globe.

2.3 Freedom in research

We have to ask ourselves what a holistic science has to look like in order for it to get closer to the real reality, far away from any world views or religious views. For me the most important foundation of such a science is freedom. Every scientist should have the freedom to ask any question, to develop any theory, to put forward any hypothesis, to verify or falsify it, to present his findings to the public without fear of consequences. But what sounds so self-evident here unfortunately does not correspond to common practice in our world. The freedom of research is held in chains by a materialistic dogmatism. Science and research should always be allowed to admit all justifiable possibilities first. Through falsification the falsehoods can then be discovered and discarded as possible explanations. But if the ideological materialist world view that prevails among natural scientists limits the set of possible solutions from the outset, then the question arises as to what kind of reality scientists want to discover. It is precisely this issue of giving scientists the freedom to conduct holistic research, that is to admit spiritual and supernatural realities and subjective experience as possibly accounting for certain phenomena, and to shake up ideologies and world views with good arguments, that in our current university and research landscape is greeted by strong headwind. I myself have been intensively involved in various research and development projects as a scientist at the Fraunhofer Institute and would like to give a picture here of how research works for the most part these days (at least in Germany).

Before you can even begin to do research, the first thing you have to do is secure funding. So research proposals are meticulously written and finally submitted to the Federal Ministry of Education and Research or a similar institution in the hope of getting a piece of the money pot. If the application is finally approved funds are usually available for the three years of the project's duration. Most scientists are actually paid through fixed-term annual contracts and the success of a research proposal is therefore of existential importance as it secures their livelihood, at least in the short term. Anyone who has read such a research proposal or - like me - even written one, will be blown away by the effort and scope involved. Resources, processes, strategies, methods and utilisation are planned and explained down to the smallest detail. Anyone who wrote in such a research proposal that spiritual or supernatural realities could play a role would have the proposal slapped in the face by his superior or the head of the institute because that would immediately put him out of the running for the funds to be distributed. Such realities are considered so absurd, especially in our higher education landscape, for ideological reasons alone, that anyone mentioning them is more or less labelled as crazy. Dogmatists are not only in the churches we find – they can also be found in the universities and research institutions. Ben Stein is a US actor, presenter, author and long-time journalist at the Wall Street Journal and the New York Times. In his powerful documentary film about the current research landscape, *Expelled*, he shows how top scientists have been ridiculed by their universities and employers and fired for ideological and political reasons simply for thinking outside the box of materialistic science.[33] In the Middle Ages findings that might change the prevailing view of the world got you burned at the stake. Today you lose your reputation, your career and your job. Anyone who follows these cases and the discussions in the social networks will discover that this topic is highly emotional. This also seems to me to be the reason why apparently no one from the faithful materialist camp feels even the slightest incentive to deal with the new scientific findings of these researchers; they could possibly shake their world view, and that is not allowed under any circumstances.

Instead of facing a public scientific discussion with an argumentative objectivity one encounters a completely unacceptable degree of malice based on prejudice and ignorance. Almost every scientist who does not conform to the materialist world view is accused from the outset of attempting a theocratic infiltration of society, creationism and religious fanaticism. In order to forestall any accusations that might be made against me, I would like once again to distance myself firmly from any religion or religious community at this point. I come from a secular family and even on Christmas Eve I go to the forest with my family and not to church. I don't let myself be limited in my view by any religion or by pre-determined world views. I think we would all do well to get over the hatred and agree simply to follow the path of best arguments, best evidence and greatest probabilities regardless of what world view it leads us to. Unfortunately, many scientists walk the path in exactly the wrong direction without realising it.

I think it is very important briefly to introduce here some courageous, almost rebellious scientists who have risked their careers in the name of the true values of science.

Dr Günther Bechly

- PhD in Palaeontology
- University degrees in biology, zoology, parasitology and palaeontology
- Over 150 scientific publications
- He has described over 160 new animal species
- Ten animal groups have been named after him by other scientists
- He was advised to terminate his employment by his long-time employer, the Stuttgart Museum of Natural History, because he lived according to what I have presented above as the freedom of research. 'I was told quite clearly that I was a disruptive factor, had a risk potential and undermined the credibility of the house.'[34]

Dr Richard von Sternberg

- PhD in Biology
- PhD in systems science (theoretical biology)
- Over 30 publications in peer-reviewed scientific books and publications.
- Fired from the Smithsonian National Museum of Natural History in Washington D.C. for giving credence to Intelligent Design. His department head called him an 'intellectual terrorist.'[35]

Prof. Dr Brian Josephson

- Professor of Physics at the University of Cambridge
- Received the Nobel Prize in Physics in 1973 for the discovery of the Josephson effect (tunnel effect of quantum physics).
- Later worked on mind-matter interaction and supported research for parapsychology. His former colleagues distanced themselves from him saying, 'Josephson is nuts.' Journals such as *Nature* eventually stopped publishing his papers.[36]

I find it very frightening that science is apparently no longer allowed to be science. In my view, this is a very worrying state of affairs. The freedom of science is in existential danger, and our society simply accepts this. The American physicist Julius Robert Oppenheimer formulated the idea of the freedom of science very aptly:

> *'The scientist must have the freedom to ask any question, to doubt any assertion, to search for any possible proof and to correct any errors.'*[37]

2.4 Paradigm shift

Completely unnoticed by much of the public, an incredible outcry and perhaps a turning point occurred in the scientific world in the summer of

2018. So I felt that there might indeed be some hopeful light at the end of the tunnel of scientific freedom when, in July of that year, there was a major revolution in the scientific world, one that had been barely imaginable for decades. For the first time a positive peer-reviewed study on psi abilities was published in the *American Psychologist*, one of the most prestigious psychology journals in the world. This official journal of the *American Psychological Association*, it is highly respected and articles published in it enjoy wide acceptance.

> *'This article clarifies the domain of psi, summarizes recent theories from physics and psychology that present psi phenomena as at least plausible, and then provides an overview of recent/updated meta-analyses. The evidence provides cumulative support for the reality of psi, which cannot be readily explained away by the quality of the studies, fraud, selective reporting, experimental or analytical incompetence, or other frequent criticisms. The evidence for psi is comparable to that for established phenomena in psychology and other disciplines, although there is no consensual understanding of them. The article concludes with recommendations for further progress in the field.'*[38]

In the shadow of this study I can quote the physicist, computer and cognitive scientist Douglas R. Hofstadter who publicly commented on an article in the *New York Times* about the psi-scientist and PhD social psychologist Daryl J. Bem and his parapsychological study in a very disrespectful way:

> *'If any of his claims were true, then all of the bases underlying contemporary science would be toppled, and we would have to rethink everything about the nature of the universe. For that reason, publishing an article like this is a very serious act, and it reveals that the editors are unlikely to have understood what the implications of such an article are. (…) The reason you would not even consider publishing it is that you believe deeply in science and this deep belief implies that*

the article is necessarily, certainly, undoubtedly wrong in some fashion, and that the flaws in it should be found and exposed, rather than publishing it prematurely.[39]

No one prevents Hofstadter from looking for the alleged shortcomings of Bem's study and publishing counter-arguments. Instead, however, he prefers to write an article for the *New York Times* that is completely devoid of any substantive discussion of the study. He speaks of deep faith in science, but his careful choice of words, *unsupported by any argumentation*, points more to a materialistic dogmatist than to someone who takes the trouble to read and examine such studies carefully. Would Hofstadter and the *New York Times* go so far out on a limb again after the publication in the *American Psychologist* of the peer-reviewed Cardeña study on psi phenomena cited above? Hofstadter denounces publications that in his eyes are false and premature, and the fact that he has now scored an own goal is probably an irony of fate. In Hofstadter's own words we can conclude that the Cardeña study has toppled all of the bases underlying contemporary science. Actually his study and his findings should have been on the front page of every daily newspaper and in all the news in the world, but the opposite is the case. I have the feeling that the results of the study are deliberately marginalised so that they do not spread. From my point of view the publication of psi studies in scientific journals may therefore not be desirable as it leads to a dead end. A large number of materialist scientists continue to refuse on principle to deal seriously with such findings. Even if it clearly changes nothing, even if experts confirm the authenticity of psi phenomena, I hope that this study is only the beginning of many more to investigate psi phenomena with established methods. I fear, however, that the old world views are so entrenched in the minds of materialists that not much will change at first. But it is the beginning of something new. Our world is unmistakably changing. I have hope that a new generation of open-minded scientists will grow up with a different consciousness, a distinct fairness and an unprejudiced openness towards these issues. For this to happen, however, we need to start teaching the basics of a holistic and open form of science to our children in schools. However, as long as dyed-in-the-wool materialists dogmatically cling to the traditional teaching content, the teaching of a holistic view of our world will be extremely difficult. Recently I had a small dispute with the Ministry of Education and Schools of the State of North Rhine-Westphalia about content on the subject of macro-evolution and the presumably alternativeless presentation of the origin of species via Darwinism. In Chapter 4.1: *Materialistic/naturalistic origins* I will go into more detail about this sobering attempt at scientific dialogue.

2.4.1 Our society is one step ahead of science

Our society is already quite a bit further ahead than classical science in terms of psi phenomena and spirituality and may be in the middle of a paradigm shift. More and more people are becoming aware that *there must be more to it*, and I have the feeling that the times when people looked askance at this and condemned the spiritually-minded as lunatics are slowly coming to an end. The subject of spirituality is becoming respectable, a fact which is also reflected in the popularity and success that many spiritual teachers and mediums have experienced in recent years. This trend is certainly no coincidence, but an expression of a changing society. It is not without reason that Pascal Voggenhuber, Swiss medium and bestselling author, had already published fourteen books by 2021 and that all of them were in the Swiss top ten bestseller list for non-fiction. I would also like to mention Tyler Henry here. He also has outstanding skills as a medium which he has often been able to present in his books, live performances and his TV series (notably *Hollywood Medium*) and there are many others. Many of them have been filling large halls with their lectures and seminars for years. With breathtaking afterlife contacts in live demonstrations and several TV appearances they are increasingly reaching a young audience with an easy-going and fresh manner. A medium has long since ceased to be just an old crazy person, but a normal, open-minded young person, a person like you and me. In an interview, Voggenhuber once reported that the last time in 2012 a client had to wait seven years for a consultation appointment with him. No one would wait seven years for an afterlife contact if they were not convinced of the medium's abilities and proof-heavy methodology and credibility.

Another indication that our society is becoming more and more open to such spiritual topics is the great success of the book *Proof of Heaven*[40] by the US neurosurgeon and brain specialist Dr Eben Alexander. As a classically trained doctor he long thought that the survival of the soul after physical death was out of the question. When he fell ill one day with meningitis, the doctors who treated him had very little hope for his recovery as his brain gradually lost more and more of its function. But during this process he had the impressive near-death experience which he recounts in his book. This book was published on 23 October 2012 and immediately landed at number one on the *New York Times* bestseller list for paperback nonfiction as a newcomer on 11 November 2012. According to my research, the work was listed in the top 20 for a total of 114 weeks with few interruptions, until the end of June 2015, including 46 weeks at number one. A book by a madman with a fictional story would never have successfully stayed on the bestseller list for so long. We can be grateful that courageous people like Eben Alexander dare to go public with these experiences and reveal how they change a person in an incredible way.

Let us now take a look at the 'Spirit Summit 2019' online congress organised by the Swiss online publisher PSI ONLINE, where 66 renowned spiritual teachers offered online lectures and seminars for the German-speaking region. The success of this event was enormous as the following figures from the organiser show. 'Spirit Summit 2019' had 51,779 participants and 652,337 video views with a total of 190,000 hours of videos watched. That's the equivalent of 21.7 years. Afterwards, 98.12 per cent of the participants said they had received helpful content for their lives. PSI ONLINE organised another online congress the following year in March 2020 called 'Flow Summit 2020' with 175,000 participants and 3 million video views. This equates to 850,000 hours of video consumption, the equivalent of about 100 years. The development of the Thanatos

TV YouTube channel[I] with currently (2023) over 136,000 subscribers (English + German channel) also shows a clear trend towards more interest and openness for these topics. Where in 2018 1.3 million videos were viewed, in 2019 there were already 5.6 million clicks. In just one year, the number of hours spent watching videos on this channel has increased from 260,000 to 1.4 million hours in 2019, the equivalent of almost 160 years. My interview about the EREAMS study (English + German) reached over one million views on this channel alone within the first four months - and in 2023 more than 1.7 million views[II].

The change in society is unmistakable and I find it most interesting that both the predictions from the Vedic[III] scriptures and those of the Mayan calendar about the dawn of a new age fit coherently into the current picture of change. In Vedic cosmology, a distinction is made between four ages, the so-called Yuga cycles. We are currently in the fourth cycle, which, like all yuga cycles, is subdivided into sub-cycles. However, there is no uniform division; the cycles and sub-cycles vary in length and are consistent with cosmological events. The two physicists Paul J. Steinhardt of Princeton University and Neil G. Turok of Cambridge University confirm in their book *Endless Universe - Beyond the Big Bang* that the cosmological time indications in the Vedic scriptures show astonishing similarities to the findings of contemporary astronomy.[41] So we are not talking about some invention by a primitive people but, on the contrary, in the Vedic scriptures we find a concentrated mystery knowledge of the first human advanced civilisation, knowledge of cosmology but also of spirituality and many other areas (see also chapter 4.3 below, *Involution and Vedic Mystery Knowledge*).

We are currently in the final phase of the Kali Yuga sub-cycle, which is also called the sub-cycle of the dark age or strife. The Sanskrit term Kali

---

[I] https://www.youtube.com/@ThanatosTVEN and https://www.youtube.com/@Thanatos-Television

[II] English: https://youtu.be/9e1SLF7Kg8Y and German: https://youtu.be/41uN9zv4etQ

[III] Vedas = ancient Indian sacred Sanskrit scriptures from the tradition of Hinduism

goes back to the Hindu demon Kali and can be translated as quarrel or strife. Meanwhile the Indian counting of the Kali Yuga and the start of the great cycle in the Mayan calendar (13 times 144,000 days = 5,200 years of 360 days) began practically at the same time, namely around 3,100 BC.[42] The date of the winter solstice on 21 December 2012 was very present in the media, especially due to the many reports and articles, but above all also due to the Hollywood movie *2012*. The reason is the misinterpretation of the Mayan calendar. It was believed that this date defines the end of the world, but exactly the opposite is the case. This date marks the beginning of a new cycle and thus the chance for a new beginning. Two ancient advanced civilisations, completely foreign to each other, independently give almost the same duration of about 5,000 years for this dark age, which - as we can now confirm looking back on the last 5,000 years - was determined by division and separation from the spiritual source, exploitation, power, suffering, war and a perpetual materialism. But now we are on the threshold of a new age. As it says in the Vedic scriptures, time as we know it will come to an end and after a relatively short transitional period a new age with satya-yuga-like conditions will begin. The satya yuga is the first and perfect cycle of the four yuga subcycles, it is also described as the golden age. In the Satya Yuga, people lived ethically responsible and very spiritual lives. They possessed a different condensation and vibrational frequency so that they could approach the spiritual levels. However, the term vibrational frequency is not to be interpreted here in the physical sense. It is rather an attempt to describe this phenomenon of approaching levels of consciousness appropriately. 'Satya' can be translated as truth or righteousness. It means that the vibrational frequency of the earth is being raised more and more which makes it possible for more and more people to gain access to this spiritual world. One may or may not believe the Vedic prophecies, but one should ask oneself where the people in this early period of human culture got their knowledge from? They knew about cosmology and healing, some of which we only rediscovered in our modern scientific research in modern times. How can it be that different advanced cultures that are foreign to each other are able to make similar statements about the ages at the same time? We should value this ancient knowledge and pay attention to it. It is definitely more than just invented mythology and it is not a fantasy. The timing is interesting here, and more than appropriate, because shortly after I finished writing the last paragraph above certain events in our world began to unfold. I am writing these lines in April 2020 and the Corona virus is spreading unstoppably. It is paralysing large parts of our lives and thousands of people are falling victim to the virus every day. At the moment northern Italy and New York are particularly badly affected. The rest of Europe is also at a standstill. There are contact bans, curfews, and shopping is only possible with safe distancing and a face mask. The supermarket shelves are still well stocked and only tinned of food, pasta, flour and toilet paper are constantly sold out. It is already foreseeable that the world will be a different place after the pandemic. This little virus suddenly teaches us all what really matters. Everyday things suddenly take on great value: hygiene products, food, medicine, a visit to the hairdresser and being close to our loved ones are no longer things we take for granted. The virus suddenly makes us all the same. It doesn't distinguish between rich and poor or whether we come from the West or the East. The work of cashiers, rubbish collectors, harvest workers, lorry drivers and many other professions that have hitherto received little attention from society is suddenly seen in a completely different light. We are just realising how important each and every one of us is, no matter where our place may be. I am firmly convinced that the Corona virus is part of the change. The only question is whether it will also be a change towards a more conscious and better world for all living beings on Earth. I hope so, and if we believe the predictions of the Vedic scriptures and the Mayans we may put aside our worries and our fear of lack and loss and allow a sense of hope and trust to germinate within us.

The death researcher Dr Elisabeth Kübler-Ross wrote a remarkable section in her book *On Life after Death* which, it seems, predicted the situation of the Corona Crisis:

'But my real task - and here I need your help - is to tell people that there is no death. It is very important that humanity knows this, because we are at the beginning of a very difficult time, not only for America, but for the whole planet Earth. Blame it on our own destructiveness, blame it on nuclear weapons, blame it on our greed and materialism, blame it on our behaviour in terms of pollution, blame it on us for destroying so many of nature's gifts, and blame it on us in that we have lost all true spirituality. I exaggerate a little, but certainly not too much. The only means that can bring about a change for a new age is for the earth to begin to tremble, that we may be shaken up.'[43]

2.4.2 European Values Study 2017

The European Values Study (EVS) is a series of transnational empirical long-term study on European ideas about family, work, religion, politics and society. The surveys have been conducted every nine years in so-called waves since 1981. In 2017 the fifth wave was completed and published; in total over 70,000 people in Europe were interviewed.[44] With this figure one can certainly speak of a representative sample.

***Table 2-2:** EVS 2017 - Questions of faith*

Question	GER	AT	CH	EUR
Belief in God	60.1 %	74.7 %	73.2 %	75.1 %
Belief in life after death	45.8 %	57.7 %	56.4 %	51.1 %
Belief in rebirth	24.8 %	31.8 %	27.9 %	26.7 %

I have examined the data on religious and spiritual views for Germany (D), Austria (AT), Switzerland (CH) and Europe as a whole (EUR). The fact that in a modern, predominantly materialistically oriented European society, three-quarters of all people believe in God and more than half believe in a continuation of life after death was, to be honest, very surprising to me. It is also interesting to note that Germans are significantly more reticent about these questions than Austrians, the Swiss and Europeans as a whole (11 to 14 percentage points, see Table 2-2). A survey commissioned by *SPIEGEL* (German news magazine) in 2008 shows a very similar result. According to this, 52 per cent of Germans believe in the immortality of the soul.[45]

The idea of rebirth, that is that we have already lived before this physical life and enter the earth through ever-new cycles of reincarnation, was something I would have thought would only have been believed in by highly spiritual people. But the percentage of people in Germany who believe in this is 24.8 per cent. With 83 million inhabitants (estimate of the Federal Statistical Office from January 2019), that's over 20 million people in Germany alone who believe in reincarnation. If we take a look at Europe with a total population of 746 million (estimate of the German Foundation for World Population 2018) at a rate of 26.7 per cent, there are almost 200 million people living in Europe who believe in reincarnation.

Table 2-3: EVS 2017 - What corresponds most closely to your faith?

country	personal god	spiritual world	don't know	nothing
Germany	20.6 %	42.2 %	13.5 %	23.6 %
Austria	28.5 %	47.0 %	11.2 %	13.3 %
Switzerland	20.2 %	59.8 %	11.0 %	9.0 %
Europe	42.0 %	33.2 %	12.6 %	12.2 %

Table 2-3 summarises which set of beliefs was most likely to be true for the respondents. When comparing the data from Table 2-2 on the question Belief in God with the results from Table 2-3, it becomes clear that for most people on this item the concept of God must have an overarching character. Thus not only a belief in a personal, biblical God is meant, but also a belief in a spiritual world. Incidentally, there is great diversity in

Europe on the subject of the spiritual world. In most Western European countries, the percentage of belief in a spiritual world is between 29.2 per cent (Spain) and 59.8 per cent (Switzerland), whereas in Eastern European countries there are enormous fluctuations. In Armenia, for example, only 1.3 per cent and in Georgia 5.6 per cent of the population believe in a spiritual world. Switzerland is the front-runner in this study when it comes to the subject of the spiritual world. Switzerland has a long tradition of spirituality, many of the world's most renowned mediums and spiritual teachers come from Switzerland where the topic is already widely accepted by the population. There are also renowned organisations such as the *Baseler Psi-Verein*. I am sure that this acceptance will continue to increase and will prevail in coming generations. Against the background of these figures we should no longer be afraid to discuss these topics freely, even in public. The paradigm shift towards a world in which spirituality is also seen as quite natural can no longer be denied.

3 Matter

'When we count the galaxies of the starry world or prove the existence of elementary particles, these are probably not proofs of God. But as a researcher, I am deeply impressed by the order and beauty I find in the cosmos, as well as inside material things. And as an observer of nature, I cannot reject the idea that a higher order of things exists here in advance. The idea that all this is the result of chance or mere statistical variety, that is totally unacceptable to me. There is an intelligence given here on a higher level, beyond the existence of the universe itself.'[1]

Carlo Rubbia, Nobel Prize in Physics 1984

In Chapter 1 above (*And suddenly everything was different*) I told you about the death of Joma in an accident, an event which touched and changed me in such an incredible way. Since this tragic occurrence the following thought has accompanied me: all the love that this girl had for her parents, her smile, her joy in life and everything that made her who she was can't have simply disappeared now. I suddenly realised that the matter our bodies are made of could never contain all that. I am not the first person to have this kind of thought. Rupert Sheldrake calls it a centuries-old argument about the soul-body or mind-brain problem. While for the materialists there is nothing but matter and thus no consciousness, the mechanistic dualists consider only the body as unconscious, inanimate and lower matter, and detached from it there exists the eternal, immaterial ‚conscious mind.[2] To get to the bottom of the matter, I began later to research what matter actually is and at what point matter becomes alive and whether a consciousness with feelings such as love, joy and sorrow can arise from it. But perhaps the very question of how consciousness could arise in matter is fundamentally wrong; for it is possible that consciousness exists outside the space-time dimension we know and that it has always been there and only temporarily enters into a physical connection within the concept of incarnation.

In 2005, the 125 most important questions still unanswered by science were published in a special edition of *Science*, the journal of the American Association for the Advancement of Science.[3] As it turned out the most important question was: 'What is the universe made of?' Much more interesting, however, is the question in second place: 'What is the biological basis of consciousness?' As you may have guessed I consider this second question to be fundamentally wrong. At least it must not be asked in this way, because in its present formulation it implies that there must obviously *be* a biological basis, one that only needs to be discovered precisely. This question shows quite clearly that a purely materialistic view of the world is negligently limiting and prevents us from asking the right questions at all. I hold the same view here as Pim van Lommel; the question should rather be: 'Does consciousness have a biological basis at all?' and he quite logically supplements this question with two others: 'Can we then speak of a beginning of our consciousness? And does our consciousness ever come to an end?'[4] In Chapter 5 below (*Consciousness*) I will elaborate on this topic.

In the list of the most important questions just discussed there are other interesting topics that I try to answer in this book. Thus, in twelfth place is the question: 'How and where did life arise on earth?' Not only do many scientists, lecturers and teachers believe that this question was answered long ago, but some of them come up with such incredibly flimsy, even naïve explanations, whose probabilities have been proven to be practically zero. But since these explanations fit into the materialistic paradigm set in stone they are taken as proven facts without any encouragement for people to think for themselves. The really bad thing about this is that these people are not only responsible for their own knowledge but have the responsible task of educating young people. In my view it is highly irresponsible for students and pupils to be taught these incomplete, unproven theories as a matter of course and without any alternative, as the only possible view of a modern, enlightened person. The historian of science Ernst Peter Fischer has already described it very aptly (in German): 'Ein Paradigma ist das Brett, das alle vor dem Kopf haben (...) Voraussetzungen, die keiner mehr hinterfragt.'[5], which means that a paradigm makes people blind blockheads and no one questions presuppositions any more. In Chapter 4.1.1 (*How did life originally come into being?*) I will take a closer look at this topic and show, among other things, that in our dogmatic education system there is no room allowed for scientific discussions because in the eyes of those in charge everything that is not materialistic must presumably be religious fanatical ideology. However, the fact that the question of the origin of life appears in this list at all shows that fortunately there must still be a few sensible scientists who demand further verification or falsification here.

If the materialists claim that everything we are is just the interplay of unconscious dead matter, then surely we should find answers, or at least clues about it, when we fathom the consistency of matter. In my research I have found breathtaking and surprising answers that I would never have imagined. I now see our material world with completely different eyes. You will find the results of my insightful journey in this chapter.

3.1 Where does matter come from?

There are three wonderful statements that are indisputably used again and again by esotericists and physicists alike:

- We are all stardust.
- We are pure energy.
- We are vibration.

Whereas the esotericist recognises a certain romanticism and spiritual depth in this, the physicist sees things quite soberly and hopes to have them scientifically clarified. Both have their charm, and the wonderful thing is that we can uncover great synergies here.

3.1.1 Big Bang, stars and nuclear fusion

13.7 billion years ago, our universe was created in a brutal expansion from a very hot dense point in the form of the Big Bang. This theory is generally considered to be widely confirmed[6] even though there are alternative hypotheses that can be taken seriously; but I will not go into detail on that here. In 2006, George F. Smoot was honoured with the Nobel Prize in Physics for his COBE experiment which impressively confirmed the Big Bang theory by measuring the cosmic background radiation.[7] In his TV programme *α-Centauri*, Prof. Dr Harald Lesch (most famous German TV scientist) refers to the Big Bang as 'the day without yesterday, (...) the beginning of everything'[8] although I would like to supplement this quotation with the words '.... in the material world!' because with the Big Bang, matter, energy, space and time came into being. For me, therefore, it seems to be a logical conclusion that there must then obviously also be something that exists without space and time, for the Big Bang, as I understand it, cannot possibly have come into being out of nothing. The question 'What was there before the Big Bang?' sounds very interesting at first but it is inadmissible in this form. The word 'before' implies that time must have already existed whereas the scientific consensus is that time only came into being through the Big Bang itself. For me this is already a first indication that there must obviously also be dimensions in which there is neither space nor time and quantum mechanics confirms this assessment. I will explain this to you in Chapter 6 (*Quantum Mechanics and Spirituality*) using the example of quantum entanglement and the quantum eraser, but let us return to the Big Bang and focus on the formation of matter. Our human body, weighing an exemplary 80 kg, has approximately 10^{28} particles (proton masses) from 60 different elements, and approximately 97 per cent of the mass is determined by only four elements: oxygen, carbon, hydrogen and nitrogen.

Table 3-1 shows the elemental composition of the human body, the trace elements (such as iodine, zinc, iron, fluorine, copper, manganese, selenium, chromium or cobalt) only occur in tiny amounts and are therefore summarised with a total share of < 0.5 per cent. So our body is made up of these building blocks. But how did they come into being?

Table 3-1: *The chemical elements of the human body according to Anne Marie Helmenstine*[9]

Element	Element-symbol	Mass percentage
Oxygen	O	65,0 %
Carbon	C	18,0 %
Hydrogen	H	9,5 %
Nitrogen	N	3,2 %
Calcium	Ca	1,5 %
Phosphorus	P	1,2 %
Potassium	K	0,4 %
Sulfur	S	0,2 %
Sodium	Na	0,2 %
Chlorine	Cl	0,2 %
Magnesium	Mg	0,1 %
Other	-	< 0,5 %

After the Big Bang the universe began to expand and it is still doing so today. In the first few seconds the still young universe had an enormous energy or mass density with unimaginably high temperatures of several billion degrees Celsius. However, the expansion led to a cooling. In the process, the first atomic nuclei were formed. First hydrogen, the earliest element in the universe, was formed from protons. When the protons joined with the neutrons the hydrogen isotopes deuterium and tritium were formed, a process which finally gave rise to the second element helium. There was a small period of three minutes at the beginning of our universe in which the elements hydrogen and helium could be created. Hydrogen with one proton and helium with two protons and two neutrons are at the very front of the periodic table, all the other elements behind them are therefore called the heavy elements, those which were therefore not created in the Big Bang but were 'hatched' in the stars by nuclear fusion.[10] If we now take a look at the elemental chemical composition of our bodies we must conclude that most of our physical elements must therefore have been created in large stars only after the Big Bang. The stars themselves were and are formed by the gravitational fusion of gas clouds in space. Gravity causes the material to clump together more and more until the gas cloud finally collapses under its own weight. Due to the enormous mass, and thus also energy density, a nuclear fusion process is set in motion. At the beginning a star like our sun fuses hydrogen into helium. However, if the mass of the star is large enough, the nuclear fusion process can continue after the helium. But the star must have at least five solar masses for this to happen, so that the heavy elements above helium can eventually be created, especially carbon, oxygen and nitrogen. The nuclear fusion process works until the star has reached the element iron. Iron is the last element in the periodic table for which energy can still be produced in the fusion process. After that, the nuclear fusion process ends and an iron core the size of our earth finally emerges, which shrinks in a flash under its own weight to a size of ten to twenty kilometres in diameter. The star has become a neutron star and the outer shells of its former solar structure are hitting it with a tremendous force. The German physicist and mathematician Dr Josef M. Gaßner compares this shell collapse onto the iron core to a trampoline effect. The collapsing stellar spheres are thrown back at several thousand kilometres per second.[11] In the course of this supernova explosion the original luminosity of the star increases billions of times. In the process all the heavy elements that are above iron in the periodic table are created.[12] So when someone says that we are made of stardust, it is not metaphorical but actually literal.

Isn't the thought incredible that the atoms and molecules of our bodies must have been created in a star and its supernova? It's not just our bodies, of course, but also everything else around us and everything we eat or breathe on a daily basis. However, we must not lose sight of the fact that our bodies are subject to constant change. All the molecules in our body (except for DNA) are completely replaced within days or weeks.[13] Every second of our lives, 500,000 cells are broken down and renewed.[14] The matter in our body is continuously transformed by a constant process of exchange. Even the cell membranes of our neurons, to which materialistic scientists ascribe great importance in the emergence of consciousness, are exchanged at the molecular level in a fortnightly rhythm. The idea that our consciousness is based on particles that are continuously exchanged seems to me to be just as far-fetched as the idea that consciousness arises from nuclear fusion processes in the suns. Perhaps the question of the *emergence* of consciousness is also fundamentally wrong, because an emergence implies that there can have been no consciousness to begin with. There is also the possibility that consciousness has always existed and was rather the origin for all these processes.

3.2 Matter is not material

What is matter made of? The question of the structure of matter is thousands of years old. In ancient Greece in the fifth century B.C. the philosophers Leucippus and his student Democritus coined the term *atom* (indivisible = Greek *atomos*)[15]. In their view, everything had to consist of the smallest indestructible parts and even the human soul was regarded as the product of an atomic composition that disappeared with death, whereby the atoms, as eternal particles, could form new compounds again.[16] After centuries of stagnation, it was not until the 19th century that the question of what matter is actually made of was raised again.

We are all very familiar with the mass of matter in our macroscopic world. We touch things, we use them, we can separate them from each other, we can ingest matter or hurt ourselves on it. But when we leave our macroscopic world and penetrate deeper and deeper into matter, we enter a new world that is determined by energies and nothingness. Albert Einstein already formulated the equivalence of energy and mass with his most famous formula $e = mc^2$, the constant c for the speed of light (here even squared) may be safely omitted for the representation of this connection. This is comparable to the O-notation in computer science for describing the growth of a function. Constants play no role for the fundamental consideration of a function and its growth behaviour. In other words, mass and energy are the same thing according to Einstein.

But how exactly can we understand this? If I bump into the bedpost with my foot while still half asleep in the morning after getting up, it hurts like hell, and the post is undoubtedly not energy, at least in my perception, but extremely massive and hard. But let's now get to the bottom of the matter. Let's look at a solid and smooth tabletop. Imagine that we zoom in closer and closer to the tabletop, just like in a close-up photo. Slowly, we leave the macroscopic world and the smooth surface becomes more and more like a jagged mountain range. We zoom in further and further, lattice-like molecular structures appear, which in turn consist of atoms.[17] Now we have in principle reached the level that the ancient Greeks defined as the smallest structural unit of matter. But we zoom further into the atomic shell and find, besides a lot of nothing, even more building blocks. In the centre is a tiny atomic nucleus that makes up almost the entire mass of the atom. Around this atomic nucleus, in the shell, there are, with certain probabilities, the even smaller electrons, which have a relatively huge distance to the nucleus. To visualise this, Lesch and Gaßner compare the size ratio of an entire atom to its atomic nucleus with that of a large football stadium (let's say the Signal-Iduna-Park in Dortmund) as an atom and a grain of rice in the centre of the kick-off circle as its nucleus.[18] However, while it is always very lively and atmospheric in the Signal-Iduna-Park where great football teams fight for victory and more than 80,000 euphoric fans cheer the game, in comparison there is yawning emptiness in the atomic shell except for the negatively charged electrons. We zoom in further and reach the atomic nucleus, which consists of the positively charged protons and the electrically neutral neutrons.

These nuclear building blocks determine the mass of the entire atom, so let's take a closer look at them. It doesn't matter whether we look at neutrons or protons, the following applies equally to both. We take a look inside a proton and thus reach an area where, at least according to the current state of research, we find the really smallest indivisible elementary parts, the quarks. In every proton there are three quarks (two up quarks and one down quark) and the gluons (derived from the word glue) that hold them together, and these generate one of the four fundamental forces of physics with this strong interaction. These elementary particles interact permanently with a force field that acts equally everywhere in the universe, the so-called Higgs field, named after the Scottish physicist Peter Higgs. Including this Higgs field, which was experimentally detected in the Large Hadron Collider, it turned out that all elementary particles of a definitely massive proton or neutron must be completely massless. Yes, you read that right! Where solid matter should actually be, there is de facto no mass. How is that possible? How can an atom have mass if it consists of a whole lot of nothing and massless elementary particles? Do you remember Einstein's formula? Mass is the same as energy, so the mass of matter is not solid substance, but the kinetic and binding energy of quarks and gluons. Isn't it fascinating when we look at the smallest of things that we are made up of 100 per cent energy? So it is not esoteric nonsense to say that we are pure energy. It has even been physically proven. The quantum physicist and former head of the Max Planck Institute for Physics in Munich Prof. Dr Hans-Peter Dürr even concludes that there is no matter at all:

> *'... what a surprise, we have to realise that matter basically no longer exists. In the end, there is only a kind of oscillation. Strictly speaking, there are no electrons, there is no atomic nucleus, they are actually only oscillation figures. A kind of oscillating figure like your mobile phone conversation in the electromagnetic field, nothing material in the actual sense. At this point we have lost matter.'*[19]

3.3 Mind and matter

Why did I deal with the subject of matter in the first place? I was looking for an answer as to whether Joma's soul is an integral part of the matter of her body and whether the soul also dies with physical death. Believers, philosophers and materialistic scientists have been arguing for decades about whether the matter of our body is actually involved in the emergence of our consciousness. One explanatory approach, advocated among others by the American philosopher John Searle, is that the mind arises from matter through molecular structures that become more complex. It can be compared to two hydrogen atoms and one oxygen atom, which in themselves have completely different properties from their molecular composition as a water molecule. The properties of individual atoms are not necessarily reflected in the molecular compound; completely new material characteristics are created through reorganisation and the formation of compounds. According to Searle, consciousness is also said to have arisen during such emergent processes in the brain.[20]

Some materialists even see evolutionary processes involved in the emergence of consciousness. The British psychologist Nicholas Humphrey, for example, describes the existence of consciousness as having evolutionary advantages in terms of chances of survival and reproduction, which is the only reason why it arose in the first place. According to his assessment, the brain generated feelings and desires. However, this was not real, but a production of the brain and pure imagination.[21] I share the opinion of Rupert Sheldrake, who comments on this as follows:

> *'Well, when we say consciousness is imagination, that is not an explanation of consciousness, it presupposes it. Imagination is rather a functionality of consciousness.'*[22]

The interaction of matter and atoms with mind and consciousness is also described in panpsychism[I], among other theories. One of the best-known representatives of panpsychism is the American philosopher Thomas

[I] from the Greek: pan: everywhere and psyche: spirit/soul

Nagel who in his book *Mind and Cosmos*, published in 2012, put forward the thesis that all elements of the physical world are also mental.[23] This therefore means that all atoms and molecules are said to have at least a lower form of a spirit or consciousness. The British philosopher Galen Stawson does not ascribe human consciousness to the atoms individually, but in his view an increase in the complexity of a system can also lead to the formation of a complex mind.[24] This interpretation ultimately leads to a seamlessly ensouled universe. In this context, the term World Soul is often mentioned. We find an astonishing parallel to this in the ancient Indian philosophy Vedanta[I], which is considered the basis for Hinduism and Buddhism. In it the highest concept of God (called Brahman) is described and this stands for the unchanging, immortal Absolute and the primordial ground of all being. It exists without beginning and without end. Brahman stands for the ultimate One which itself has no cause but from which all spiritual and material things have arisen.[25] Thus Brahman establishes all animate and inanimate matter.

I think that panpsychism with its animate atoms can be refuted quite easily in a critical debate. In Chapter 3.1.1 (*Big Bang, Stars and Nuclear Fusion*) I have already described how the human body is subject to constant change. Every few weeks all the atoms and molecules of our bodies are continuously and completely exchanged, but our soul shows itself to be completely unimpressed by this almost complete atomic change. It cannot therefore be possible that our spirit is the product of the atomic and molecular substance of our physical body.

The physical approach with energy and the Higgs field opens up far greater perspectives. The Higgs field is a force field that has no local source - it is non-local and equally present everywhere in the whole universe. It acts on the elementary particles of our matter which themselves consist of nothing and energy. Harald Lesch described the discovery of the Higgs field as a 'real bombshell' because 'the Higgs field is one of the initial conditions of the universe.'[26] I consider this verified interaction of the Higgs

---

[I] Literally translated: end of the Veda (completion of all Vedic knowledge)

field with the quarks to be a credible basis for the idea that there may well be other energy fields, perhaps also from spiritual planes, which can interact with the energy of our matter free of time and space. The Swiss philosopher Armin Risi describes it similarly:

> *'Theistic science postulates that the infinity of matter is embedded in an absolute, eternal field of consciousness and that this field of consciousness animates matter, fills it with IN-FORMATION and thereby allows it to take on form.'*[27]

The Higgs field has already been experimentally proven in the particle accelerator at CERN, but with the field of consciousness it is somewhat more difficult. Nevertheless, I consider this non-local and timeless field of consciousness and an animate material body that serves as a puppet for consciousness to be the most plausible approach.

4 Origin and evolution of life

'Any foolish boy can stamp on a beetle, but all the professors in the world cannot make a beetle.'[1]

Arthur Schopenhauer

One of the main reasons I wrote this book is to give comfort and hope to bereaved people in their grief and desperation. But something can only be truly comforting if it is real and true. A large proportion of people in our western world have been brought up secularly and have grown up in a purely materialistic view of the world through the influence of our school and university education and the reporting of the public media. This world view is deeply rooted and prevents an openness to spiritual topics which are usually rejected with deceptive rationality and with full conviction. The primordial theory of the origin of life and Darwin's theory of evolution are, in my opinion, the main causes of this, because they provide people with a supposedly natural explanation for our existence that is never questioned. I can only release these people from their unsound convictions if I can show them with scientific arguments that these theories do not have the steadfastness accorded to them and even contain gross errors. Only then will predominantly sceptical people be able to listen to and believe in my spiritual research. This is the reason why we cannot avoid looking at some chemical, biochemical and biological expertise in detail, because otherwise my arguments are not credible and not strong enough to shake the materialistic world view and put the natural scientists in explanatory trouble. In the following chapter you can therefore expect many technical terms and scientific approaches, but I would like to encourage you, even if you are not particularly familiar with them, to let me guide you through this sometimes difficult subject. My aim is to give everyone access to these arguments.

The question of the origin of life and the origin of species is one of the greatest mysteries of humankind. It is the irritant par excellence, and anyone who has followed the discussions between Darwinists and creationists about creation in the social media will have been almost literally struck by the viciousness and aggression from all camps. I have given up participating in discussions in this context; irrelevance and hatred prevail there and it leads nowhere. What I find astonishing, however, is that this emotional pre-occupation with the subject even extends into academic circles; even at specialist conferences and in serious scientific literature sharp hostilities can be found, giving me the impression that many materialistically-inclined scientists demonstrate a special talent in this respect. I would like to give you a small sample from my biology book *Biology for Physicians, Pharmacists and Chemists*, which was recommended to me by my university as an official textbook during my medical studies.

> *'The continuous evolution of plant and animal species since the origin of life is today the well-documented basis of our world view. But in the last century, when the doctrine of the constancy of species became untenable, the introduction of the knowledge of evolution appeared as an intellectual revolution, the aftermath of which reached into the 20th century. Even today, there are isolated exotic eccentrics who, for ideological reasons far removed from scientific knowledge, oppose the facts of evolution.'*[2]

Objectivity looks different from this and the fact that something like it is written in a university textbook published by *Georg Thieme Verlag*, one of the largest providers in the field of German-language medical publications, is incomprehensible to me. I find it significant and highly questionable. Apart from the fact that everyone who thinks differently is called an 'exotic eccentric' here and is accused of having ideological bias, the authors even claim in a tone of unimpeachable matter-of-factness that the whole of evolution has been *proven.* But this is simply not the truth; the alleged facts of evolution do not stand up to closer scrutiny at all well in many areas. The Darwinian theory of evolution is, as the name suggests, a theory, and there is some absolutely serious criticism of it. This criticism may and must be heard, especially since it comes from proven specialists and not from some ideological crackpots. In 2001, the Discovery Institute published a list under the title *A Scientific Dissent From Darwinism*[3] with the names of renowned scientists from all over the world who contradict the prevailing opinion on the Darwinian theory of evolution. This list now contains over 1,000 signatories, mainly scientists with doctorates and professors from some of the best-known universities such as Yale, Princeton, Stanford, MIT, UC Berkeley and UCLA. Time and again Darwinists try to ridicule this list by making false statements that the people on it are made up or are deluded creationists who would argue far from science. After doing the work and looking at the scientifically sound arguments that speak against Darwinism, I have also allowed myself to be added to this list. I can assure you that I am not made up and that I had to apply for this list with a letter of motivation and proof of my academic titles. Not just anyone can apply for it or use fake names and titles. One is intensively vetted before admission. Therefore, this list is absolutely authentic. I am neither a creationist nor do I belong to any religion. I have allowed myself to be included in this list solely for the sake of better arguments. Unfortunately, a scientifically sound criticism of the theory of evolution, as formulated by the scientists on this list, is all too readily associated by the public with a fundamentalist religious doctrine. Of course, it cannot be ruled out that there are also some creationists on the list, but this does not justify questioning the list as a whole. To make matters worse, if creationists hold to a literal interpretation of the Bible (with Adam and Eve and all the rest), they are ridiculed as being out of touch with reality, which is not surprising. This makes it easy for Darwinists to ridicule these people, and ultimately this list, and to let all arguments (even good ones) fall flat.[4]

I would now like to join you on the path of *objectivity* and look at the situation with common sense, holistically and detached from any special world views, and examine the various arguments which support other theories of creation, without bias. Incidentally, I consider abiogenesis and Darwin's theory of evolution to be the decisive factors why a large part of our society is convinced of a materialistic world view. Therefore, I will deal with these theories in detail. I will put scientific knowledge to the test and compare different approaches including abiogenesis and Darwin's theory of evolution, Intelligent Design, involution and Vedic mystery knowledge. Ultimately, I want to find out how exactly, and from what point in time, life began with a consciousness or a soul and whether consciousness instead arose at some point as a by-product of evolution or perhaps acted as the starting point of all developments. Basically the question arises to what extent all this can be explained exclusively by the gross material world. In a holistic view, I will therefore also include subtle materiality in my considerations. I will describe the concepts of gross and subtle materiality in more detail later in this chapter, but there is one thing we should never lose sight of: none of us was present at the origin of life. Nor has anyone succeeded in creating life in the laboratory, although scientists are regularly celebrated for this in the press, for example in the famous Urey-Miller experiment, which I discuss in more detail in Chapter 4.1.1 below (*How did life originally arise?*). In the experiment a few simple amino acids were produced, though in a biochemically unusable form, a fact which was concealed. But even if the correct amino acids had been produced as building blocks of proteins, the way to a protein and from a protein to a living organism would still be so far that the success of this experiment would honestly be a mystery to me. We will see that the insurmountable hurdles here are in the details. One thing we can agree on, however, regardless of our world view: We humans are obviously more specialised in destroying life than in creating it.

4.1 Materialistic/ naturalistic origin

The theory of a materialistic or naturalistic origin for life and for species through exclusively physical-biochemical processes within the scope of chemical and biological evolution corresponds to the current scientifically recognised state of affairs. It is taught in schools and universities (usually as a proven fact) and is not questioned by an enlightened secular population. Dr Lars Jaeger writes in his book *Wissenschaft und Spiritualität* (*Science and Spirituality)* that the view that humans, animals and plants were created by an external intelligence can no longer be seriously held by any informed person today. In his view, all living beings are the result of an evolution that began about 3.5 billion years ago.[5] I find it interesting that Jaeger does not give any room to a life-creating external intelligence, but calls those people who believe in a physical-biochemical theory of the origin of life with evolution '*informed*', although this theory contains events at several points that have a probability of zero (I describe exactly what these are in Chapter 4.1.1 below: *How did life originally arise?)*. A reasonably well-informed person should know that an event with a probability of zero definitely cannot occur, yet the theory is held on to against all logic. It is strange that spiritual people are ridiculed for their beliefs and not those who multiply their naturalistic term of life by zero and are firmly convinced that something other than zero will result. The renowned American philosopher Prof. Dr Daniel Dennett is a convinced atheist. In an interview on the YouTube channel *UnBelievable?* he says that he does not believe in anything supernatural.[6] However, I have to disagree with him, because he very much does! He's just not aware of it. One cannot free oneself from it by simply declaring oneself an atheist; that is a fallacy. For he has to believe that events which are completely ruled out from a statistical point of view, for instance the purely random formation of amino acids and proteins, have nevertheless occurred. To be honest, I find that very supernatural. This raises the question of who actually believes in the greater miracles here?

Is there scientifically comprehensible evidence for Jaeger's statement?

What exactly does he mean by an informed person? Apparently not someone who is able to overcome the confining walls of materialism. I think he rather means a typical person of our secular western civilisation, someone who has had the materialistic world view and Darwinism instilled in him at school as the absolute truth without any reference to possible weaknesses of this theory. For my part I rather consider an informed person to be someone who not only has a comprehensive education but who has not lost his own thinking and common sense. A truly informed person checks and questions the things they believe in. But we seem to have been taught not to question things at school. I was no different. Until my profound spiritual experience after Joma's accident I accepted the common doctrine on the origin of life as a matter of course for 43 years without a hint of doubt. Especially because of my medical studies I considered the current doctrine of a purely physical-biochemical origin with evolution to be an absolute and irrefutable truth that needed no further questioning. After all, recognised researchers, doctors and professors have arrived at these findings within the scope of their scientific methodology. Why should a reasonable, enlightened person doubt such a thing? And if someone had tried to teach me about the origin of life and species with an explanation other than this I would have declared them crazy, not because I had heard or checked their arguments - that seemed far too ridiculous - but because I was one hundred per cent convinced of my own knowledge and education. It was clear to me that, far from scientific knowledge, these people had only one thing in mind, namely to spread their religious views. But my spiritual experiences and feelings after Joma's accident were of such tremendous impressiveness that my thinking about it changed completely. Anyone who has experienced something like that is no longer the same person afterwards. I began to look at things more closely. Is the naturalistic explanation of the origin of life really so certain and conclusive that one can believe it without reservation? Which arguments speak for it, which against it? How does life arise from dead matter, at what point does chemistry become biology? How does highly developed life full of complex, well-coordinated processes with an intellect and feelings emerge from primitive single-celled organisms? Did the diverse creatures and plants in our world really come into being through evolution alone? To answer this, I have divided this topic into two parts. First, we deal with the fundamental question of the origin of life and then we will look at the emergence of species through evolution. In all these ways of looking at things, I don't want to lose sight of my main motivation. Joma's love, her laughter, her preferences, desires and feelings must have come from somewhere. Can the theory of evolution provide clues to the origin of her and our consciousness?

4.1.1 How did life originate?

> *'Molecules don't care about life. Organisms care about life. Chemistry, on the contrary, is utterly indifferent to life. Without a biologically derived entity acting upon them, molecules have never been shown to evolve towards life. Never.'*[7]
>
> *Prof. Dr. James Tour, Professor of Chemistry, Professor of Materials Science and Nanotechnology at Rice University in Houston/Texas*

In Chapter 3 (*Matter)* we saw how matter most probably came into being in our universe. But atoms and molecules are not alive. So we had discovered the organic-molecular basis for living systems and with the Darwinian theory of evolution we had a construct at hand, which we tried to transfer from the animal and plant world to the molecular level. But there is no empirical data or knowledge whatsoever, nor even any evidence, that there was evolution at the molecular level for the emergence of life. This idea is solely the result of an extrapolation of Darwinian evolutionary thought. The chemical facts speak in every respect against an evolutionary emergence of complex molecules such as proteins, as I will show later. The question arises as to how life can arise from dead matter, and further: Is matter alone the basis for life?

Let us first answer the question of what life actually is. There is no official, all-encompassing definition of life because there are associated aspects that are too complex. Depending on whether you ask a biologist, a chemist, a physicist or a philosopher, you will definitely get different answers for the phenomenon of life.[8] However it seems to me, at least when it comes to defining the earliest and most primitive life, that the research group around the Chilean biologist Francisco Varela has found a suitable explanation with their term *autopoiesis.*[9] 'Autopoiesis generally describes the self-creation and self-preservation of a system. According to this, living organisms are autopoietic systems - i.e. networks of processes that are active in delimited units and that are capable of producing more of themselves and maintaining themselves.'[10] Of course a complex living being such as a human being cannot be described with this definition alone. But for the time being we are only concerned here with the original transition from dead matter to a living cell. Thus, four core characteristics crystallise for my definition of life:

1) **Delimited unit:** The simplest form of life would be a single cell that forms a compartment, that is to say a space which is delimited from the environment, with a cell membrane.
2) **Self-preservation:** In order to survive a cell requires an active metabolism for the exchange of substances and energy with the environment.
3) **Reproduction:** A living cell is able of replicating itself by passing on its genetic information to the child generation of cells in a copy. This is also where the idea of evolution comes in; because random mutations in the genes can lead to altered offspring that may be able to feed and reproduce better and prevail over the original variant (at least that is the theory of evolution).
4) **Intrinsic system:** Intrinsic means from within, of its own accord. Neither membrane formation nor metabolic processes nor replication may be initiated or maintained by conscious external materially conditioned actions.

In 1958, Francis Crick published the central dogma of molecular biology, which is still accepted today - note the choice of the word 'dogma'. In it he describes DNA[I], RNA[II], proteins and the flow of information between them as the basic building blocks of life. Simplified, the scenario can be described as follows. DNA is the central information carrier of the genetic material of a living being. It contains a kind of blueprint for the composition of proteins and is found in every cell in the form of a rope-ladder-like double helix. The rungs of this strand are formed by base pairs (adenine-thymine and guanine-cytosine) and they encode the necessary information. Human cells are equipped with a twofold chromosome set of 23 chromosomes. This results in a total of around three billion base pairs.[11] DNA is not capable of producing the proteins encoded on it itself.

When a cell needs a certain protein, the information stored on the DNA for the production of this protein is first transferred into messenger RNA (mRNA). This process is called transcription. The mRNA finally delivers the blueprints for protein synthesis to the ribosomes which are located in the cytoplasm outside the cell nucleus. Ribosomes are the cellular protein factories. According to the information encoded on the mRNA the amino acids and finally the proteins are synthesised through the support of transfer RNA (tRNA). This step of protein biosynthesis is called translation. The proteins ultimately convert the information from the DNA into biological function.[12] According to modern science, the origin of life could be proven by the fact that DNA, RNA and proteins could actually arise from the atoms of the primordial soup. The moment when the replication of DNA started would be the starting signal of evolution.

I consider this assessment that the mere existence of DNA, RNA and proteins could explain the origin of life to be highly negligent because it implies that *every corpse would have to be alive*. Moreover, DNA does not contain the entire blueprint of a living being, it merely codes for the synthesis of proteins. DNA cannot explain why and how specific tissue cells, complex anatomical structures or new organs arise from pluripotent em-

---

[I] Deoxyribonucleic acid

[II] Ribonucleic acid

bryonic stem cells which can develop into any tissue. Who or what actually determines that these or those stem cells should become nerve or blood cells, brain, heart muscle or lung? Coordinated and complex processes take place that cannot be explained by the presence of proteins alone. Dr Kerstin Wagner from the Leibniz Institute for Age Research in Jena in Germany conducts research in the field of biomedical and molecular mechanisms on processes of ageing. She confirms that the mechanism underlying the specific cell formation from pluripotent stem cells is not yet really understood.[13] Life must definitely be more than DNA, RNA and protein synthesis. Apparently it is also taken for granted that DNA is not some random assembly of base pairs but contains encoded highly complex information. Complex and meaningful information is never the product of happy coincidences, even if you give it millions of years. Long periods of time are one of the most important arguments used by Darwinists to justify developments. But as I will show in a moment through concrete calculations on the time required, the time argument speaks more against chemical and biological evolution than in favour of it.

The postulated long periods of time of the materialists are in fact an argumentative own goal. Complex and meaningful information is always an expression of intellect (see Chapter 4.2.1, *Information*). There are no known natural processes that could produce this kind of information. The following comparison certainly cannot be transferred one-to-one to biological reality but it tends to show the impossibility of a random emergence of complex and meaningful information in natural structures such as DNA. Imagine taking a Harry Potter book and cutting out every single word and putting them in a bag. Then you pull one word after the other out of the bag. What is the probability that you will pull the words out of the sack in exactly the right order so that the fully readable meaningful story emerges again? A meaningful structured overall text would emerge effectively *never*. The Harry Potter book *Order of the Phoenix* has almost 200,000 words. Thus, there are 200,000-factorial many ways to combine them. The factorial of n (written n!) is given as the product of 1 to n, so for 200,000 that would be $200{,}000! = 1 \cdot 2 \cdot 3 \cdot \ldots \cdot 200{,}000$. This number is so unimaginably large that I cannot show or describe it. To get a feel for it, let us consider here the factorial of 5, of 10 and of 20:

- 5! = 120
- 10! = 3628800
- 20! = 2.432.902.008.176.640.000

So if the book had five words, statistically I would need 120 attempts until I had drawn the correct arrangement once. If I needed one second to draw five words for a possible solution (which would be very fast), I would have found the correct arrangement once in two minutes. With ten words, it would take me 42 days, and with 20 words, an incredible 77 billion years. The factorial has a super-exponential growth; with a mere 20 words we already exceed the age of the earth by a factor of 17. What would it look like if we tried the entire Harry Potter book with 200,000 words? And DNA contains many times more information - it is not the size of a book but of a whole library. Anyone who looks at these numbers can no longer seriously be convinced that chance and long periods of time are an adequate explanation for the emergence of complex information. The French biophysicist and philosopher Pierre Lecomte du Noüy puts it in a nutshell:

> *'Events that (...) need infinitely more time than the assumed age of the earth to at least have a chance of taking place can - as it seems to me - be regarded as impossible from the human point of view.'*[14]

In work conducted in the summer of 2020 the team led by Prof. Dr Reinhard Heckel from TU Munich managed to store the first episode of the Netflix series *Biohackers* on synthetic DNA. The tiny amount of just one picogram (10^{-12}) was enough for the research team to store 100 megabytes (10^{6}) of video data. If you extrapolate this to one gram of DNA, it corresponds to an unimaginable amount of data of 100 exabytes (10^{18}), which is 100 million terabytes (10^{12}) or 100 billion gigabytes (10^{9}).[15] The biochemical company *Twist Bioscience* has calculated that 20 grams of DNA are enough to hold all of mankind's currently digitised data.[16] DNA has an incredibly high data density and stability. Whereas the first data losses can occur after about ten years on previous data carriers, it is assumed that DNA can be read without errors for at least 1,000 years. The world's largest SSD hard drive currently (in the year 2023) available on the market is called *ExaDrive DC100* by the manufacturer *Nimbus Data.*[17] With a capacity of 100 terabytes, it seems almost ridiculous compared to the 100 million terabytes in a gram of DNA.

The origin of the first life is still completely unexplained today. Nevertheless, there are many scientists who are convinced otherwise. As I will show, many of the findings of these so-called origin-of-life scientists are based on incomplete and erroneous interpretations and procedures. Chemical facts are often simply passed over out of convenience or ignorance. But not by me and not here. I look at the relevant details from the outset and do not shy away from questioning scientifically accepted concepts and addressing misinterpretations. It is therefore essential that I sometimes have to delve into the scientific depths of chemistry and biochemistry because this is the only way I can credibly point out the mistakes that are usually made at the very beginning of the account. My argumentation here is purely scientific and so I am, of course, open to counterarguments and criticism and I welcome a factual exchange. It is not my intention to be right at all costs or to be the 'winner'. Instead I would simply like to point out errors and help us get a little closer to the truth.

Before I explain the concept of chemical evolution, however, I would like to paint a picture of what beliefs about the origin of life are prevalent outside the scientific community. In a study by Dr John Narcum, assistant professor of marketing at the Technical University of Arkansas, 715 people were asked about the origin of life, among other things.[18] The results were astonishing and at the same time frightening because, contrary to apparently widespread opinion, we are in fact very far from being able to create life in the laboratory. This was the first question Narcum asked this subject area; it required a 'true' or 'false' answer:

> *'Scientists engaged in research into the origin of life were able to create complex life forms from scratch, i.e. they created a primordial atmos-*

phere of the Earth in laboratory experiments and added chemical substances that they believed existed there before the first life. They were eventually able to create complex life forms, such as frogs.'[19]

41.40 per cent of the participants answered this question with 'true' and 58.60 per cent with 'false'. I am amazed, even stunned, that over 40 per cent of people really believe that we can create frogs from dead matter. But the result of the next, very similar question is even more worrying.

> *'Scientists engaged in research into the origin of life were able to create simple life forms from scratch, i.e. they created a primordial atmosphere of the earth in laboratory experiments and added chemical substances that they believed existed there before the first life. They were eventually able to create simple life forms, such as bacteria.'*[20]

An incredible 72.73 per cent of participants were convinced that we were capable of creating bacteria from scratch in the lab. Only 27.27 per cent of the respondents thought this was 'false'. The average age in the study was 38, and 80 per cent of the participants had a college or university degree. Obviously, a false image is being conveyed in our schools, colleges and universities, but also in the public media. Especially our biology professors and teachers, but also other origin-of-life researchers, are not willing to provide clarification. Instead they lose themselves in over-motivated, personal, fundamental convictions rather than factually presenting scientific reality. An example of this can be found in the *Unbelievable?* podcast in the interview between host Justin Brierley and Lee Cronin, one of the best-known origin-of-life researchers in the world.[21] Justin Brierley reflected on his school knowledge of the primordial soup:

> *'There is some kind of a primordial soup millions of years ago on the surface of earth. Chemicals swimming around, maybe bolts of lightning going off and somehow something happened and poof, you've got your first sort of very simple cell. Is that view essentially correct or fundamentally wrong?'*[22]

Lee Cronin gave the following answer to this question while Denis Noble, biologist and professor of physiology, who was also present, nodded his head in agreement:

> *'So, you're not wrong. Your GCSE chemistry is not too bad at all...'*[23]

I find it highly alarming that even the greatest specialists in this field do not provide honest enlightenment but primarily focus on wishful thinking without critical examination. Unfortunately, such behaviour is not an exception but the rule.

According to the origin-of-life scientists the following scenario is supposed to have taken place about 3.5 billion years ago. The first life in the primordial soup of the young Earth is said to have arisen through so-called chemical evolution. Randomly floating atoms had to come together in a first step to form organic molecules which were needed as the basic building blocks for the formation of longer molecular chains such as amino acids, proteins, sugars, nucleic acids and lipids. According to Jaeger, this organic matter, especially hydrocarbon compounds, should have come together with a high probability through external energy sources (such as volcanic activity and lightning) to form chain-like macromolecules.[24] However, he does not explain why this probability should be high. Gaßner also makes it clear in conversation with Lesch that life could not have arisen without external energy. He explains that initially small molecules formed into larger and larger chains, and that this happened by chance. In his opinion this also initially resulted in compounds with bad molecular constellations that were unfavourable for life. These compounds were repeatedly broken up by the harsh UV radiation of our sun and new constellations were formed. A protective ozone layer was not yet in place. According to Gaßner, the following phenomenon should have occurred: Exactly then, when the molecules had coincidentally come together to form a meaningful chain, the separation was suddenly stopped by the sun's rays (only: How? By what or by whom?). In his view, a molecule must have finally sunk into the primordial soup, to a point where UV rays could no longer reach it.[25] For what reason did precisely this one meaningful molecule among all the countless possible constellations know that it had a meaningful arrangement? And why should it then lower itself for protection? After all, every other variant molecule always remained nicely on the surface to expose themselves again to the destructive effect of the UV rays. If this is really what happened there must either have been a physical reason for the molecule to sink (but no such reason is known) or the decision to sink or to prevent the molecular chain from unravelling was made consciously by the molecule itself or by an external intelligence. That chance alone would have brought about the emergence and, above all, the stable maintenance of amino acids is not an admissible option and is excluded by the low probability.

In the same conversation, Lesch makes it figuratively clear to the viewer that different molecules had to recognise their mutual presence as advantageous:

> *'One molecule says to the other: "Stay near me. It's good if you stay near me." And the other molecule says, "Oh, it's true, it's good for me to be near you and it's good for you to be near me." And then there's a circular process.*'[26]

By talking of the circular process Lesch is alluding to Manfred Eigen's model of the hypercycle which I will discuss later. Of course, the molecules didn't really talk to each other and Lesch didn't literally want to express that with his elaboration, but he wanted to point out that in his view the molecules were able to distinguish the advantageous and the non-advantageous from each other. Such a distinction is a property of biological evolution or of a consciousness, but neither of these existed yet on a prebiotic earth. So how could an atom or molecule have achieved this evolutionary or cognitive feat? Did it have a consciousness? As I see it, there is no evidence whatsoever for the idea that molecules could recognise a benefit in their association. That would necessarily mean that molecules have intentions and goals in mind. However, this is not possible without information processing and evaluation by a consciousness. As I understand it, Gaßner's and Lesch's attempts at explanation are not conclusions from scientific findings but simply the attempt to justify a chemical evolutionary origin of life under all circumstances.

The chemist Dr Mai Thi Nguyen-Kim from the Terra X Lesch & Co[I] team also claims extremely optimistically that the first organic molecules were formed and chemical reactions took place 3.5 billion years ago, and that 'with this, the first building blocks for life, such as amino acids as building blocks for proteins and nucleotides as building blocks for DNA and RNA, were certainly already created.'[27] Jaeger already saw a high probability for these processes and now Nguyen-Kim goes one step further and describes them as *certain*, but she offers no explanation as to *why* this is actually so certain. The chemical facts in fact prove exactly the opposite, as I will show in this chapter. It is quite astonishing that the most important passage in the origin of life is simply expunged by Nguyen-Kim with a small subordinate clause as if it were a matter of course and without a hint of a critical examination. We scientists have a responsibility to present a complete and honest picture to the public. Yet, once again, the materialist paradigm weighs more heavily than showing the truth. There is absolutely no evidence for the claimed processes of formation. Yet it is scientifically accepted without a hint of doubt as proven fact.

In my view the strongest scientific objection to chemical evolution is so-called homochirality. The exact spatial shape of vital molecules is of decisive importance for the functionality of biological systems. Every molecule has a mirror image - in this context one also speaks of enantiomers or mirror image isomers. Figure 4-1, for example, shows the two enantiomers of the basic structure of each amino acid (NH_2=amino group, COOH=carboxy group, H=hydrogen, C=carbon and R=remaining side chain). The basic building blocks of organic chemistry (sugars, amino acids, lipids, etc.) occur in nature only in one mirror-image form, or only one form is useful in a particular organism or for a particular function, the other is not. This is called homochirality. (chiral: handlike, e.g. like left and right hand). Enantiomers are very similar, but they cannot replace

[I] Well known scientific German YouTube channel produced by the public television station ZDF

each other. The letters 'L' and 'D' denote the absolute configuration; that is, they are distinguishing marks for the type of spatial arrangement of a chiral molecule. Almost all natural amino acids (e.g. L-lysine) occur in the L-form. The D-form is extremely dominant in natural sugars (e.g. D-glucose). Homochirality means that only one of the two enantiomers is found. A 1:1 (one-to-one) mixture of two enantiomers is called a racemate. Vital molecules do not occur as racemates but always in homochiral form. Racemates are biologically useless.

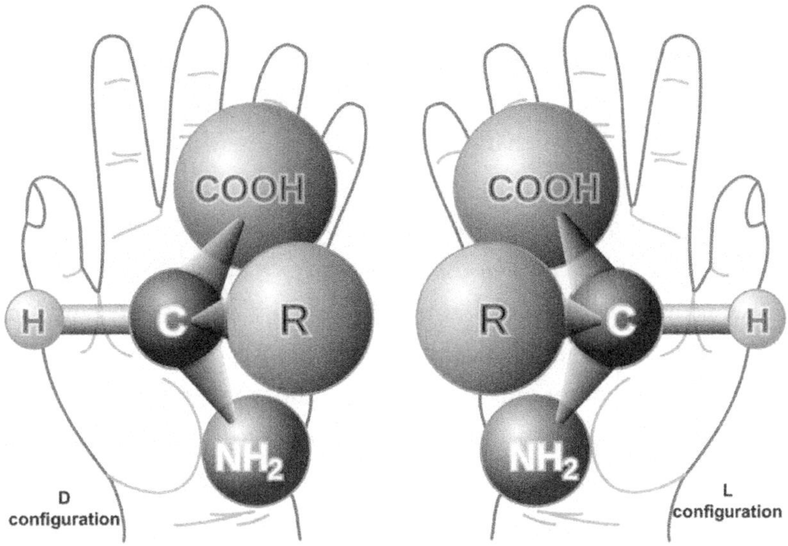

Figure 4-1: Chirality (handedness) - here the mirror image isomers (enantiomers) of an amino acid

How did nature manage to decide on a certain enantiomer? If you want to explain the origin of organic chemistry, you have to solve the problem of homochirality! Homochirality is an unsolved riddle, because the probability for a chiral molecule to have both L and D enantiomers is exactly the same. Prebiotically, there is no competition between molecules, no enantiomer has a prebiotic advantage over another, yet nature has chosen exactly one pure enantiomer for all basic building blocks. Moreover, racemates can only be separated at a later stage into enantiomers with great technical effort. The probability that there are natural processes that carry out such separations of enantiomers completely uncontrolled is practically zero.

What do our biology books say about the necessity of homochirality of amino acids, sugars and lipids? Nothing! But instead, without a single reference to the lack of evidence, it is claimed as a matter of course that life arose from the primordial soup. By what right is this being done? As you can see, there are unsolved problems here already - at the very beginning of the story. In my eyes this is no longer science but dogmatism and is, by the way, extremely dishonest towards our pupils and students. Instead of pointing out this unsolved fact, all the schoolbooks and textbooks in the world would much rather show the Urey-Miller experiment of 1953, which is still used to serve as 'proof' for the primordial soup theory.

The world-famous Urey-Miller experiment caused a sensation in the scientific world at the time. In their laboratory, Stanley Miller and Harold C. Urey created a primordial atmosphere in a glass flask that was very similar to the Earth's atmosphere 3.5 billion years ago. The flask was filled with inorganic elements and water vapour, and it was exposed to UV radiation and artificially generated lightning by electrical discharges.[28] This experiment was repeated many times with improved and more authentic compositions of the gases involved, and each time it was shown that organic molecular chains were formed. However, the majority of these reaction products were irrelevant to living organisms, and some were even harmful. To a small extent, however, some of the 20 standard proteinogenic[I] amino acids that occur in living organisms were actually formed. However, only racemates were produced and, as we have seen, racemates are biologically ineffective. The homochiral form of an amino acid has never been produced in even one Urey-Miller experiment, and this information is not to be found in any biology book. In fact, I am sure that

[I] involved in the building of proteins

most biology teachers know nothing about it. Despite these glaring weaknesses the Urey-Miller experiment, which was effusively celebrated in the scientific world, is still considered groundbreaking today. It was said to have created the basic building blocks of life by generating amino acids. The choice of words is very important here, because this statement was obviously intended to give the impression that the mystery of the origin of life had now been solved. *But amino acids are not the basic building blocks of life.* They are the basic building blocks of some organic compounds. But organic matter does not automatically mean that life is present. Yet this fallacy is indoctrinated into people's consciousness almost like propaganda. Gaßner - like many other scientists - sees this experiment as proof of what the first steps towards the emergence of life looked like.[29] Current schoolbooks and textbooks still teach it this way. However, this theory of the origin of life is far too optimistic; because the path from an amino acid to a living being is still very long, besides which there are other criticisms of these experiments. For example, the experimenters were only able to detect the actively sought amino acids in the first place after additional preparation of the primordial soup[30], and no more than 13 different proteinogenic amino acids (out of the 20 needed) were ever found in one reaction mixture. Be that as it may, it basically does not matter at all whether amino acids really came into being in this way or not, for even if all twenty amino acids necessary for the construction of human proteins were actually present we are still no closer to what we call life.

The primordial soup has been shown by various simulation experiments to have properties that counteract the formation of long amino acid chains. In particular, the abundant water in the primordial soup poses a major problem. When amino acids are concatenated to form proteins, a water molecule is necessarily split off. But due to the large excess of water in the primordial soup, this reaction would be very unlikely to occur in the course of chemical equilibrium under prebiotic conditions without enzymes. Rather, the opposite reaction would occur, namely a hydrolysis, that is, a splitting of the amino acid chains with the consumption of water.[31]

The primordial soup is thus not a suitable medium for the formation of proteins; it even massively counteracts their formation. Apart from the rather obstructive composition of the primordial soup, the much-invoked coincidence must also play a role once again, whereby the chemical evolution advocates are happy to remain steadfastly true to their line against all reason and scientific knowledge, even with probabilities of zero. What is the probability of even a single protein being created by chance through the concatenation of amino acids? Let's start with a small human protein that consists of a chain of 150 amino acids. Even this small number of amino acids means that there are an unimaginable 20^{150} different possible combinations, whereby a functioning protein is not only determined by the correct arrangement of amino acids alone but also by a specific folding of the molecular chain, with 10^{300} folds possible for a typical protein.[32] For orientation, I point out that the number of all atoms in the universe is estimated at 10^{90}. Only one wrong arrangement or folding in the amino acid chain would immediately render the protein useless. In our example we have 20^{150} or expressed as a power of ten over 10^{195} different possible combinations of random arrangements. That is a 1 with 195 zeros. This unimaginably large number is called the dotrigintilliard.

10000000000000000000000000000000000000000000000000000000
00000000000000000000000000000000000000000000000000000000
00000000000000000000000000000000000000000000000000000000
0000000000000000000000000000

In comparison, one billion: 1,000,000,000

We usually find it very difficult really to understand the dimension of very large numbers. Whether someone owns a billion or a trillion euros no longer makes any noticeable difference to us. To get a feeling for this immensely large number of 10^{195}, imagine the following situation. You want to meet a friend for dinner, he suggests the following time: 'We'll meet in a million seconds.' That is 10^{6} seconds, which corresponds to eleven days. If we now go three powers of ten higher, 10^{9} seconds, then that is already 32 years. At 10^{12} we are at 32,000 years and at 10^{18} at 32 billion years, which is more than twice the age of our universe. But now we have 10^{195} possible combinations for the formation of a simple, small protein! That is an unimaginably large number, and that doesn't even include the foldings! Now please answer the question honestly for yourself, how likely is it that exactly one particular arrangement and folding will arise undirected by chance from all conceivable possibilities, just the exact arrangement that carries concentrated meaningful information and functionality? And even if it did happen, it would not be enough for it to arise only once, it would have to happen very frequently, and as prebiotic nature knows only chance it would not be able to *remember* the correct order. In the example above, we only wanted to form a small protein. Let's take a look at the largest human protein known to us, titin from human muscle cells. This protein consists of more than 30,000 linked amino acids. The probability that this protein would form by chance is $20^{30,000}$. I will refrain from presenting this unimaginably large number here. So it would take more than a miracle for a single meaningful protein to be formed at all. But we have over 200,000 different types of proteins and over 2,000 enzymes in our cells.

After fourteen years of research, molecular biologist Dr Douglas D. Axe published an article in the *Journal of Molecular Biology* that answered the research question of how frequently or rarely functioning sequences (for example proteins) occur in comparison to the number of all possible combinations of amino acids. In his quantitative estimation for small proteins (with 150 amino acids), he comes to the conclusion that there are 10^{77} functionless combinations for one functioning, correctly folded protein.[33] You would be more likely to get six right numbers in the lottery ten times in a row than to get a functioning protein only once. The probability of such a protein being created by chance is therefore practically zero. The ever-popular argument of long time spans for evolutionary development also plays no role here. With a seemingly ridiculous age of a mere 4.5 billion years of our earth this time span is not sufficient by far to come remotely close to statistically justifying the emergence of proteins.

In addition to the basic building blocks of amino acids or proteins, sugars (carbohydrates) play a decisive role on the path to organic chemistry and the life that supposedly emerges from it. Carbohydrates serve cells and organisms as a source of energy and scaffolding substance (for example D-glucose, D-fructose or D-ribose as scaffolding for DNA and RNA). The synthesis of simple sugars (monosaccharides) is extremely difficult; even with the most modern methods in laboratories it has never been possible to produce a homochiral monosaccharide from scratch. There are indeed a large number of scientific publications in which one sometimes boasts of having produced not only amino acids but also monosaccharides. However, in every paper I have researched so far, it always comes down to the fact that only a mixture, that is, a useless racemate, was produced. But, for the experimental follow-up steps in the origin-of-life research, the scientists concerned never continue to use these racemates as a starting material. They always just state that they created the desired component, which they really did, but at the same time they also created a lot of other components such as enantiomers, isomers (partial reflections) and other substances that make further processing impossible. Afterwards, they usually dispose of this contaminated primordial soup, only to buy the purified, solvent-free, homochiral form of the required amino acids and monosaccharides produced by industry for further processing. It is not exactly credible simply to circumvent the problem of homochirality in this way. The early Earth could not simply buy homochiral building blocks. Incidentally, the industry does not obtain these homochiral amino acids and sugars through artificial syntheses, but directly from nature itself. For this purpose, proteins and carbohydrates are taken from nature and broken down into their individual parts. Isn't that significant? Obviously, it is anything but easy to produce these starting materials, yet it is all supposed to have happened completely undirected and by chance under a rock or in a pond on the prebiotic earth. For me, this is not in the least believable.

The linking of monosaccharides to polysaccharides (polymerisation) is even more difficult than the linking of amino acids because even a simple sugar such as D-glucose can occur in different arrangements: as an open system, a ring of five or a ring of six. Each arrangement has several mirror images (isomers), because the complete molecule can be mirrored (enantiomer) but so can certain partial structures of it. For example, a single ring structure of D-glucose has thirty-two different isomers. If only six D-glucose molecules were to be linked together, this would already result in over a trillion (10^{12}) different possibilities for linking them together.[34] There is hardly anything more difficult in synthetic chemistry than the polymerisation of sugars. Even for specialists in perfectly equipped laboratories the effort is enormous. In the rest of this chapter, I will describe such a polymerisation process in detail so that you can get an idea of the enormous complexity. These processes for the polymerisation of complex carbohydrates, but also of lipids, are highly specific and require constantly changing conditions (in terms of temperature, pressures, gases, solvents, pH value, and so on). The emergence of organic matter postulated by the chemical evolutionists can definitely not have taken place in this way. Every scientist can calculate, understand and comprehend this, and yet a large proportion of these people continue to hold to the theory of chemical evolution. I'm sorry, but that makes no sense. Where is the science in that? And when people then continue to cling to a material origin of life brought about by chemical evolution despite this clear falsification it reminds me of pseudo-religious fanaticism. The pseudo-religion of a material world view seems to make one blind and ignorant.

I don't expect any scientist to consider a God, a Creator or spiritual worlds as the cause, but it is at least time to admit that chemical evolution, as universally described, cannot have occurred in the way most scientists think. And even if it did occur we would have produced nothing but dead organic matter, that is to say something which has nothing to do with life. Life needs organic matter in this gross material world in order to be able to function. But that does not suggest that organic matter is the reason for life. Yet that is exactly what is proposed in all of natural science for reasons I do not understand. I am also very upset that in my schooling and medical studies I was not shown that there are legitimate criticisms and major improbabilities regarding chemical and biological evolution. Why was I deprived of these insights? Instead, I have been taught things based on hypotheses that have zero probability. It is a scandal that our schools and universities are completely silent about these clear criticisms about the probabilities - or rather improbabilities - in the origin of life. I would have liked to have been enlightened about this in my studies. This is where our current science crosses an illicit line. For its own protection it has shed its honesty. Science should be open and honest, always and unreservedly, otherwise it does the same as religions and becomes an ideological faith movement. That I am not entirely wrong in my assessment of this is made clear by the following quote in *The New York Review* of 9th of January 1997 by Richard C. Lewontin (Professor of Biology at Harvard University):

> *'We side with science, despite the obvious absurdity of some of its constructs (...), because we cannot allow a divine foot in the door.'*[35]

It is astonishing that science does not want to admit a divine foot but accepts probabilities of zero without batting an eyelid and, what is even worse, serves them up to pupils and students as proven facts, just for the sake of maintaining its dogmas. Lewontin also makes a distinction when he uses the expression the 'scientific side' – a distinction that is incomprehensible to me. Why should there be different 'sides' at all? Are a spiritual world and psi phenomena not part of science? This makes it unmistakably clear that current science has long since left the path of empiricism, objectivity and reason. What is at stake here is the defence of a rigid materialistic world view and the belief in it. So faith also plays a big role in science.

The latest scientific explanation for the origin of life is the RNA world hypothesis, which is considered the missing link between dead organic matter and the beginning of selection and evolution. In the 1980s, Thomas Cech found out that RNA is not only an information carrier, but can also catalyse chemical reactions. Thus, RNA would combine the functionality of DNA and proteins, of which it is said to have been the precursor. According to this hypothesis, RNA would have everything one would need for life.[36] However, in this view, known chemical facts are simply pushed aside or not taken note of. The random formation of nucleic acids such as RNA would contain chemically incompatible processes; some synthesis steps would require very high and others very low reaction temperatures. How could this have happened at a single site? Homochiral building blocks would be needed, and the multi-component nature of the nucleotide building blocks would make the formation even more difficult than was already the case with proteins.[37] D-ribose, which forms the basic structure of RNA, is a pentose, that is, a sugar with five carbon atoms. A carbon atom is represented by the symbol C (for carbon) and numbered from one to five according to its position in the sugar molecule. However, in the construction of the RNA and the associated concatenation of the D-riboses, the compounds can occur not only at the regular carbon atoms C3 and C5, but with equal probability at the carbon atoms C2 and C5. The problem with this C2-C5 connection is that it no longer produces normal RNA, but siRNA (small interfering RNA). siRNA suppresses the expression of genes and stops replication, which is the exact opposite of what the hypothesis tries to explain. RNA is also very unstable. It decays extremely quickly in the course of autocatalytic degeneration. To protect it from this, at least for a short time, it would have to be cooled to minus 80 degrees Celsius.[38] How could the prebiotic earth solve all these problems? We don't know, and no biology book in the world enlightens students about it.

Richard Dawkins, one of the best-known evolutionists, has an interesting explanation for this, which I do not want to leave unmentioned because it shows the desperate, almost naïve search for a possible answer for the origin of RNA or DNA. In the interview with Ben Stein, he makes it clear that we do not know how the first life arose. I find that a very honest admission, but I wonder why this admission is nowhere to be found in the biology books of this world. He even thinks it is possible that there are intelligent designers. These designers would have to have been extraterrestrial intelligences who initiated the decisive steps for the emergence of life on Earth. But these extraterrestrials themselves would have arisen in a completely natural way through chemical and Darwinian evolution.[39] I think this quotation shows wonderfully how much Dawkins and his supporters lack holistic foresight. Blaming the origin of life and intelligence on extraterrestrials makes no sense. It does not answer the origin question. Why should aliens be materially similar to us? There could also be gaseous beings, or perhaps these aliens are pure forms of energy that do not need a material body. How far away would Dawkins' assessment of the extraterrestrial intelligent designers be from a creative spiritual world that is nothing other than the interplay of different forms of energy?

> *'I really believe that physicists underestimate the leap in complexity that comes with biological processes. (...) If you look at it (the complexity,* author's note*), then a cell like this is already a universe away from what a nuclear physicist deals with.'*[40]
>
> *Harald Lesch*

The simplest form of life is the cell, although can one really still speak of 'simple' after this quotation from Lesch? Most people and even scientists are not even rudimentarily aware of the magnitude of this complexity. The sum of all protein-protein interactions in a cell is called the interactome. These are non-covalent (for example electrostatic) interactive connections in a living cell between proteins. It is completely unexplained how a living cell could emerge functional from this extremely large number of possible combinations of its molecular components. You can't just put any proteins into a cell and proclaim 'it's a go'. The proteins that belong together must always find each other and interact with each other because this is the only way to guarantee the functioning of the cell. Peter Tompa and George Rose from the Free University in Brussels and John Hopkins University in Baltimore published an article on protein-protein interactomes in *Protein Science* in 2011. They concluded that in a single simple yeast cell alone there are an unimaginable $10^{79,000,000,000}$ (10 to the power of 79 billion!) different possible combinations for protein-protein interactions.[41] This crazy large number is beyond anything humanly imaginable. All the biology books in the world are also completely silent on this subject.

A living cell is therefore the starting point of all mutation and selection processes postulated in the theory of evolution. For once you have a living cell, according to evolutionists, the evolutionary machinery could be set in motion, and multicellular living beings would emerge from single-celled organisms. But this scenario already starts with a big problem: Where should the living cell, which according to Lesch is as complex as its own universe, actually come from? Dr Stephen Meyer, co-founder of the Discovery Institute's Center for Science and Culture, earned his doctorate at the University of Cambridge with a methodical interpretation of various studies on the origin of life. He is the author of the New York Times bestseller *Darwin's Doubt: The Explosive Origin of Animal Life and the case for Intelligent Design.*[42] At a lecture, he satirised this problem of where the first cell, which already had to carry biological information, actually came from with a wonderful story.

> *'Once upon a time there was an absent-minded scientist. One day he was walking home from university and was preoccupied in deep thoughts about the origin of life. That day (...) he fell into a pit, for he was not watching where he was going. But "No problem!" he said to himself. "I know exactly how to get out of this pit again. I just need to go home, get a ladder, then come back, put the ladder in the pit, jump into the pit and climb up."'*[43]

In Lesch's video contribution entitled *Entstehung des Lebens aus toter Materie (Origin of Life from Dead Matter)*[44] he presents an attempt to explain the origin of the first life. He says that life is defined by certain proportions of substances and their organisational form with feedback mechanisms. Ultimately he describes an existing metabolism that will only later be enclosed by a cell membrane. But this assumption can hardly be correct because, according to the renowned origin-of-life researcher Prof. Dr Neal K. Devaraj and his team, a cell membrane must have been present from the very beginning when the cell was formed. Without a membrane, there is no proton gradient and thus neither energy nor metabolism.[45] In order for the atoms and molecules described by Lesch to form such a required form of organisation, they must assemble into increasingly complex molecules. He says that these molecules could improve over other molecules, for example in terms of synthesis rates, by making slight changes in large time windows. These improved molecules would therefore reproduce better compared to the other molecules and dominate the population.[46] However, Lesch does not say a word about how these molecules, which in his description are apparently already supposed to have functionality, came into being in the first place. Furthermore, he uses terms of biology such as population and reproduction which have no relevance in a prebiotic earth, that is, in a time before biology. By what and why should these molecules be able to reproduce at all? He ultimately traces his explanations back to the model of the hypercycle[47] described by Manfred Eigen. Eigen described a kind of first evolutionary replication system for nucleic acids and protein syntheses via a feedback reaction cycle. In the simplest case, two RNA molecules and two enzyme proteins couple together in a cycle in such a way that one RNA molecule produces an enzyme that catalyses the replication of the other RNA molecule. And this in turn produces an enzyme that catalyses the replication of the first RNA molecule. Such a cycle could actually be demonstrated under controlled conditions in a specially designed reactor. But this no longer has much to do with prebiotics. This cycle was able to evolve evolutionarily. Mutations led to altered molecules and in some cases to improved synthesis rates, so that the mutated molecules prevailed over the slower synthesised molecules. On the way to the emergence of life, these hypercycles were supposed to become increasingly complex. There is also talk of the self-organisation of matter. Hydrothermal vents ('black and white smokers') with their pyrite crystals are said to play a decisive role as possible next steps towards the formation of a true first cell with compartment formation.[48] Another theory considers development in ice crystals.[49] All in all these are interesting findings but they do not sufficiently satisfy my definition of simple life. A hypercycle has so far only been hypothetically attributed to a compartmentalisation with a membrane, and it is not an intrinsic system. One must also not forget that the initial state of this cycle presupposes already functioning proteins and RNA, whose random emergence, as I have already been able to show, must be regarded as impossible. Moreover, under controlled conditions in the reactor, energy-rich molecules are deliberately added to the hypercycle from the outside in order to keep the cycle going and to positively reinforce it.[50] The conception and initiation of the hypercycle with appropriate reagents is controlled by an external consciousness (of the experimenter). The initiation and maintenance of the system is not an intrinsic property of the hypercycle, but the consequence of a conscious induced action. Prebiotic conditions and the instability of RNA are also completely ignored. But assuming, despite my objections, that we had created a functioning hypercycle, what exactly could it do? Basically, it is a mathematical model, a kind of race. The fastest synthesisations and replications prevail more and more as a logical consequence. However, I do not believe that speed in synthesisation is a quality characteristic for the emergence of life. The process of emergence is, in my view, much more complex. Ultimately, a well-constructed and finely tuned composition of a functional cell with the 'complexity of a universe' must emerge, with a wide variety of cell organelles, cytoplasm, cytoskeleton, membrane and countless other components and processes. In my opinion, this cannot come about through a race of synthesisations, but must rather be the expression of qualitative and sense-giving criteria. However, the source of meaning and information is completely ignored by materialistic scientists.

Lesch's argument that 'we are dealing with large periods of time', and therefore that this unbelievable development into a functioning living cell can be justified, is not tenable from a statistical point of view. We would need periods of time that would not only exceed the age of the earth, but the age of the entire universe many times over. Moreover, the formation of RNA is inevitably tied to the formation of homochiral sugars. The problem of homochiral precursors cannot be solved with a lot of time, it is of a fundamental nature.

In 2010, a team of researchers led by the genetic engineer Craig Venter published an article on the creation of artificial life in the scientific magazine *Science*.[51] This was celebrated in a number of articles in the world press and media landscape, some with exuberant headlines. *Spiegel online*

(Germany's leading news site) wrote: 'Breakthrough - Researchers create artificial life for the first time - A vision has come true'[52] and *Die Welt* (the German national daily newspaper) even flaunts the headline 'Researcher Craig Venter creates artificial life - WE ARE GOD! '[53] But let us be clear: these claims are simply not true, they are the result of an outrageous exaggeration and a wild headline rush. The press always loves to pounce on such scientific reports only to make an even bigger hype out of them. There is no doubt that Venter had achieved an incredible feat. He had succeeded in producing an artificial genome with one million base pairs and transferring it into an existing bacterium. You could call it a genome transplant. Venter's claim, however, that he had thus created a 'synthetic cell' can certainly be interpreted as an expression of his exaggerated euphoria. Many of his colleagues disagreed with him. In response to Venter's interpretation and the hullabaloo in the press an article then appeared in *Nature* in which eight experts in synthetic biology had their say with far more sobering views. Martin Fussenegger, Professor of Synthetic Biology at ETH Zurich, assesses it as follows: 'Venter has actually only used established technologies. What he does is called genetic engineering. This always involves the reprogramming of organisms into which one introduces foreign genetic material. A 'normal bioengineer might do that with up to 5,000 base pairs. Venter puts together pieces of 100,000 base pairs in such a way that a genome of one million base pairs is created. (...) This order of magnitude is new.'[54] In the end, he copied DNA fragments based on the model of a natural genome and, for the next step, nature had to come to the rescue again. Natural yeast cells finally assembled these fragments successively, but without really creating anything biologically new. In order for the synthesised genome to unfold, he also still needed an intact cell. The synthetic genome of the bacterium M. mycoides was implanted into the intact cell of the related species M. capricolum, so that from then on M. capricolum only synthesised proteins that were typical for the donor bacterium M. mycoides.[55] Venter was thus dependent on a completely intact cell, without which it would not have worked. '99 per cent of what makes up a cell - proteins, sugar structures, fats - were therefore not artificially synthesised, but contributed by nature.' The experts' conclusion:

an impressive technical achievement, but far from being synthetic life.[56]

If I had to describe it from a computer scientist's point of view, Venter didn't actually do anything other than copy the operating system from one perfectly functional computer over to another perfectly functional computer only to claim that he had created the second computer with all its hardware and software from scratch. But he didn't. The second computer already existed and was running before the copying, just like the bacterium which previously existed completely structured and, above all, was alive.

There is no end to the hype of scientists and the media, and an incomplete and manipulated picture is constantly being brought to the public's attention. On 4 September 2022, for example, *Bild* (the daily newspaper with the highest circulation in Germany) published an article with the following headline: 'Is the origin of life in this laboratory flask? Mankind is still puzzling today: How did life on Earth come into being? Researchers at the University of Jena have now come a significant step closer to finding the answer: at the Institute of Inorganic and Analytical Chemistry, chemists succeeded in forming biomolecules under prebiotic conditions!' Prof. Dr Wolfgang Weigand explains that life was certainly based on the reactions from his experiment. He says: 'Our experiment proves that these organic substances, which easily react further to proteins, lipids, sugars and DNA, could have formed in warm pools on the Earth's surface around 4.2 billion years ago.[57] This sentence alone is a paradox because it uses the word 'prove' together with the subjunctive 'could'. This shows once again that there is a lot of wishful thinking involved here. He even claims that proteins, lipids, sugars and DNA would 'easily' arise from his primordial soup. This statement is unbelievable! If it is so easy, then please let him show it. I wonder if Weigand has ever dealt with the subject of homochirality, unprotected side chains or the origin of information? It is irresponsible to make such claims. I offered *Bild* my comments on this article saying I would like to present my counter-arguments. However, the newspaper had no interest in this because headlines that brag in bold letters about the origin of life in the laboratory are more spectacular and go down better with the readership than an article about the mistakes scientists make.

I find it amazing how quickly and easily such media-grabbing headlines can emerge. When you then go into the details you realise that the journalist in question could hardly have exaggerated more. With such media-effective disinformation you can of course win over many readers, and unfortunately it takes a lot of persuasion and effort to refute these exaggerations with objectivity and real facts. But the press then doesn't care much. A headline revealing that 'we are God' and that we can create artificial life inevitably sticks in people's minds. The explanation that it is simply *not like that* mostly comes to nothing. Thus the strategy of the materialists has worked once again. So religious fanaticism is not the only fanaticism. Materialist fanaticism is in no way inferior to it. I wonder why the media do not run such a headline as 'Breakthrough! Darwin's theory of evolution finally disproved! Multiple probabilities of zero bring theory down.' I am sure neither *Spiegel online* nor *Die Welt* nor any other editorial office in our western world would run such a headline although I have been able to show in this book, through the work of many renowned research colleagues, that it is factually justified (especially in chapters 4.1.2, *Darwin's theory of evolution* and 4.1.3, *The origin and evolution of whales*).

So: let us leave chemical evolution behind us and consider the situation in which we have a living cell (wherever it may have come from). Then, in the eyes of Darwinists, the power of mutation and selection over time should be strong enough to produce almost nine million different species of plants and animals. Our current science once again invokes the Darwinian idea that successively more complex life must have arisen from simple life and this idea is then simply projected back to molecular structures. Apparently it is in the nature of man to consider only a slow, gradual evolution from simple to complex as possible. However, the fact that certain structures and processes in nature, due to their complexity, cannot have evolved successively through slow change is something we will look at in more detail in Chapter 4.2 (*Intelligent Design*) when it comes to Intelligent Design and non-reducible complexity. However, before anything could evolve at all, something living would first have to have been there.

Evolution therefore does not begin at zero, but with a living cell created as if by magic. Thus, the question of the origin of life remains unanswered from a scientific point of view.

At this point I will put aside all previous considerations, theories, experiments and scientific papers, as they can also be found 1,000-fold in the *Journal of Molecular Evolution* (JME), because none of them can adequately explain the origin of life, as Behe also confirms in his book:

> *'Yes, not a single paper published in JME since this journal first appeared (1971) has ever proposed a detailed model within the scope of which a complex biochemical system could have emerged in a gradual, step-by-step manner à la Darwin.'*[58]

The German biochemist Prof. Dr Klaus Dose (head of the biochemical laboratory of the Max Planck Institute in Frankfurt, professor of biochemistry at the universities of Frankfurt and Mainz) has also done intensive research in this area and gives an honest assessment of the subject:

> *'For over 30 years experimental research has been conducted in the field of chemical and molecular evolution regarding the origin of life. However, this has not led to any solution, but has rather contributed to a better understanding of the magnitude of the problem of the origin of life on this earth. At present, all discussions of principled theories and experiments in this field end either in a dead end or in an admission of ignorance.'*[59]

Prof. Dr James Mitchell Tour is an expert in synthetic organic chemistry and nanotechnology. He is Professor of Chemistry and Professor of Materials Science and Nanotechnology at Rice University in Houston/Texas and was named one of the top ten chemists in the world by Thomson Reuters (formerly Reuters News Agency) in 2009. He has published over 750 scientific articles and is one of the most cited scientists in his field (over 100,000 citations); his 2005 journal article *Directional Control in Thermally Driven Single-Molecule Nanocars*[60] is the most accessed article in the entire American Chemical Society.[61] He says that with each new day of exploration of the cell, new complex processes and structures are discovered. The situation is much more like a perpetual discovery of new details rather than a successive increase in knowledge. He points out that his chemist colleagues agree with him and have recognised that chemistry cannot account for the origin of life. In his view it is mainly the biologists who believe in and hold to a chemical evolution of life. Tour is one of the best specialists in the world when it comes to the development of complex functional molecules. In his lecture *The Secret of the Origin of Life*[62], for example, he presents the details of this. He describes how extremely elaborate and difficult the synthesis of such molecules is and names many different synthesis problems that had to be overcome by him and his team, but also by prebiotic nature in a presumed chemical evolution scenario. For example, it is essential that the correct order is followed when adding the reagents. You can't just throw all the components into a pot or a volcanic pond and hope that everything will come together as it should if you just wait long enough. Complex molecules have to be assembled successively by adding the appropriate building blocks. Errors in the sequence can no longer be corrected in most cases; to correct them it would be necessary to return to the first step of the synthesis. In addition, highly specific environmental conditions are required for each individual synthesis step. Among these are: a specific temperature, a specific pressure, a specific solvent, specific gas constellations, a specific pH value and very specific elements in specific quantities in specific time periods are needed. For example, there are reactions that can only take place at a temperature of -50 degrees centigrade, whereas other steps require temperatures of +5, room temperature or even +130 degrees centigrade. To make matters worse, sometimes the required temperatures are only allowed to act for a certain period of time and the yield of the desired product is extremely low. Some steps run at a ph value of nine, others at a ph value of one. There can be hundreds of such steps on the way to a complex molecule. Each individual reaction must be deliberately and specifically implemented by the chemists with all the required preconditions exactly in place; if only one parameter is not right the synthesis step cannot take place. The publications on such molecular syntheses usually contain a detailed molecular characterisation, which can often be two or three hundred pages long. This is a detailed description of the countless highly specific individual steps and requirements for the stepwise development of this molecule. The synthesis of such complex molecules, regardless of whether it is to be created in the laboratory or in nature, is highly complex, costly and without alternative. This means that a putative chemical evolution must have taken on the same enormous effort for all the individual steps in the molecule's development as is the case today in modern laboratories. How could we now imagine the emergence of a complex functional molecule in prebiotic nature, when countless highly specific synthesis steps must be implemented, each with highly specific environmental conditions?

Enzymes that could simplify and implement such syntheses did not yet exist in prebiotic times. No one can explain how this could have worked. We have absolutely no idea. Nevertheless, there is a large community of biologists who stubbornly claim the opposite and believe that what chemists are constructing in laboratories today with all their intellect and technical equipment and with great effort, miraculously happened all by itself in a pond or at a hydrothermal spring billions of years ago, completely uncontrolled and by chance. Many scientists are not clear about the chemical basics and details so they publish books and papers in which they sell speculations and wishes as scientific reality out of full conviction, without being aware of it. For example, Jaeger claims the following in his book *Wissenschaft und Spiritualität (Science and Spirituality)*:

> *'However, there were places where the circumstances for the first molecules of life were almost perfect: volcanic springs in the deep sea (black smokers). Here, many biologists assume, the 'chemical gardens' developed in which the appropriate reactions took place that gave rise to more complex 'molecules of life', among them the macromolecules that still play the essential role in the metabolic reactions of all life today.'*[63]

I don't think Jaeger ever thought about the homochirality of these building blocks or how amino acids could link together in the deep sea, splitting off water. Nor could the polymerisation of complex sugars or lipids, which requires hundreds of constantly changing environmental conditions (temperature, pressure, ph, gases, and so on) have possibly happened in just one place like a black smoker. In addition, black smokers are too hot and toxic for life, at these temperatures of over 400 degrees centigrade the organic molecules would degenerate into CO_2 in no time. They are very unstable; within a few decades they grow and collapse. That is too little time for anything useful to develop. Even the white smokers, which are much colder at 40 - 90 degrees centigrade, cannot be considered. They consist of porous rock, which should provide membrane-like compartments. But porous rock is useless as a membrane substitute. Rock membranes are over 100 times thicker than phospholipid membranes. The presumed energy production via the ph gradient would never be able to provide enough energy. The high ph would also remove carbon, which life needs. How the proteins could form a meaningful interactome remains as unaddressed as the formation of membranes. Therefore, a white smoker is certainly not a perfect place! The problem is that biologists in particular do not bother to look at the chemical conditions in detail. This is how such highly speculative theories then arise, and even doctors and professors then just parrot each other's ideas. Although I have been able to show the impossibility of this theory in this chapter, the assumptions of biologists obviously have a higher value and importance in the public domain than the chemical facts.

The fact is, the origin of life definitely could not have been as the biologists assume. The probability is indisputably low. So why are these obvious weaknesses ignored by science? Every single biology teacher, professor and lecturer in the world tacitly agrees that, contrary to chemical behaviour and contrary to the nature of molecules and contrary to observations, they have to believe as a matter of course in a series of miracles and improbabilities of exorbitant proportions. I am sure that most biologists are not even aware of these facts which argue against chemical evolution to the highest degree. I am shocked that this miracle of presumed chemical evolution is blatantly allowed to be taught as a proven fact in our schools and universities. Scientific knowledge is being trampled on here. I am ashamed of this science.

Biologists like Lee Cronin keep affirming that they will make a breakthrough in the next few years.[64] Yet even with all their intellect they have never succeeded in creating a simple living cell and have never even been close to doing so. How then could this creation have worked billions of years ago, without intellect, under a rock or in a pond? As simple as the biologists' answer is, it is also naïve. 'You just have to give it enough time' they say. But even the simplest bacterium with its 256 protein-coding genes has not been produced in the laboratory. Tour explains that even if, against all probabilities, biologists were given all the building blocks in nature, such as amino acids, proteins, DNA, RNA, lipids, fatty acids and whatever else they would like, they would not manage to make a single living cell out of them.[65] In Lee Strobel's book *The Case For Faith*, Tour is quoted as follows:

> *'I earn my living by creating molecules. You cannot imagine how difficult this work is. I stand in awe of God because of what he has done through his creation. Only a beginner who knows nothing about science would say that science leads away from faith. If you really study and do true science, it brings you closer to God.'*[66]

In my search for the origin or existence of our consciousness, I have now reached the depths of the chemical and biological science of creation. In my research on this topic, I have positioned myself between the argumentative but also polemical fronts of creationists and materialistic evolutionists, and I am most amazed at the scientific depth in which this discussion is being fought out. However, I am primarily interested in where our consciousness comes from, and I think that both creationists and evolutionists will certainly agree with me that on these chemical and biological levels of the precursors of life and the first cells we will certainly not find anything in this respect. All discussions around the topic of the origin of carbohydrates, proteins, nucleic acids and lipids are, in my view, not necessary at all, because the essentials are not being considered. For life clearly does not consist solely of visible and tangible matter. Let us assume, despite all the improbabilities of chemical evolution, that all the organic molecular chains relevant to life would be completely present. What would we get? We would definitely not get life, just a pile of dead organic matter. Armin Risi confirms this view:

> *'The assumption that organic matter at some point produces 'life' and, in humans, consciousness as a by-product, is thus contrary to all observation and logic.'*[67]

At a 2011 lecture, Lee Cronin said he would be able to create artificial life within the next two years. He would only have to find the right chemical composition once, then it would be possible to create life in a few hours.[68] More than 12 years later, he is still completely clueless and almost obsessively seeks the solution exclusively in matter. If all he wants is the right chemistry, then why don't we look at a simple cell that has just died, or the body of a freshly deceased person. His corpse is full to the brim with carbohydrates, proteins, enzymes, DNA, RNA, lipids in complete cells, and what just a moment ago miraculously worked together has suddenly stopped working. Metabolism no longer takes place. Replication no longer takes place. The cells are without function. The organic matter is the same as before, yet life has disappeared. Life is more than the organic matter of the body. There must be an invisible subtle energy, a spirit, which breathes life into this complex mechanism and also takes it away again.

4.1.2 Darwin's theory of evolution

> *'The fact of evolution is the backbone of biology, and biology thus finds itself in the peculiar position of being a science based on an unproven theory - is it then a science or a faith?'*[69]
>
> *L. Harrison Matthews, British zoologist*

What if we actually found incontrovertible arguments explaining why evolution could not have been the explanation for the origin of species? Could perfectly comprehensible logical arguments, arguments which could not be falsified even by empirical research, really dissuade evolutionary theorists from their research goal of a completely naturalistically explainable evolution? Experience shows that this will not happen. It seems probable that biologists would never let the theory of evolution fail unless they personally had spiritual experiences similar to the one I had after Joma's accident. The evolutionary theorists have internalised a rigid basic conviction that is by no means empirically based but rather an expression of a fundamental world-view decision.[70]

In 1859 the English naturalist Charles Darwin (1809-1882) initiated the scientific triumph of the idea of evolution with the publication of *On the Origin of Species by Natural Selection*[71]. This happened at a time when the scientific naturalistic approach was already welcome among intellectuals as a countermovement to church doctrine. The educational urge towards enlightenment and being able to explain all things by natural, physical, biological and chemical processes naturally suited the development of a theory of evolution very well. In principle there is nothing wrong with this as long as one truly and objectively follows the circumstantial evidence and findings and disregards wishful thinking. In his work Darwin describes a detailed theory of evolution with many examples which he compiled, among other things, on a journey across the Atlantic and round South America lasting several years. He explained how species can change, and the emergence of new species from existing species, by the mechanism of natural selection. His theory states that the offspring of a species can show certain physical differences within the scope of variation. If a physical change turns out to be disadvantageous in terms of reproduction or food intake, this specimen so affected would be weeded out by natural selection. Conversely an advantageous change helps the animals to assert themselves more effectively in the struggle for survival against the competitors of their species. According to the motto *survival of the fittest* only the fittest prevail. Darwin's hypothesis was that over millions of years constant small changes of this kind had led to the emergence of new species.

Probably his best-known 'proof' of his theory was his demonstration of changes among the 'Darwin's' finches from the Galápagos Islands, birds with a high degree of variation that were subsequently named after him (see Figure 4-2).

Figure 4-2: Darwin finches with differently shaped beaks

There are fourteen different species of Darwin's finches, all descended from a common parent species from the mainland. The finches differ in body size, plumage colouration and beak size and shape; this Darwin attributed to the different requirements and food specialisations on the individual islands. Grain-eating finches had large chunky bills, whereas insectivores tended to develop pointed narrow bills. Despite this variance and adaptation to habitat, however, the finches still remained finches. The birds observed by Darwin in no way show evolution for speciation, but only adaptation and variation.

Before I take a closer look at the issue of speciation through evolutionary mechanisms, let's go back to the beginning. Let us assume that we are at the point in our evolutionary history where the unicellular organisms have already arisen (however and from wherever). The unicellular organisms are divided into the two categories of prokaryotes and eukaryotes. In a typical Darwinian approach, the simply structured prokaryotes (for example bacteria) are nowadays regarded as the predecessors of the eukaryotes which have a much more complex structure with their cell nucleus and various organelles and are found in multicellular organisms. But why should a prokaryote be a precursor of a eukaryote? Here our science is once again searching for truths by extrapolating backwards from Darwinian thinking. Just because something is simply structured, it does not necessarily have to be a precursor of something more complex. The most current explanatory model for the transition of a prokaryote to a eukaryote is the so-called endosymbiont theory. This theory states that a primordial bacterium absorbed a smaller bacterium. This small ingested bacterium produced chemical energy that the surrounding bacterium could use, in return for which the small bacterium received more protection through a second membrane, a classic win-win situation. The ingested bacterium eventually developed into the first cell organelle, the mitochondrion, which produced the energy carrier ATP[I].[72] There is certainly good evidence to support this theory in, for example, exchanged DNA sequences between nucleus and mitochondria. However, there are equally valid arguments against it, for example the direction of protein transport in mitochondria, which contradicts the theory.[73] Current science estimates a period of two billion years for this first presumed step in the evolution from prokaryotes to complex eukaryotes.[74] The first unicellular organisms are estimated to be 3.85 billion years old, based on fossil finds on Greenland. So this first step from prokaryote to eukaryote took half an earth age just to produce a non-specific unicellular organism from which the multicellular organisms would eventually emerge. If so much time was needed for this step alone, I find it very difficult to believe that in less than the same period of time the world's estimated 8.7 million species of eukaryotic

---

[I] Adenosine triphosphate

organisms in their diversity and perfection have emerged from this unspecific unicellular organism. Each individual species also has many different specialisations of cells. Humans are made up of about 220 different types of cells, and each individual type has a specific function to perform. Altogether, we are made up of about 100 trillion cells that, strung together, would circle the earth one hundred times.[75] How could this perfected turbo of evolution be ignited? Mutation, selection and time alone are not enough to account for the emergence of highly specialised cells that form complex systems in association over this period of time. Empirical data from a wonderful experiment support this view. In February 1988, Prof. Dr Richard Lenski began a long-term experiment in his laboratory at Michigan State University in which he grew twelve identical populations of the bacterium Escherichia coli. As a supporter of the theory of evolution, he wanted to prove evolution experimentally and observed the bacteria over many generations to see what new functions would evolve. The 70,000 generations of Escherichia coli bacteria are comparable to more than a million years of human existence. Time enough, then, that at least minor changes should manifest themselves. Trillions upon trillions of bacteria have been born and have died, but new functional genes and proteins or even new complex structures have not emerged.[76] For 70,000 generations, these bacteria have produced nothing other than their own kind. According to Prof. Dr Behes and Prof. Dr Minnich's interpretation of the experiment, the mutations only had a *de*volving effect, that is, a loss or reduction of certain functionalities, but a new ability did not emerge.[77] Based on this experiment, there are certainly studies that report evolutionarily newly developed abilities. But this is never due to the generation of new genetic information, only to its loss. How can *de*volution lead to a new ability? Imagine that the E. coli bacterium is a car. Through a mutation, descendants of this car lose the ability to form a body. Due to the loss of the car body, the car now weighs less than before and the fuel consumption decreases. Although this makes movement more efficient, it is only one aspect of the overall system. On the other hand, the car would lose the protection provided by the body, the occupants and seats would get completely wet in the rain, metal parts would start to rust more quickly, unprotected cables would become porous more quickly, so that the life of the car would ultimately be shortened. Nevertheless, materialists like to sell this as a benefit and proof of evolution. But it is exactly the opposite. Moreover, evolution would mean that new genetic material would be created, but that never happened in this experiment, there was only ever a loss of genetic information. This experiment could not even come close to proving that evolution produces perfectly coordinated functionalities and new species in a constant process of optimisation.

Another point is the problem of the complexity of a multicellular living being. Assuming that, with a lot of luck and chance, endothelial cells[1] had developed from the original non-specific eukaryotes, these cells only make sense if there were also blood cells and tissue cells at the same time. These different cell types only form an orchestrated collective if they are used in a coordinated, simultaneous and meaningful way. Without a blueprint that has a concrete goal for the system as a whole the scenario is inconceivable; otherwise, several interdependent mutations would have to have occurred simultaneously in order to accomplish this miracle of probability calculation. It doesn't make sense if a few blood cells come into being first if no circulatory system exists yet. Or why should muscle cells come into being when there are neither bones nor joints nor nerve cells to innervate them? It is more than obvious that a slow successive emergence of these structures would be completely pointless and would only produce half-finished organisms that would have no chance in the evolutionary struggle for survival. Darwinists encounter processes that cannot be explained solely by mutation, selection and a lot of time, especially since not every single-celled organism has followed this hypothetical path of evolution. Because even today there are still single-celled organisms that apparently wanted to remain single-celled organisms. This raises the question for me why some unicellular organisms of the early Earth should have evolved while others did not. You don't need to be a qualified biologist or medical doctor to see this: common sense is enough to realise that it couldn't have

---

[1] Cell layer lining the inside of the blood vessels

happened that way. Of course, there are materialists who see things completely differently and they should not remain unmentioned here. The German physicist and cabaret artist Vince Ebert makes no secret of the fact that he can only smile at critics of the theory of evolution. With a cabaret-like haughtiness he sees the theory of evolution as proven beyond doubt and critics in his eyes must therefore necessarily be uninformed and fanatical Bible-believing Christians.[78] The really uninformed, however, are mostly the materialistic natural scientists who do not even bother to deal with the scientific counter-arguments. With the following quotation, Ebert correctly draws attention to the fact that banal statistics are important sources of knowledge: 'Evolution does not work with fixed plans and targets, but with open possibilities. If some special ability or trait increases the number of offspring, then this ability will prevail over time. This is a banal, statistical calculation.'[79] Why does he not simply calculate the statistical probability of the multiple occurrence of interdependent mutations? Or the probability of the random chaining of amino acids into complex proteins? The probability is high that he would not like these probabilities of zero. What the special ability he names to produce more offspring has to do with the emergence of new species (which is, after all, ultimately what evolution is all about) is beyond me. Obviously, it is not as simple as Ebert would like it to be. Because, last but not least, there are overwhelming counter-arguments in this book that have nothing to do with a religious conviction but which are themselves quite banal logical calculations. However, since these calculations do not fit into Ebert's world view, they do not receive any attention. Ebert reports that many of his audience members would come up to him after his events and tell him that the theory of evolution is only a theory after all. He would always reply: 'Of course evolution is ›only‹ a theory. Gravity is also 'just' a theory. Nevertheless, nobody jumps off the roof because it is 'only' a theory.'[80] Well, gravity can be observed experimentally. Anyone jumping off a roof will inevitably hit the ground and most likely be dead. Even if gravity is only a theory, I can observe the effects. If I can observe it, I can believe it. With the theory of evolution, however, it is completely different. Macroevolution in the form of one new species emerging from another can neither be observed nor forced by experiment. The emergence of a new species has never been proven, so it is more than legitimate to question the theory of evolution. Ebert's argument on the purely evolutionary emergence of the eye, which advocates of Intelligent Design like to take as an example of an irreducibly complex system, is based on a computer simulation developed in the 1990s and published in a scientific paper by Daniel Nilson and Suzanne Pelger.[81] Ebert describes this research with great euphoria: 'Nilson and Pelger started a computer simulation, which they programmed in such a way that the sensitivity to light would always improve slightly per generation. After going through about 100,000 generation steps, the original light-sensitive spot had turned into something amazingly close to the human eye.'[82] Now, as a computer science professor, I know a lot about computer simulations and programming, and I can guarantee that a simulation only simulates what the programmers have programmed into it with their algorithms. Such a simulation can only be a very simplified representation of reality. You can also imagine that these algorithms have been programmed in such a way that the wishes and intentions of their developers have been incorporated. If you want to understand nature you cannot programme it according to limited human ideas and then think you can draw meaningful conclusions from it in the context of a simulation. What value can such a simulation have? I prefer to observe nature, because it is real and not dependent on human algorithms. And if you observe nature, you will find - as for example with the 70,000 generations of Escherichia coli bacteria - a completely different truth, a truth without evolution, and this truth is neither simulated nor created by humans.

In the 1920s and 1930s, Darwin's selection mechanism was expanded by new findings from the field of genetics with mutation, recombination, gene transfer and other factors to form the so-called synthetic theory of evolution. The fact that evolution is nowadays regarded as the 'well-proven basis of our world view'[83] and is taught in schools and universities without a hint of critical questioning is based solely on the vague assumption that new species are created by random copying errors during cell division and that these mutations usually only lead to minor changes. Most mutations, by the way, are harmful or neutral to their carriers. Only very few actually lead to a minor improvement.[84] Such mutations, as well as the recombination of genetic material at fertilisation, are entirely undirected; they occur completely randomly, regardless of living habits and environmental conditions. Selection, on the other hand, functions directionally. According to this theory, selection-positive mutations that give their carriers advantages in survival eventually prevail over time.

In the following, I would like to subject the described mechanisms of mutation and selection to a first critical examination. In this context, I would like to take a human being with a disability as an example. From a purely biological point of view, this human being possesses selection-negative changes from the point of view of Darwinists. However, I look at it in a completely different way. Disabled people are a great enrichment for many people. There is definitely no selection here, but for us compassionate people they trigger deep emotions, and not only the person with the disability, but many of his companions grow far beyond themselves with this situation and gain strength and love. The opposite of selection is at work here, namely integration. As a rule, evolution is only attributed to the physical abilities of individuals (longer proboscis, better camouflage, curved beak, and so on). But animals, and especially we humans, are more than the product of our mechanical actions. Evolution must be viewed holistically if it is to be authentic. In evolution, our social bonds and empathy in particular play a crucial role. What evolutionary power do people with a disability have in helping the people around them to have so much love, compassion and social responsibility? Such people are evolutionary boosters in our social unity and connectedness. But in the classical view of evolution, they would fall victim to selection pressure. What a false and limited view of the world that is. The following quotation from Hans-Peter Dürr confirms my view:

'This strange 'survival Darwinism', according to which the strongest gets the gold medal, is in my opinion a completely nonsensical concep-

tion. It is not about the competition of approaches, but about the creativity of cooperation. Higher quality does not come from two others competing, but from them working together.'[85]

In raven research, it can be impressively observed that individual skills and egoism are not required, but that teamwork and cooperation lead to success. The behavioural scientist Thomas Bugnyar was able to observe that ravens, through co-ordinated teamwork, took the killed animal from a pack of wolves. Some ravens bit and pecked at the wolves' tails every second, causing them to constantly turn away from the carcass and turn around. Meanwhile, the other ravens stole some 90 per cent of the carcass.[86] Selection is a concept of selfishness. Selfish ravens that would only think of themselves could hardly steal the carcass from the wolves. Here the idea of selective evolution fails completely.

Richard Dawkins commented on the criticism of a medical doctor who was of the opinion that Darwinism assumes that we came into being by blind chance in the following way: 'For the umpteenth time, natural selection is exactly the opposite of a random process.'[87] Well, just because you repeat something x times, it doesn't make it any more right. Selection is not creative, it can only sort out from what already exists, but never create. Selection is always embedded in a larger scenario. It cannot be considered or evaluated separately, because it is directly dependent on random mutations and other evolutionary factors that must inevitably precede it. As a formula, it could be expressed somewhat simplified as follows:

mutation + selection + a lot of time = evolution

If even one of the three summands (here mutation) is determined by chance, then the result (here evolution) must necessarily also be random, and selection can no longer change this. In order to be able to reflect correctly the observations of nature and the results of experiments I would like to adapt the formula somewhat. However, this requires a subdivision of the concept of evolution into the two terms microevolution and macroevolution.[88]

Microevolution: Microevolution is also called infraspecific evolution, which means evolution within species. This means changes, adaptations and variations of already existing organs and body structures within the respective species through mutation and selection. Microevolution can be verified by experiments and observations and is not questioned by anyone.

Macroevolution: Macroevolution is also referred to as trans-specific evolution, that is, evolution beyond species boundaries. This is understood to mean the emergence of completely new forms of life with organs and structures that did not exist before. Qualitatively new genetic material is created not only for the formation of new species but above all for the formation of completely new genera, families, orders, classes and phylums (see Figure 4-3, on the concept of taxonomy, that is the hierarchical division, for instance of the animal kingdom, into categories). Macroevolution cannot and could not be found in nature, in the fossil record or experimentally and is an expression of evolutionist wishful thinking.

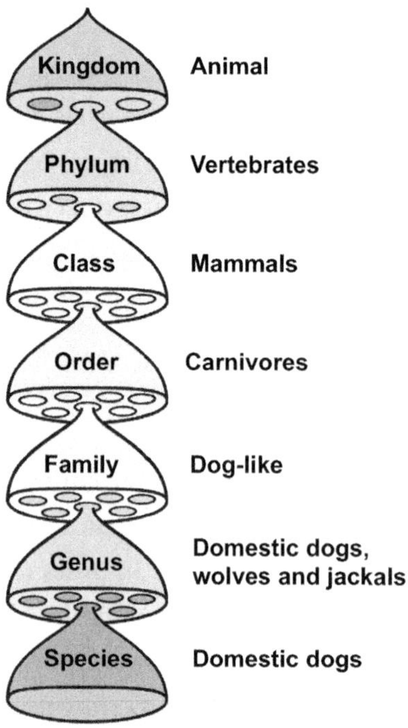

Figure 4-3: *Taxonomy using the example of dogs*

The variants of Darwin's finches I described above are an example of microevolution. Despite different expressions, they are ultimately still finches and birds. No new organs or anatomical new constructions were created. The changes are ultimately processes of variation within a basic type. The situation is analogous, for example, with dog breeds, which, just like Darwin's finches, can still interbreed. The development of breed-specific characteristics within the scope of variability (for instance dachshund or poodle from the original dog or from the wolf) rather shows that the original forms possessed complex, diverse sets of genes, and concerning evolution there was no increase but rather a thinning out of genetic diversity. A poodle can no longer give rise to a wolf. Macro-evolution would call for exactly that, but it shows exactly the opposite.

Should the evolutionists be right, despite all the absurdity, there would have to be a transition from microevolution to macroevolution. So at some point such a change must take place in a species that this mutated creature would be the first and only one of its kind. This creature could now no longer mate with the animals from which it emerged. In order for it not to die out again immediately, the identical mutation for an opposite-sex specimen would have to have arisen in the same region, because otherwise the poor mutated animal would not only be the first but equally also the last of its kind. Within the scope of phylogenetic development this would then often have to have happened again and again, even for all hypothetical intermediate stages. The evolutionary process must once again have the much-invoked coincidence on its side here, and another probability of zero is once again completely ignored.

Finally, an attempt was made to prove macroevolution experimentally. With the fruit fly Drosophila melanogaster, they chose an experimental animal in which 60 per cent of its genes also occur in a similar form in us humans. It takes one to two weeks for a new generation to emerge, and a female fly lays around 100 eggs per day. In one year, about 25 fly generations can thus be created.[89] In this experiment, the mutation rate was artificially increased in order to accelerate the evolutionary process. But despite this intervention, the flies showed no trace of macroevolution even after numerous generations. The flies remained flies, they only showed variations, for instance a change of bristles or eye colour and shape, but never new structures. Rather, degenerate specimens appeared that had legs as antennae or malformed wings.[90] Neither observations in nature nor experiments with E. coli bacteria or fruit flies could provide even hints, let alone evidence, that would point to macroevolution. There is only one logical interpretation: microevolution has only limited potential, its effect is limited. A transition to macroevolution does not take place.

I find it astonishing how great the willingness is to cling to a materialistic Darwinism against all logic, observation and probability. Our current science is treading the path of knowledge the wrong way round in many places. Starting from a Darwinism that has never been questioned, attempts are instead made to construct a truth in a backward-looking argumentation that leads to the desired result. This is commonly referred to as circular reasoning or petitio principii, when the actual conclusion is made the premise of the argument. Darwinists do not arrive at their findings because they have consistently interpreted the facts and observations, but because they have worked out the steps necessary for their supposed truth in such a way that there is no break with the paradigm. Those who act in this way follow an ideology in my eyes, but they are allowed to call themselves serious scientists in our Western-orientated society.

If macroevolution had really taken place then there should be countless indications of transitional forms between species in the fossil record. To date, the picture is very sobering, as Steve Jones, Professor of Genetics at University College London, has also noted:

> *'The finds do not at all reveal the multitude of intermediate forms that would be expected due to natural selection and the slow progress resulting from it, but many species appear without warning, remain in a fixed form and eventually disappear again without leaving any descendants. Geology certainly does not show us a finely graduated chain of living things. This is the most serious objection that can be brought against the theory of evolution.'*[91]

There are many other high-ranking experts who assess the fossil situation quite similarly, including Prof. Stephen Jay Gould, palaeontologist, geologist and evolutionary researcher at Harvard University:

> *'The fossil record, with its abrupt changes, cannot provide support for gradual change. (...) All palaeontologists are aware that the fossil record contains precious little in the way of intermediate stages; the abrupt transitions between major groups are characteristic. (...) What, then, could imperfect initial stages of useful structures be used for? What do you do with half a jaw or half a wing?'*[92]

Gould raises a very important point in his last sentence, for how exactly are we to imagine intermediate forms? Would intermediate forms make any sense at all? Would such intermediate forms with incompletely formed body parts and functionalities even be able to survive? Armin Risi has given a wonderful lecture on this subject, in which he very aptly illustrates this absurdity using the example of bats.[93] The oldest bat fossils appear abruptly and diversely about 52 million years ago, and the bat structural plan has remained almost constant since this sudden appearance in the geological strata up to the present day.[94] Bats are not some rare special case in the animal kingdom that has been pointedly selected here. Bats are quite representative, since with about 1,100 species in about 200 genera and 18 families they are the second largest mammalian order after rodents.[95] Risi takes the Darwinists at their word; there must have been intermediate stages, and even if there are no fossil finds, it would be enough for him if someone gave him a sketch of a bat precursor. He asks himself what such a transitional form, starting from a rat-like primordial mammal, would have looked like? This primitive mammal would have had to develop longer thin fingers and incipient flight skins at some point through mutation. Hearing, with the ability to hear ultrasound, would also have to have been at least somewhat functional. This animal would not be able to move around properly or orientate itself with half an ear. In addition to ultrasonic hearing, the ability to emit ultrasonic sounds would also have to have developed. So not only isolated mutations, but several complementary and interdependent mutations must have taken place. The probability of this is practically zero. Risi is absolutely right: 'The bat, which is only 98 per cent complete, would be 100 per cent incapable of life. It would slam into the wall, it could not fly properly, it would be eaten by the birds of prey.'[96] Dawkins, however, is of a completely different opinion in his book *The God Delusion*, writing: 'Half a wing is not as good as a whole wing, of course, but it is still better than no wing at all.'[97] I consider Gould's and Risi's views much more plausible, however. With half a wing, one may be more likely to survive a fall from a tree than without wings (this is Dawkin's reasoning), but the animal can neither fly well nor run well with it, it would fall prey to predators from the air or on land in no time. As another example, consider the woodpecker. This bird hammers on tree trunks up to 12,000 times a day during courtship; the typical drumming noise can also be heard across the forest when searching for food and building a nesting hole. Like a jackhammer its beak hits the hardest wood about 20 times per second at an impact speed of 25 km/h. The beak is also used for searching for food and building a nesting hole. How can it be that this animal does not suffer a concussion? A human being would probably be incapacitated for weeks after just one such head butt. Among other things the woodpecker has a special skull anatomy whereby its brain is not located directly behind the beak, but slightly above it. The force of the impact is thus not directly transferred to the brain. Furthermore, it has very little cerebrospinal fluid, so its brain has little room to move when it hits the top of the skull. Julian Heiermann of the Nature and Biodiversity Conservation Union of Germany describes a kind of shock absorber function in the woodpecker's anatomical structure which is designed (sorry) so that the blows can be well cushioned. He finally comes to the conclusion that evolution has ensured that the woodpecker does not get headaches.[98] I must clearly doubt this statement. How could evolution have turned a conventional bird, very slowly over millions of years, into a woodpecker that hammers wood? I imagine it as follows: the first precursors of woodpeckers probably pecked at trees very tentatively at first, but without much success. So they could neither find food nor build nesting holes. They fell victim to selection. However, when the later generations (wherever they may have come from) could already hammer a little harder, most of them got a concussion, because their shock absorber function was not yet fully developed. The specimens without concussion could only peck half nest cavities into the wood, while their conspecifics that were still building nests in the treetops were able to raise their brood well. And again they fell victim to selection. The selection so much praised by Dawkins would immediately sort out such intermediate stages.

So selection is not an argument for macroevolution; selection *prevents* it. Yet there are much clearer counter-arguments than the half wing or the woodpecker. How could one explain a slow, gradual emergence of the life cycle of a butterfly? The development from an egg to a caterpillar via a pupa to the finished moth, which in turn lays eggs, is highly precisely coordinated. This cycle can only function if it has been laid out in its perfect wholeness from the outset. It is impossible to explain this life cycle by a step-by-step development. Dawkins was able to explain away half a wing with a lot of imagination, but what is a half life cycle of a butterfly supposed to look like? Were there only eggs and caterpillars to begin with? But caterpillars are sexless and cannot mate or lay eggs. Or was there only the butterfly, which was initially viviparous until some specimens started laying eggs? Why lay eggs if the further steps with caterpillar and pupa did not yet exist? No matter how you want to spin it, there is no plausible explanation for a slow, gradual emergence of this cycle. It can only be done completely or not at all. This is a beautiful example of a system with a non-reducible complexity, a concept I will explain in more detail in Chapter 4.2, *Intelligent Design*.

The Cambrian explosion

The Cambrian is a period in Earth's history that began about 540 million years ago and lasted about 60 million years. If we put this period in relation to the total Earth age of 4.5 billion years, we get a very small period that occurs at about 8/9ths of the time axis (see Figure 4-4). What is so special about this period? It is that the so-called Cambrian explosion took place in this period. Suddenly, almost out of nowhere, the basic forms of all animal and plant species known to us today appear in the geological layers of this epoch on the entire Earth. No fossils worth mentioning are found in the underlying rock strata of the Precambrian, that is from the time before the Cambrian.

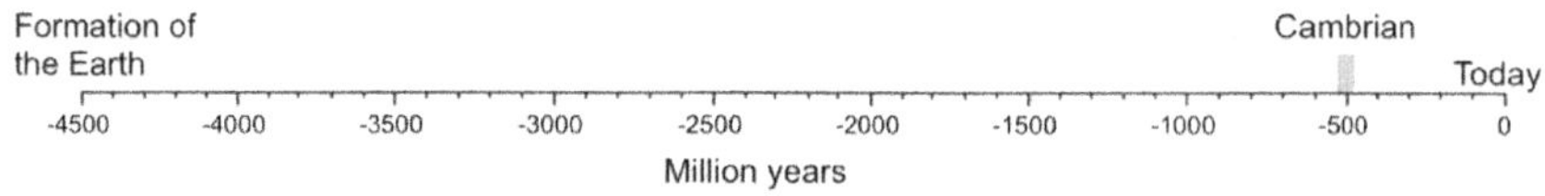

Figure 4-4: The Cambrian (grey period) in the Earth Age

In his TV-show *α-Centauri*, Lesch explains this phenomenon of the missing Precambrian fossils and thus also the missing precursors of the animal world as follows:

> *'This (the Cambrian explosion,* author's note*) seems to have taken place within a few million years, if you believe the fossil record. For the first real skeletal fossils are only known since the Cambrian. (...) There is a strange dating gap between the time before the Cambrian and the Cambrian itself. We are missing 200 to 300 million years of (geological) layers, they are simply not there. What happened there? We don't really know. It seems to have to do with the fact that large erosional processes destroyed large parts of the Earth's history. But exactly those that we are missing, those must be the precursors for the explosion of life that we observe there in the Cambrian, that is, in the fossil layers, (...) that must have taken place in these earlier phases. But we don't have them, that's what we're missing. So to speak, the steps from the single-celled organisms to the multi-cellular organisms, to the more complex organisms, precisely this transition, that is what we are missing.'*[99]

How does Lesch come to the conclusion that there must have been erosion processes here that wiped out all fossil transitional forms? There is no evidence for this assertion. Such claims are only made because Darwinian theory demands it. It seems to me that Darwinists have once again taken the wrong path of knowledge because in their understanding Darwinism and therefore also the fossil transitional forms *must have existed in any case.* So they construct this extremely improbable scenario for the sole reason of preserving the materialistic world view and Darwinism at all costs, no matter what observations have been made. Isn't it strange that the very geological layers that should have contained all the transitional forms have foolishly disappeared without a trace, all over the Earth? Another of those incredible coincidences! It's almost funny the things materialists and Darwinists have to be prepared to believe just to avoid breaking with the paradigm. But what else should a dyed-in-the-wool Darwinist think? It can only have been that way in their eyes.

Now, how would an unbiased scientist assess this situation? The Precambrian strata show no fossils, not a single hypothetical precursor, as demanded by Darwinists, is found in the geological strata around the entire globe. Logical and obvious would be the conclusion that there obviously could have been no such transitional forms for the Cambrian variety. But the evolutionary theorists construct flimsy attempts at explanation in order to be able to maintain their theory with the transitional forms under all circumstances. They are of the opinion, in all seriousness, that there were quasi gapless and area-wide erosions throughout the entire Earth and that therefore no fossil traces of the millions of hypothetical precursors of all living beings and plants of the world can be found anywhere. Others claim that the transition from single-celled organisms to the complex diversity of the Cambrian must have taken place in such a short period of time of about ten to fifteen million years and that it was not enough to create a fossil record. But this is contradicted by findings from the most extensive fossil discovery to date from the Cambrian in Chengjiang in southern China. In 1984, an extremely extensive and well-preserved fossil fauna was found in the Maotianshan Shale, the so-called Chengjiang faunal community, which was even designated a UNESCO

World Natural Heritage Site in 2012.

This fossil fauna has an age of 525 to 520 million years, so that the period of the Cambrian explosion in this region was obviously much smaller than previously assumed. In 2000, the Discovery Institute invited the world's leading Cambrian palaeontologist, Prof. Jun-Yuan Chen from China, to give a talk at the University of Washington. Dr Stephen Meyer, whom I will introduce in more detail later in this chapter, reported on Chen's impressive presentation as part of his talk at the 2014 Ligonier Ministries West Coast Conference. Chen brought many incredibly well-preserved, previously completely unknown fossils from the Maotianshan Shale for this talk. He reported that in a period of only five million years, a tremendous variety of animal species had suddenly emerged without any precursors. He then held his hand in the air with fingers spread out to symbolise Darwin's bottom-up evolutionary tree. He used this to make the point that, according to Darwin, everything started with the palm of the hand as a simple life form and that diversity eventually branched out further and further into the fingertips through random mutation and selection. He then said that the Cambrian Maotianshan layer showed something completely different. He then folded his hand down so that the fingers pointed downwards. His conclusion was that it was the other way round. The layers show an incredibly great variety of perfectly formed animal species, which rather decreased gradually over millions of years.[100] During the final Q&A session, one of the professors from the University of Washington spoke up and asked: 'Prof. Chen, that was a very fascinating lecture, but aren't you worried about freely expressing your scepticism about Darwinian evolution when you come from a communist country like you do?' After a special silence in the hall, Chen smiled and replied, 'Well, in China we are never allowed to question our government! But Darwinism, we are allowed to question it. In America, you may question the government, but never Darwinism.'[101] With this statement he made it abundantly clear that freedom in research and science in the Western world is held in the shackles of materialism.

Political freedom may not exist in China, but freedom in science and research is far ahead of us in this respect. Moreover, it becomes clear that this is not about science versus church, for instance evolution versus creationism. Chen after all comes from a cultural and religious sphere that is completely foreign to us. This is exclusively about correct and logical conclusions, based on sound reasoning. It is incomprehensible to me why a serious scientific discussion on Darwinism is not possible in our western world. For what reason are its critics portrayed as cranks and religious fanatics? It is mainly the materialists who are deliberately propagating a kind of religious fundamentalism in public to protect their own world view. They simply claim that Intelligent Design (or any criticism of evolution) is not based on science but on theism, which is simply wrong. In doing so, they make it extremely easy for themselves, because this untenable accusation in a way exempts them from having to provide proper counterarguments. I must admit that with these portents I sometimes wonder to what extent a scientific dialogue would make sense at all. Materialists are dyed-in-the-wool dogmatists; their materialistic world view is usually a fundamental decision to which they stubbornly cling. No argument in the world could convince them of anything else. Max Planck (1858-1947), 1919 German Nobel Prize winner for physics and founder of quantum physics (see Chapter 6, *Quantum Mechanics and Spirituality*), uttered something that radically supports my doubts about such discussions:

> *'A new scientific truth does not establish itself in such a way that its opponents are convinced and declare themselves to have been taught, but rather in such a way that the opponents gradually die out and that the younger generation is familiarised with the truth right from the start.'*[102]

However, as long as there are people like Dr Günter Bechly, Dr Eben Alexander or even me, people who have completely changed their scientific view of the world, hope for insight and understanding is not lost. Planck addresses a very important point, addressed to the upcoming generation. For me this is the most important course we must set for our future. Schools, colleges and universities have an enormous responsibility and we would do well finally to start looking at the world as a whole. All arguments and counter-arguments of the theory of evolution should be discussed, detached from prevailing world views and prejudices. Let's give our children back their freedom in research and science instead of keeping them dogmatically imprisoned in a materialistic world view.

Dumbing down in our schools

When I leafed through the biology book used in my daughter's school, a volume entitled *Linder Biology*, I was particularly struck by an illustration on the adaptive radiation of species. Adaptive radiation means that starting from a primordial insectivore as a non-specific ancestor of mammals about 250 to 200 million years ago, there was a gradual fanning out into the animal species we know today. From a geological point of view this is thought to have happened in a relatively short period of about 200 million years. This figure shows how, for example, elephants, primates, bats or whales evolved from this small primordial mammal. In Chapter 4.1.3, *The origin and evolution of whales* I will show you, using the example of whales, that this fanning out and formation of a family tree cannot have taken place in this way and that there is no evidence for this development. I would also like to show you how much materialistic science influences our children in schools and creates its own world view. I suspect that this one-sided influence is not even intentional but is the result of a taken-for-grantedness and a view that is never questioned. This prompted me to send an email to the Ministry of Schools and Education of the State of North Rhine-Westphalia.

'Dear staff of the Ministry of Schools and Education,

I would like to politely ask you to comment on my following concern. It is with great concern that I have noticed that in the subject area of biology, some theories that have not been scientifically verified are being taught as proven. Specifically, this concerns the scientific understanding of the origin of life and evolution. In all our textbooks it is postulated as a matter of course that life originated from dead matter and that the origin of man and the diversity of species can be explained by Darwinism. Our children are falsely taught that this is scientifically proven. But this is not the case.

If one wants to continue to use this content in the textbooks, please provide it with the indication that these are merely unproven theories and that there are scientific arguments in favour of them and that there are equally arguments against them. I don't mean that everyone should suddenly be educated to creationism, but we should honestly teach our children and make it clear what we definitely know from a scientific point of view and what is only speculative theory. We owe that to our children so that they can decide for themselves, without bias and based on real facts, which view of the world they think is correct.

I am aware that even at universities the Darwinian theory of evolution is regarded as the status quo and the current state of science; after all, I studied medicine myself. But that is precisely the problem, that here people dogmatically cling to a world view that has long since wavered. This is being elevated unchecked, almost ideologically, to the status of scientific reality and distorts the view of the facts. Why do we do things differently with the theory of evolution than we do in other areas of science, where we have to deliver hard research results? Darwinian evolutionary theory shows how mutation and selection lead to adaptations within a species, but there is no evidence that this could prove the emergence of completely new species or even humans. Yet this is exactly what we teach our children without reference to the lack of evidence. I find this frightening and scientifically grossly negligent.

I would be interested to know what you think about this as the person responsible for our education system.

Yours sincerely, Prof. Dr. rer. medic. Dipl.-Inform. Oliver Lazar'

I actually received a reply to my enquiry in which I was referred to findings in palaeontology and molecular biology without any scientific references. They said that there was fossil evidence for evolution and that evolution could have been directly proven in viruses. I was very surprised, because the lack of fossil evidence is the greatest weakness of Darwin's theory. Darwin himself had even admitted this. In chapter 4.1.3, *The origin and evolution of whales* I present further scientifically founded criticisms of the fossil situation. That there is evolution in microbiology cannot be denied. But this is microevolution, which does not prove macroevolution with the emergence of completely new species. When I asked for scientific references for the fossil evidence and proof of the emergence of new species, I did not receive any more answers. In the end, my statements on the origin of species could not be refuted argumentatively, so I guess they refrained from further discussion. A scientific dialogue is not sought, but mostly rejected a priori with the accusation of a creationist ideological manipulation attempt. Our science and education system are largely determined, even at the highest levels, by blinkered dogmatists who are not only hostile to progress but also hinder it. For me science also means further development and the correction of errors when new findings are available. As a rule, however, corrective proposals have a particularly hard time if they would consequently shake up a prevailing world view. Arthur Ellison, Professor of Electrical Engineering at City University London, President of the English Society for Psychical Research, commented on the subject of change in science as follows:

> *'I don't think any real scientist would ever claim that something cannot happen under any circumstances. Especially in the 20th century, many things have happened that previous generations thought were impossible. So when second-rate scientists (as I call them somewhat rudely) claim this can't be possible, as is often the case with the paranormal, they are basically saying that our current scientific knowledge provides a complete and exhaustive explanation of human nature and the universe, so to speak, which is of course absurd and ridiculous.*

Science and its theories are constantly changing, and we must expect them to continue to do so.'[103]

Dawkins, too, presents his view of change and correction in science in *The God Delusion*:

'Fundamentalists know they are right: They have read the truth in a holy book and are certain in advance that nothing will dissuade them from their convictions. (...) If, on the other hand, I as a scientist believe in things (for example, evolution), it is not because I have read a holy book, but because I have examined the evidence. That is really something quite different. You don't believe in books about evolution because they are sacred, but because they describe an overwhelming wealth of evidence that supports each other. In principle, any reader can trace the path back and check the evidence for themselves. If a scientific book is wrong, at some point someone will find the error and it will be corrected in subsequent books. That this does not happen with holy books is obvious.'[104]

I fully agree with Dawkins on correcting errors, but he lacks a bit of self-reflection here, because his definition of fundamentalism refers exclusively to the religious, but not to the materialist fundamentalists. He says that he has examined the evidence - for instance for evolution. However, I wish he would look at the scientific papers on spirituality and their evidence as well. But he denies this subject its credibility, not because he has examined it himself and been able to refute the evidence, but a priori because he neither can nor wants to believe it. He is talking here about a holy book (*On the Origin of Species*) and its followers who ignore contradictory evidence. To protect himself and his Darwinian theory Dawkins takes refuge in the religious-scientific duality. He brings a purely religious motivation into the focus of the discussion. I think he is immune to the realisation that he is dealing with scientific counter-arguments and not religious ones. The fact that he even has his own holy books with his literature on evolution, to which he clings just as dogmatically as the believers he criticises cling to their holy scriptures, despite the lack of or insufficient evidence and several probabilities of zero, does not seem to interest him. He calls himself a scientist, a phrase which implies that he does not consider those he criticises to be scientists. This is a fatal error. There is an ever-increasing number of high-level, qualified scientists who manage to combine the natural sciences with spirituality at a high level. Many of them had spiritual experiences of their own, e.g. in the book *Spiritual Awakenings*[105] 57 scientists and academics describe their experiences in detail. Also worth mentioning here is Prof. Jeffrey J. Kripal of Rice University in Houston/Texas, who in his book *The Flip*[106] reports on the spiritual awakenings of rationalists and the consciousness research of philosophers and neuroscientists. Knowing full well that such psi studies and their scientific results are subject to particularly critical scrutiny, the quality and meticulousness of the study design and execution are usually at a disproportionately higher level than studies in the classical fields. Dawkins says in his quotation that every reader can check the evidence for himself. I therefore invite every reader to check the evidence of our EREAMS study on afterlife contacts (see chapter 7, *Is there evidence for a spirit world?*). Checking the evidence is not the sole preserve of materialistic natural science, even if Dawkins obviously sees it that way. By the way, I am not alone in my view of the anti-Darwinian evidence; many scientists far more competent in evolutionary biology have checked it, examining for example the origin of life and species, and they have discovered errors. But I am sure that for ideological reasons there will be no corrections in subsequent books by Dawkins or anything that shows that he has actually 'traced the path back and checked the evidence'.

Holy books are not rewritten, but if, like Dawkins, you have a firmly anchored world view in your head that threatens to collapse if the errors in your world view are proven, then unfortunately this refusal to re-write also applies to the scientific books he refers to. The only problem is that unfortunately this is not obvious and lay people, our schoolchildren and students among them, are served up unproven theories as a matter of course presenting a 'reality' without alternatives. When even Dr Richard

David Precht, one of the most brilliant thinkers and philosophers in Germany, writes as a matter of course several times in his book *Wer bin ich und wenn ja, wie viele? (Who am I and if so, how many?)* quite naturally and without any doubt that Darwin has proved that we humans are descended from animals[107], in my opinion this is not due to the result of his own examination of the theory of evolution but to his blind trust in the natural sciences. This confidence even goes so far as to call dissenting philosophers and scientists 'stubborn'.[108] Precht's statements about a presumably proven theory of evolution show that the materialists' strategy has worked. They have managed to get a majority of people in our society and even great thinkers to internalise Darwin's theory of evolution as an incontrovertible reality and a matter of course. I am sure that most of them do not even know of the criticisms and weaknesses of this theory. Nevertheless, they are convinced of their half-knowledge. The two psychology professors David Dunning and Justin Kruger call this phenomenon the *Dunning-Kruger effect* (see Figure 4-5).

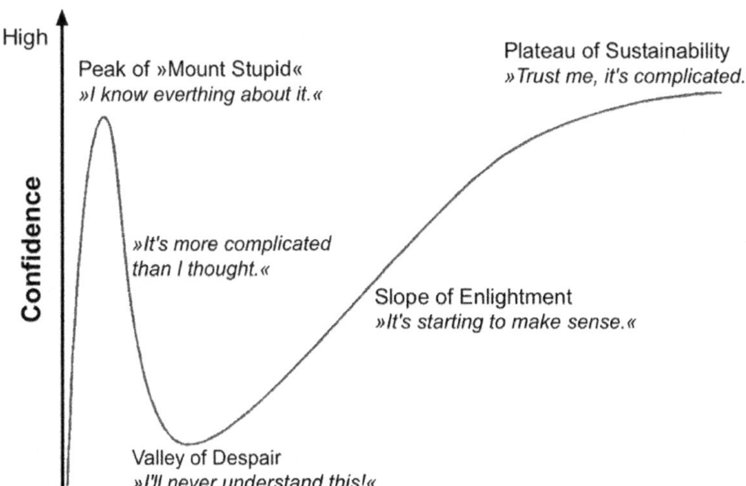

Figure 4-5: Dunning-Kruger-Effect

The effect states that there is a distortion in many people's self-perception of their knowledge and ability. Ignorance and a lack of overall picture eventually lead to self-overestimation. The fatal thing is that these people, in their unconscious overestimation of themselves, are completely convinced of themselves and their knowledge. In the chart, this is called the *Peak of Mount Stupid.* If these people are also academically respected personalities whose word carries weight, then there is a very great danger of misinterpretation and false world views.

The criticism of the theory of evolution in this book is scientifically based. It is not about the Bible or any religion. It is not a battle between science and religious ideology, but between good and bad science. Unfortunately, when it comes to the origin of life and species, we are teaching our children very one-sided and demonstrably bad science. Who would it hurt if we openly and honestly presented all the pros and cons of the theory of evolution in our schools and universities and showed that there is serious research that has discovered insurmountable hurdles in the theory *far from religion*, that there is a difference between micro- and macroevolution, that there are zero probabilities at several points, and so on? It would broaden our children's scientific horizons, not infiltrate them ideologically. Geisler and Turek confirm this:

> *'But Darwinists will always go to great lengths to ensure that this is exactly what does not happen. They would rather suppress the evidence than allow it to be presented honestly. Why? Because this is the one area where Darwinists lack faith - they lack faith that their theory will still be believed when our children have seen all the evidence.'*[109]

After all the arguments I have presented, I wonder about the sceptics who even organise themselves into associations and yet tolerate this kind of science without criticism. Where is the scepticism here? It would be appropriate here. But they prefer to remain on the peak of 'Mount Stupid' of the Dunning-Kruger curve and do not even think of critically questioning the scientific findings; instead they prefer to focus their attention on spiritual issues. This is basically understandable, because scepticism about scientific findings requires expert knowledge, which the sceptics usually do not dare to approach themselves, they blindly trust the peer review. Expert assessments are important and good. However, they are not the measure of all things. The experts will always assess according to their own world view and knowledge. A lateral thinker who possibly turns established knowledge on its head is mercilessly excluded. A reviewer who promotes lateral thinkers runs the risk of being in the line of fire of criticism himself, and hardly anyone is willing to put his own reputation on the line for such scientific revolutions. So criticising science is difficult - only specialists are able to do it - but strangely enough when it comes to spirituality everyone thinks they are an expert and can sharply criticise things they usually don't even know anything about. I wonder by what right they do this. I too am sceptical, and my scepticism has revealed to me all the misinterpretations and errors in origin-of-life research, errors which I present in this work in a factual and argumentative way. Scepticism is good and important, but one must not make the mistake of directing it exclusively at topics that do not fit into one's own world view. If ignorance and lack of knowledge are the basis of scepticism, then scepticism quickly becomes dogmatism.

4.1.3 The origin and evolution of whales

I think it is time to take a closer look at the arguments of the Darwinists as well, because in their opinion macroevolution has, after all, long been proven. No doubt there is extensive research in this area, but is the argumentation really conclusive? With millions of animal species it should surely be easy to find many more millions of preliminary and intermediate stages in order to be able to show macroevolution palaeontologically as well. After so many years of research, however, it turns out that it is not so simple, even if Dawkins sees it differently:

> *'Many developmental transitions are very elegantly documented by more or less continuous series of fossils with gradual changes. In some cases this is not the case, and these are then the famous 'gaps'. (...)*

Creationists rave about 'gaps' in the fossil record, just as they love gaps in general. (...) Gaps are automatically filled by God in the minds of creationists. (...) It would be easy to imagine that there are no fossils at all, and even then the evidence for evolution, for example from molecular genetics or geographical distribution, would still be overwhelmingly strong.'[110]

Dawkins writes of many transitional forms in the fossils that document the gradual changes, but I think the scientific reality is different. My research has shown that there are very few publications with truly complete transitional stages. Why he then speaks of 'many' is beyond me. From my point of view it would also be very helpful if we could define what exactly is meant by a continuous and complete fossil record in this context because Dawkins complains that critics of evolution would require almost every single step of the stepwise development of an animal species to be proven, which of course is not feasible. I agree with him there. But are five fossil intermediates enough to prove macroevolution from a piglet-sized land-dwelling small mammal to a blue whale (at up to 33 metres long and weighing 200 tonnes, the heaviest and largest vertebrate ever to have lived on Earth) over a period of about 40 to 50 million years? Or do we rather need ten, twenty or a hundred such intermediate stages? There is no general answer to this question. It certainly depends on the respective complexity of the transformation, and the transformation from the small land mammal to the whale can hardly be surpassed in complexity. In my view, five intermediate stages are definitely far too few, and to call this 'continuous' and 'seamless' seems a bit too euphoric to me. Moreover, I think it is not just the number of intermediate stages that matters but rather that the overall argumentative package is coherent. To this end, it would be helpful if the fossils which have been found, in particular, showed significant anatomical transitional structures and clearly demonstrated the required transformations, for example a whale's dentition that contained both teeth and baleen[I]. But such obvious stages of transformation are not found in the fossils. The Darwinists only ever show us milestones of a hypothetical evolutionary sequence, that is, already fully developed and independent animal species with perfectly formed structures, and then, according to their biased intentions and looking through the glasses of Darwinism, arrange these into a phylogenetic sequence that suits them. This does not necessarily have to be wrong, but there are certainly other views and interpretations that lead to a different result, one far from a Darwinian wishful thinking that is the foundation of these findings. But let us first look at what arguments Darwinists have for macroevolution. Then we can form an objective judgement.

Basically, the Darwinists all refer to one and the same example, namely the evolution of whales. According to them, the gradual emergence of whales has been proven without any gaps. The paper *The origin and early evolution of whales. Macroevolution documented on the Indian Subcontinent* by the team of whale researchers around the Dutchman Johannes Thewissen is the hottest iron in the fire of the evolutionists. In the paper, the researchers boast in the following words: 'The origin of whales is most likely the best understood example of macroevolution in the fossil record.'[111]

Travis Park, an expert on prehistoric whales at the Natural History Museum in London, even outdoes this arrogance: 'Whales are an iconic example of evolution. They evolved from small mammals with hooves to the blue whales we know today.'[112] So if the evolution of whales is the best Darwinists have to offer on the subject of macroevolution then this should stand up to critical scrutiny and thorough examination without any doubt. Since whales are mammals, they, as well as the entire variety of mammals, are descended from land-dwelling rat-like small mammals according to the theory of evolution. Allegedly, these land mammals went through many intermediate stages of (almost) complete anatomical remodelling before finally becoming whales. This transformation began about 60 million years ago in the Tertiary period, with the first complete

[I] Baleen whales have lamellar bristles in their upper jaws, which they use to filter food (especially krill) very efficiently from the water.

animals of modern whale groups appearing in the geological strata about 34 million years ago. Before I subject whale evolution to a factual and critical evaluation, I will give you an overview of the individual presumed stages of development as they are currently described by evolutionary theorists as proven facts.

50-48 million years ago (living on land)

Indohyus (see Figure 4-6) was an exclusively terrestrial vegetarian genus of cloven-hoofed animals the size of a raccoon. There is a strong resemblance to today's deer piglets.

Figure 4-6: Indohyus

Pakicetus (see Figure 4-7) was slightly larger than Indohyus and resembled a wolf with its stature and typical teeth of a carnivore. Pakicetus lived exclusively on the land.

Figure 4-7: Pakicetus

47-42 million years ago (living on land and in water)

Figure 4-8: Ambulocetus natans

Ambulocetus natans (see Figure 4-8) had a length of about three metres and lived both on land and in the water. It somewhat resembles a crocodile. An almost complete skeleton was found in 1992 in Pakistan by Johannes Thewissen. In 2011, a very similar specimen was discovered in Peru. With a length of four metres and an age of 43 million years, it was named Peregocetus pacificus. This animal bore a strong resemblance to today's sea lions.

41-35 million years ago (living in water)

Figure 4-9: Basilosaurus isis and Dorudon atrox

With a body length of 18 metres, Basilosaurus isis was the largest mammal of this time. It was a carnivorous predator. Thus, remains of the smaller Dorudon atrox (see Figure 4-9) were found in its stomach.[113] Dorudon grew up to five metres long. Both lived exclusively in water. They had small hind limbs that were not connected to the rest of the skeleton. Thus they were unsuitable for locomotion on land. Evolutionists see these as rudiments, that is, regressed non-functional remains of the hind legs of land mammals. Another legitimate assumption is that these structures played an important function in mating. According to Gingerich, one of the world's best-known whale researchers, Basilosaurus was an evolutionary dead end. Therefore, the Dorudon is also considered more of a precursor to modern whales because of its physical proportions.[114]

34 million years until today (modern whales)

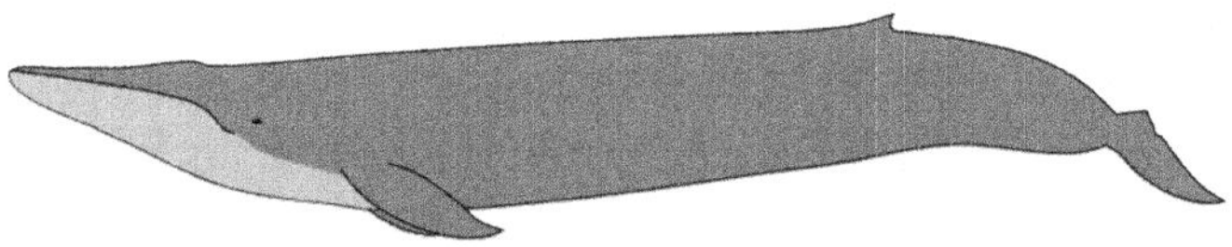

Figure 4-10: Blue whale

Basilosaurus and Dorudon disappeared from the fossil record 36 million years ago. At that time, they were the only hypothetical whale precursors for which there were finds. Then, 34 million years ago, the first fossil finds of modern whale groups suddenly appeared.[115] Two theories exist for the origin of the baleen whales, which also include the blue whale (see Figure 4-10). They are said to have evolved from toothed whales, whereby according to the first theory, toothed whales developed fan-like teeth that acted like a kind of sieve.[116] Theory two assumes that some toothed whales first lost their teeth completely and only later formed the baleen.[117]

Figure 4-11 shows the stepwise hypothetical development of the small raccoon-sized land-dwelling Indohyus to the blue whale, the largest and heaviest vertebrate on Earth. Looking at this illustration, one must legitimately ask why the natural scientists chose exactly these preliminary stages? After all, they are definitely not obvious. These animals could hardly have been more different in size and anatomy. Nevertheless, they are firmly convinced that it is true.

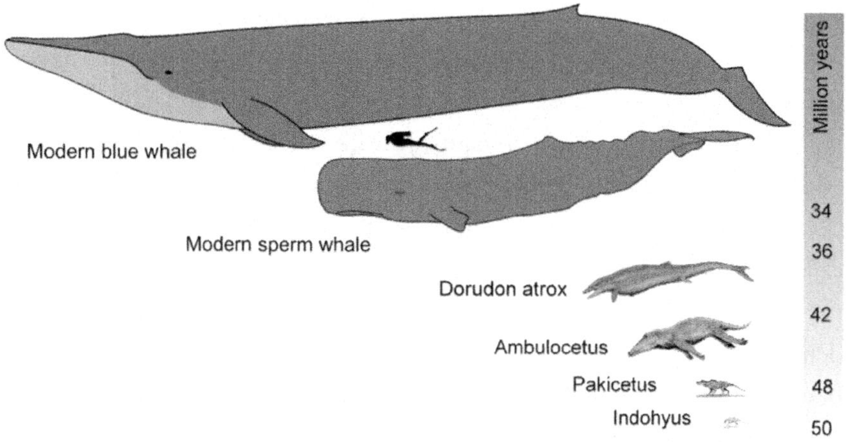

***Figure 4-11:** Size comparison of the individual hypothetical development stages*

I think we can all agree that the very sparse fossil sequence of the alleged whale precursors presented here is not a very weighty criterion in this argument on its own. All the species found could easily represent independent species that simply died out. But what makes evolutionists think that the small Indohyus, of all things, is a precursor of whales?

They found ossicles in the Indohyus that also exist in a similar form in the whale. From this it was concluded that Indohyus must be an ancestor of the whale.[118] In order to make the (non-existent) argument of evolutionists clear to everyone at this point I will gladly repeat it. The evolutionists claim that there was a complete morphological and anatomical transformation from the small aardvark to the gigantic blue whale. In this change of exorbitant proportions, really everything(!) has changed *except these ossicles*. This small structure has always remained the same throughout all the enormous transformations and that is why Indohyus is said to be a precursor of the whales. Everything is said to have changed, except this one detail. And it is precisely this detail that is then used as proof of descent. But this argument is paradoxical and absurd. It shows once again that it is only the desire to preserve phylogenetic evolution that determines the interpretation and that the obvious is ignored at will. In my opinion it is much more likely that the ossicles are a convergent structure, that is, an anatomically similar feature that formed in parallel in both phylogenetically unrelated organisms due to similar functionality and similar requirements.

Whales also have an oesophagus, just like sharks, frogs, birds, reptiles and many more. Does it make sense to assume a common ancestor just because they all have an oesophagus? In the eyes of evolutionists, these so-called homologies are one of the most important proofs for the validity of the theory of evolution.[119] Lesch also cites this point of homology as evidence for evolution. He shows the viewer an illustration with the hand bones of man, the dog, the pig, the cow, the tapir and the horse (see Figure 4-12) and claims that these are always the same.[120] Out of a self-confidence that is inexplicable to me one is now apparently supposed to believe that because there are similarities in anatomical construction, there must be a phylogenetic relationship. Similarities in anatomical construction are surely no proof of common descent! Without a spark of self-reflection on what is claimed and without a syllable of critical debate, a single limited view of the materialistic theory of evolution is being served up to a large audience as the only valid and serious truth.

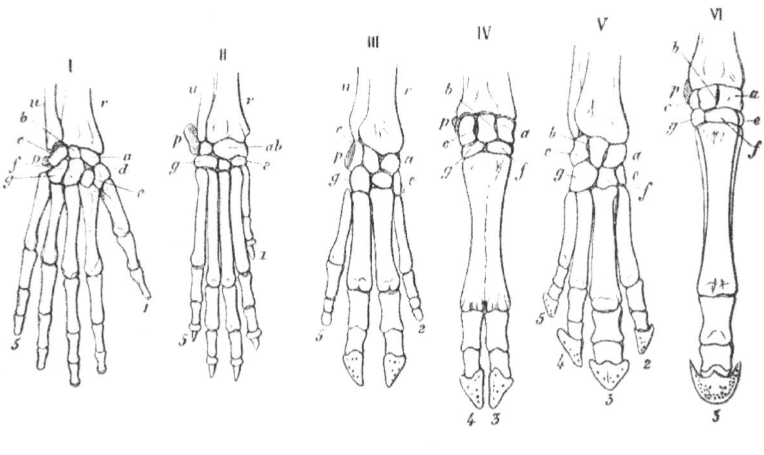

Figure 4-12: *Homology of hand bones in different mammals. I Human, II Dog, III Pig, IV Cow, V Tapir, VI Horse*

With the following comparative example it becomes obvious that the evolution theorists have fallen for a pseudo-argument. The Austrian physicist Robert von Lieben and the US inventor Lee de Forest invented the electron tube for generating and amplifying electrical signals at the same time and completely independently of each other in 1906. Here the same functionality in a similar structure was developed by two men completely independently of each other, because precisely the same requirements and the same environmental conditions lead in a completely natural way to similar solutions and functionalities. For evolutionary theorists, such a parallel invention of the electron tube must not have existed. In their eyes, a common predecessor must have existed.

Another example comes from computer science: If I transfer the argument of homology as a proof of descent to the world of software development, I would have to conclude that the operating systems Windows and Linux have a common predecessor, because both work with window views, directory structures, user administration, system configurations, and so on. I can assure you that new software is not created by taking an existing solution and rewriting it. Of course, programmers always use established design patterns that have proven themselves in programming and therefore parallels can naturally be found in the source code of different software solutions, but this does not mean that there must have been a common ancestor source code. Proven structures are simply used again and again in completely new designs. Why should it be any different in biology? After all, in biology we also deal with source code (DNA).

Anyone who simply believes and adopts the assertions on homology without criticism may call himself a serious scientist, and anyone who dares to draw attention to this obvious misinterpretation that contradicts logic is labelled a crank or a fanatical creationist. Evolutionary theorists no longer even tread on thin ice with their claims when arguing, they try to walk on water just to justify their irrefutable Darwinism.

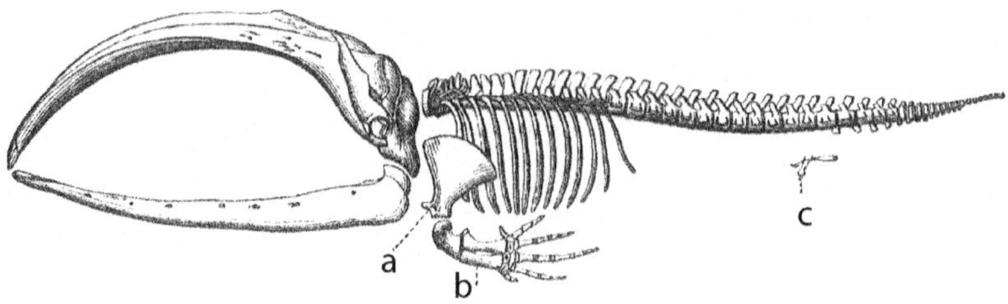

Figure 4-13: Skeleton of a baleen whale (a - shoulder blade, b - front leg, c - rest of the (alleged) hind leg)

To get back to the whales, I would like to use another sequence from Lesch's video contribution on homology. He holds up a large picture of the skeleton of a whale to the camera and claims: 'There is really no clearer example against an Intelligent Designer than the whale.'[121]

He uses the term *Intelligent Design* here, meaning an intelligent creative source, which I will discuss in more detail in Chapter 4.2, *Intelligent Design*. The whale has pectoral fins that contain bony structures (see Figure 4-13 a and b). These structures show anatomical similarities to the arm and hand bones of the land-dwellers presented earlier.

In Lesch's eyes, 'something better than this could have been designed'. But he does not give us a suggestion as to how it could have been done better. The blue whale weighs 200 tonnes. I think it is an advantage that the fins have a stable bony structure. Anything else would be poorly designed. Therefore, the criticism of a bony arm structure inside the pectoral fins of the 200 tonne colossus is incomprehensible to me. Moreover, the interpretation of design is always dependent on the evaluation criteria of the observer, criteria which do not necessarily have to coincide with the criteria of the designer. Design is often also the result of compromises that have to be made in complex systems. If you design the fastest car in the world, you will certainly not be able to build the safest car at the same time. Conversely, I cannot blame the design of a heavily armoured vehicle for having poor aerodynamics and not being able to reach high speeds. Often, after all, it is best to choose a happy medium, and then one-sided criticism is simply not legitimate.

Another 'proof' of descent for a land mammal, according to Lesch, are the 'vestigial hind legs' (see Figure 4-13 c).[122] However, these allegedly 'vestigial hind legs', which have also been found in a similar form in Basilosaurus and Dorudon, are not rudiments of an earlier land life. Darwinists are often hasty in their judgement when they find structures that might somehow fit the paradigm. In this specific case, they simply call this structure 'vestigial hind legs' and everyone believes it. But this bony structure is actually called the chevron bone, which has a very important function. The muscles of the sexual organs are fixed to the chevron bone, especially in the male whale the retracting muscles of the two-metre-long extendable penis.[123] Armin Risi finds the right words to debunk such misinterpretations:

> *'Although the chevron bone of whales has a clear function, evolutionary theorists call it a "rudiment of hind legs". This is another of the many Darwinian circular arguments: One takes the postulates of evolutionary theory as fact, projects these assumptions onto the chevron bone of whales and declares that this bone is a rudimentary structure (= remnants of hind legs), and that this "fact" is evidence for evolutionary theory.'*[124]

There are other findings that speak against this extreme evolutionary complete transformation from Indohyus to today's whale. Let's take a look at the mutations required for this and their probabilities against the background of the time available. If the population size and the mutation rate are known, we can calculate how long it will take for a mutation to occur at a certain point. However, for such massive transformations as in the hypothetical emergence of whales to have occurred, it does not always require single mutations occurring one after the other. For certain transformations, several suitable mutations would have to occur simultaneously, otherwise many of the new structures could not have arisen. The problem with this is that, from a statistical point of view, it would take more time than the universe is old for two randomly occurring mutations to occur simultaneously in mammals. Now, in the evolutionary formation of the whale, we would need not just two, but *hundreds of thousands* of such parallel mutations, and because this would create a new species, these mutations would have to occur equally in at least one opposite-sex specimen in the same region.[125]

From a statistical point of view, for the umpteenth time, we have a probability of practically zero, and, also for the umpteenth time, this does not seem to interest any evolutionary scientist because this finding does not fit their theory. Objectively speaking it is simply wrong that probabilities of zero can be embedded quite naturally in postulated processes of serious research. It really is crazy! The biologist and palaeontologist Dr Günter Bechly said in an interview that he certainly has colleagues who shared his doubts about the theory of evolution. For fear of the consequences, however, hardly anyone dares to say so publicly. 'According to the textbook, whales (...) are supposed to have evolved within a mere five million years (meaning the transition from land to sea mammals, *author's note*)'. For Bechly it was obvious that the story could not be true. And he was not the only one who noticed inconsistencies. On one occasion an atheist colleague confided secret doubts to him behind closed doors: 'Gosh Günter, from a land creature to an aquatic creature in five million years - that's impossible!'[126] Thomas Mörs, palaeozoologist at the Swedish Museum of Natural History, reports in an article of the *National Geographic News* about an astonishing find in Antarctica. The oldest fossil of a complete whale was found there, with an estimated age of 49 million years. He concludes that the evolution from land mammals to marine whales must have been much faster than previously thought.[127]

I wonder how much shorter this period of time has to become before we realise that evolution can no longer explain it? No matter what is observed and discovered our scientists cling almost obsessively to the theory of evolution. This no longer has anything to do with reason, it is rather the irrepressible will of the Darwinists that feeds their belief in evolution. Moreover, how can one reconcile a 49 million year old, fully-evolved whale with the presumed time scale of whale evolution presented above? 49 million years ago, we were still in the phase of Indohyus and Pakicetus.

After this find in Antarctica, the US biologist and author Jonathan Wells even speaks of only one million or fewer years for the transition from the land-based, running form to the completely marine whale.[128] Now one to five million years may sound a lot at first glance, but in terms of developmental history it is only the blink of an eye. Anyone who can deduce this and is not afraid of the consequences can only conclude that the whale evolution described could not have happened in this form.

For me it is much more plausible that these alleged transitional forms were in fact independent lineages of a formerly much bigger diversity of flora and fauna, just as Prof. Chen impressively showed in his lecture. Genetic diversity used to be much greater than it is today, some lineages simply died out, others eventually evolved through adaptation, variation and selection into the lineages of animal species we have today. Actually, exactly the opposite of evolution happened: no new structures were developed by chance and diversity was rather gradually reduced. This conclusion is consistent with all observations of nature and all experiments. At any rate, this cannot be used by Darwinists as an explanation for macro-evolution. So while creationists, according to Dawkins, obviously fill the gaps described with God, Darwinists do it with flimsy and demonstrably constructed stories that are the expression of a Darwinian interpretation.

Many Darwinists do not even realise that they have to muster a much greater faith than those who postulate an intelligent creative source. If we were to assume that Darwinism had never existed, and that the theory of evolution did not haunt the backs of the minds of materialistic scientists, would the observations and findings of alleged transitional forms be taken for granted as it now is? Or would one not rather find independent animal species that suddenly appeared in the geological strata and eventually also disappeared again? Certainly, there are other aspects of whale research that cannot be exhaustively examined within the scope of this work, but the criticisms of whale- and macro-evolution that I have presented here are more than convincing in themselves. In the end, one must conclude that the scientific findings on whale evolution, which, remember the hottest iron in the fire of evolutionary theory, cannot stand up to critical scrutiny. The entire argumentation regarding macroevolution is nothing more than a string of artificially constructed interpretations, aimed from the outset at supporting the presumably untouchable, unquestionable theory of evolution. Observations, probabilities and obvious findings are ignored at will to protect Darwinism, or in some cases deliberately misinterpreted, just because the theory demands it and not because it would be a logical consequence. If you look at the shaky foundations on which the theory of evolution stands you have to be very surprised that all this is taught in our schools and universities without critical examination.

4.1.4 Junk DNA and morphic field

On 25 April 1953, James Watson and Francis Crick published an article entitled *A Structure for Deoxyribose Nucleic Acid* in the scientific journal *Nature.* In it they described the double helix structure of our genetic material for the first time, work for which they were awarded the Nobel Prize for Medicine in 1962.[129] DNA is the central information carrier of the genetic material of a living being, it contains a kind of blueprint for the composition of proteins. It occurs in the form of a ladder-like double helix in every cell and consists of deoxyribose and phosphate molecules. The rungs of this strand are formed by base pairs (adenine-thymine and guanine-cytosine), which are usually abbreviated with the letters A, T, G and C. They encode the necessary information for the composition of proteins. Human cells are equipped with a double chromosome set of twenty-three chromosomes, resulting in a total of about 30,000 genes with about three billion base pairs.[130] DNA is a perfect information carrier. In Chapter 4.1.1, *How did life originate?* I was already able to show that one gram of DNA material can store an incredible 100 million terabytes of data. Dawkins describes in his book *The Blind Watchmaker*[131] that even the DNA of a tiny amoeba contains 1,000 times more information than all 30 volumes of the *Encyclopedia Britannica.* This means that an amoeba has about 30 times as much DNA as a human being. Incidentally, most plants possess significantly more DNA (50,000 genes on average) than mammals (25,000 genes on average). Human DNA was completely decoded for the first time in 2004; it differs from the DNA of a mouse by only one per cent and from that of a chimpanzee by two per cent. In terms of DNA alone, we are therefore more similar to a mouse than to an ape.[132] Nevertheless, many Darwinists argue that because of the great similarity between human and ape DNA, there must be an evolutionary connection and this is proof that humans are descended from apes. This claim is based solely on wishful thinking because it fits so well with evolutionary theory. Wouldn't it be more logical to say that we should look more like mice than apes? The human genome is 50 per cent the same as a banana and 70 per cent the same as a dandelion, so why don't we look at least half like a banana? Nor have I yet come across a human dandelion. Incidentally, 99.5 per cent of all humans have an identical genome.[133] It is hardly conceivable that the entire human diversity should be determined by only 0.5 per cent of the DNA. If we consider all these numbers and phenomena, we can undoubtedly conclude that the size of the genome correlates neither with the complexity of a living being nor with the degree of consciousness. Nor does the similarity of a genome allow any conclusions to be drawn about phenotypic appearance or the degree of consciousness. DNA uses four letters in its language: A, T, G and C. These four letters are used to encode information. Darwinists claim that the similarity in sequence would allow conclusions to be drawn about evolutionary and phylogenetic relationships. But we are entering the stage of information here, which is the field of computer scientists, not biologists. Our language, like the DNA code, also consists of letters, only there are a few more. We can also use them to encode information. Let's look at the following two short sentences as a counter-example to the similarity argument:

Peter finds inspiration in cooking, his family and his dog.
Peter finds inspiration in cooking his family and his dog.

Both sentences are almost the same length, they contain 98 per cent identical signs and positions of these signs. Nevertheless, the meaning they contain, that is, the semantics, could hardly be more different. Only the comma is missing in the second sentence and that turns family man and dog owner Peter into a cannibal and dog eater. This example clearly shows that the similarity of two coded sequences is no measure of the similarity of the meanings they contain.[134] It is therefore illogical, wrong and downright tricky to want to draw conclusions of any kind from the similarity of codes.

In my opinion it only becomes really interesting when we leave the realm of previous findings anyway because they are based on a vanishingly small proportion of only about 1.5 per cent of human DNA. Only 1.5 per cent (!) of human DNA actually codes the proteins for cellular protein syntheses. These sections are also called exons. What the remaining 98.5 per cent of the DNA is needed for is still unknown, which is why these sequences were initially given the name junk DNA or intron.[135] So when someone claims that the chimpanzee genome is 98 per cent the same as the human genome, they are only referring to the known 1.5 per cent of the DNA, which clearly puts the matter into perspective. So what makes this junk DNA so interesting? For many years, junk DNA was regarded as meaningless genetic rubbish that had successively accumulated in the course of evolution. For many years, this was manna for the Darwinists who in their perpetual battle against the creationists could now show that the supposedly omnipotent and omniscient creator God had designed quite a mess. What kind of God would create a human being who had a superfluous 98.5 per cent genetic rubbish in him? In their eyes this was clear evidence that everything had to have come into being purely materialistically over long periods of time through evolutionary mechanisms. But when the *Encyclopedia of DNA Elements Project (ENCODE)* was launched in 2003 by the National Human Genome Research Institute in Maryland, U.S.A., a different way of looking at junk DNA emerged. After nine years of research the scientists in this project believed they could show that junk DNA performs regulatory functions in switching genes on and off. This switch functionality is apparently necessary to keep the genome alive. 'The mystery of the genetic junk that was no longer junk seemed to be solved, and scientists assumed that the non-coding sequences were indispensable for controlling genome activity.'[136] When these findings were published in 2012 creationists were able to counterattack: now God had apparently assigned a function to junk DNA after all. But the scientific world of findings is very changeable, for the tide was to turn again shortly afterwards. A research team led by Enrique Ibarra-Laclette published an article in the scientific journal *Nature* in 2013 that set all the findings on junk DNA back to zero.[137] The research team was able to show how a small aquatic plant called a humped bladderwort (Utricularia gibba) disproves the scientific theory of the ENCODE project. With only 80 million base pairs, the humped bladderwort has the smallest known plant genome. The grape, which belongs to the same order, has more than five times the number of base pairs, but not as many as the 28,500 genes of the humped bladderwort. The DNA of the water plant contains only an astonishing three per cent junk DNA, which shows that gene regulation obviously works even without junk DNA. In the humped bladderwort gene regulation sits in the middle of the genes.[138]

So basically we are back at square one on the subject of junk DNA. However, there is circumstantial evidence that ascribes a completely different functionality to this junk DNA and I would like to put forward a speculative hypothesis in this regard as follows (the same idea was also formulated in a similar way by Pim van Lommel in his book *Consciousness Beyond Life*[139] and by Christina von Dreien in her book *Christina - Die Vision des Guten (The Vision of Good)*[140]. The impression is that a highly developed organism with consciousness always has a large proportion of junk DNA. The functionality of this DNA could be determined by an external consciousness. The junk DNA is possibly a kind of antenna for non-local (that is to say available virtually everywhere, regardless of location) information or non-local consciousness, something which is also described as a morphic field. This is an energy field that, as a cosmic consciousness, carries information about the morphology, structures, processes but also about the knowledge of living beings. The morphogenetic field postulated by the English biologist Rupert Sheldrake is part of the morphic field, and it can be perfectly harmonised with this hypothesis. This is a higher, non-local field of information that controls the behaviour and shaping of all living organisms. Armin Risi believes that 'this field corresponds to what is traditionally called the etheric body or vital body.'[141]

The etheric body has been known in many traditional teachings such as Ayurveda for thousands of years. The Sanskrit term *Pranamaya Kosha* also ultimately describes this energy sheath that animates body and mind. I consider this energy sheath to be the interface between the gross physical body and the subtle and spiritual spheres. It appears that there is an exchange of information between DNA and this information field. The hypothesis formulated here is not only confirmed in several experiments but also by the quantum physicist and Nobel Prize winner Erwin Schrödinger, who as early as 1944 expressed the assumption that DNA was a 'non-static macromolecule' and could be used as a quantum antenna for communication with the non-local information field.[142] Schrödinger thus believed that quantum mechanical processes with DNA as the receiver could be responsible for the transfer of information between a non-local information source such as the morphic field and the sub-molecular structures of living organisms. According to Sheldrake's definition of the morphogenetic field, all formative and functional information of living organisms is present and stored as a wave function in non-local space, and once we are in the realm of waves, we enter the quantum world, as presented in Chapter 6, *Quantum Mechanics and Spirituality*. In his hypothesis of morphic resonance he describes a kind of collective memory, outside space and time, from which living beings can equally draw and contribute.[143] Now, if DNA were able to resonate with the morphic field, this could explain the complex structures and evolutionary development of living organisms.

With this hypothesis, we now have for the first time an reasonable model for an interaction of a physical material body with an immaterial information field. With my hypothesis I would like to go a bit further than Sheldrake who primarily considers form-giving and functional information with his morphogenetic field. I consider it quite possible that a soul can also go into resonance with DNA, as I will show with the example of transplantation studies. As already described in chapter 3.3, *Mind and Matter*, all atoms and molecules in the cells of our body are completely exchanged in a perpetual process within a few weeks, only the DNA is not. Thus a presumed exchange of information between DNA and the non-local information field or a soul would never be impaired, which would be the necessary precondition of such an interaction. I'll now give a few examples that support this hypothesis on the resonance between DNA, morphic field and souls amazingly well.

First, let's take a look at the human immune system which is controlled by our DNA. So-called antigens from bacteria, viruses and cells foreign to the body must be recognised by our immune system so that the specific antibodies, our defence cells, can be produced. The antibodies produced fight the invaders as part of an immune response and the underlying information about this is stored in immunological memory. This can ultimately lead to lifelong immunity against certain pathogens and diseases. For example, if you had measles as a child, you get lifelong immunity. So you can't get it again because your immunological memory already knows the appropriate defence strategy. Now the question arises as to where exactly this immunological memory is located in the body, whose atomic composition is constantly changing. Van Lommel is of the opinion that the immunological memory, which is also subject to constant change, cannot be stored in the DNA itself. In his estimation, it would have to be stored in non-local space, and thus there would be a permanent transfer of information between the information field in non-local space and the DNA of each cell.[144] I consider van Lommel's estimation to be logical and plausible, especially since he supports this theory with an article from the journal *Nature.* In it, the research team around Moira Gilliver reports on a resistance development of bacterial strains against certain antibiotics in wild animals that lived in complete isolation. Although these animals, living in complete isolation and could not possibly have come into contact with antibiotics, they had nevertheless developed resistance.[145] Where would the bacteria in the wild animals have obtained the information about antibiotic resistance? A very plausible explanation for this phenomenon is that the already-resistant bacterial strains fed this information into the non-local information field so that the bacteria in the wild animals resonated with it and were eventually able to take up this information again via their DNA and convert it into functionality.

In another astonishing experiment it was shown that rats from several successive generations learned how to escape efficiently from a water maze. The amazing thing was that over time, even completely foreign rats from other laboratories around the world were able to do this more and more quickly.[146] The knowledge of a suitable strategy for escaping from the water maze must therefore have somehow been transferred to all rats in the world. Without a non-local field of consciousness, this phenomenon is difficult to explain. Statistically significant results could also be made with an experiment on so-called *conditioned aversion* in chicks. Newly hatched chicks were shown a small yellow light in the form of a light-emitting diode, whereupon they began to peck at it. Meanwhile, the chicks were given a substance that induced nausea in them. Finally, after a while, the chicks stopped pecking at the yellow light. Subsequent generations of chicks actually showed a significant aversion to the yellow light. Apparently, the first chicks had stored their aversion in collective memory, and through the effects of morphic resonance, the later chicks reverted to this pattern of behaviour.[147]

In Chapter 4.1.1, *How did life originally arise?* I reported on pluripotent embryonic stem cells that can develop into any specific tissue. The exact reasons and processes for this have not yet been scientifically clarified. The morphic field, especially the morphogenetic field it contains, could provide a plausible answer to the phenomenon of stem cell development. The information it contains about the form and functionality of the material body could be transmitted to the cells via the DNA. Thus, with the help of the morphic field, we would be able to explain the specialisation of stem cells into specific tissues.

Another interesting experiment was carried out by Cleve Backster in 2003. He was able to demonstrate that cells of the same living being remain connected to each other even over long distances.[148] To do this, he took white blood cells from the cheek mucosa of his test subjects and kept them alive in a nutrient medium. The experiment was now designed in such a way that he showed his subjects very distressing or sexually arousing images in order to observe whether there were changes in the white blood cells. As soon as the subjects were confronted with the images, the white blood cells did indeed show a measurable reaction instantaneously, and this reaction remained even when the subjects and their extracted cells were far apart (between twelve and twenty kilometres). Backster even electromagnetically shielded the separately stored cells, but even then the reaction still remained. The cells of a living being obviously react to the thoughts and feelings of their owner regardless of whether they still exist in the compound or have been separated.[149] Following quantum entanglement (see chapter 6.1.2, *Non-locality - entanglement in space*), it would be quite appropriate to call this phenomenon *DNA entanglement.* Entanglement means that there is a non-local connectedness between DNA molecules and that spatial distances and time spans dissolve. This is another indication that we are moving into the world of quantum processes in this topic.

In my opinion, the clearest sign that our soul aspects are connected to the physical structures via the DNA can be seen in the so-called memory transplantation. This phenomenon involves patients who have received a donor organ transplant and who experience a subsequent change in their nature and can partly perceive the thoughts and feelings of the donor within themselves. The American Claire Sylvia was one of the first organ recipients to publicly report such experiences. She received a heart and a lung from a donor through a transplant at Yale-New Haven Hospital in 1988. As is common with transplant she did not know the donor's personal detail but, as she reports in her 1999 autobiographical book *A Change of Heart*[150], she noticed a strange change in herself after the organs were implanted. She felt a presence and it was as if a strange soul had taken up residence in her body. Later, strange dreams accompanied her about a young man named Tim, with whom she felt inexplicably connected in great love. Although she used to detest it, she suddenly became passionate about eating chicken nuggets, drinking beer and had an urge to be active that was completely uncharacteristic of her. She suddenly loved riding motorbikes and even went on a bike tour of France. She experienced these changes so impressively that she went in search of the donor's family to find out more about them. She was indeed able to locate the relatives and she told them about her changes in character and her dreams about the young man called Tim. The relatives were finally able to confirm to Claire

Sylvia that all the described personal characteristics of the deceased matched him exactly and that they could clearly recognise him in them. It turned out that the organ donor's name was indeed Tim, that he liked beer, loved chicken nuggets and was a passionate motorcyclist. Tim died in a motorbike accident at the age of 18. The journalist, author and operator of the very successful Thanatos TV format Werner Huemer describes other documented cases:

> *'In the meantime, many other cases have been documented, (...) for example, an 18-year-old organ recipient named Danielle developed a distinct enthusiasm for music, learned to play the guitar and began to sing. The heart she had received came from an 18-year-old boy who had been a musician and had written poetry. (...) Another spectacular case, also suggesting contact from the afterlife, involved a ten-year-old girl who had received the heart of a murdered eight-year-old. The girl had to be treated psychiatrically because she had suffered from severe nightmares since the implantation. During the sessions, the child gave such detailed and realistic accounts of how she was killed in her dreams that the police were called in. To the astonishment of all involved, the information about the course of events turned out to be true incidents. The murderer of the eight-year-old girl, from whom the heart came, could actually be identified and arrested!'*[151]

In his study published in 2000 on personality changes in organ recipients after heart transplantation, the cardiologist and psychologist Paul Pearsall of the University of Hawaii confirms the phenomena described.[152] In his view, the effects of immunosuppressant drugs, stress after the surgical procedure and statistical coincidence are not sufficient explanations for the observations. His study was criticised by many materialist doctors; he had allegedly not adhered to valid standards in the survey and the cases described were only exceptional cases. In an article in the *Süddeutsche Zeitung* (the large German newspaper) of 24 October 2007, Oliver Decker, psychotherapist at the Transplant Centre of the University Hospital Leipzig, gives the following assessment on this subject: 'Many patients adopt the perspective of distanced self-observation and also fantasise about their organ. The fantasies go into the mystical superstitious.'[153] In the same article, the author speaks of imagined preferences that the organ recipient would have developed partly out of gratitude and partly out of feelings of guilt towards the donor. Professor Hans-Werner Künsebeck, a psychologist in the Department of Psychosomatics and Psychotherapy at the Hannover Medical School, gets almost grotesquely carried away in his rejection of the phenomena described:

> *'Everything can be explained rationally. (...) The immunosuppressive drugs - these are the drugs that prevent the body's own cells from attacking the foreign tissue - sometimes cause a change in the sense of taste. Former favourite dishes may then no longer taste as good, while other dishes are suddenly perceived as delicious. (...) Those who attribute this to the organ donor develop strategies to deal with the newly won life. But there is nothing mystical about this, it can be explained.'*[154]

According to Künsebeck, it was Claire's immunosuppressant medication that triggered Sylvia's craving for chicken nuggets and not her emotional attachment to Tim. I have great doubts about this rational explanation. The materialists' attempts at explanation show once again that they do not want to see the truth because it does not fit into their world view. For them, the world stops at the cell wall. If the phenomena described were only imagination and had materialistic causes, how can it be explained that some organ recipients, of all the possible behaviours in the world, adopted exactly those that were proven to match the donor? How can it be explained that correct names and descriptions of persons could be given even though the organ recipient did not know the donor beforehand?

A rationalist should realise here that the probabilities for this kind of explanation are once again close to zero. The phenomena described cannot be explained using the methods of materialistic natural science. Their attempts at explanation are clumsy and testify to ignorance and scientific dogma. Even the argument that this phenomenon is only the exception does not change the underlying finding. After all, such phenomena show up in Pearsall's study in 17 out of 73 people[155] and '79 per cent of patients in an Austrian study said they felt and behaved no differently than before the operation. 15 per cent said they had actually changed, but blamed it on the life-threatening experience. Only six per cent said their character had changed because of the new organ.'[156] Even if these phenomena happened to only one in a thousand people they aren't something that can simply be wiped away. There are perfectly plausible explanations for the fact that these behavioural phenomena do not occur in everyone after a transplant. Every person is differently sensitive to spiritual events. Someone who is very sensitive can perceive the high-frequency vibrations of the subtle world, as I call it, well, but others feel nothing because their sensitivity is less pronounced or they pay no attention to it. If one is not closed to spirituality the following interpretation could be considered a comprehensible explanation:

I do not believe that the phenomena mentioned are a kind of cellular memory, the term used by many authors to refer to them. The cells themselves do not contain the memories but rather form a place of resonance with their DNA and function like a soul antenna. I suspect that in the organ recipients who experienced the phenomena described there is a soul connection to their donor. Here I use the terms vibration and frequency because they describe the spiritual phenomenon most aptly. I explicitly do not use them in a physical sense but there are no better terms in our language. The souls of donor and recipient may vibrate on a similar frequency, so the organ recipients would be able to resonate with the foreign DNA. In this way of a synchronised vibrational frequency, the souls find access to each other and to the morphic field. If the recipient and donor souls are not connected to each other via their vibrational frequency, there is no resonance. Accordingly, these patients do not feel any feelings or perceptions of the deceased person. Conversely, the soul of the deceased will also have no interest in making itself felt by the foreign recipient, since a connection does not exist in this case. Therefore, I am firmly convinced that Claire Sylvia has a close soul connection to Tim, and this connection existed long before the two of them incarnated.

4.2 Intelligent Design

> *'If it could be demonstrated that any complex organ existed, which could not possibly have been formed by numerous, successive, slight modifications, my theory would absolutely break down.'*[157]
>
> *Charles Darwin*

Before I explain the term *Intelligent Design* in more detail, I would first like briefly to introduce what I consider to be the three most prominent and scientifically renowned representatives of this theory. The term Intelligent Design was decisively coined by the biochemist Prof. Dr Michael J. Behe. In his bestseller *Darwin's Black Box*[158] published in 1996 he presents serious biochemical objections to the theory of evolution in a profound scientific argument. This book received a great deal of attention from the public as well as from critics and experts and was controversially discussed. In addition to Behe, Dr Stephen Meyer, co-founder of the *Discovery Institute's Center for Science and Culture*, is also a very well-known proponent of this theory. He is the author of the New York Times bestseller *Darwin's Doubt: The Explosive Origin of Animal Life and the case for Intelligent Design.*[159] As a third leading figure of the Intelligent Design theory, I would like to mention the renowned molecular biologist Dr Douglas D. Axe who has published his studies and findings in many scientific journals such as the *Journal of Molecular Biology, The Proceedings of the National Academy of Sciences* and *Nature* as well as in his book *Undeniable: How Biology Confirms Our Intuition That Life Is Designed*[160]. Behe, Meyer and Axe are three highly renowned scientists, competent in their fields, who through observation and logical reasoning alike have discovered Intelligent Design to be the most likely explanation for the origin and evolution of life. In particular, they were able to show very convincingly that certain structures and processes in biological evolution could not possibly have been implemented without intelligent planning. This is ultimately what gave rise to the name Intelligent Design. Who the intelligent designer is supposed to be in the end is usually left open. Materialists conclude from this that only God can be meant. There are, however, alternative possibilities, such as the morphic field postulated by Rupert Sheldrake (see chapter 4.1.4, *Junk DNA and morphic field*) as the source of experience and information. But how exactly is Intelligent Design to be imagined? At first glance, this admittedly does not sound very serious and certainly not scientific. And if you don't take the trouble to deal intensively with the arguments you will very quickly come to hasty misjudgements and prejudices. Many materialists see Intelligent Design as just another attempt by creationists to spread their beliefs under a new label. In his video *Hat Gott die Welt erschaffen? (Did God create the world?)* from the series *Terra X Lesch & Co*, Lesch confirms my assessment:

> *'These (the creationists,* author's note*) are the people who say that we only need to look at the Bible, and if we now interpret the Bible literally, then we can see what is the case. And they don't call themselves Christian fundamentalists of the particularly literal interpretation of the Bible, but they call themselves, in order to avoid a bit of the problems with science, adherents of the Intelligent Design theory. And the argument goes like this: Everything we see around us is of such complexity, it can't have come into being on its own. It must have been made. God willed this world and made it.'*[161]

Ebert also thinks he knows what Intelligent Design is. He describes it as follows:

> *'The concept of Intelligent Design (...) has no approach at all. It simply lives from the fact that it declares the theory of evolution to be implausible. But even worse: the supporters of Intelligent Design sell their ideology as science. An ideology that suppresses demonstrable findings and is based on ignorance and dogmatism. Thus, the doctrine of Intelligent Design involves not only the abandonment of scientific thought, but also the abandonment of freedom and democracy.'*[162]

I could list countless more such quotations, but let this suffice for now.

How do you feel when you read these quotations? Do they sound like a scientific, argumentative and factual debate? Unfortunately not; I wish that materialists would develop an openness and impartiality towards this topic so that a scientific discussion could emerge. Because this is where the problem begins: many materialists deny Intelligent Design its scientific nature. You may choose to call it science or not, but if factual arguments, great probabilities and logical conclusions put the previous findings in explanatory trouble, then they should be taken seriously. Incidentally, there are many things in our reality that cannot be grasped scientifically, for instance the origin of our moral sense, our passion for something or our infinite love for certain persons. It is a fatal misjudgement to regard as legitimate reality only that which is demonstrable via current scientific methodology. Anyone who has studied the subject of Intelligent Design intensively would not seriously claim that the arguments are unscientific anyway. The fact that Ebert does not even give the Intelligent Design theory any credit is, for me, more an indication that he has not really studied the subject. Yet it is he who accuses Intelligent Design proponents of ignorance and dogmatism. At this point I give all materialists a good advice. If one really wants to refute the arguments of Intelligent Design then there is only one way: the arguments must be presented honestly and in detail and finally refuted by counter-arguments. In any case, you cannot convince any halfway intelligent viewer or reader with contentless assertions and polemics. I find the style of discussion between materialists and Intelligent Design representatives very disconcerting in many places, as it is characterised by great emotionality, polemics and fanaticism. First of all, emotionality is not a bad thing; I admire Dawkins, for example, for his dedication and passion in his books. You can feel in every line that he is really moved by the problem and that he stands fully behind what he writes. I have the greatest respect for his achievement, but nevertheless one is allowed to disagree. However, one should be allowed to present one's opinion argumentatively, with pleasure and even emotionally and passionately, but always with the necessary respect. I have noticed with Lesch, Ebert and many other critics of Intelligent Design that they neither name nor explain the concrete arguments of this theory.

If anything they stick to very general and superficial statements. I have not yet explained the arguments of Intelligent Design either, but this will follow below. I also find it astonishing that most materialists immediately talk about God and religious ideology in their books and lectures as soon as the subject of Intelligent Design comes up. Neither Behe nor Meyer nor Axe argue with or about God. God and the Bible play no role at all in their arguments, they use only scientific methods and logical conclusions. So why is it that many materialists claim that Intelligent Design has no approach and that it is a religious ideology and a rejection of freedom and scientific thinking? In my view, there are only two legitimate explanations for this. Either they simply do not know the arguments of Intelligent Design or they have no counter-arguments. They mostly know what the basic idea of Intelligent Design is, but the details of the argumentation, at least this is my impression, are rather unknown to them. Which brings us back to the Dunning-Kruger effect. Mostly these scientists have made a fundamental decision in favour of a materialist world view and other views cannot possibly be true for them, which is why, in their eyes, any discussion of these arguments would be a waste of time.

A few years ago this assessment would have been true for me as well, but when Joma opened the door to a larger world for me I was ready to invest time and effort in new ways of seeing and thinking and I found not waffle but solid arguments. Understanding the scientifically-sophisticated arguments of Behe, Meyer and Axe is tedious and time-consuming, but at the same time worthwhile, and if you want to criticise them, even if you are reluctant, you must have read their books. With most materialists, however, I have the impression that they have not taken the trouble. I have read Dawkins myself, otherwise I would never allow myself to criticise him. In my opinion it is only honest criticism if one presents concrete arguments for Intelligent Design (for example the implications of the flagellar motor of bacteria) and then refutes them in argument and with solid facts. But this does not happen in most cases. Those who do not know the arguments *for* Intelligent Design cannot formulate any serious counter-arguments. To protect their own world view they take the easiest way out of this dilemma and accuse Intelligent Design of being a theory for religious fanatics with a literal interpretation of the Bible. With this pseudo-argument they protect themselves from having to get into an embarrassing scientific discussion using real evidence. An uncritical audience or readership can easily be convinced by such an approach that they are dealing with religious nutters, which makes further discussion otiose and you, the scientist, look like a clever. I can assure you that I do not belong to any religion, neither the Bible nor the God described in it play any important role in my life, nevertheless the arguments of Intelligent Design convince me more than those of the Darwinian theory of evolution. In the following, I would like to present the arguments of Intelligent Design in more detail.

Intelligent Design is based on the observation of nature and the discovery of systems that have an irreducible complexity. What is meant by this? The basic idea of evolution is that everything must have evolved through successive, slow change, step by step, through random mutation and selection. Many small changes should eventually lead to small improvements, so that the system can always become a little bit better and more complex from generation to generation. Now, however, in many places in nature one finds systems that have such great complexity and so many interdependent components that a slow, linear emergence is in contradiction with the evolutionary argument. 'Irreducible' means that a highly specific complex system depends on each of its individual components. If only one component is absent the entire system cannot function. Each component considered on its own is also without function and only in the compound of the whole system does the function finally become active. Imagine an old mechanical clock. You only have to remove a small cogwheel or a spring and it no longer works. So what sense and selective advantage would there be if all the other components of the clock were to come into being very slowly and gradually, one after the other, by chance, without benefit? It's not as if the clock would work a little better with each new component. No matter what component was added to the clock, it would not run and there would be no benefit or progress. Only when the last part of the system was be added would the overall system get its function. To my understanding this process can only be explained meaningfully if the overall system was planned in this composition from the outset. For Dawkins, this idea of intelligent planning is nothing more than an illusion that is the result of natural selection.[163] I consider his assessment to be fundamentally wrong. Selection does not have the potential to explain a stepwise further development of an irreducible complex system, it rather prevents it since it would select out all predecessor stages of such a system as functionless and unnecessary ballast. Such irreducibly complex systems (and also processes) require creativity and foresight. This is something that selection cannot do.

The most prominent example of an irreducibly complex system is the bacterial flagellum. Some bacteria have a kind of outboard motor for locomotion, a flagellum (a thread-like tail) that is driven by a rotary motor located in the cell membrane. The flagellum rotates at around 3,000 revolutions per minute, although there are also species that can operate at up to 100,000 revolutions.[164] Figure 4-14 shows a cross-section of the cell membrane of a bacterium with the rotational motor for the flagellum embedded in it. The rotation motor is formed by about forty proteins and needs forty more to be controlled.[165] It has components that are also known from mechanical motors developed by human engineers. Among other things, it has a rotor, a stator and various ring-shaped sliding and sealing bearings. How great is the probability that such a complex system, which resembles our mechanical motors in many places, slowly evolved via useless intermediate stages and then only randomly obtained a function in the last step of the mutation? In my opinion common sense is enough to realise that the probability of this must be extremely low. The flagellar motor quite obviously corresponds to an intended specification, since the individual components work hand in hand in a coordinated manner and are mutually dependent. If the probability of a complex system arising by chance is extremely low and a specification is recognisable, then in my opinion this clearly indicates design. This does not have to mean that God did it, that is a different discussion, but first of all it is to be noted that intellect, skill and design are clearly required for the achievement made.

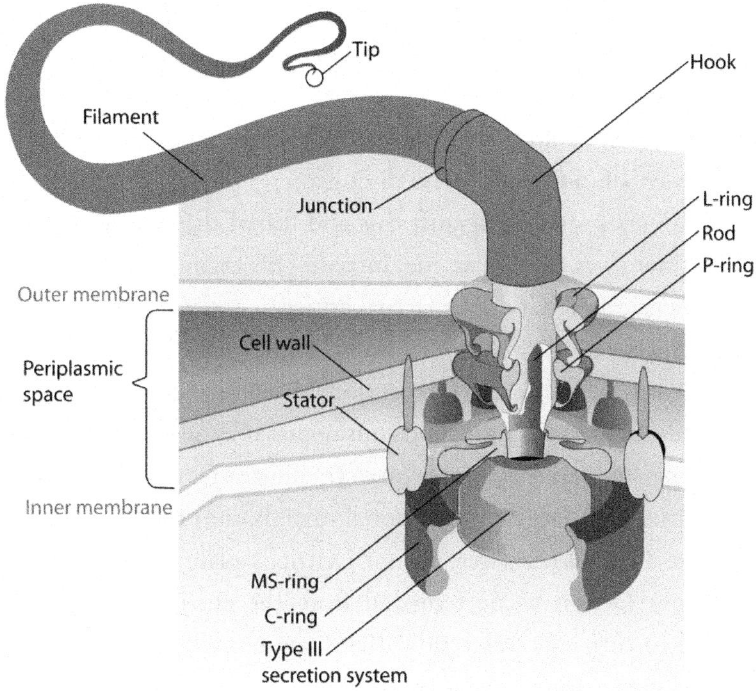

Figure 4-14: *Flagellum of a gram-negative bacterium*

In 2004, curious scenes took place in Dover (Pennsylvania, USA). In the local school board there were convinced representatives of Intelligent Design. They went so far as to want to introduce the findings of this theory into the curricula of state schools. I am an absolute supporter of this because there is nothing reprehensible about drawing attention to the scientific arguments against Darwinian macroevolution. This is not about religion, the Bible or God, it is about training a critical scientific eye and distinguishing between good, bad, probable and improbable arguments. I see it as our duty to point out all the advantages and disadvantages of both Intelligent Design and the theory of evolution. Probably further scientific discussions and a sensitisation for the topic in our society are necessary so that Intelligent Design can establish itself as a serious theory far away from religious fundamentalism in argumentative objectivity. When the Dover

Area School District's biology curriculum was published, it contained references to the fact that there were gaps in the Darwinian theory of evolution and that further research was needed in this regard. Intelligent Design was mentioned as an alternative approach, with a reference to literature on the subject that could be found in the school library. This triggered an enormous wave of indignation and discussion.

Many parents protested against this and feared that the separation of church and state was no longer guaranteed. This argument alone is completely nonsensical. What does a factual criticism of the Darwinian theory of evolution have to do with the church? In the eyes of these critics this curriculum was therefore unconstitutional. Many materialist scientists also opposed Intelligent Design and thus opposed Behe who involuntarily became the personified representation of Intelligent Design. Even the Discovery Institute, the largest institutional organisation for Intelligent Design, criticised the Dover Area School District's plans. They even asked for Intelligent Design to be removed from the curriculum again. But things were to turn out differently. Behe saw himself and his theory of Intelligent Design taken to court in 2005. Several parents (including Kitzmiller) filed suit under the direction of chief attorney Eric Rothschild. The case, titled *Kitzmiller versus Dover Area School District*, became known around the world. It turned out to be about much more than a biology curriculum. This court case really became a big, staged show to validate materialist science and the theory of evolution in its unqualified validity. In the end the court case was no longer about whether or not the biology curriculum at Dover could contain Intelligent Design. It was about Intelligent Design itself and whether it was a science.

For me a court hearing like this made no sense. I could understand that the inclusion of Intelligent Design in the curriculum was the subject of a trial, because the time was not yet ripe for it. But the question of whether Intelligent Design was a science or not clearly went too far for me. I assumed that science was actually decided by scientists, not judges, especially since Judge John E. Jones, a former criminal defence lawyer and head of the State Liquor Control Board, obviously had no expertise in this area.[166] What value could his decision have on the scientific level? Here the legal issues were far beyond understanding. Be that as it may, the trial began, and at the centre of the trial was the flagellar motor of bacteria which thus quite unexpectedly gained a certain popularity. Materialist scientists wanted to show that the individual components of the flagellar motor were also independently functional without having to be embedded in the overall system. This would invalidate Behe's assertion that the components were only designed for the purpose of the complex overall system and had no function individually. The flagellar engine could therefore have evolved in a sensible, comprehensible way, piece by piece and component by component. The plaintiffs' main argument concerned a component of the flagellar motor called the Type III Secretion System (T3SS), which can also be seen in Figure 4-14. The T3SS is characterised by a 'needle' complex that allows the bacterium to inject its own proteins into a host cell as if with a hypodermic. The T3SS is a central component of the flagellar motor and the materialist scientists saw this needle complex as confirming their claim of an evolutionary origin of the flagellar motor. In their eyes, the needle complex already existed as an independent system and was merely integrated into the flagellar motor in the course of evolution. It was thus clear that the individual components of the flagellar motor had independent functions without having to be part of the overall system. The case was thus decided (although it clearly had been before), Judge John E. Jones upheld that the Dover curriculum was unconstitutional and that Intelligent Design was not science. Many materialist scientists thanked Judge Jones for his decision, saying that reason had finally triumphed. *Time magazine* even featured Jones on its cover on 8 May 2006 as one of the most influential people in the world of scientists and thinkers.[167] I honestly find this event very sad, because this was science being trampled under legal feet. I understand when the judiciary has to intervene to protect ethical values and the integrity of humans, animals and nature. But here we are dealing with a scientific theory about the origin of life and species. What value and use can a judicial decision have on this issue? Jones is definitely not a scientist, certainly not in the field of biology. He is not qualified to weigh the scientific arguments, as he almost certainly cannot understand them in the necessary depth. His judgement is worthless from a scientific point of view. Science is decided by scientists, not judges. So let's leave the legal insanity behind and take a detailed look at the T3SS needle complex to deal with the only relevant thing, which is the scientific issue.

Did proponents of evolution really hold the greatest trump card? Was the T3SS needle complex really present before the flagellar motor and thus an evolutionary precursor? The microbiologist Prof. Dr Scott Minnich, together with Meyer, was able to show that the flagellar motor definitely arose first and only later the independent T3SS needle complex.[168] Their findings were confirmed in 2012 by Sophie S. Abbey and Eduardo P. C. Rocha from France with their publication *The Non-Flagellar Type III Secretion System Evolved from the Bacterial Flagellum and Diversified into Host-Cell Adapted Systems*[169] in the peer-reviewed journal *PLOS Genetics*. It could be shown that the genes for the flagellar motor have a greater mutation density than the genes for the T3SS needle complex. An increased mutation density is generally considered an indication of greater age. The T3SS needle complex shows a very low mutation density, it is definitely a younger structure and therefore arose after the flagellar motor. The needle complex is rather a devolved flagellar motor and not a precursor of it, i.e. the original flagellar motor has regressed with loss of functionality. Thus, the main argument of the court's decision is refuted by scientific knowledge. It is in the nature of science that new knowledge is constantly being gained, a process which always leads to the previous theories having to be questioned. That is why a judgement cannot be the last word. It even contradicts the idea of free research. Science is a living process, it requires constant exchange, discussion and evaluation. What seems true and conclusive today can be replaced by something new tomorrow. This is how it has always been and how it will be in the future, and no judge in the world can change this.

An irreducibly complex system can also be described by an irreducibly complex process. From this point of view, I would now like to present the life cycle of butterflies. These filigree, graceful and wonderfully pretty animals, which often weigh less than a gram, have always fascinated me.

They seem embody something magical, and in Aztec and Mayan mythology the butterfly was the symbol of life and death. The ancient Greeks gave the butterfly the name *Psyche*, the word for soul. They saw in the animals the embodiment of the human soul. Today, too, the butterfly is often regarded as a symbol of transformation and a bridge to the souls of deceased children. Perhaps this also explains my great attachment to these animals. When I was a little boy, I built a caterpillar breeding box in which I put fresh food for the caterpillars every day. This way I could observe this incredible metamorphosis from a small caterpillar to a chrysalis to a flying butterfly at close range. Mostly it was the caterpillars of the peacock butterfly that I had collected from nettles in the area. The small black caterpillars were spiny and ate and ate all day. After moulting several times, they chose a suitable spot where they pupated upside down. After about two weeks, the already finished butterfly shimmered through the shell of the pupa, which finally burst open. It was hard to believe: a completely new creature, it seemed, hatched and ready, its colourful wings shining in the most dazzling colours. How is that possible? That is probably the question everyone who has witnessed this fascinating metamorphosis asks. According to the theory of evolution, every living creature ultimately evolved from single-celled organisms that, through mutation and selection over long periods of time, very slowly developed more and more into the species we know today. How should we now explain the life cycle of the butterfly? What came first? The egg and the caterpillar? The caterpillar has no sexual organs, which makes it a bad candidate for reproduction. Even the pupa does not make reproduction any more likely because in the pupa the caterpillar liquefies almost completely and a large number of its cells go into cell death. These so-called larval cells are thus digested and finally form the building material for the butterfly, which receives completely new organs and structures. Why would a caterpillar pupate and liquefy completely if it did not know that it would continue afterwards? This step into cell death contradicts the basic idea of selection, because selection cannot look into the future and realise that this is happening for a specific purpose. This is also admitted by Dawkins: 'Nature has no eyes and does not look into the future. It does not plan ahead. It has no imagination, no foresight, it does not see at all.'[170] But this is precisely what is needed to explain the developmental cycle of the butterfly. Dawkins owes us an explanation in this respect. This process cannot be implemented by chance through small individual steps over millions of years. A development cycle that is only 50 per cent complete makes no sense. Either it is completely implemented or not at all. There is no such thing as a little egg and a little caterpillar or a little liquefaction to become a butterfly. It requires a plan, a look into the future with a specific goal and intentions. That such a complex process would come about by chance and that every little change along the way would also bring evolutionary advantages must be strictly ruled out for logical reasons alone.

Evolutionists would argue that the origin of this life cycle has not yet been discovered, so there is no reason to consider intellect, planning and design as a starting point. Nevertheless, one has to ask how it could have worked. I am not even asking for proof. A coherent theory would be enough for me. That is why I ask that any evolutionist, with all his creativity, formulate just one possible, purely theoretical scenario that explains in a comprehensible and logical way the emergence of the life cycle of butterflies solely through mutation, selection and many small individual steps over millions of years. This is not a sophistry on my part, but a good opportunity to give the idea of evolution a credible and rational basis. Most evolutionists, however, do not think about this in detail. They are convinced that all of this must somehow have arisen naturally over millions of years. But that is precisely the point. The idea of how something like this could come about in a purely evolutionary way already fails in theory. Apparently, the Darwinists are prepared to muster a far greater faith than that which they always accuse the Intelligent Design advocates of.

In addition to their life cycle many butterfly species exhibit other incredible abilities that are difficult to explain in terms of their emergence through mutation and selection. For example, the monarch butterfly, which is native to North America, lives through two to three generations in a summer, and each of these survives for about four weeks. Thomas Emmel, professor of zoology, reports that the last generation produced in late summer lives for nine months - nine times longer than the previous generations, which is why it is also called the Methuselah generation. It is suspected that there is a change in the DNA. Only the animals in the Methuselah generation possess some six corresponding genes that lead to this extension of their lifespan.[171] This extended lifespan is necessary because the monarch butterfly hibernates as a butterfly (and not as an egg, caterpillar or pupa). Billions of monarch butterflies make their way to Mexico in autumn, sometimes thousands of kilometres from Canada, to remain motionless in the coniferous forests of Mexico's trans-Vulcanian mountains for several months. Every single one of these billions of monarch butterflies has flown this route for the first time in their lives. In spring, the animals fly north again to mate, lay eggs and die shortly afterwards. This means, therefore, that in autumn there is no animal alive that already knows the flight route to Mexico, and yet the butterflies always arrive at exactly the same spot in Mexico every year. Where can this knowledge come from? Was the flight route written into the animal's DNA piece by piece by random mutation? And why does the winter generation have different genes than the summer generations? Why don't the overwintering butterflies pass on their Methuselah genes, since the summer generations no longer have them? I am firmly convinced that the information about which generation lives longer, when to fly, which route to take and which destination to fly to comes from the morphic field. The morphic field contains the experiences and knowledge of previous generations, and animals have access to it through morphic resonance.

4.2.1 Common objections to Intelligent Design

Many convinced materialists, whether they are scientists or not, repeatedly raise the same objections to Intelligent Design. Then they usually reject further discussion categorically, considering only they themselves rational and informed. Anything else far removed from the scientific status quo is laughed at by them and dismissed as religiously-motivated crankery. Inspired by the book *I Don't Have Enough Faith to Be an Atheist*[172] by Dr

Norman L. Geisler and Dr Frank Turek, I present these common objections below. I have deepened Geisler's and Turek's counter-arguments with my own thoughts and commented accordingly.

Objection 1: Intelligent Design is not science

That Intelligent Design is not science was legally sealed in 2005, as already explained, by Judge John E. Jones. I have already expressed what I think of this judgement. It is not so important to me whether it can officially be called a science or not, because the only thing that matters is whether it is true. The love for my daughters and my wife is definitely real, but science will not be able to prove it to me. It doesn't need to, because I know it anyway. Science does not have a monopoly on knowledge and truth. So, although it's not really important, I still believe that Intelligent Design is definitely a science. As a theory it derives its arguments from empirically-verifiable facts obtained by recognised methods (for instance the low mutation density in the T3SS needle complex), from the consideration of probabilities and logical conclusions, and not from sacred writings. The findings of Intelligent Design are published and can be discussed by the scientific community. Therefore, Intelligent Design fulfils all the necessary requirements to be recognised as science. However, the concept of science is narrowed down by Darwinists from the outset in such a way that intellect is categorically excluded as a cause of information and not, for example, as a consequence of knowledge. In this way, Darwinism is shaped from the outset towards a materialist view of the world. What truth can such a science possibly find? My definition of science is free of religion and world views, and every halfway-intelligent person knows that this is the only possible form of science. In section 4.2.2, *Information* I will show that forensic scientific methodology is used in researching historical events from the past (for example the origin of life). This methodology provides great evidence for Intelligent Design. It is the same methodology that Darwin used to justify his theory of evolution. So those who accuse Intelligent Design of not being science must do the same for Darwin's theory of evolution, because both are the result of the same scientific methodology.

Objection 2: Intelligent Design is religiously motivated

Many Darwinists claim that Intelligent Design is just another and modern term for creationism, and therefore all its proponents are exclusively religiously motivated. I am definitely not religiously motivated, my motivation is to find the truth. If you look at the books of Behe, Meyer, Axe or other Intelligent Design scientists, you will also find that none of them starts their arguments with God or the Church; instead they argue scientifically. However, it cannot be ruled out that there are also some representatives who are actually religiously motivated. Geisler and Turek have given an excellent answer to this:

> *'So what? Does that make the thesis of Intelligent Design wrong? Does the religious motivation of some Darwinists make Darwinism wrong? No, the truth is not in the motivation of scientists, but in the quality of their research and the validity of their evidence. A scientist's motivation or bias does not necessarily mean he is wrong.'*[173]

The journalist Christoph Krachten, one of Germany's best-known online TV producers and YouTuber of a science channel with over 600,000 subscribers, published a video on 14 May 2017 entitled *Evolutionstheorie endgültig bestätigt - Kreationisten auf verlorenem Posten* (*Evolution theory finally confirmed - Creationists at a loss)*. In it, he claims that the theory of evolution has been clearly proven beyond any doubt. That this is far from being the case I have already shown several times on a scientific basis in this book. He also claims that the Discovery Institute's list *A Scientific Dissent From Darwinism*[174], which I mentioned earlier, with over 1,000 highly renowned professors and doctors who distance themselves from the theory of evolution, is fake.[175] I am also on this list and can guarantee that I had to apply for it with a letter of motivation and proof of my degrees. He calls this list a 'very bad attempt at manipulation and it is bullshit'. To claim that the people on the list neither exist nor work at the universities mentioned or are not scientists at all is patently not true; I am living proof of that. He wants his viewers to understand the principle of science and not fall for propaganda. He even calls the critics of the theory of evolution perfidious. However, a serious journalist who wants to exude scientific competence should know and understand the things he criticises. For contrary to Krachten's prejudice, Intelligent Design perfectly adheres to the rules of science. In his eyes, however, Intelligent Design is nothing more than ecclesiastical propaganda, and he calls on all proponents of Intelligent Design to finally come to their senses and give up, because the Catholic Church admitted evolution long ago.[176] What, pray tell, is the Catholic Church supposed to have to do with this? Not once does he mention or explain the term 'irreducibly complex system'. He focuses solely on the presumed religious motivation rather than on a logical scientific discussion of how the emergence of such systems could have been explained quite naturally. This, however, would have been the only legitimate way to question Intelligent Design. But once again it ends in the typical picture: a substantive discussion is dispensed with, or to speak more clearly, *has* to be dispensed with, because the journalist responsible either has no knowledge of the scientific arguments of Intelligent Design or deliberately ignores them.

The term Intelligent Design causes a big stop sign to appear in the minds of many materialists, telling them: 'Stop! Don't look at it any closer! None of this (whatever it actually is) can be true because it's religiously motivated.' By the way, there is no correlation between motivation and truthfulness; anyone who nevertheless claims and believes this cannot have scientifically honourable intentions. So because Intelligent Design doesn't fit into the materialist world view, most journalists and scientists obviously don't even bother to look at the arguments in detail, and the Dunning-Kruger effect strikes again. I wish that these people, before rushing to criticise, had invested time and effort in reading Michael Behe's book *Darwin's Black Box*. After all, in the first instance, Intelligent Design doesn't care about God or the Church at all. It is a purely scientific approach to the subject. I myself do not belong to any religion, yet I consider Intelligent Design to be much more plausible than Darwinism. No god or faith has forced me to do this, I simply follow the best scientific evidence and arguments. That is also the only viable way. The world view and faith simply must not play a role in the objective consideration and evaluation of arguments.

Objection 3: The argument of imperfection

The argument of imperfection is probably the most frequently used objection in the discussion about Intelligent Design. It is raised again and again by renowned scientists, but also by philosophers and Darwinists of all kinds. Darwinists see the intelligent designer as nothing more than an alias for God Almighty. Surprisingly, they see God in it much more than the representatives of Intelligent Design themselves. This makes it easier for them to argue against it. Intelligent Design proponents see only an intelligent source as the cause of irreducibly complex systems and thus of life and the origin of species. This is a serious difference. Whether ultimately God, a morphic field, a spirit world or something else is behind it is a completely different discussion. Darwinists thus regard a possible designer only as a trick so that the creationists' presumed attempt to justify everything with God does not immediately attract attention. The objection of imperfection thus begins with an alleged God who is, after all, omniscient and omnipotent. They then go on to ask how it can be that his creations are not all perfect. In their eyes, the designer has made many mistakes; an intelligent designer should be able to develop perfect systems. Vince Ebert elaborates on this question: 'If we are supposed to have been created by a clever, omnipotent designer, why did he develop something as unnecessary as the appendix?'[177]

First of all, it should be said that the appendix does have a physiological function. Loren G. Martin, professor of physiology at Oklahoma State University, explains that the appendix plays a very important role, especially in embryonic development, in children and young adults. In the embryo, which is about eleven weeks old, glandular cells migrate into the appendix mucosa and start producing biogenic amines and peptide hormones which are responsible for various biological control mechanisms in growth. In adulthood, the appendix takes on the function of a lymphatic organ. It is thus part of the Immune system and produces B-lymphocytes (a form of white blood cells) and a certain class of antibodies (immunoglobulin A [IgA]).[178] Would it actually be permissible to ask why evolution has not managed over millions of years to make the supposedly superfluous appendix disappear through mutation and selection? But there are many other examples of a very similar nature. I have already presented Lesch's objection regarding the pectoral fin of the whale. Darwinists also like to point to the presumably poorly designed human eye. On the one hand, they wonder why there are so many people who wear glasses, and on the other hand, the so-called blind spot is an expression of bad design. The blind spot (papilla) is the place on the retina where all the nerve fibres from the inside of the retina meet and bundle together to form the optic nerve. This exits through the retina and leads to the brain via the visual pathway. Since this exit point of the optic nerve has no receptors, it is also called the blind spot. According to Darwinists, a good designer would not have allowed such a blind spot. However, I don't think you can make any sweeping statements about the quality of a design if you don't know the designer's intentions. But there's one thing you definitely can't overlook, even a presumably bad design is still a design in the end. Even an apparently bad design can certainly not have been put together by chance and the forces of nature. In the real physical world, however, complex systems often have to make trade-offs. This is something Darwinists tend to overlook. You can't accuse an 11-inch 'notebook' of being poorly designed because the screen is far too small. The designer created it for mobile use and ultimately chose a compromise between compact dimensions and functionality. The fastest car cannot also be the safest and the safest cannot also be the fastest. You cannot pick out individual criteria and evaluate them independently of the overall system, certainly not without knowing the designer's goals. Intelligent Design is not at all about creating perfect systems, but about the realisation that there are irreducibly complex systems that require an intelligent creator. From my point of view, it is in any case a false basic assumption of Darwinists to demand something like perfection at all. For observation of our world shows us that a designer who would undoubtedly be able to realise a better design clearly does not necessarily do so. There are many examples in production where components are deliberately manufactured in such a way that they do not last as long as they could. Either it is not necessary because the intended use of the product was not planned for a longer duration, or because the manufacturer wants a new product to be bought because of wear and tear or destruction. Perfection is not the goal in such production processes. I also don't always give my children the best car, the best clothes, the best flat or all my money (even if it sometimes seems that way to me). They should not experience perfection, but rather learn the value of things, master difficulties themselves, be allowed to fail sometimes and be able to grow from their tasks. This would not be possible in a perfect world. The objection of an imperfect design negligently disregards the fact that the planner could have many different motives, whereby the perfection of the system may even be undesirable or simply play a subordinate role.[179] Considering that we are all souls who are allowed to have experiences, imperfect systems are indispensable in some situations. Otherwise, how could we as humans experience ageing or illness if our bodies were perfect? We incarnate into this imperfect world not to be perfect but to master our learning tasks. The whole discussion about whether a system is perfect or imperfect and whether it has a good or bad design only makes sense if the designer would tell us his intentions personally. Since this does not happen, the objection of imperfection is neither legitimate nor relevant.

Objection 4: Intelligent Design fills knowledge gaps with God

This seems to be Dawkins' favourite objection, because in his books he repeatedly accuses the intelligent-design advocates of trying to explain every gap in knowledge with God. This accusation is somewhat reminiscent of earlier eras, in which people attributed a divine origin to all the things they could not explain. For example, the Vikings considered the northern lights to be reflections of moonlight in the shields of the Valkyries (female spirit beings), and Canadian Indians saw in them the luminous appearance of their god. Today, thanks to scientific findings, we know that after a solar flare, charged particles fly in the solar wind towards the Earth and are guided to the poles by the Earth's magnetic field. Upon entering the Earth's atmosphere, air molecules are then excited, causing the breathtaking glow in the night sky (aurora borealis). If Dawkins and the other Darwinists had their way, this is exactly how it should always happen. In their eyes, it is always only a question of time until science has found an explanation for a certain phenomenon. And as long as one has not yet found a rational explanation for something one should not, after all, make the mistake of filling this knowledge gap with God like our primitive ancestors. However, the conclusion that intelligent-design advocates only come to the conclusion that irreducibly complex systems and the origin of life and species require an intelligent originator from the lack of a natural explanation is not correct. It is not the lack of an explanation that gives Intelligent Design its foundation, but an abundance of empirically verifiable facts (for example E. coli and fruit fly experiments) and the observations of the nature of information based on forensic research (more on this in chapter 4.2.2, *Information*). In the history of mankind, it has never been observed that even a single specific piece of information has been generated by completely natural processes. All our observations and experiences show that information always comes from an intelligent being. It is therefore scientifically legitimate to draw this conclusion, because it is based on repeatable observations and verifiable empirical values and not on a gap in our knowledge.

In contrast to Darwinism, Intelligent Design can be falsified. If a law of nature were ever discovered that could explain the purely natural emergence of specific information, the Intelligent Design theory would have to be considered refuted. As long as this does not happen, however, one must consequently regard Intelligent Design as clearly the better interpretation of the available facts. While proponents of Intelligent Design are open to both natural and intelligent causes, Darwinists persist in insisting on exclusively natural causes. Because they do not consider any other possibility of creation, their theory, unlike Intelligent Design, is not provisional and thus not open to correction. Darwinists are quick to criticise church doctrine for its dogmatism, but they themselves are no less dogmatic.[180] As I have been able to show, Intelligent Design does not use the gaps in knowledge to fill them with God. Rather, it is the observations and empirical facts that point to an intelligent source. Conversely, however, Darwinists have a huge knowledge gap, because they are far from being able to give a useful explanation for the emergence of irreducibly complex biological systems endowed with specific information. They fill their own knowledge gap, which they are mostly not even aware of, by always selling mutation, selection and a lot of time as the solution to the problem, contrary to the probabilities and logical connections. I have already been able to show several times in this book that random mutation and a backward-directed sorting selection do not have the creativity and the potential to explain the emergence of complex information. The much-maligned long periods of time also do the Darwinian theory no favours from a statistical point of view. Geisler and Turek put it in a nutshell:

> *'Moreover, they (the Darwinists, author's note) wilfully ignore the positive, empirically demonstrable evidence for an intelligent Creator. This is not science, but religion, which invalidates scientific observations!'*[181]

4.2.2 Information

> *'The problem of the origin of life is clearly and fundamentally equivalent to the problem of the origin of biological information.'*[182]
>
> *Bernd-Olaf Küppers, German physicist, philosopher and theoretical biologist*

When I drafted an initial outline for this book, it was clear to me that there had to be a chapter on the origin of life and evolution. At first I assumed that this would require the medical scientist in me. I thought I would certainly have to argue with my knowledge of anatomy, chemistry, biology, biochemistry, physiology and physics in order to be able to evaluate the previous theories and draw my own conclusions. But as I have researched and written for this book and looked more and more deeply into all the scientific knowledge about my topic one thing has become clear to me: What it ultimately boils down to, what is absolutely decisive for the original origin of life and species, is INFORMATION. So it is not the medical scientist, but the computer scientist in me who obviously has to deal with this subject. In order to substantiate this insight, we will have to look at what information actually is and how it can be defined. I find the starting point of my views remarkable, because here there is an unexpected consensus between the materialists and their critics. All agree that DNA carries complex coded information. But how did this information get there? We will examine which theories could account for the origin and evolution of this information.

I would like to start with a negative example of how information can definitely **not** be explained. In his book *Information und ihre Bedeutung in der Natur (Information and its Meaning in Nature)*, the German computer scientist Dr Wolfgang Johannsen presents his evolutionary-energetic information model, the basis of which is (completely unproven) biological evolution.

> *'Information, insofar as it carries meaning, is biological, and it is bound to energy. It is biological because it arose with and through biological evolution. Semantic information is therefore only found in living beings (eukaryotes, archaea, bacteria) of biological evolution. (...) Information is a product of evolution. Nowhere else than in the organisms of evolution does it exist - as far as we can conclude this within the limits of our horizon of knowledge.'*[183]

When Johannsen speaks of 'our horizon of knowledge', he actually means the horizon of knowledge of the materialists. I do not agree at all with his generalisation of this assessment to the whole of humanity. My horizon of knowledge, and that of many others, is at least sufficient to recognise that the normal scientific theory of the origin of life and macroevolution must be rejected on statistical grounds alone. If Johannsen's horizon of knowledge is already limited from the outset by his materialistic view of the world the question arises as to whether it makes sense to set up models and assertions that lack any basis in a holistic approach. He claims, without a hint of evidence, that meaningful information arose with and through biological evolution. But alleged evolution requires a functioning initial state that already carries information, because the hypothetical process of random mutations and selection cannot simply start from scratch. Anyone who claims that information is a product of evolution must, as I have already shown in this chapter, accept a probability of zero several times in his theory. But of course Johannsen does not mention this. If one tries to explain the origin of biological information for a living being by saying that it arose through biological evolution itself, one is going round in circles. If one were to ask where the biological information of a living being came from, Johannsen would have to answer: 'From the evolution of the living being.' And if one were to ask how the emergence and evolution of this living being could be justified, he would have to answer: 'They are the result of the existing and mutated biological information.' It is hard to believe that a serious scientist can be satisfied with such a circular argument. Evolution (more precisely *macroevolution*) has not been proven at all, it is a theoretical construct on very shaky ground. This raises the question of what value a new information theory has if it is based on another completely unproven theory. Another counter-argument for Johannsen's theory is to be found in my afterlife contacts with Joma, contacts in which the mediums involved were able to provide me with information that they could not possibly have known. Where should this information, for example about Joma's accident history or her winning two equestrian tournaments, have come from? The biological basis of this information postulated by Johannsen is undoubtedly no longer present in this case. Joma is biologically no longer materially existent, yet the information clearly comes from her. This finding is not an isolated case, but the rule, as we were able to prove impressively with the highest significance in our EREAMS study. Basically, the materialists commit a fatal error in the question of the origin of information, because in their view, only matter alone can be considered as the sole cause of information and life. The graduate engineer Prof. Dr Werner Gitt, for many years head of the Department of Information Technology at the Physikalisch-Technische-Bundesanstalt (PTB) in Braunschweig, Germany, draws the logical conclusion from this:

> *'If random physical and chemical processes are the sole sources, then intention, morality, free will and responsibility are also just random events and have no meaning in themselves. Indeed, the assertions of all materialist-minded authors run precisely in this direction.'*[184]

Gitt has conducted research for over 30 years and has constantly developed his information model of *Universal Information (UI)*. It is a continuation of Claude E. Shannon's information model of 1948, on which modern computer science is based.[185] Gitt has lectured on this subject at universities on all five continents and numerous discussions and scientists have helped him develop his concept of UI. He considered his greatest breakthrough to be the realisation that information is a separate, non-material entity. Even after countless national and international lectures, no one has yet succeeded in disproving the natural laws of information he formulated, based on his information model of UI. I consider his concept to be the best model for defining information insofar as it is observable and coded. As we will see, especially in the context of clairvoyance (and clairsentience and so on.) or telepathic communication, there is also a possible exchange of information without any visibility or coding.

The term 'information' is not exactly defined; it is used in various ways in scientific and technical contexts. There is a lack of a clear, precise and universally valid definition. If we are to derive valid arguments and conclusions from the nature of information in what follows, it is an indispensable prerequisite to have an exact and complete definition of information. Gitt's information model of UI, in my view, fulfils precisely this requirement.[186]

Three necessary conditions for Universal Information

Suppose we have discovered something and we want to know whether it contains information. As a first step, we need to make three checks in terms of the symbols used, the sequence and the arrangement. Gitt illustrates this check of the necessary conditions very nicely with the ancient Egyptian hieroglyphics, which we now know contain information. But if we didn't know, how could we tell whether the figures shown have a deeper meaning and are not simply decorations like a wallpaper pattern? So we start with the verification. The first condition requires that the information uses different characters. This is definitely the case with hieroglyphs (owl, eagle, water waves, and so on). In addition, these characters must appear in an irregular sequence, because this distinguishes them from artistic design with similar shapes and ornaments strung together. This second condition is also fulfilled by the hieroglyphs because no periodic repetition of symbols is recognisable. Condition three requires a representation of the symbols in a recognisably ordered manner. Gitt speaks of rows, columns, rings or spirals as possible arrangements. As can be seen in Figure 4-15, the symbols are arranged in columns. This means that this third necessary condition is also fulfilled.

Figure 4-15: Hieroglyphs from the Sarcophagus of Anchnesneferibre, British Museum

If all three conditions are fulfilled, this is still not proof that we are actually dealing with information, it is merely the basic prerequisite. It is quite possible that the ancient Egyptians simply decorated their buildings and tombs in this way. It was not until the discovery of the Rosetta Stone in 1799 that the hieroglyphs could be identified and translated as a language. The Rosetta Stone is a very special stone tablet dating from 196 BC. It shows inscriptions in three different languages (hieroglyphics, Demotic and Ancient Greek) all carrying the same meaning, carved in honour of the Egyptian King Ptolemy V. The Rosetta Stone, or rather its trilingual inscription, is considered the most important building block for deciphering the hieroglyphs. It made clear that the hieroglyphs were a language that contained information.

Five levels of universal information

The information model of the UI is based on the three necessary conditions mentioned, but these only form the beginning of what is needed. Gitt completes the model with five characteristics of information. According to his interpretation, information is always present when all of the following five hierarchical levels occur in an observable system (see Figure 4-16):

> *'Statistics, syntax, semantics, pragmatics and apobetics. Information is represented as language (it is formulated, sent and stored). An abstract alphabet containing individual symbols is used to form words (codes). Then the meaning-bearing words are combined into sentences according to the rules of the relevant grammar (syntax) to convey the intended meaning (semantics). Universal information must of course also contain the actions expected by the sender (pragmatics) and its intended goals (apobetics). Pragmatics and apobetics can be explicitly formulated or also implicitly recognisable without being verbally described.'*[187]

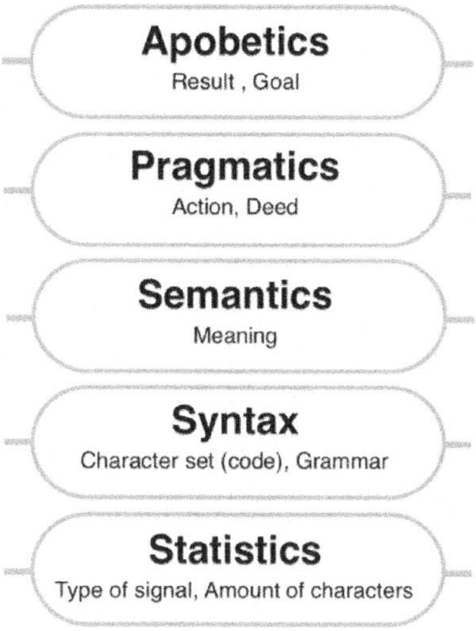

Figure 4-16: The five levels of Universal Information according to Werner Gitt[188]

Level 1: Statistics

This lowest level of information corresponds in principle to what the American mathematician and electrical engineer Claude E. Shannon (1916-2001) published as the foundation of the first information theory in 1948 in his work *The Mathematical Theory of Communication.*[189] In it he considered the concept of information exclusively against the background of what is important for transmission and storage. His goal was to send information as quickly as possible through the transatlantic cable. To this end he looked at information purely quantitatively asking how many letters, digits and words there are in the system. Other aspects of his consideration were the characters used in the underlying alphabet (e.g. A to Z with 26 characters, binary with 0 and 1 or A, G, C and T of DNA) as well as the frequency of these characters and the words made up of them. Whether these characters and words carry a meaning in themselves was irrelevant to Shannon; it was inconsequential to his goals. According to his theory, the information content increases solely with the number of characters. It is obvious that this approach cannot come close to describing the true content of information. The following example shows the consequences of Shannon's approach:

a) Twenty divided by four equals five
b) 20 / 4 = 5

According to Shannon, variant (a) contains more information than variant (b), although both statements are the same in terms of content at the level of meaning. In order to take the *meaning* of the information into account, Shannon's information theory must therefore be extended by further levels. The next level in Gitt's information model is the level of syntax.

Level 2: Syntax

Syntax refers to the lexical and grammatical rules of information representation. In principle, this second level comprises, on the one hand, the system of characters used and, on the other hand, the set of rules on how these characters are to be combined. The combination of individual characters must make sense in order to create valid sequences. With our English alphabetic character system, the following two strings could result:

- trdgjkl asoptbnxy kl aqoghr
- This is a correct sentence.

The top line does contain valid characters, but they have not been properly combined. Obviously, only certain combinations of characters are allowed so that valid words can be formed from the vocabulary. The term syntax, however, not only includes the formation of lexically correct words for vocabulary formation but also the correct concatenation of these words to form whole sentences. The formation of sentences must follow certain grammatical rules. The meaning of such sentences, however, does not play a role at this syntactic level, which is why the following sentence is lexically and grammatically correct, but devoid of meaning (semantics):

- The singing shoe drinks the sad car.

A correct syntax thus forms the basis for the representation of meaningful information, but is itself completely free of interpretation and meaning. I think it is obvious that a code system can never arise from matter by itself. All our observations and experiences contradict this and show that a code system is always the result of a mental process and has a creative and intelligent originator.

Level 3: Semantics

Semantics is the decisive criterion and the core of information, because it represents the meaning contained in the information. Semantics ultimately gives information its meaning, its significance. As the recipient of a message, one is mostly interested in its content and meaning and not in the character combinations and grammatical skills used. A code system is therefore also interchangeable, while the meaning of the information remains the same. In extension to Gitt's model, for me, information is not necessarily dependent on the first two layers (statistics and syntax), it can also exist without code. Only when it comes to representing, storing or transmitting information in the material world is coding necessary. As an example of the fact that there can also be an exchange of information without coding we can refer to the non-material world. In communication with the spiritual world, an exchange of information takes place between a medium and spiritual beings on a telepathic level via so-called clairvoyance (see chapter 7, *Is there evidence for a spiritual world?*). Through clairvoyance the medium suddenly possesses foreign knowledge through the connection to the spirit being and without having to go through the diversions of a language or coding. This shows quite clearly that information does not have to be material, nor does it need matter in any form. Gitt formulates two important sentences of experience in this regard:

a) *'Every Universal Information requires a spiritual source as its originator. If the transmission takes place via several physical links (e.g. via car radio, antenna, transmission mast* [author's note]), *then there must be a spiritual source (transmitter) at the beginning of the transmission chain.*

b) Universal Information cannot arise from random, uncontrolled physical-chemical processes."[190]

Level 4: Pragmatics

Gitt describes the level of pragmatics as the receiver's reaction to the information expected by the sender. He says that every piece of information invites the receiver to act in order to achieve a certain goal. However, Gitt describes the goal aspect of the sender separately in the fifth level as so-called apobetics. I think, however, that not every piece of information that is sent requires action on the part of the receiver. If a piece of information sent has the goal of providing the receiver with an insight, this is not a call to action. In my view, a more appropriate description of pragmatics would be to define it as information that causes something in a receiving system. Thus, pragmatics can equally refer, for example, to the construction of proteins, the intuitive but also intelligent action of a human being and to passive understanding. UI has a profound, purposeful meaning at this level compared to uncontrolled physical-chemical processes. Contrary to the endeavour of physical and chemical systems always to achieve the lowest-energy and most stable state according to their natural laws, processes triggered by UI are usually rather brought into higher-energy and unstable states of disequilibrium (for example protein formation in aqueous solution; because from an energetic point of view the proteins in water would have to break down again into their amino acid components by hydrolysis).

Level 5: Apobetics

Gitt calls the highest level of information apobetics. This term is new and was formed by him in reference to the Greek word *apobeinon* (= result, success, outcome). The apobetic aspect of information is orientated towards the planned objectives of the originator. The sender thus wants to achieve feelings and /or a concrete goal. At this level we have the *origin* of information. An intelligent mind, the originator of a goal, creates information that has to access the four other layers below it in the course of a transmission to the receiver. I would like to add that outside the material world layers one and two (statistics and syntax) are not necessarily required, since an exchange of information can also take place telepathically via the psychic senses.

Figure 4-17 shows a representation of Gitt's information model that I have supplemented. In particular I consider the border between levels two and three to be very important (dashed line), as it represents the transition between spiritual and material levels. Gitt has already described it in a similar way. Information can exist without any problem only in the non-material levels three to five; only the storage or transmission in the material world makes the material levels with syntax and statistics necessary.

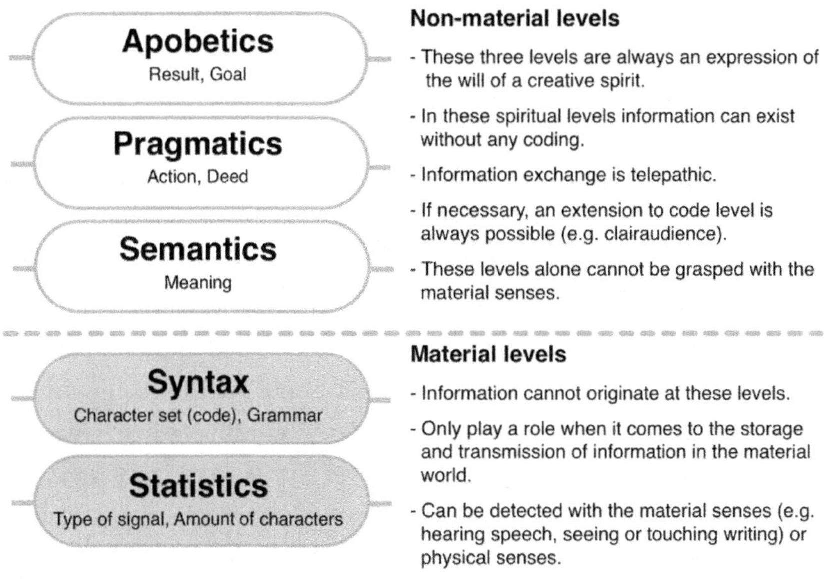

***Figure 4-17:** The Five Levels of Universal Information, adapted from Werner Gitt*[191]

The deciphering of code (for instance hieroglyphics, the source code of software, or DNA) always starts at level one. The observation is then successively extended to the fifth level. However, code is never the original beginning of information, it happens top down, starting at level five. This inevitably means that when we discover and trace information, we always encounter an intelligent source, a creator. All our observations in the world around us confirm this insight. Gitt poses an enormous problem for materialistic scientists because 'there is no known law of nature, process or procedure in the material world whereby Universal Information can arise by itself in matter.'[192] In 2011, a symposium was held at Cornell University (New York) with 29 high-ranking scientists to discuss the origin of biological information. For the first time renowned specialists from the fields of theoretical computer science, computer technology, numerical simulation, thermodynamics, evolutionary theory, organic biology, developmental biology, molecular biology, genetics, physics, biophysics, mathematics and linguistics were brought together at the highest scientific level. The impressive presentations of the symposium were summarised in the book *Biological Information - New Perspectives.*[193] The unanimous consensus in the 25 published papers is that biological information can only be created by intelligence. Lesch also comes to the conclusion that natural science cannot explain the meaning of its systems. It can only examine the text of nature for its grammatical rules. Using the example of a Goethe text he makes it clear that natural science can examine every single letter of the work, even the printer's ink of the letters, down to the smallest detail, or the grammar, but the interpretation of the content is not one of them. He says we have to read, understand and interpret the whole piece, even read between the lines to some extent, to understand what the creator of the piece wants to express. According to Lesch, natural science cannot do all this.[194] Layers three to five (semantics, pragmatics and apobetics) above 'syntax' in Gitt's information model are thus neither tangible nor explicable by the classical natural sciences. At the beginning of information there is always the meaning and purpose of a mind, and in the 100th broadcast of α-Centauri, Lesch makes it clear that physics and natural science cannot incorporate this into their theories:

> *'Physics has no concepts like purpose and meaning at all. These are not scientific terms. (...) Physics demands that the systems it studies are*

reproducible, that the experiments are repeatable, in any place at any time. Only we humans, we are not physical systems in that sense. Because we are not repeatable. You can't put us from one place to another without us changing. Even when time passes, we change. (...) Physics cannot explain the world. Physics can explain how the world works, but it cannot explain why it works the way it does. (...) We (physicists, author's note*) cannot even understand why the world started in the first place. (...) That is one of the biggest and worst problems we have in physics, that we always seem to have to go beyond physics in order to be able to justify physics itself. (...) We get, as the saying goes, to the moon with physical thinking, but not to heaven.'*[195]

Precht comes to a very similar conclusion when it comes to the topic of meaning or apobetics:

'Sense is not a scientific unit of measurement, an object or an electrophysiological process.'[196]

So if natural science has no concepts like meaning and purpose, how could it account for the meaning-giving information in DNA? The answer is obvious: not at all!

If we now want to understand the origin of the DNA code, we have to realise that this is an event from the past. We cannot travel back in time and observe the original emergence of DNA. So both the Darwinists and the Intelligent Design advocates face the same problem here. They are trying to figure out something that lies in the past. Thus the question arises, what are the permissible ways and methods in science to fathom such past events?

Questions of origin are typically investigated with forensic methods. Geisler and Turek have compiled an overview (given in Table 4-1) that shows the differences between empirical and forensic research. There are scientifically recognised methods for investigating historical events. They are called *the analysis of competing hypotheses* and *inference to the best explanation.* But how can researchers determine which explanation for the origin of information in DNA is the best? A fitting answer to this question comes from a contemporary of Darwin, the geologist Charles Lyell. He said that if you want to study the past, the present is the key. If we can no longer observe the past causes, then the best thing to do would be to look for explanations in current processes and causes and then apply them to historical events.

Table 4-1: *Empirical vs. forensic research according to Geisler and Turek*[197]

Empirical research (function)	**Forensic research (causes)**
explores the present	explores the past
examines regularities	examines individual cases
Explores repeatable processes	explores non-repeatable events
Testing through repeatable experiments	Test by uniformity (uniformity principle)
explores how things work	explores how things began
Examples: *How does the universe work?* *How does life work?*	*Examples:* *How did the universe come into being?* *How did life come into being?*

If we now ask the question which current processes and causes are responsible for the emergence of information, we can say on the basis of our everyday and observable experience that it is always an intelligence. Whenever we recognise a piece of information in our current life, be it a software code or a radio signal, and trace this information back to its source, we never find a material process at the end, but always an intelligent creator, be it a programmer, an editor, an engineer, an author, a composer or any other creative spirit. Thus legitimate recognition of an Intelligent Design uses the same forensic methodology to argue here as the Darwinists. Yet Intelligent Design is denied scientificity by many people (and one U.S. District Judge). Consistently, one would have to do the same with Darwinism.[198]

The fact that a purely natural material process with random mutations and population-influencing selection cannot be considered for the emergence of meaning-giving complex information is something I would like to illustrate from the perspective of a computer scientist. It would be as if I were to teach my students programming as follows: 'Please type randomly on the keyboard of your computer. Once a day, stop for a moment and examine the code you produce. In the sense of selection, keep only the code that is understood by the compiler[I], and delete everything else. There is no need for creativity or pre-planning, blind chance and the subsequent sorting out are sufficient. (Note: In reality, however, selection cannot consciously sort out, because it only works population- and not sense-driven). After that, you type on your keyboard again completely randomly and the game starts all over again. You only have to do this long enough and at some point you will have programmed a great operating system, video editing software or a flight simulator.' As a computer science professor, one would not only be ridiculed by the students with this teaching content, one would also quite quickly, quite rightly by the way, receive a dismissal for incompetence. But if a biology professor tells his students exactly the same thing, he is considered extremely serious and competent with such statements. This insanity is completely incomprehensible to me and cannot be rationally understood. Even if you were to make random changes to an existing working code you would never create even better software. There would only be a degrading effect, the code would lose functionality, a small hello world programme[II] would never become the greatest 3D flight simulator. That is the case in computer science, and it is no different in biology. Anyone who thinks that this may be true for computer science but that biology is something completely different is, in my opinion, mistaken. Allocations to subject areas are irrelevant, because what is at stake here is the general nature of information. It is astonishing how Darwinists are prepared to believe in such miracles as a matter of

---

[I] Translates the code into an executable programme

[II] The Hello World programme is a very simple programme that simply outputs the string 'Hello World'.

course, against all logic and observation, just so that their view of the world is not shaken. The really bad thing about it, however, is that all this is done in the name of an empirical science and is carried along in blind obedience by our lecturers, teachers, students and pupils.

I consider the opening quotation for this subchapter by Prof. Dr Bernd-Olaf Küppers to be one hundred per cent correct: 'The problem of the origin of life is clearly and fundamentally equivalent to the problem of the origin of biological information.'[199] Where I must vehemently disagree with Küppers, however, is his attempt to view information as a scientific structure similar to matter. Many of his colleagues in evolutionary biology also assume that information can arise in matter on its own. But such a creative process has never been demonstrated by anyone in reality. And as a computer scientist, I can only shake my head at the following quote from Eigen: 'Information comes from non-information.'[200] This statement is not only highly illogical, it contradicts all observation and experience. The following statement by Küppers is also interesting. To the question 'What is life?', he gave the following equation as an answer:

'Life = Matter + Information'[201]

It is easy to show that this formula is fundamentally wrong. Let us consider the corpse of a freshly deceased human being. The corpse consists of matter, of cells and biological information in the form of DNA and RNA. But life is not present. Küpper's formula is thus falsified. Life is much more than that.

Information is a non-material. We were able to show with great evidence through our EREAMS study that our deceased can continue to exist and transmit information even without their material bodies. Information can therefore exist completely detached from physical structures. Gitt proves this finding that information is non-material with the help of the International System of Units (SI[I]). This system defines seven basic units

[I] Système international d'unités

that are independent of each other. All other conceivable physical units that relate to the material world can be derived from these base units. By multiplying or dividing different base units, these are finally described.

Table 4-2 shows the seven basic units. A unit derived from this is, for example, speed (length/time = metre/second = m/s). Without exception, all material units can be described using combinations of these basic units. However, Universal Information cannot be described using these basic units, so Universal Information must be a non-material unit.

Table 4-2: *The seven SI base units*[202]

(1)	Length	(unit: metre, *m*)
(2)	Mass	(unit: kilogram, *kg*)
(3)	Electric current	(unit: ampere, *A*)
(4)	Temperature	(unit: Kelvin, *K*)
(5)	Amount of substance	(unit: mole, *mol*)
(6)	Light intensity	(unit: candela, *cd*)
(7)	Time	(unit: second, *s*)

Gitt describes that other aspects such as consciousness, free will and life cannot be described by the SI system either. Therefore, these must also be non-material units. He describes it as a central problem that the materialistic way of thinking accepted in science is the cause of serious errors as long as non-material quantities are treated as if they were material.[203]

4.2.3 Architecture in the universe

> *'Even we, who no longer fear vengeful gods, feel awe and wonder at this unexpected precision of a growth pattern of nature.'*[204]
>
> *John Gowlett, Hungarian architect and botanist*

Many structures in nature and in our universe show an extraordinarily precise architecture. In the most diverse areas, both in the very smallest and in the very largest, we find the same construction features again and again. The whole thing can be traced back to the so-called golden ratio. Another name for it is divine proportion. This is an extremely fascinating principle that is constantly repeated in the universe, in nature, in science, but also in art. The golden ratio and its derivatives such as the golden spiral, the golden triangle or the golden angle can be found in seed patterns and leaf arrangements of flowers, in the human inner ear, in DNA, in works of art, in snail shells or in galaxies, to name but a few. The golden ratio is represented by the Greek letter Φ (Phi); it is calculated as $(1+\sqrt{5})/2$ or represented by the irrational number 1.6180339.... One can visualise this proportion plastically as follows.

$$\frac{AB}{AC} = \frac{AC}{CB} = \Phi$$

Figure 4-18: *The golden ratio*

Figure 4-18 shows a straight line between points A and B. This distance is divided in the ratio of the golden section if the whole distance to the larger section is the same as the larger distance to the smaller one. So in the example, the ratio of the distance AB to the distance AC is the same as the ratio of the distance AC to the distance CB. This ratio is usually perceived as very aesthetic and harmonious, which is why we find architecture and art particularly attractive when it contains features of the golden ratio. However, I find the appearance of the golden ratio in nature much more astonishing. In the meantime the Fibonacci series is completely undisputed as a recognised pattern of growth and development in the plant world.[205] The Fibonacci numbers are directly related to the golden ratio and are found remarkably often in nature. They are also part of my lecture on procedural programming and algorithms, because this sequence of numbers is excellent for covering the topics of iteration and recursion very clearly. Every computer science student in the world will be confronted with this topic at least once in their student life. But that should not be the problem here.

Instead, we look at what exactly this sequence of numbers is and how you can find it everywhere. It was first described by Leonardo of Pisa (Fibonacci) in 1202 in his book *Liber Abaci*. It is an infinite sequence of natural numbers that begins with a zero and a one. All subsequent numbers are then the sum of the two preceding numbers. For example, the eighth Fibonacci number with the value 13 is calculated by adding its two predecessors, i.e. 5 and 8 (5 + 8 = 13), the ninth Fibonacci number with the value 21 is then the sum of 8 and 13 (8 + 13 = 21), etc.

0 1 1 2 3 5 8 13 21 34 ...

If you now put the two summands in proportion to calculate the next Fibonacci number in each case (e.g. 21/13 or 89/55), the result is approximately the golden ratio.

Figure 4-19 shows the seed arrangement in the head of a sunflower. Each seed is at the same time part of a left-turning and a right-turning spiral arm. The number of left- and right-turning spiral arms in all sunflowers in the world are always two neighbouring Fibonacci numbers, frequent combinations are 21/34, 34/55 or 55/89. The specific arrangement of the seeds in the head of the sunflower also results directly from this. This arrangement is not random, but mathematically exactly offset by 137.5° each. This is the golden angle, calculated from the full circle, i.e. 360°, divided by the square of Φ. Only in this arrangement is the maximum number of nuclei accommodated in the head of the flower. This principle is not only found in sunflowers, but also, for example, in daisies, in fir and pine cones, in pineapples and many other plants.

Figure 4-19: Sunflower seeds with left- and right-turning spiral arms

Spirals play a very important role in nature. They can also be traced back to the golden ratio. These so-called golden spirals are logarithmic spirals whose growth factor is Φ. This means that a golden spiral becomes wider by a factor of Φ with every quarter turn. Figure 4-20 shows such a golden spiral, made approximately using squares of Fibonacci numbers.

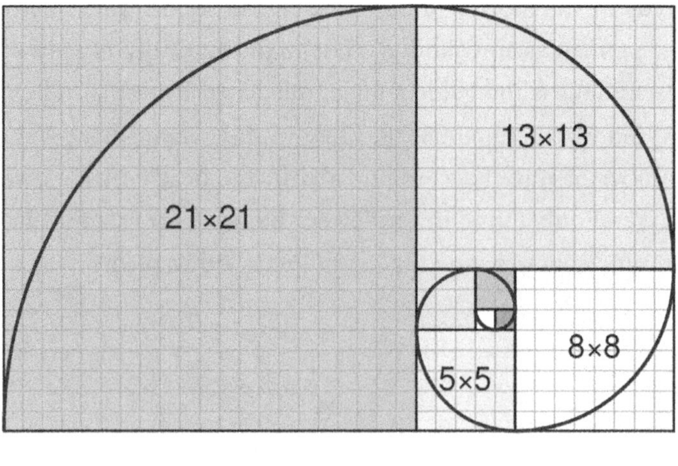

Figure 4-20: Golden spiral - Fibonacci numbers

Figure 4-21 shows an example of a nautilus shell and the disc galaxy NGC 3147. Just like many other shells and snail shells and countless disc galaxies (for example our Milky Way) they also all contain the structure of the golden spiral. There are countless other examples (or example ferns or whirlwinds) but it would go beyond the scope of this book to cover them all.

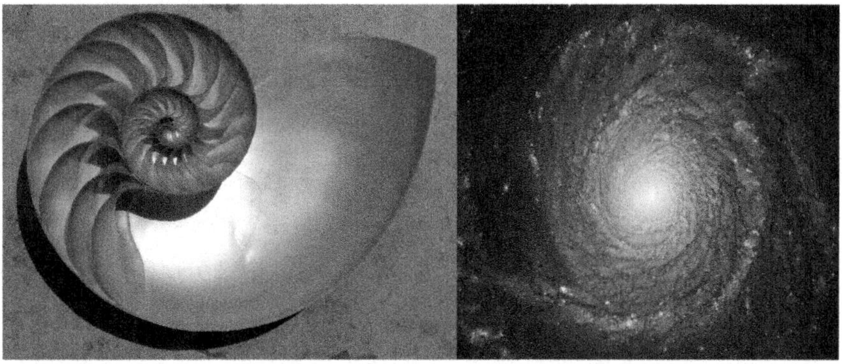

Figure 4-21: *Golden spirals in the Nautilus case (left) and in a disk galaxy (right)*

After the golden ratio shows up in the largest structures we know, such as galaxies, we also find it in the smallest, for instance in our DNA. 'A DNA molecule measures 34 ångström[I] in length and 21 ångström in width in each full cycle of the spiral of the DNA double helix.'[206] The numbers 34 and 21 are adjacent Fibonacci numbers; put them in the ratio 34/21 and they approximate the golden ratio Φ. 'The Fibonacci series shows that the golden section is not only the product of human aesthetic sensibility, but occurs as an objective pattern of development in nature.'[207]

All these observations and findings are, of course, not necessarily proof that these structures must have an intelligent originator, yet it always astonishes most people who see this for the first time. In my opinion this astonishment stems from the fact that we intuitively recognise that something like this cannot be a product of chance or purely chemical physical

[I] One ångström corresponds to the ten millionth part of a millimetre.

processes. For me, the phenomena described around the golden section rather contain clear indications of a conscious all-encompassing architecture.

4.3 Involution and vedic mystery knowledge

> *'Realise also, Arjuna, that everything from the natural world (...), has its origin in consciousness itself - the one supreme divine consciousness. In the natural world, the supreme consciousness divides itself into many forces, both material and spiritual-soul - which combine and recombine with each other in endless variety. Everything known or recognisable originates from the highest consciousness.'*[208]
>
> *Krishna talking to Arjuna about the world of nature, Bhagavad-Gītā*

Materialists consider the emergence of life as being completely detached from consciousness. For a materialist it seems quite self-evident that life had to begin simply and primitively from matter and then successively develop into more complex systems; consciousness only came later as a by-product. This process is seen - without questioning it and without considering alternatives - as a necessary fact. However, this bottom-up evolutionary process is not without alternatives, as I will show. Neither Darwinism nor Intelligent Design endeavours to answer the question at what point and in what form consciousness exists. But for my understanding this is precisely the crucial point. Consciousness is an integral part of our lives. It is as much a part of our human existence as the functionality of our cells or our heartbeat. Leaving it to the side and considering it unimportant or a mere side effect in the explanation of life is, in my view, the completely wrong approach. Who actually says that consciousness must have been added to life at some point and somehow at a later stage of development? This interpretation is again a typical reflection of the Darwinian way of thinking in a material world view.

A true scientist looks at the diversity of all possibilities and carries out an objective evaluation with a holistic view. Those who allow themselves to be limited from the outset by a world view can only find the presumed truth that conforms to this world view. One must not disregard the option that consciousness does not have to emerge, but that it has always existed outside of space and time. Intelligent Design at least suggests that there must have been a conscious designer beforehand. This means that Intelligent Design is not limited to the rigid boundaries of materialism and I think this is a step in the right direction. No current science is able to explain the emergence of consciousness. Therefore, the assumption that consciousness is rather the reason and source of life and not its product is a perfectly legitimate way of looking at it. In fact my first impression is that this seems to be a far better explanation because it does not require us to believe in zero probabilities or in a macroevolution that has never been observed. Possibly, by looking into the past through the mystery knowledge of the ancient advanced civilisations, we can find deeper knowledge and new answers.

The Sanskrit scriptures of the ancient Indian civilisation are considered the oldest written language in the world. The traditional original texts are called vedas or vedic scriptures[I]. They contain astonishingly precise and modern knowledge on medicine, astronomy, spirituality and many other areas concerning human life and cosmic existence. In Chapter 2.4.1, *Our Society is One Step Ahead of Science*, I presented the cosmological time data from the vedic scriptures, confirmed by contemporary astronomy. It suggests that the contents of the vedic scriptures must have come from an intelligent and informed source. If such specific information as cosmological timing is described precisely and correctly there is a legitimate reason to believe that the other contents also contain some truth value. Even if we cannot prove everything scientifically it is at least as right to consider and take these contents seriously as to take chemical and biological evolu-

I Sanskrit word veda = divine knowledge, sacred teaching

tion seriously. This accumulated knowledge cannot be attributed to primitive ancients, it rather points to a spiritually highly-developed culture. The question inevitably arises as to where this knowledge, which is over 5,000 years old, came from. In esoteric circles it is assumed that the people of this age were in a different vibration, one which probably enabled them to gain a certain access to higher spiritual levels. However, the term 'vibration' is not to be interpreted in the physical sense. It is about different dimensions of consciousness converging, and the term 'vibration' should rather be seen as a figurative paraphrase of this. It is in the context of this spiritual convergence and connectedness that this culture may have arrived at its knowledge. In any case, I find it very unlikely that in the Neolithic age a primitive people could have acquired such great and profound scientific and spiritual knowledge without access to higher sources. However it may have happened it is in any case highly remarkable. The opening quotation to this section is from Krishna, the Hindu form of the divine and the embodiment or true incarnation of infinite cosmic consciousness. According to tradition he is said to have formulated the *Bhagavad-Gītā* in 3141 BC, the text also known as the Bible of India. Krishna speaks to his friend, the prince Arjuna, who, as a leader and warrior, begins to reflect on life before a forthcoming battle. In this conversation, Krishna reveals to him his divine knowledge of the world and the meaning of life. In what follows, I will take a closer look at the concepts presented by Krishna on the origin of life, nature, the cosmos and the meaning of consciousness.

What particularly impresses me in the *Bhagavad-Gītā* are the statements on the absence of time and space because these, rather amazingly, fit in coherently with the findings of quantum physics. I will explain my thinking on this topic in Chapter 6, *Quantum Mechanics and Spirituality*, using the example of quantum entanglement and the quantum eraser. What follows here is a rare example of looking at life from a position far away from matter. Concepts such as meaning, morality, feeling, subtle and gross matter, consciousness, spirit and soul are placed at the centre from the very beginning. For unlike Darwin's theory of evolution in which everything has a material cause and, over long periods of time through random mutation and selection, ever more complex life emerges very slowly in small steps and at some point brings forth consciousness as a by-product, in the vedic scriptures the emergence of life is viewed in exactly the opposite way. According to the veda all life ultimately arises, top-down, from consciousness.

4.3.1 The realm of nature and the life force

According to Krishna, the essence of divinity consists of two aspects, he calls it his lower self and his higher self and describes it as follows in the *Bhagavad-Gītā*:

> *'My lower self is the realm of nature (prakriti) (...) and it is composed of eight basic components: Earth, Water, Fire, Air, Ether (Space), Spirit, Intellect and I-Consciousness. Note that these basic components are arranged in ascending gradational order, from gross matter (physical and chemical elements) to the subtler and finer: Mind, Intellect and Ego-Consciousness (which is the basic sense of existing as a physical I). And note that these eight components all belong, even the very subtle ones, to prakriti, the cosmos, the world of nature. Beyond this world of nature, I possess a second, higher aspect, distinct from and yet interacting with nature as a whole. This is my spiritual realm (purusha). Purusha is the life force, the source of consciousness in all beings and the animator of all life. This mysterious power sustains the whole universe. The intermingling of these two realms, nature (or matter) and spirit (or consciousness), is the womb of all beings. Life itself has its origin in this union of nature and spirit. The whole universe unfolds from these two aspects of me and will eventually dissolve into me. I am pure consciousness, Arjuna, the underlying essence of all elements and creatures.* [209]

Here, for the first time, we find exactly what I so vehemently missed in all the chapters before this one: *purusha*. This term also exists as *prana*; in Tibet they speak of *Sog Lung*, in Japan of *Ki*, in China of *Chi* or *Qi* and the indigenous people of North America call it *Manitou.* What they all have in common is their translation as breath of life, life energy or life force. Bruce Elijah, Chief of the Oneida Iroquois, made a very appropriate statement about current science:

> *'They measure what they see. At the same time, they know from experience how little they are able to see. But nevertheless they are absolutely convinced that there can only be what they see and that what they do not see does not exist. They know down to the last molecule what a plant, an animal or a human being is made of. But put all these substances side by side. What makes this heap of chemistry a living plant, a living animal, a living human being? They cannot see, they cannot measure this life force that we call Manitu. And that is why they ignore it. Can you really be more stupid? They move in a world that exists only and solely through this life force. They themselves exist through it down to the last of their hair. And they ignore it because they are too blind to see it, too numb to feel it, too deaf to hear it. And they believe that they are the smartest and wisest specimens of homo sapiens! The stupidity of this science is more boundless than all of cosmic space!'*[210]

In Chapter 4.1.1, *How did life originally arise?* I explored the question of why the corpse of a freshly dead person is actually dead, because all the organic compounds (DNA, RNA, proteins, enzymes, etc.) and cells that biologists consider to be the sole basis of life were still present, yet life disappeared. The life force purusha gives the appropriate answer to this. It is the invisible force, a high divine aspect that can give matter the breath of life but also take it away. Krishna explains that nature (prakriti) alone is the cause of all material things in the universe; the human body also emerged from it alone. But the cause of being alive, perceiving oneself as an individual and feeling joy and sorrow in an individual body is the divine spirit (purusha).[211]

'Again and again I stimulate Nature to bring forth her multitude of forms and beings, infusing spirit into their matter and subjecting them to the laws of their respective natures. None of these actions binds me in any respect, Arjuna. I remain unattached and uninvolved, indifferent to the fruits of these actions. Nature - in its nearness to God - carries on the activities of creation. Under my watchful eye, the laws of nature take their course. Under my supervision of the actions, the animate and the inanimate manifest and the wheel of the world is set in rotation. (...) I am the source of everything in creation, the origin of all beings, of all life phenomena.'[212]

In line with Krishna's explanations, Armin Risi formulates the origin of physical life on earth with the concept of *Involution* in his book *Ihr seid Lichtwesen (You are light beings)*. He describes Involution as an explanatory model that combines the oldest knowledge with new insights and thus leads far away from Darwinism and creationism to a holistic science of life.

'At a time when humanity has become bogged down in religious and atheistic one-sidedness, the knowledge of the spiritual origin of man (involution) becomes a revolutionary revelation: life on earth did not evolve from matter, but from the spiritual primordial roots of the cosmos. The cosmos is multidimensional, as is the human being. The visible material world is embedded in higher, 'invisible' worlds. Light beings are a living reality, and human beings are also light beings, not only symbolically and mythologically, but also biologically and anthropologically. What is happening on earth today has a long prehistory that began in the higher dimensional realms of the universe.'[213]

Risi uses the concept of involution to describe how man appeared on earth. He introduces the concept of materialisation. This is a process that can condense subtle matter into gross matter through the action of consciousness. But what do we actually understand by subtle and gross materiality? Subtle materiality is not a scientifically recognised term, it comes rather from esotericism and refers to the immaterial level to which terms such as ethereal, spiritual and mental are assigned. I am therefore not surprised that materialist science has nothing to do with this term. The gross materiality, on the other hand, comprises our physical, material world, and from an esoteric point of view, these levels are distinguished purely energetically by different degrees of densification. However, from my point of view, the use of the term densification is not to be interpreted literally, because densification suggests that one could capture and measure the associated energies with the means of physics. But this is not the case (at least not yet). However, no other qualified term exists to describe the change from the subtle to the gross and vice versa, so I will stick with the common word choice of *densification*. Involution can be understood as an extension of this concept. In this process there is a hierarchical condensation of light worlds and light beings out of the respective next higher dimensional worlds. According to Risi, when the boundary from the subtle-material to the gross-material is crossed in this process of creation, involution leads to materialisation.[214]

> *'Involution is an interdimensional-hierarchical process of creation: the successive condensation of the second dimensional world from the first, the third from the second up to the seventh, the cosmos visible to us. (Most traditions speak of seven 'worlds' or levels of creation). With these definitions we can summarise the spiritual origin of man in a single sentence: The first human beings came into being through a materialisation of light beings.'*[215]

The term *light beings* is an image for the souls created by divinity from cosmic consciousness. Incidentally, there is much convincing evidence for the concept of materialisation and dematerialisation, two pieces of which I would like to present here in a little more detail. I will begin with a report by the death researcher Dr Elisabeth Kübler-Ross.

On the way to her office, she was approached by a woman asking if she could accompany her, she needed to talk to her. Kübler-Ross recognised the lady, it was Mrs Schwarz, an old patient of hers. The strange thing, however, was that Mrs Schwarz had died ten months ago. Kübler-Ross could not believe what was happening to her, she thought she was hallucinating, but she could actually touch the woman. She describes this incident as the most unbelievable thing she ever experienced. She kept hoping that this entity would finally disappear but Frau Schwarz stayed by her side. Once in the office, she asked the lady for proof of authenticity and had her write something handwritten on a piece of paper. With the most loving smile, the lady telepathically connected with Kübler-Ross and conveyed to her, 'Are you satisfied now?' She delivered the message that Kübler-Ross must not stop her research on dying and after-death experiences, that she would be supported and that her real work was only beginning.[216] After the lady disappeared, Kübler-Ross immediately obtained Mrs Schwarz's old files. The signature on the medical chart matched exactly the signature on the document she had just received.[217] She said that this event had prompted her to continue with her research work. This report may sound very strange, perhaps even crazy, and some may think that we have now finally left the path of serious consideration. There is no proof that the phenomenon described really happened this way, but I consider Mrs Kübler-Ross to be a serious scientist. Why would she make up such a story, knowing that hardly anyone would believe her? With such a story, you embarrass yourself at best and attract the laughter and malice of the sceptics. That's why I think it's absolutely authentic. Only if it is really true do you put up with all that because you are deeply convinced and impressed by what you have experienced.

The Dutchman Arnold Gerrit Henskes (1912-1948), better known by his stage name Mirin Dajo, performed every evening in the summer of 1947 at the famous Corso Theatre in Zurich, Switzerland and demonstrated his physical invulnerability. He had his assistant pierce his naked upper body several times with a pointed foil in front of the present and often shocked audience. He let this procedure pass in complete silence and felt no pain, not a drop of blood flowed, and this despite the fact that the blades penetrated several organs. He had himself pierced and extensively examined in front of the eyes of doctors and forensic doctors in the Cantonal Hospital of Zürich and the Bürgerspital in Basel, among others. Even after physical examinations, ECG and X-ray examinations, the doctors could not detect any injuries. Stunned, they had to admit that it was no trick. These examinations were carried out in public, led by the Swiss internist Professor Rudolph Massini. It would be foolish to assume a conspiracy or staging here because there were simply too many different people involved in these events. Fraud can definitely be ruled out. I will refrain from photos at this point; however, those who want to get their own picture will find detailed information and photos in the books by Armin Risi *Ihr seid Lichtwesen (You are light beings)*[218] and by Luc Bürgin *Das Wunder - Mirin Dajo: Der unverletzbare Prophet und seine phänomenalen Kräfte (The Miracle - Mirin Dajo: The invulnerable prophet and his phenomenal powers).*[219] There is also a video recording of his appearances and of the medical examination. Swiss television, together with *Mysteries magazine*, made the original recordings available to the world public. I would like to highlight a scene in the video in which Mirin Dajo, with a sword sticking out of his abdomen, presents himself in stoic calm to the people present. Professor Massini, unable to believe what he is seeing, grabs his head several times in bewilderment.[220]

Mirin Dajo always declared 'that his experiments and demonstrations have a high aim, namely to give materialistic people an insight into the superiority of mind over matter.'[221]

> *'It is my task to show people the power of the spirit. God has given me my invulnerability so that I can tell people about the power of the spirit over matter - and about my mission, the goal of which is worldwide peace. These divine powers are not only effective in me, but in everyone.'*[222]

Mirin Dajo explained his invulnerability with the terms de- and re-materialisation. When the sword was thrust into his body, his flesh dematerialised around the foreign body and formed a kind of channel. When pulled out, the tissue rematerialised. He also used the term supermaterialisation. According to Armin Risi's interpretation, Dajo most likely meant a materialisation from other dimensions, something which seemed to the spectators to be like a materialisation from nothing. This phenomenon is comparable to the concept of involution, a materialisation of light beings from higher dimensions.[223] Admittedly, this story about Mirin Dajo's work sounds very crazy. Science has sometimes tried to explain these phenomena with entirely natural causes, but these attempts at explanation are so absurd and even so ridiculous that one can only shake one's head. It has even been claimed that, with careful handling, anyone could be pierced in this way, or that piercing channels were present in the body. It was claimed in all seriousness that Dajo had piercing channels through his chest and abdomen, even piercing organs such as the lungs and heart! I studied medicine, so I can say with absolute certainty that such channels cannot be driven through the body without seriously injuring or even killing the person (death for example brought on by a pneumothorax or an internal bleeding). Dajo's later autopsy report clearly confirmed that no fistulas were present.[224] It is inconceivable what nonsense these self-proclaimed rationalists spout just to avoid breaking with the paradigm. So, if the scientific attempts at explanation come to nothing, the only correct conclusion is to believe in the authenticity of Mirin Dajo's abilities. Those who deny such things find themselves in the awkward position of having to accept highly complex staged frauds involving hundreds of initiates from various circles of people or ridiculous-looking medical explanations.

Mirin Dajo not only possessed self-healing powers, he could also use his ability to give healing to others. But what actually happens during such a spiritual healing and how is its functioning best described? If one interprets the observations correctly a dematerialisation of the diseased or defective organs and structures takes place. One can perhaps imagine it like the beaming in the Star Trek movies only it is not the entire body that is transferred into another energetic form, just the affected body parts. As I was already able to show in Chapter 3, *Matter*, matter is not material. Everything is pure energy. A spiritual healer seems to be able to initiate this process through his consciousness and his connection to higher spiritual levels, or at least to be available as a channel for healing. After dematerialisation, there is a rematerialisation of healthy tissue. Organs, stiffened knee joints or blind eyes virtually dissolve in the subtle materiality and reconstruct themselves in their anatomically and physiologically correct arrangement to be later condensed and materialised again in full function. It is quite possible that the morphogenetic field plays a role in rematerialisation as a source of information. I am aware that as an enlightened Western European one can hardly imagine the scenario described and that most of us would probably only believe it if we had been present to witness it or had experienced healing ourselves. I myself am quite critical of the events described. It has something of mystical magic about it and one might think that a professional stage magician was at work here, deluding and deceiving his audience. But on closer inspection there is simply too much to be said against this view. It is impossible to involve so many different people in public in a fraud of this magnitude. Serious medical professionals could not see any deception at close range, even with the help of X-rays, and certainly could not give any explanation for the proven healing successes.

Weighing up all observations and contemporary reports it seems most plausible to me that the events described are indeed authentic. It is much easier for me to believe in de- and re-materialisation or involution than in the chemical and biological theory of evolution which has the weaknesses I described earlier. Unlike the emergence of life from dead matter and macroevolution, the principle of de- and re-materialisation could at least be truly observed, and observation is, after all, the basis of all empirical research. Intelligent Design is, in my view, the first step in the right direction. It is argumentatively far superior to the materialistic concepts and puts the evolutionists in great explanatory trouble. Intelligent Design leaves the specific naming of the designer open, but it boils down to a conscious, intelligent source. This is the crucial point. Consciousness does not emerge at the end of development as the accidental product of presumed evolution; consciousness is the origin and controlling agency of all these developments. The deeper you look into the scientific details of this the clearer it becomes that matter alone cannot justify life. *From the outset* consciousness and intellect are needed.

After all the unbelievable and impressive experiences and feelings that flowed through me after Joma's accident, after the highly significant results of our EREAMS study on afterlife contacts, and after weighing probabilities, logical conclusions and conclusive reasoning with regard to the emergence of life and complex, meaningful information, I come to the conclusion that consciousness did not originate or 'emerge' within the scope of material processes in the course of time but must be the starting point of all these developments. Everything that makes up the world and us humans in our innermost being comes from beyond matter and when our physical end approaches our soul also becomes aware again of its infinite existence beyond time, space and matter. I am therefore absolutely certain, after my intensive study of the origin of life, that Joma was not the product of material processes. Her consciousness existed before her material body, and it still exists now, after her physical death. The body, in my understanding, is only a phasic follower in our eternal existence, enabling us and others to have experiences that help our souls to grow. In this holistic view I consider the concept of involution, in addition to the vedic scriptures, far from any religious sentiment, to be the most convincing explanation when it comes to the origin of the world, of man and of life in general. Rationalists may smile at this insight and dismiss it out of ignorance as mysticism or esoteric nonsense. But most of them do not realise that they have to have much more faith in order to maintain their own materialistic view of the world. I, for one, am not willing to believe in all the necessary miracles that science so cleverly manages to hide from its students and pupils.

The materialist theory of evolution sees no meaning in life and interprets everything as a product of pure chance, but I would like to contradict this and conclude this chapter with a quotation from Krishna from the *Bhagavad-Gītā* on the meaning of human life:

> *'All life revolves around this sacrificial law (sacrifice = selfless action, author's note) called "the yajna wheel". Those who digress from it and*

instead seek to give free rein to the senses for personal pleasure, ignoring the needs of others, live in vain and waste their lives. Why do I, the creator, set this in motion? Because this world is a field of learning, a place for the education, training and elevation of all beings. If we refuse to learn, we cannot gain the benefit of training.'[225]

5 Consciousness

'The spirit, consciousness, the soul must fundamentally be regarded as something independent of the body, as something existing outside the central nervous system. Spirit and consciousness are not, as some scientists claim, 'the excretions of the brain' and thus extinguished as soon as the brain ceases to function, but the spirit has only gradually created the brain, the entire body, and will continue to perfect its instrument.[1]

Sir John Carew Eccles, Australian Nobel Prize winner for medicine at the World Congress of Philosophy in Düsseldorf in 1978

For most brain researchers there is no doubt that our feelings, our thoughts, our memories, our creativity, our plans for the future, our imagination, our intuition but also our mental disorders originate in our brain on a materialistic basis. That which constitutes us in our innermost being, with all our individual characteristics, is radically reduced to biological, biochemical and physical processes. Quite unscientifically but highly intuitively, I would like to subject this hypothesis to an initial evaluation. For me, it is inconceivable that love, for example, as the highest of all feelings, could arise through neuron activity in the brain. This incredible love that one feels for one's own children, for example, or the love of music or the creative development in art cannot be a product of action potentials and biochemical processes in the synaptic cleft. Whether I am right in my intuition or whether science can provide overwhelming evidence for its claims is something I will examine in more detail below.

In his book *Neuromythologie (Neuromythology)* the pharmacologist and science journalist Dr Felix Hasler speaks of a neuro-hype and a certain arrogance that current brain research has developed as it pretends to know exactly about the biological processes that lead to our thinking and feeling. This arrogant thinking unfortunately has serious consequences, especially for patients with mental disorders whose cause is seen entirely as a biological or physiological malfunction in the brain. It isn't too big a stretch to suggest that the pharmaceutical companies have an interest in fuelling this way of looking at things. After all, they can use it to justify the use of expensive drugs. Hasler was able to show very impressively that the pharmaceutical industry has *always* managed to bring drugs onto the market by manipulating research results. Moreover, pharmaceutical companies have invested a lot of money in popularising and marketing new mental illnesses.[2] I find it a devastating development that today seven times as many psychotropic drugs are prescribed as 25 years ago[3] , especially against the background that a recent large study by the psychiatrist Klaus Munkholm and his colleagues concluded that almost no measurable advantages of antidepressants over placebo could be demonstrated.[4] Contrary to prevailing opinion and practice, this would mean that there is no scientific evidence for the use of antidepressants. But there is also a positive trend to be observed, as Dr Gabriella Hunziker writes in the *German Medical Journal* that 'fortunately, a new generation of critical neuroscientists is emerging who are well aware of the limitations of brain research.'[5]

5.1 Does consciousness arise in the brain?

'However, the hypothesis that consciousness and memories are generated and stored exclusively in our brain is still unproven. Direct proof of whether and how neurons in the brain produce the subjective core

content of our consciousness is still entirely lacking. (...) The materialistic point of view falls short in many respects and can no longer be maintained in its present form. It is becoming increasingly clear that consciousness cannot be explained exclusively by the activity of the brain. [6]

Pim van Lommel

The fact that the interaction of neurons is causally responsible for the generation of consciousness is still completely unproven scientifically. In addition to the Dutch cardiologist and near-death researcher Dr Pim van Lommel, Mario Beauregard, professor of psychology and radiology at the Neuroscience Research Center of the University of Montreal, is also convinced that materialism is no longer tenable as an explanation for the origin of consciousness from a neurobiological and neurocognitive point of view.[7] On the other side of the argument the German philosopher Dr Richard David Precht refers to current findings from brain research in his book *Wer bin ich und wenn ja, wieviele? (Who am I and if so, how many?)* He describes the measurement and localisation of brain activity in MRI scanners in response to certain emotional triggers (for instance. sexually arousing or upsetting images) as the big hit among neurobiologists. He even claims that all our feelings, thoughts and actions are created with the help of chemical signalling substances.[8] For me, this claim is completely incomprehensible, especially since it lacks any logical conclusion. That chemical signalling substances are involved in our feelings is beyond question, but to call them the reason for the emergence of feelings is completely unproven and, in my opinion, completely wrong. Unfortunately, scientists rarely point out that it is nothing more than an unproven conjecture; for most of them it is taken to be a proven fact. Serious mistakes are being made here - with fatal consequences, as I will demonstrate below.

Today's brain research tries to prove the emergence of consciousness and feelings through the detection of increased activity in certain areas of the brain. Neuroradiological procedures (for instance EEG[I], PET[II] or fMRI[III]) are the main methods used here. In particular, science assumes the origin of feelings in the brain area of the limbic system with amygdala and thalamus. However, it is a fatal misinterpretation and almost naïve to conclude that increased activity in certain brain areas gives rise to certain feelings. That these brain areas are involved in certain feelings has already been shown in many studies. But to also locate the *emergence* of feelings there is not a permissible conclusion. In my view, this way of thinking is grossly negligent and an expression of materialistic wishful thinking.

Let us imagine the following situation: we hear a wonderful, soulful song on the radio. Its melody is breathtaking, its lyrics touch our heart. Now we want to find out where this song originally came from. How can we explain the act of creation, the composition of the song? Where did the melody, the rhythm and the lyrics come from? Now a classical scientist sets out to investigate the radio set that played this song. What does this scientist do now to find the origin? Using the strategy of the brain researchers, he puts the radio set through a tomograph and discovers that certain components in it are active when the song is played. Current flows in the device through resistors, capacitors and coils. Components get warm or start vibrating. So he thoughtlessly concludes that the song must have originated precisely in these components. But this is quite obviously a fallacy: the radio is, after all, only a receiver. A song is never created by the device. What I have described here corresponds, figuratively speaking, roughly to the level of our current scientific brain research. Our brain is not the creative source of our feelings; it is rather comparable to the radio device just described. From my point of view, therefore, the findings of our brain research regarding the origin of feelings and consciousness are worth nothing. The equation*: increased activity in a certain area of the brain = origin and localisation of feelings and consciousness* is naïve and unconvincing. Thus, the brain too is rather a mediator, a receiver for the

---

[I] Electroencephalogram

[II] Positron emission tomography

[III] Functional magnetic resonance imaging

earthly, physical connection to the soul as a carrier of feelings and consciousness. Pim van Lommel has collected evidence-heavy and haunting accounts of experiences through his studies with patients who have had near-death experiences. These reports allow only one conclusion, namely that consciousness can be experienced independently of the brain and body.[9]

In connection with research into near-death experiences it is often suggested that NDErs have not really died and therefore these near-death reports are not necessarily meaningful. Because of this objection we went one step further in our EREAMS study (see chapter 7, *Is there evidence for a spiritual world?*) and investigated the possibility of contact with the consciousness of the actually deceased with the help of reputable, well-trained afterlife mediums. This produced some astonishing and convincing evidence. In more than 86 per cent of the cases the deceased were able to prove themselves impressively beyond doubt by means of clear, highly specific messages about events or secrets that only the they themselves and their relatives were in a position to know. The bodies and accordingly also the brains of these deceased people have long since ceased to exist due to the decomposition process or cremation, yet it was still possible to communicate with their consciousnesses and experience their feelings.

The fact that the brain is not needed for a functioning consciousness has also been shown in various other studies. For example, the British neurologist John Lorber examined people with hydrocephalus to check their intelligence. In hydrocephalus the skull is filled with too much cerebrospinal fluid (CSF) while the brain is much too small and underdeveloped due to atrophy. Lorber examined a total of 600 patients. In 60 of them the findings were extreme and the cerebrospinal fluid occupied a volume of more than 95 per cent of the inside of the skull. While half of this group showed severe mental disabilities the other half had an IQ of over 100. He also reports a young student who received an excellent university degree in mathematics. His professor noticed that he had a somewhat enlarged skull and sent him to Lorber who was a neurologist. When Lorber examined him it was found that the brain mass between the internal ventricles and the cortical surface of the brain was only one millimetre instead of the normal 4.5 centimetres. This man thus possessed a first-class university degree and an IQ of 126, exhibited quite normal social behaviour, and all this in principle without a brain.[10] The Canadian brain physiologist and neurosurgeon Wilder Penfield was able to produce acoustic and visual sensory impressions or long-past memories in patients by electrically stimulating certain areas of the cerebral cortex with a thin needle. Despite these results, however, he made it clear that 'there is no place in the cerebral cortex where electric shocks bring a patient to a conviction or cause him to make a decision (...) or cause anything that could be called mental activity.'[11]

The results published by the British neurobiologist Steven Rose in his study of chick brains were also interesting. The chicks learned via an induced nausea stimulus that they should not peck at small coloured lights, even though they naturally peck at everything. The learning process was successful and the research group found that there was strong development and activity in the chicks' brains during learning in the left forebrain.[12] From this, it was concluded that the memory of what was learned must be contained in the corresponding nerve cells. When the brain area in question with the active nerve cells was removed from these chicks, it was assumed that the learned behaviour would be lost. But this was not the case. The chicks retained their memory of what they had learned. The same was reported by Penfield, who found that even after the surgical removal of large areas of the cerebral cortex in humans there was no impairment of the patient's consciousness.[13] The neurosurgeon Eben Alexander suffered a severe meningitis caused by the bacterium E. coli. While he was in a coma his entire cerebral cortex was severely attacked by the bacterium.[14] The cerebral cortex is considered to be the seat of the highest integrative functions of the brain and, although Eben Alexander's neocortex showed absolutely no activity, he had the most impressive and conscious experience of his life during it. Later he regained his full cognitive ability. Obviously, our consciousness is not the product of brain activity. It can exist completely detached from it.

5.2 Love

'Love itself cannot die, it is a constant that remains with us for all eternity. If you have truly loved people, you will never lose them.'[15]

Gordon Smith

After the Joma episode I was allowed to break through the limitations of the earthly emotional world and experience unconditional infinite love on the soul level. It became clear to me that loving souls cannot be separated by anything or anyone, neither by death nor by a life in which one has never met. Love is ultimately the only relevant thing in our infinite existence, and yet science is unable to explain love and nothing will change in the future. Hans-Peter Dürr has recognised the higher nature of love well:

'If you try to explain love, you destroy something; because the moment you think you have understood love, you have destroyed it.'[16]

True love of the heart does not come from the material world - so conventional, classical and materially-orientated science will never be able to find evidence of its origin as long as it focuses exclusively on biochemical and physical processes. The Hamburg psychology professor Heinrich Berbalk writes about love that much has been thought about it but little research has been done.[17] This prompted me to conduct a literature search on the subject of research into love using a respected search system for scientific databases and library catalogues. Using the search term 'marketing' I got 6.7 million hits, and a search for 'love' returned three million results. But when I then looked a little more closely at the sources I found on the subject of love there was almost nothing on the love of the heart I reported above. It was almost always only about the love of a job, love and dating apps or the love of earning money. In fact, a tiny percentage of publications on love relationships were limited to finding a suitable partner, sexual attractiveness and psychological analyses of behaviour between men and women. Research into deep heartfelt love, such as exists between parents and their children, is almost non-existent. If one were to ask humanity what they would like to know more about, *either* the origin and nature of love for people who mean infinitely much to them *or* new marketing strategies in the textile industry, I am sure that hardly anyone would choose marketing. I am convinced that in order to explore love of the heart one must accept that this love cannot be explained via materialism but is of a higher spiritual, perhaps even divine nature.

5.2.1 The brain - an organ of love?

> *'One loving person is in a coma, and the other brings him back to life with his love and constant care.(...) As clear as the scientific and medical explanation may sound, now I know from experience: love heals and brings back to life. Julia (Nawalny's wife,* author's note*), you saved me, and they should write that into the neuroscience textbooks.'*[18]
>
> *Alexei Nawalny after he woke up from his coma following his Novichok poisoning.*

In my research on the scientific study of love all the articles I found always had two things in common. The brain researchers exclusively investigated partnered love between a man and a woman, and they always located the origin of love in the brain. In my opinion, it is first necessary to specify the concept of love more precisely. Love is not equal to love, and science looks exclusively at the one aspect of falling in love with a life partner. Philosophers use the ancient Greek term *eros* for this passionate form of desiring and erotic love. Studies inevitably focus on concepts such as happiness hormones, arousal and sexuality, all of which are properties of the material world. Of course, this is also a form of love, but there are other levels that are completely ignored by research. For example, there is the love of family and friends. You can love your pet, your hobby, your car, music, nature and much more. In what follows, however, I would like to highlight two very special forms of love, ones which are the greatest possible manifestations in this world and beyond. In 2014, Disney Studios released a remake of the film *Sleeping Beauty* starring Angelina Jolie as the dark fairy Maleficent. In the story, she places a curse on the king's newborn daughter Aurora out of anger with the king. On her 16th birthday, Aurora will prick herself on a spindle and then fall into a death-like sleep. The curse, and Aurora's coma, can only be lifted by true love's kiss. Aurora grows up loving the moorland, nature and all the creatures that lived there in the realm of the dark fairy. Aurora and Maleficent unexpectedly become close and build an intimate and loving relationship. Maleficent raises Aurora and eventually loves this child as her own daughter. She has to watch helplessly as her self-imposed curse, against which she was also powerless, is inexorably fulfilled. When Aurora actually pricks herself on the spindle at the age of 16 and falls into the death-like sleep, the curse can only be broken by a kiss of true love from Prince Philip. But when he kisses her, nothing happens. Aurora does not wake up. Desperate, deeply in love and heartbroken, Maleficent says goodbye to Aurora's lifeless body. As a farewell, she breathes a tender kiss on Aurora's forehead through her tears. Aurora then opens her eyes and the curse is broken. So the kiss of true love does not come from the potential love partner Prince Philip, but from a mother. This story is, of course, only a fairy tale, but anyone who has children of their own will be able to relate to it. Under normal circumstances, there is no greater love in an earthly life than the love of one's own child. Of course, the love for one's partner can certainly take on similar proportions, and I hope that everyone may experience this happiness. But the love for one's own child usually has an even higher value. This kind of love does not lead us into a libido-hormonal state of arousal, which is the subject of scientific research in particular; instead it is a pure, unconditional form of infinite soul connection.

If one goes beyond this realm of earthly experience, one finds yet another level of love, which, however, remains denied to most people during their lifetime. It is the form of love that has its origin in higher dimensions of the spiritual world, a love as I described it in Chapter 1, *And suddenly everything was different.* This infinite, unconditional and all-surpassing love cannot be adequately described in human words. Only those who have really felt this love themselves can understand it. This love is absolutely real - it is mentioned, for example, in countless reports by people with near-death experiences. I too was (and am) allowed to feel this love again and again, and whoever has experienced it only once will feel an everlasting longing for it. In my opinion, these different levels of love reflect different qualities that also need to be taken into account in research. Unfortunately, a scientific consideration of the levels of love beyond partnered Eros simply does not exist, so research results so far do not get to the core of true heartfelt love.

In the 1990s the American anthropologist Prof. Dr Helen Fisher was one of the first researchers to study the interplay between love and brain activity. The following quotation from her makes it more than clear that she has a very limited view of love; once again it is only about reproduction and endocrinology. She describes love as 'one of the central brain structures that evolved to control mating and reproduction.'[19] But I can safely testify that my love for my children, for my animals or for nature does not come from wanting to reproduce. The German Press Agency reported a study in which 35 per cent of dog owners said they loved their pet more than their partner.[20] Here the assumption that the mating instinct is at the origin of feelings of love fails completely. How could this view also explain, for example, the love between homosexual couples? Two people of the same sex fall in love because of love and not because they hope to procreate. Could it be that such a scientific approach even subliminally puts the stamp of a disease on homosexuality? I think that the scientific attempts to explain Dr Fisher's love are already wrong in their approach and are only an expression of the materialist paradigm. Love is not an auxiliary tool for procreation to occur, it itself is the greater, the more important principle.[21] Mating and procreation are certainly aspects of partnered love but they do not originally produce it. Fisher, like the neuroscientist and psychiatrist Prof. Dr Dr Manfred Spitzer from Ulm, concludes that the brain is the organ of love.[22] They base their findings on biochemistry and on the results of functional magnetic resonance imaging (fMRI), an imaging procedure that makes brain activity visible. The fMRI does not measure neuronal activity directly, it shows local differences in blood flow. Dr Francesco Bianchi-Demicheli, a psychiatrist and sexologist at the University Hospitals in Geneva, and Stéphanie Ortigue from Syracuse University in the USA even developed a neurological analysis procedure called *Neuro-Imaging of Love* to study love in the brain, which also works with recordings from fMRI.[23] They used the same strategy as the two neurobiologists Dr Andreas Bartels from the Max Planck Institute in Tübingen and Prof. Dr Semir Zeki from University College London to examine love test subjects by showing them photos of their beloved partners while examining their brain activity using fMRI. They were able to determine that four limited brain regions were active during the feeling of love (the anterior cingulate cortex, the insular lobe, the caudate nucleus and the putamen).[24] In addition to neuronal activity, the release of neurotransmitters in the brain also plays a supporting role, as Prof. Dr Michael Berner, Director of the Karlsruhe Clinic, explains.[25] The most important hormones here are noradrenaline and dopamine. Noradrenaline activates the body, makes people euphoric and is similar to cocaine with its stimulating effect. The neurotransmitter dopamine conveys positive emotional experiences; it stimulates the reward system in the brain as it does in addicts and is therefore also called the happiness hormone. According to the researchers this creates a kind of addiction to love because the need arises to stimulate the reward system again and again. From the research point of view, longing and desire for love are thus primarily explained by hormonal factors.

Can these findings really enlighten us in our search for the origin of love? Definitely not. The conclusions that scientists have derived from their observations do not contribute anything to solving the question of origin. They call the brain the organ of love and claim that love and also other feelings originate in the brain. Hormones are also said to be significantly involved in the development of the feeling of love. As I have already criticised, I think it is absolutely illogical and not legitimate to consider increased activity in certain areas of the brain as the sole reason for the emergence of feelings such as love. Increased activity does not necessarily mean the emergence of these feelings, but only shows an involvement in the process. The reason for this interpretation lies solely in the fact that the brain represents the highest level in the human body that is still physically ascertainable and measurable . But if we consider, as I do, that matter is not material (see chapter 3, *Matter*) and ultimately nothing more than an energetic oscillation pattern, the question arises why one simply stops looking at the boundaries of the brain when tracing back to the origin. The possibility that the energy of brain matter is not the uppermost limit but that further levels of consciousness exist beyond it is completely ignored by our science. Scientists are here once again discarding their honesty, for if they were honest they would have to express themselves more cautiously, for example thus: 'In the course of our investigations, we were able to detect increased activity in certain areas of the brain. These areas are the highest level that we can measure with the equipment currently available. Holding a purely materialist view of the world we assume that love or other feelings and desires must originally arise in these regions of the brain, because there is no other material structure in the physical body that is superior to these areas. Exactly what this original process of formation looks like inside the brain cannot be answered at present and is therefore only a conjecture conforming to our current world view.' That would be an honest description of the situation. But unfortunately this is not what happens. Instead, materialism once again claims the sole right to scientific reality and articles are published in which scientists claim, in a matter of course way that is completely incomprehensible to me, that love originates in the brain. I also consider it fundamentally wrong that biochemical processes are supposed to be an explanation for the causal emergence of love. The hormones involved, just like the activated areas of the brain, play a major role in the interaction of the physical body with the soul or consciousness, but they are merely interfaces, concomitants and consequences, yet they are chosen by materialist science as the cause.

5.2.2 Love from a philosophical spiritual point of view

Does a philosophical or spiritual view of love fulfil the scientific claim at all and could one really explain love fundamentally with it? I am absolutely convinced of this, because the limits of materialism must not play a dominant role in the search for truth. I would like to remind you that science alone is no guarantee for the discovery of truth. There are levels of reality that science, merely by definition, can never reach; for these you need a holistic view.

Plato describes love as 'the longing for wholeness'. However, while he still defined wholeness through Eros, I would like to give it a new and expanded interpretation. Longing for wholeness must necessarily mean that one is obviously separate from the whole with which one would like to be one. And when one has finally become one, one has reached the goal of eternal infinite love. Love is the most intense feeling in the world and it shows itself through a boundless great affection for another person or soul, combined with the desire to do everything for the good of that person or soul without asking anything in return oneself. To evoke happiness in the other soul is in turn the greatest possible self-experienced happiness. Naturally, there are souls very close to us, such as family and friends in the earthly incarnation, but sometimes also souls from the soul family, whom we do not necessarily have to get to know in our present incarnation. For these souls we feel the greatest love, and especially in loss and separation we feel the strength of this feeling. No one else but the truly loving can descend into the infinite depths of grief, sorrow and longing. Sigmund Freud said that 'we are never more unprotected against suffering than when we love' and Thomas a Kempis already knew that one cannot live in love without pain.[26] This pain is the longing for wholeness, which brings us back to Plato. Ultimately, it is the desire to be reunited with the people you love.

In a holistic approach other aspects are added. I would like to start with a quotation from Jesus, who in my eyes possessed a greatly expanded consciousness and was a highly gifted medium. In the Gospel of Matthew 22:39 he said, 'You shall love your neighbour as yourself.' As I understand it he did not mean that you should be nice to your neighbour living next door. Rather, it means, 'Recognise yourself in the other.' Other people are incarnate aspects of the Divine just as you are an aspect of the Divine. It is about recognising that we are all parts of the Divine and that love is our interconnectedness. At the end of our evolution all aspects will reunite in divinity. Mahatma Gandhi also formulated this realisation in such a wonderful way: 'You and I - we are one. I cannot hurt you without hurting myself.' Separation is an illusion that we are deceptively presented with in our three-dimensional world. But love is the way to higher dimensions where there is no more separation; there we are all one. One of the most important passages in the *Bhagavad-Gītā* confirms this view and makes it clear that love has its origin in the one all-encompassing soul of divinity:

> *'That is Brahman, the Divine, which lies beyond time, which does not perish even when being itself dissolves!*
>
> *This eternal, absolutely divine is the highest goal.(...) All those who reach this highest home reach me, never to be separated from me again, never to return.*
>
> *This immortal state can only be achieved through love, through unswerving, exclusive devotion to me (the Divine). Just as the individual wave has no being independent of the sea, the individual soul has no real being separate from me, the all-embracing soul.'*[27]
>
> *Krishna in conversation with Arjuna about immortality, Bhagavad-Gītā*

By love through 'unswerving, exclusive devotion to the divine', Krishna does not mean that one should religiously or fanatically devote oneself to an individual supreme god. What is meant is that every human being, and thus every individual soul, is an aspect of divinity, and the point is to love every human being, every soul. Selfless souls who are free from ignorance and egoism can tread this so-called northern path and leave the wheel of incarnations to unite finally with divinity eternally.

5.2.3 Love is …

'Love is the light
scaring darkness away.
…
The power of love
a force from above
cleaning my soul.'

Frankie goes to Hollywood - The Power of Love

The answer to what deep heart love really is is found neither in the material structures of our brain nor in hormonal processes. Scientific attempts at explanation are far too weak in terms of their arguments when it comes to looking at origins. When it comes to the origin of love, science has to admit that it simply knows nothing about it. In the protection of endocrinological correlations and functional magnetic resonance imaging the exact opposite is claimed in an exaggeratedly euphoric manner. I think I have been able to show in a factually neutral analysis that this argument lacks any basis. If one sets out in search of the origin of love one must be prepared to transcend the boundaries of the physical. Only in a holistic view will we be able to approach the truth, and to this end I am not developing a dry, non-practical theory here, nor am I philosophising in an esoteric crazy way about possible realities in spiritual dimensions. I am drawing conclusions from my personal experiences – the experiences which came so impressively into my life after Joma's accident. The results of our EREAMS and some further studies are also able to support my impressions in a highly significant way. We were able to show with the strongest evidence that the consciousness and love of a deceased person continue to exist even after the death of the physical body. Our results are so clear that as a scientist one has to ask oneself whether it makes sense at all to continue to search for the causes of love in exclusively material structures of the body when it obviously also exists completely detached from it. The essential of our self is not the body, but love. I do not have the slightest doubt about this; I do not need faith for this realisation, it is my knowledge. Within the scope of my own mediumistic training I have already been allowed to make contact with the deceased of various bereaved people myself on several occasions. I would therefore like to tell you a little about my personal feelings.

Professional and experienced mediums can certainly report on this in much more detail than I can, but I would like to shed more light on the experience from a scientist's point of view. I cannot say for sure whether my perceptions are universal - I can only speak for myself. However, I know from other aspiring and also professional mediums that they feel much as I do. When deceased people from the spiritual world connect with me love is the first and strongest feeling I can perceive. This love of the deceased is very clear and it does not originate within me, rather it is felt by me through resonance. I am entirely sure that in a mediumistic connection this love is not a feeling generated or imagined by myself and that it is actively brought to me from the outside. Tingling sensations and goose bumps, which I can in no way consciously induce, accompany these presences. The experience of being in contact with another consciousness feels absolutely real, it is highly impressive and indescribably moving. Well-trained mediums can receive very precise information from the deceased in such a connection. There will be more about this later in our account of the EREAMS study. Death does not end a person's existence and love, death merely frees the soul from the chains of physical incarnation and allows it to shine in its true, original radiance. Consciousness and love are indestructible, infinite and eternal. The spiritual world is absolutely real without the slightest doubt.

If I can now summarise my findings on love: we are on the way back to the origin beyond matter, an origin in the spiritual world. The love of souls is undoubtedly still present even without a body but this insight does not yet tell us anything about its origin. Basically, we have merely taken the next step from the brain to the immaterial soul in the spiritual world, but where does the path now lead us further? It seems most plausible to me that the love of the heart has its origin in the one all-embracing soul of divinity, and anyone who has only once felt this divine love himself will not doubt this.

Original version in German

Für immer

Nicht in deinem Kopf.
Nicht in deinen Sorgen.
Nicht in deinem Schmerz
und auch nicht tief verborgen.
In keinem Botenstoff,
auch nicht in Neuronen.
Brauch' weder ein Hormon
noch flinke Elektronen.
Nicht in deinem Körper,
auch nicht im Verstand.
Es ist nicht verloren,
was uns einst verband.
Nicht in den Atomen,
ich bin nun befreit.
Ich bin ein Gefühl
und deine Ewigkeit.
Auch ohne einen Körper
bin ich dir so nah.
Wir sind nicht getrennt,
vertrau mir, es ist wahr.

Oliver Lazar

English translation by analogy

Forever

Not in your head.
Not in your worries.
Not in your pain,
nor hidden deep.
Not in any neurotransmitter,
nor in neurons.
Don't need a hormone,
nor nimble electrons.
Not in your body,
nor in your mind.
It is not lost,
what had us combined.
Not in the atoms,
I am now free.
I am a feeling
and your eternity.
Even without a body,
I am so close.
We are not separated,
Trust me, it's true.

Oliver Lazar

6 Quantum mechanics and spirituality

What exactly does the physics of quantum mechanics have to do with the topics of spirituality, the emergence of consciousness and the spiritual world? If you take a look at esoteric literature QM seems to have a lot to do with the spiritual hypothesis. Astonishingly often one finds references to quantum mechanics and it is often used as proof for the existence of spiritual realms. I agree with the conservative physicists in their criticism of this literature. I also have the impression that many presumably spiritual teachers, esotericists as well as philosophers interested in physics, driven by an indispensable will to find scientific proof for the existence of the spiritual world, of the principle of spirit creating matter, or even of quantum healing, have pounced on this topic of quantum mechanics with rather naïve expectations. Under the protection of the language of physics and using mathematical formulae they seem to be argumentatively on the safe side. Which esoterically-interested person could ever doubt these explanations when physicists themselves find the phenomena of quantum mechanics incomprehensible? The quality of argumentation in esoteric literature varies greatly, from naïve and curious to highly scientific. Even if the ctiticisms in his book and in his lectures are very one-sided and sometimes hurtful the physicist Dr Holm Gero Hümmler justifiably draws our attention to the fact that some dubious healers, shamans and philosophers are on the move in the esoteric scene where they use quantum physics and relativity theory in an unscientific way to justify their methods and views.[1] The physicist, mathematician and philosopher Dr Lars Jaeger also speaks in this context of 'laymen who misuse quantum physics to support their aberrant world views.'[2] But is this criticism of such a world view, which is sometimes very harsh, pejorative and sweeping, really always justified? Natural scientists, rather unjustifiably, like to lump esotericists all together. As is so often the case in life, esotericism has a lot of light, but it also has a very large shadow. Unfortunately, this dark side brings the entire esoteric community into disrepute and makes it doubly difficult for serious research in this field.

So let's deal with the *light* side of esotericism. For there *are* some very high-quality scientific discussions of this topic and even some serious scientists and other prominent people who are of the opinion that the material world arises from the spiritual world and from our thoughts. Even the founder of quantum mechanics and Nobel Prize winner in physics, Max Planck, was of the opinion that matter would not exist without the mind.[3] The married couple Christine and Frido Mann have written an entire book on this subject entitled *Es werde Licht: Die Einheit von Geist und Materie in der Quantenphysik (Let There Be Light: The Unity of Mind and Matter in Quantum Physics)*[4]. Christine Mann is a psychologist and the daughter of the famous quantum physicist and Nobel Prize winner Werner Heisenberg. Frido Mann is also a psychologist and the grandson of Thomas Mann. In their book they write about overcoming materialism and about a holistic view of the world and the human being and how reality is formed from our thoughts. A very similar approach is taken by the biologist, physicist, geographer and educator Dr Ulrich Warnke. In his book *Quantenphilosophie und Spiritualität (Quantum Philosophy and Spirituality)*[5] he describes extremely complex interrelationships and uses strong arguments based on Heisenberg's uncertainty principle, superposition and the very famous double slit experiment. I will explain these topics in detail below and try to answer the question to what extent quantum mechanics can confirm the emergence of reality from our consciousness against the background of current research results. But if we want to find an answer to this, we must first deal with the basics of quantum mechanics.

Quantum mechanics is admittedly an extremely challenging subject area. It will probably even turn your understanding of classical processes, causal relationships and structures familiar to you from your daily life completely upside down. I will take you on a journey into the physical science of quantum mechanics to show you that the world you think you know holds incredible and unthinkable realities and phenomena. My hope is that I can use quantum mechanics to sensitise you to new perceptions and ways of looking at our world, because then it will also be much easier to consider other realities and perhaps even spiritual realms. Unlike many esoteric authors, I do not dwell on the knowledge and statements of the last century, but include current and sobering research results on quantum mechanics in my explanations.

Isaac Newton formulated the laws of motion, establishing the foundations of classical mechanics, in 1687. In our everyday life we are used to thinking in terms of Newtonian mechanics, especially the principle of causality, and we accept that there is always a cause-effect relationship in the interaction of forces for everything that we experience. In our macroscopic world processes are usually deterministic, that is, their individual steps are predictable and unambiguous. So when I put my foot on the accelerator of my old Land Rover Series 3 vintage car, a cascade is set in motion that is predictable. Put simply, the carburettor gets more petrol, the engine speed increases, and the vehicle accelerates. However, if we leave the world of the macroscopic and dive deeper and deeper into the matter structures of atoms and molecules, things suddenly behave quite differently. Determinism dissolves almost completely as the boundaries of time and space disappear. In what follows, I will endeavour to present you with what I consider to be the relevant findings of quantum mechanics as clearly and comprehensibly as possible without getting lost in the deep jungle of scientific detail. The following quotation from Richard Feynman should also motivate us for the possible hurdles to understanding in this chapter:

'(…) I think I can say with certainty that nobody understands quantum mechanics.'[6]

Richard Feynman (US physicist, Nobel Prize winner in 1965)

6.1 What is quantum mechanics?

'Quantum mechanics begins (…) where things become fuzzy, indeterminate, where things begin to behave strangely.'[7]

Harald Lesch

At the end of the 19th century a certain complacency prevailed among physicists with regard to scientific knowledge. They basked in the glory of the achievements of Newtonian mechanics and electrodynamics and regarded all open questions of physics as answered in principle. This quotation from the Scottish physicist James Clerk Maxwell at his inaugural lecture at Cambridge University in 1871 underlines this impression: 'In a few years all the fundamental physical constants will have been approximately determined, and (…) the only occupation then left to scientists will be to push these measurements one decimal place further.'[8] But then in 1900 the German physicist and later Nobel Prize winner Max Planck set a revolution in motion. He came up with a formula for the radiation spectrum of so-called black bodies, thus showing how objects radiate heat.[9] His formula had an obvious flaw that made him doubt it himself for many years, but as so often in the history of great discoveries it was precisely his anomaly that helped us to make what I can aptly call a great quantum leap. The flaw was that the energy did not radiate continuously but instead was portioned out in packets. He called these energy packets *quanta*. Five years later, it was a little-known physicist called Albert Einstein who brought quanta worldwide fame. He put forward the hypothesis that all electromagnetic radiation occurs exclusively in quanta. But this assertion had severely shaken the physical world of the time, because it meant that light, which until then had been universally regarded as a wave, had now acquired the character of a particle. Einstein called these light particles *light quanta*, and nowadays the term *photon* is common for these.[10] Einstein postulated in his light quantum hypothesis that a photon hitting a piece of metal gives up its energy to an electron in the metal. The energy generation in our solar cells is based precisely on this effect. Incidentally, Einstein was awarded the Nobel Prize for Physics in 1922 not for his general or special theories of relativity but precisely for this discovery of the photoelectric effect. Despite his discovery of the particle character of light Einstein continued to hold on to the idea of its wave properties. After all, many experiments provided proof of this and it seems clear in the colours and frequencies of the spectral composition that we know from the rainbow. And so the world was faced with a problem. What was light then, a wave or a particle? It seems that it can be both. This dual nature of light is also known as *wave-particle duality*, and this is the starting point for all the physical, esoteric and philosophical interpretations in quantum mechanics.

6.1.1 The wave-particle duality in the double-slit

The wave-particle duality is most impressively demonstrated in the famous double-slit experiment. The experiment was first performed with light in 1802 by the English ophthalmologist and physicist Thomas Young. I am sure that this experiment will amaze you, as it resists our usual logical perception. We will realise that things in the quantum world do not behave as we know them from our everyday lives, and if someone were to think it was a trick or a deception I could well understand that. But this experiment was repeated many times under controlled conditions, and it always showed the same result. Before I describe the experiment to you, however, we must first deal with the concept of probability, because this is completely different at the quantum level from how it is in our macroscopic world.

Let's imagine two beer cans; one is full, the other is empty. Both cans are indistinguishable from the outside, and we do not know which is the full or the empty can. We can only *guess* which is the full can, and the probability of getting that right is 50 per cent. To get certainty, one would have to inspect one of the two cans. Now it may sound strange that I am emphasising this here, but there are clear facts in this scenario: one can is full, one can is empty, and this reality existed before the two cans were inspected. So checking which can is full had no effect on the reality that already existed before and still exists afterwards (assuming the experimenter did not finish the beer). In the world of the smallest, however, other laws apply with regard to probability. If we now transfer the example with the beer cans to the quantum world it turns out that the probability of finding the full can is no longer based on our lack of knowledge. Rather, it is an integral part of the quantum system, which can now give rise to several possible realities. The hypothetical quantum beer is therefore simultaneously in both cans before our examination, but also just as well in neither. The state of this quantum beer is *fuzzy*, in its case several possible states overlap without manifestation, a situation which is also called *superposition*. Only at the moment when the quantum beer interacts with another system, for example when we check one of the cans, do we force the quantum beer to assume an objectively determinable state. Our observation obviously collapses the state of superposition and reality emerges. This sounds crazy. But in a system isolated and closed from the outside world, exactly these phenomena show up.

Let us now take a look at the double-slit experiment and let us follow the whole phenomenon with real quantum particles. The experiment has been repeated countless times not only with light (photons) but also with electrons, atoms and fullerenes (complex carbon molecules), that is to say with the components of real matter. No matter what was used in the experiment the results of the wave-particle duality were always the same. The experimental set-up for the basic experiment is quite simple (see Figure 6-1).

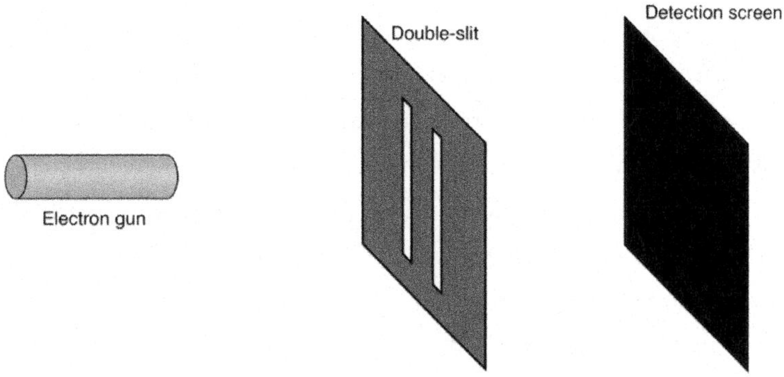

Figure 6-1: Double slit experimental setup

We use an electron beam system (electron gun) and shoot electrons at a plate that has two small parallel slits. Behind this plate is a sensitive detection screen that makes the electrons hitting it visible and detects them. Before we now carry out this experiment with quantum particles, it makes sense to look first at the experiment with particles that we know from our macroscopic everyday life. So we can briefly replace the electron gun with a sandblaster (see Figure 6-2). After activating the sandblaster, the sand grains fly towards the intermediate plate with the double slit. In the process, the sand grains that can pass through the slits form two homogeneous pattern bars on the rear detection screen.

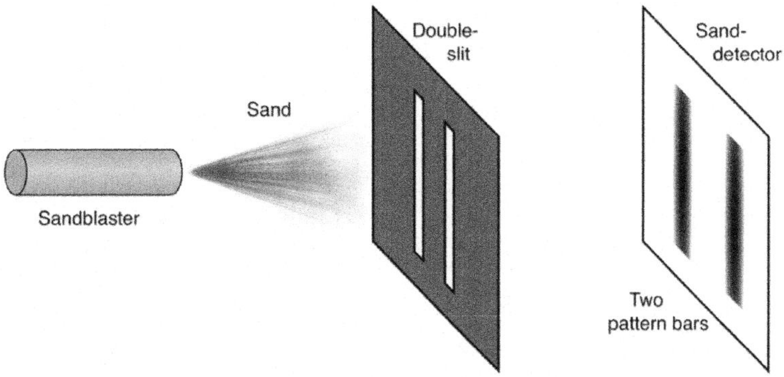

Figure 6-2: Double slit with sandblaster

This scenario is comparable to holding a stencil over a sheet of paper and then using a spray paint to transfer exactly the pattern of the stencil cut-out onto the paper. In our everyday experience this result is no surprise and fully corresponds to our natural expectations. But now we put the sandblaster away and use the electron gun instead. We fire electrons in the direction of the double slit and in principle we now expect the same result as in the experiment with the sandblaster. But in the quantum world, the particles no longer behave like their macroscopic brothers. Figure 6-3 shows the result of the double-slit experiment with electrons, in which not two pattern bars become visible, but several pattern bars with different intensities, with the intensity decreasing towards the outside. These so-called interference patterns are well known in physics as they are always a clear indication of the interaction and superposition of waves.

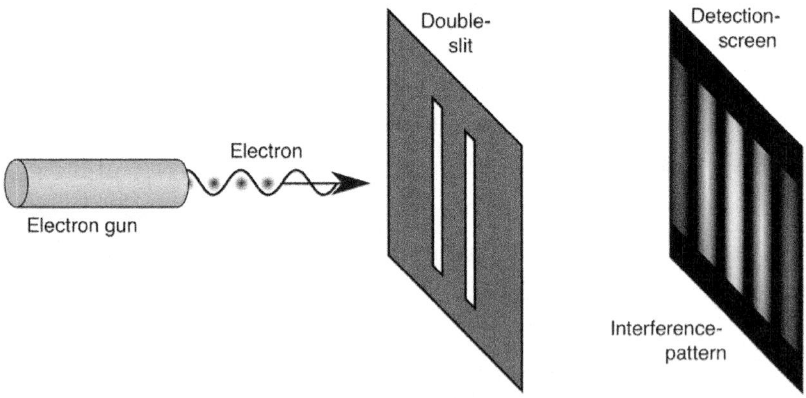

Figure 6-3: Double slit with electrons and the typical interference pattern

Imagine that the plate with the double slit is half submerged in water. If a wave were to roll towards it, it would hit the plate, and parts of the wave would pass through the two slits. Behind this, two new waves would be created, which would partially overlap, also known as interfering. Where two wave crests meet, they reinforce each other, and an even larger wave is created. If two wave troughs meet, they amplify in the opposite way and we get a deep wave trough. Where a wave trough meets a wave crest, they neutralise each other and the water surface becomes smooth. If we now transfer this effect to the double-slit experiment with the electrons, it can only mean that the electrons must obviously have wave properties when passing through the double slit. The pattern bars created on the detection screen represent the wave superpositions whereas the empty spaces in between are the result of the neutralisation of the waves.

Figure 6-4 illustrates the propagation of the waves behind the columns. Where the wave lines intersect, there is an amplification, so that we get the brightest pattern bar exactly in the middle of the detection screen, where there are the most superpositions. Towards the outside, there is less amplifying overlap, so that the intensity of the patterns becomes somewhat weaker. Between the pattern bars the wave signals have cancelled out and the screen remains black there.

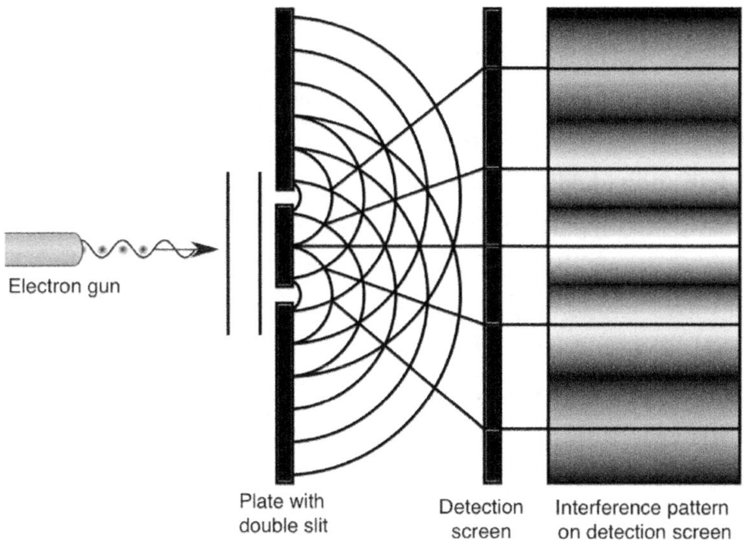

***Figure 6-4:** The two waves overlap behind the slits and create the interference pattern*

It is time to draw a small interim conclusion before we dive even deeper into the subject and extend the experiment. So we have shot electrons, to which we would ascribe particle character as building blocks of atoms, with an electron gun onto a plate with a double slit. The electrons hitting the detection screen behind it are shown in our experiment as a bright point of light. So when they hit the screen, the electrons are definitely particles. But on their way from the gun through the double slit towards the screen, they obviously behave differently. They oscillate at a certain frequency like a wave, and behind the slits their waves overlap, otherwise the interference pattern on the rear screen could not be explained. However, when the wave hits the screen, the wave property of the electrons collapses and they manifest themselves again as particles at a specific position. Incidentally, the exact position at which the electrons will manifest themselves after being fired from the electron gun cannot be predicted. Although the electron gun always shoots with the same intensity and in the same direction the electrons seem to hit the detection screen completely at random. In sum, however, the amazing interference pattern always appears.[11] In their interaction they obviously behave like superimposed waves. Next, however, the electrons were no longer shot out of the electron gun individually, fired one after the other. It was now expected that the interference pattern would disappear, since we were now dealing with single electrons that could no longer interfere with other electrons and their waves behind the slit. But the surprise was very great because the interference pattern remained unchanged even with individually fired electrons. Thus, there was only one possible explanation for the phenomenon: a single electron passes through both slits at the same time, and its wave interferes with itself behind it.[12] Now the question arose as to what actually happens to a single electron when it flies through space in the wave state? Where is it during this time? What consistency does it have in the meantime? Is the electron (as a particle) possibly *in* the wave and is it carried by it through space? Does one half of the electron fly through the first slit and the other half through the second?

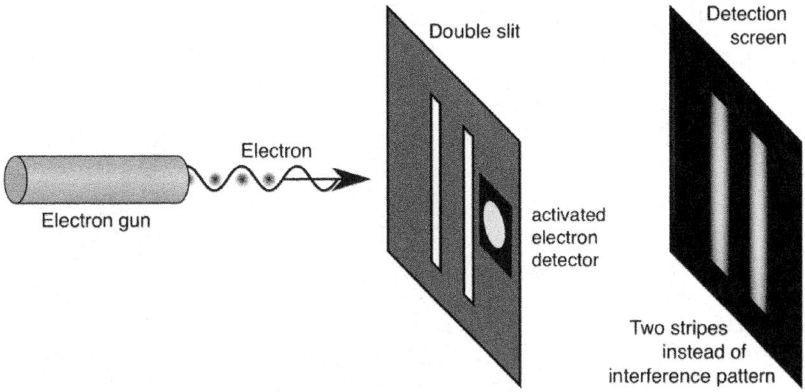

Figure 6-5: Double slit with electrons and detector switched on

To get to the bottom of the matter the experiment was extended. To determine which slit an electron would fly through, a detector was attached to one of the slits that could detect the electron as it passed through. And what happened next was the starting point of one of the greatest philosophical and physical discussions about the occurrence of reality in the last century. Figure 6-5 shows the double-slit experiment with a detector switched on at one slit.

It is hard to believe, but when we add one activated detector the interference pattern on the rear screen disappears and we get the image of two pattern bars visible to normal particles, as with the sandblaster. It almost seems as if the electron did not want to be detected coming through the slits as a wave so all of a sudden it behaved like a particle again that could actually be measured by the detector. It could be clearly measured whether an electron came flying through the left or the right slit. If that doesn't seem crazy enough, look at what happens when you switch off the mounted detector (see Figure 6-6). If the detector is inactive, the interference pattern appears again. It almost seems as if the electron has a sense for the situation we have constructed and notices whether we want to observe it or not. As long as it is not observed, the electron is in superposition as a wave function. It therefore has neither a specific position nor a specific momentum, it is dematerialised in principle at all permissible locations in the probability space. The squared wave function represents the probability of the particle's location.[13]

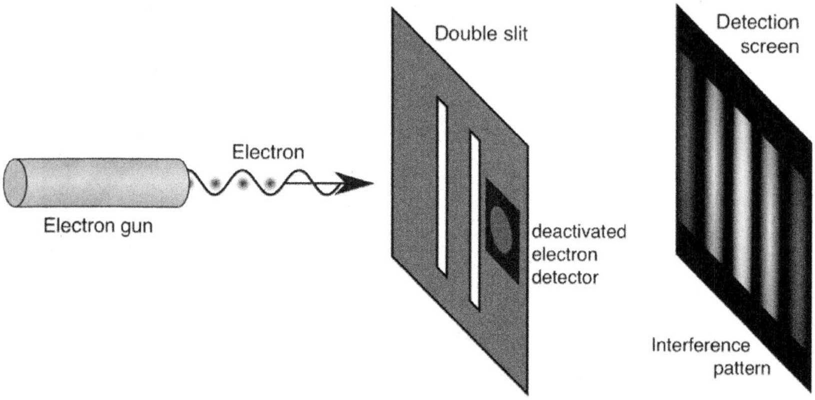

Figure 6-6: Double slit with electrons and detector switched off

Finally, it was the three Nobel Prize winners in physics, Erwin Schrödinger, Werner Heisenberg and Max Born, who described this behaviour of quantum particles via the Schrödinger equation and the Heisenberg uncertainty principle as position-momentum uncertainty. So if we do not observe the electron, it must decide on a location and manifest itself only after it has passed the double slit and hits the rear screen. But let us look again at the situation with the electron detector switched on. Obviously, the process of observing influenced the behaviour of the electron. Our conscious observing caused the wave function to collapse, the electron was forced to manifest itself, reality had to arise at this moment. But what exactly does 'at this moment' mean? The amazing thing is that the electron detector was placed behind the slit. So the electron must actually have decided *before* it crossed the double slit whether it had to fly as a particle through one slit or as a wave through both. But how did the electron know that it would be measured behind the double slit? Otherwise it could have simply passed through both slits as a wave, as before. Thus, it is also clear that the measurement itself cannot bring about the particle property of the electron on its own, because the decision as to whether it is a wave or a particle must definitely take place before it crosses the double slit and thus also before it is measured. Since the measurement took place behind the double slit, there obviously had to have been a temporal retroactive influence on the electron. Isn't that absolute madness? We have witnessed a kind of time machine. Could this possibly be the first indication that there is perhaps no such thing as time? I will present this phenomenon of retroactive influence in time in an even more impressive way with the experiment of the quantum eraser in chapter 6.1.3, *The quantum eraser - entanglement in time.*

For many years there was no satisfactory explanation for this phenomenon and this led not only philosophers and esotericists to new ways of looking at the origin of reality but also many physicists. In the current esoteric but also popular scientific literature, many authors still like to refer to these original views from the last century. It is therefore not surprising that Warnke cites the statements of two Nobel Prize winners in physics for his remarks: 'Consciousness creates reality'[14] by Eugene Wigner and 'Reality is created by observation'[15] by Nils Bohr. Of course, one can argue that there is obviously no longer any reality independent of the observer, but one must not forget one thing: the observations in this double-slit experiment were based on a closed quantum system. A closed quantum system is an artificially created idealised and isolated framework for the experiment in which the observed system in a vacuum has no interaction with the outside world. But this does not correspond to the reality in our macroscopic, material world, where interactions inevitably occur always and everywhere. In our world we are exposed to influences from our environment at all times; quantum particles collide permanently with gas molecules, photons or radiation, for example. The wave-like existence of particles in superposition in the microscopic quantum world can therefore not exist on a macroscopic level in an open, real system or in connection with a measurement, which is nothing other than an interaction.[16] This lightning-fast destruction of the quantum nature of superpositions through even the smallest interactions with the environment is also referred to as decoherence.[17] Current research in physics has made great progress, especially in recent years. Unfortunately, these new insights are seldom or never included in the complex ways of looking at esoteric approaches. Wisdom and quotations are something wonderful, but I am quite sure that, for example, a Nils Bohr with today's physical knowledge of decoherence would no longer repeat his quotation from earlier. Besides Warnke and the Manns, there are many other authors who have formulated very valuable and conclusive theories on the subject of consciousness creating reality. I appreciate these schools of thought and am very grateful for the conclusions, some of which have been worked out very precisely. However, I consider these theories rather improbable, especially against the background of current physical achievements. I see my assessment confirmed above all by the work of David Wineland and Serge Haroche. These two physicists managed to isolate individual photons from their surroundings and observe them in their superpositions without destroying their quantum state. So an observation took place that did not collapse the wave function. This is clear evidence that our observation does not create reality. With their experiment, they were even able to prove the decoherence process directly. Wineland and Haroche received the Nobel Prize in Physics in 2012 for their groundbreaking experimental method for measuring individual quantum systems. With this, we remove the ground from any observation-creates-reality philosophy, at least for the time being.

6.1.2 Non-locality – entanglement in space

Entanglement is one of the most astonishing phenomena of quantum mechanics and it completely challenges our everyday experience of spatial separation and location. Entanglement means that two particles share a state independent of location, that is, they are connected with each other even if they are spatially any distance away from each other.[18] In order to be able clearly to understand entanglement we will construct another experiment. First we have to produce entangled particles, and to do this we send single photons through a nonlinear crystal. The photon is transformed in this crystal, and two new entangled photons with half the energy each are created. Figure 6-7 shows the experimental setup and the light paths of the two entangled photons.

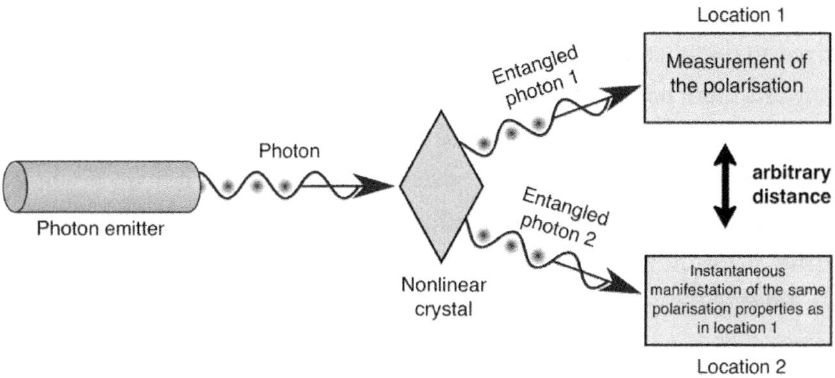

***Figure 6-7:** Instantaneous equal polarisation during the measurement process on an entangled photon*

After leaving the crystal, the two photons travel different paths, they are therefore spatially separated and undoubtedly at different locations. The entanglement of photons can be determined by their polarisation, that is to say the direction of their oscillation. The polarisation is not defined in the photon during the wave state in superposition, it only arises at the moment of measurement. In other words, the particle state of the photon, including its polarisation, is only generated and determined by the measurement process itself. If you measure one of the two photons and thus determine its polarisation, you also determine the polarisation of the other entangled photon. The crazy thing is that it doesn't matter how far apart the two particles are. Particle A could be on Earth and particle B could be somewhere in the Andromeda galaxy. The measurement process on one particle instantaneously, without the slightest time delay, produces the same measurement value on the other particle. But how is this immediately-simultaneous exchange of information supposed to work over any distance? If no time is allowed to pass for the exchange of information the speed of the exchange must be infinite. But this cannot be reconciled with the theory of relativity which states that the highest possible speed for the exchange of information is the speed of light, and this is not infinite, but is about 300,000 kilometres per second. In any case, delays would have to occur, but this is not the case with entanglement. Incidentally, Einstein was never able to accept this realisation during his lifetime; he even referred to the phenomenon as 'spooky action at a distance'. What explanation can there be for this behaviour? Obviously, the two entangled photons are not separate at all, but still form a location-independent unit. Quantum systems consisting of several particles always remain a whole, no matter how far apart the individual particles are. This effect, measured at the quantum level, also has an impact on our macroscopic world. Recently, this entanglement effect has been exploited in new technologies. In 2016, the quantum satellite Micius was launched into orbit as part of a Chinese research project; from it entangled photons were sent to two ground stations 1,200 kilometres away. With the help of entangled photons, it is possible to ensure a tap-proof exchange of quantum keys for the establishment of secure communication.[19] Entanglement is clear proof that our three-dimensional spatial world cannot be the only reality. Rather, our spatial world must be embedded in or exist parallel to a spaceless dimension. There is undoubtedly a reality in which the localisation of particles is non-existent. Our definition of place, spatial separation and distance thus collapses. This phenomenon is also referred to as the non-locality of particles.

6.1.3 The quantum eraser – entanglement in time

The astronomer, mathematician and physicist Dr Josef M. Gaßner calls the quantum eraser 'the craziest story there is in quantum mechanics.'[20] What Gaßner calls crazy here is precisely such a realisation, where we humans with our earthly minds reach a limit, a limit that Dawkins does not want to admit. The quantum eraser completely turns our deterministic understanding of cause-effect relationships of our reality in space and time upside down. I have to warn you that things will get a bit more complex and quite bizarre now, but I promise it's worth staying on the ball here. We now extend the double-slit experiment by placing a non-linear crystal directly behind the double slit. Instead of electrons, we now shoot photons at the double slit, which are converted by the crystal into an entangled photon pair each. We direct one of the entangled photons to a detection screen while directing the other to a separate detector (see Figure 6-8).

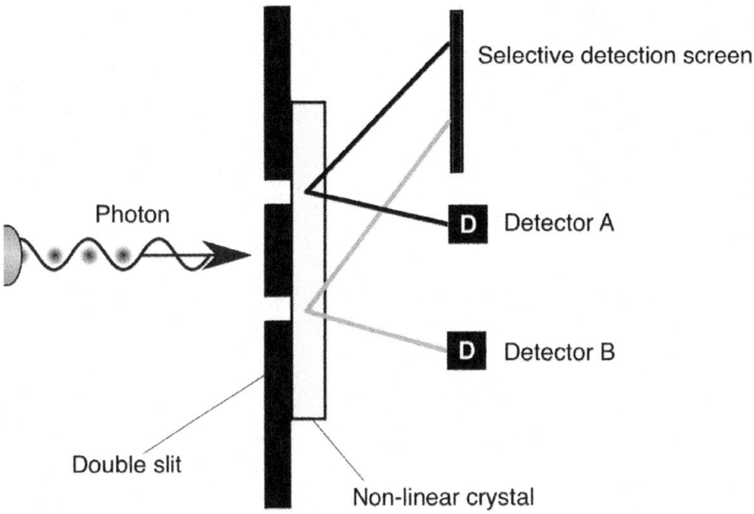

Figure 6-8: Detection of entangled photons without interference patterns (following Josef M. Gaßner[21])

Photons coming through the upper slit are directed to detector A, those coming through the lower slit are directed to detector B. Whenever we measure a photon at detector A or B, we simultaneously record the impact location of the entangled photon on the detection screen. This allows us to establish a correlation between this impact location on the screen and the respective detector. As was to be expected no interference pattern appears here, but for both detector A and B the photons each produce a single bar. Compared to our previous double-slit experiment with an active detector, this is not much new at first.

But now we modify the experimental setup with three beam splitters that randomly deflect a photon with 50 per cent probability in one direction and 50 per cent in the other direction (see Figure 6-9).

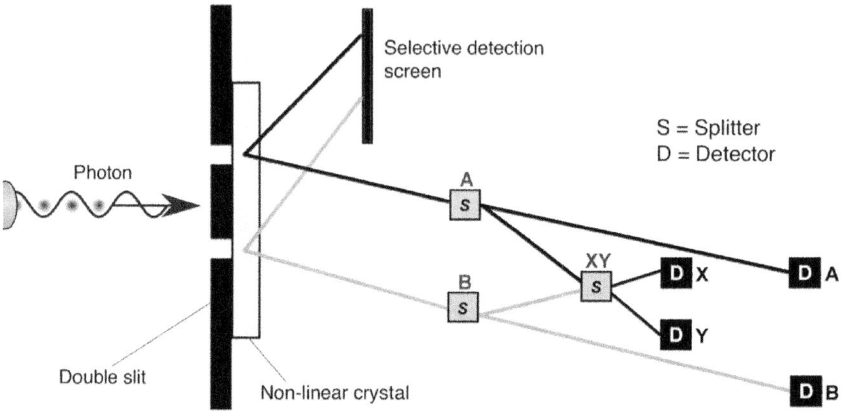

Figure 6-9: The quantum eraser (based on Josef M. Gaßner[22])

The amazing thing is that when we correlate detectors X and Y with the impact locations of the entangled photons on the detection screen we suddenly get the interference pattern again. And as if that alone were not crazy enough, the real trick comes now. Take a look at the distances from the crystal to the detection screen on the one hand and to the beam splitters and detectors on the other. The path to the detection screen is much shorter than the path to the beam splitters. Since photons always move at a constant speed of light, the photon that is directed onto the detection screen arrives much earlier than the other. So while one photon must already show itself on the detection screen, the other entangled photon is still on its way. The decision in the beam splitters as to where the photon will be forwarded has not yet been made. Nevertheless, the first photon already knows in advance whether it has to show itself as a bar or interference pattern. Thus there is only one permissible conclusion. The random decision in the beam splitters must definitely have an influence on the behaviour of the first photon, acting backwards in time.[23] This is not a magic trick, and it reveals a new reality that is contrary to our experience.

Our understanding of time is led *ad absurdum* in this experiment. Entangled photons are therefore not only non-local, they also exist outside the time structure we know.

Interestingly, there are experiments in brain research that show a very similar effect of such temporal backdating. The neuroscientist Benjamin Libet and his team stimulated test subjects with electric shocks on the back of the hand and measured on the one hand the objective perception of the time of the stimulus via the measurement of brain activity by means of an electroencephalogram (EEG) and on the other hand the subjective perception by the test person himself. It turned out that the objective perception of the stimulus, the activity recognisable in the EEG, was recognisable with a delay of about half a second. The subjective perception, on the other hand, the conscious perception of the stimulus, occurred surprisingly earlier, immediately at the time the stimulus was triggered. According to Libet, the sensory perception in the brain must therefore have generated the subjective conscious experience at the actual time of the stimulus triggering through a temporal backdating.[24]

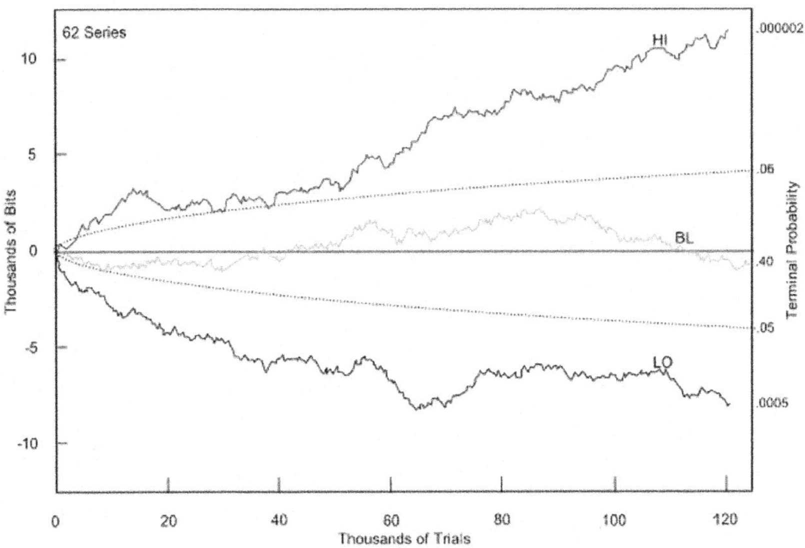

Figure 6-10: Final result of the psychokinesis experiment with a random number generator (Source: Roger D. Nelson, 2017)[27]

At Princeton University, Robert G. Jahn founded Princeton Engineering Anomalies Research (PEAR) in 1979, one of the most renowned psi research groups in the world. Until 2007, numerous high-quality and controlled studies were carried out.[25] Among others, there was a famous experiment on psychokinesis. In this experiment, the subjects were asked to influence a random generator with their thoughts. The random generator produced completely random sequences of the numbers zero and one. The number sequences were generated from the radioactive decay of a radioactive source, which could not be influenced either chemically or physically.[26] The test subjects were given the task of influencing the number sequences in such a way that either more zeros or more ones should be produced. Figure 6-10 shows the highly significant result of one participant after sixty-two experimental series.

On the right edge of the graph is the respective final result for all three types of passes after 125,000 passes each. The curve in the middle, labelled BL, shows the values of the random generator without anyone having acted on it mentally. As expected, the values are close to the zero line, which means that on average as many zeros as ones were generated. The upper curve, labelled HI, shows the result for the passes in which as many ones as possible were to be generated. The lower curve, labelled LO, represents the result for the runs in which the participants should have the random generator generate as many zeros as possible. Both the results for HI and LO are highly significant, meaning that the mental manipulation of the random numbers worked so well that it cannot be explained by luck or chance. In statistics, it is common to work with a significance level of 0.05 (= five per cent). This can be interpreted to mean that something is considered significant if there is no more than a five per cent chance that the result was obtained by chance. The five per cent significance levels are also plotted on the graph. It can be clearly seen that the HI and LO curves exceed these limits by far. From a statistical point of view, it can be ruled out in principle that these successful manipulations only occurred by chance.

The German-American physicist and parapsychologist Helmut

Schmidt conducted this experiment in a variant that takes us back to the question of the reverse-effect on time. Schmidt not only presented his test subjects with currently generated random number sequences for psychokinetic manipulation, but also number sequences that he had already recorded in advance and then fed to the participants from memory without their knowledge during the experiment. This pre-recorded data is also known as pre-recorded targets (PRT). The astonishing thing now was that these PRT experimental series also produced significant results that, statistically speaking, could not be explained by chance. How could a random number sequence stored in advance contain significantly more ones or zeros than the random distribution of the simultaneously recorded control number sequence, if the psychokinetic influence on it only took place later? Obviously, the psychokinetic influence has an effect that works into the past.[28]

Prof. Dr Gitt has a wonderful lecture which he has given many times - entitled *Origin of Life from the Perspective of Information*. In this lecture he deduces very conclusively from his natural laws of information that, according to his argument, God must be omniscient and eternal. Instead of 'God' I prefer terms like 'divinity' or 'spiritual world', but that does not change his excellent reasoning. *Omniscient* and *eternal*, to my understanding, mean that the spirit world exists outside our temporal structure and can oversee our past, present and future. While we humans can possibly still imagine that there are spiritual beings that look into our past and present, we find it immensely difficult to see how they can also look into our future. After all, we humans have free will and I can decide freely every second of my life, so how should that be possible? Gitt illustrates the whole thing in his lecture with a little story. He tells of how his wife sent him to the bakery with the request that he buy five buns. When he arrives at the bakery, he is not sure which buns to take. Because the poppy seed buns are on sale, he takes three poppy seed buns, one normal and one with sunflower seeds. Now he asks the question whether they knew in advance in the spirit world what he would choose. If the spiritual world is eternal and omniscient, it must have known beforehand.[29] But with our limited human minds we don't really get it together. How can I decide freely and yet the spirit world knows in advance how I will decide? The quantum eraser shows us experimentally that it can indeed be like this. Chance decides in the beam splitters which path the photon will take, yet the other photon entangled with it knows in advance what will happen. From my point of view, this can only be explained by the fact that there must be a dimension that exists outside of time. When intelligent spiritual beings look at our material existence from a timeless dimension, they see everything that was, is and will be at the same time. Thus, they can also see in advance which buns you will choose at the bakery. For us humans living in this space-time, this is incomprehensible, but obviously there is no before and after, there is only the now. Time is a purely humanly-experienced construct.

In my own afterlife contacts, and also in those of some of the participants in our EREAMS study, we repeatedly find statements from the deceased about our future development or about future events. Mostly it is about changes in career or love, but also about fateful events such as illnesses and personal development. Often these predictions are then confirmed afterwards. On the whole, however, the spirit world is very cautious when it comes to future topics; probably our free will must not be influenced too much by this foresight. We only receive as much information as is important for our lives. The fact that a glimpse into our future is possible is also described by the psychiatrist Brian L. Weiss in *Many Lives, Many Masters*. In this book, Weiss describes how, through the therapy of his patient Catherine, he gained access to her past lives, but also to her spiritual guides and teachers. In the trance she reported astonishing experiences from the various epochs of past lives. Again and again, highly evolved spirit beings also spoke up in these conversations and at these times Catherine spoke with a different voice. Weiss wondered whether it was possible to look into the future as well as into the past. This was clearly confirmed to him.[30]

6.2 What can quantum mechanics do for spirituality?

In Chapter 2, *Science and Spirituality* I have already described that materialist science needs certain initial prerequisites of faith in order to be able to function at all, and thus it definitely also falls into the category of a faith. According to the scientific-materialist faith, then, objectivity, causality, time and space are self-evident given facts and they are assumed to be real without a hint of doubt. It seems to me that it is therefore incoherent to define the terms science and faith as opposites. The term 'faith' is actually unfortunate because it suggests that one must *believe* and cannot know or logically reason, which is a fatal error. For it makes no difference whether one deals with faith in science or faith in the spiritual world; knowledge and logic can be applied in both. They are equivalent in my eyes and I would even interpret the concept of the Spiritual World as an intrinsic part of the concept of science. A holistic science would not only contain materialistic aspects but also the spiritual ones; in both cases we have to work according to the common rules of scientific methodology. The good thing about this holistic science is that it can question itself, at least if of freedom of research is also guaranteed and the dogmatists and reputation-fetishists are excluded. Such a science, or better, such a belief in science, differs from religion especially in that it must present comprehensible arguments in order to convince others. The findings must be published and examined in the context of a public discussion. This would be unthinkable for a religion, but not for a belief in the spiritual world.

The scientific findings of quantum mechanics have been confirmed, so the faith-like principles of classical science have not only to be questioned - they have to be seen as having been *refuted* as a logical consequence. I do not question the existence of causality, time and space, but as principles of a faith that would account for a complete view of the world they fail. The classic scientific interpretation of the nature of things is not the only permissible reality - the world is far more complex and multi-layered than current science can grasp or understand. In my view quantum mechanics has brought down the foundation of materialist science by its own methods and findings. I am convinced that belief in a spiritual world can provide good evidence for its validity through current scientific methods and can stand up to professional debate. With this book and our research I am trying to contribute to this.

I am sure that quantum mechanics provides facts that prove that the world is not as we know it. Because if you realise that matter does not actually exist and that cause-effect relationships and the dimensions of space and time are not fixed absolutes, then it is also much easier to imagine the existence of a spiritual dimension. This is precisely where I see the justification for the interplay of quantum mechanics with spiritual topics. Some scientists and philosophers go one step further and justify the emergence of consciousness by quantum mechanical processes. But I consider this approach to be wrong because in my view *consciousness does not need to arise*, it has always been there and is rather the origin of everything. I think that many esotericists and philosophers have gone too far out on a limb when it comes to quantum mechanics. Quantum mechanics is not proof of the concept that consciousness creates reality, although I am convinced that consciousness is the origin of all being and also of the material world. But the principle that conscious observation is the trigger for the emergence of reality can be considered disproved. The double-slit experiment, which still made the world of physicists, esotericists and philosophers tremble in the 20th century, was demystified by Wineland and Haroche through decoherence. They showed that one can observe a quantum system without collapsing the wave function and superposition. The crucial thing that quantum mechanics can do for spirituality is to realise that the entanglement of quantum particles reveals to us the existence of a reality without place and without time. Our space-time structure therefore represents only one layer in a multi-layered reality. These different layers of reality do not seem to be separated from each other, so our world is permeated by a non-local and timeless dimension. From the point of view of quantum mechanics there is an abolition of cause-effect relationships which are now replaced by the concept of *simultaneity*. What we perceive as the Now encompasses every moment both in the past and in the future at the same time. From the perspective of an eternal spiritual world time degenerates into nothingness.[31]

Pascal Voggenhuber's perception of the spiritual world confirms this impression of dissolving boundaries between the worlds. In his book *Botschafter der unsichtbaren Welt (Ambassadors of the Invisible World)*, he reproduces his spirit guide's explanations of the structure of the spiritual world, which can be reconciled astonishingly well with the effects of quantum mechanics:

> *'The human brain needs structures, you want to be able to classify everything somehow. In the same way, you want to classify the spiritual world. So you divide it into levels and dimensions. But in reality there is neither time nor space here. And if time and space do not exist, then there can be neither levels nor dimensions, at least not as you understand them. For your understanding you often need or want a division, that is why there are spiritual beings who try to explain our world, which is totally illogical for you, to you in a certain logic. But it does not really correspond to the way our world is.'*[32]

I would like to introduce you to another interesting explanatory approach by Christina von Dreien. This young Swiss woman has various paranormal talents including multidimensional perception. She explains the structure of the world with its dimensions as follows:

> *'It is not so easy to explain this subject to the three-dimensional mind. Dimensions are kinds of frequency ranges or spheres of consciousness. It is important to understand that there is no spatial demarcation between dimensions, but a spiritual one. The individual perception of dimensions depends on the personal energy level, the personal vibrational frequency of a living being. According to this personal vibrational frequency, the corresponding consciousness and the corresponding talents then follow.'*[33]

7 Is there evidence for a spiritual world?

'There are two ways to be fooled. One is to believe what isn't true; the other is to refuse to believe what is true.'[1]

Søren Kierkegaard

In order to be able to answer the question of evidence for the spiritual world one must first clarify the extent to which this particular area of research can be covered by science at all. So let's take a look at how scientific research is actually defined. The Springer textbook *Forschungsmethoden und Evaluation (Research Methods and Evaluation)* by Nicola Döring and Jürgen Bortz is considered a standard work in this field and it says that anyone who conducts scientific research searches for assured new findings with the help of recognised scientific methods, on the basis of the current state of research, in a targeted manner, documents the research process and the results in a comprehensible manner and presents the study to the professional public in lectures and publications.[2] Döring and Bortz divide the research world into two main categories. The first category consists of the non-empirical sciences, which include the formal sciences (mathematics, philosophy and so on) and the humanities (law, history, theology, literature and so on). The second category contains the empirical sciences, which include the social sciences (sociology, psychology, medicine and so on), the natural sciences (physics, chemistry, biology and so on) and the technical sciences (mechanical engineering, electrical engineering, computer science and so on). Table 7-1 shows this division into scientific categories.

Table 7-1: Non-empirical vs. empirical sciences (following Döring and Bortz[3])

Non-empirical sciences		**Empirical sciences**		
Formal sciences	Humanities	Social sciences	Natural sciences	Engineering Sciences
Mathematics	Law	Sociology	Physics	Mechanical Engineering
Philosophy	History	Psychology	Chemistry	Electrical Engineering
etc.	Theology	Medicine	Biology	Computer Science
	etc.	etc.	etc.	etc.

Before I introduce the field of spiritual sciences I would like to explain what is actually meant by empiricism or an empirical science. The term empiricism means experience, an empirical science can therefore be described as a science based on experience and observation. From this we can already deduce what form of research this characterises. With the help of systematic and standardised processes through quantitative and qualitative methods findings are collected in relation to research questions on the basis of observations. The empirical data obtained in this process is information about the reality of experience that is specifically selected and documented for the research problem.

Now, where could one place spiritual science in this model? Most people will probably say that spirituality belongs to the humanities and is therefore clearly non-empirical. I think one has to see it in a more differentiated way. One cannot categorise spiritual science across the board;

there are certainly aspects of spirituality that undoubtedly belong in the realm of the humanities and elude empirical research. But spirituality is very complex. For example, it also has many aspects that can clearly be classified in the fields of sociology, psychology, medicine, natural sciences and even computer science. In other words, many aspects of spiritual science can be quite clearly researched empirically. All the criteria mentioned by Döring and Bortz are, in my opinion, also applicable to spiritual research in many areas.

In our secular society with its materialistic world view there is usually no room for people for whom the existence of the spiritual world is absolutely real. Not infrequently they are labelled as religious or esoteric crackpots and ridiculed. One participant in our EREAMS study expresses his disappointment about this as follows:

> *'It is such a shame that our society is so dismissive of afterlife contacts. So many more mourners could be comforted. And sitters could talk to others about it without being called crazy.'*

Yet there are so many people who have experienced their own extrasensory perceptions or even received contact with their deceased. In 2020 an extensive study with over 1,000 participants under the direction of Evelyn Elsaesser was published on these so-called after-death contacts. This scientific study, entitled *Investigation of the phenomenology and impact of spontaneous and direct After-Death Communications (ADCs),*[4] meets a high scientific standard and does absolute justice to an established methodology. Evelyn Elsaesser has already been primarily involved in the study of after-death experiences for thirty years and for this research project she was able to attract several professors and doctors from Great Britain and the USA as project partners and scientific committees. In contrast to our EREAMS study, where we work with a medium as an interface to the spiritual world, Elsaesser investigated after-death contacts occurring directly between mourners and their deceased. These may have happened, for example, through sensing or feeling a presence, or touching, hearing or seeing the deceased. 40 to 50 per cent of the population have already experienced such an ADC, mostly while asleep.[5] However, although this phenomenon is apparently very common it is not talked about publicly. The aim of Elsaesser's work and also of our EREAMS study is to facilitate a serious public discussion on this topic. People should no longer have to fear being exposed or laughed at because of their perceptions and experiences in dealing with the spiritual world. With our scientific work we are doing true pioneering work and are placing the discussion about the continued life of our souls on a solid foundation that can no longer be ignored or ridiculed even by a modern society. But, as mentioned in the opening quotation, much of our society refuses to believe what is true. Our research is neither manipulated nor the product of esoteric wishful thinking; it clearly reflects the truth that has been elucidated by the use of scientific methodology. Although most people have been brought up from childhood with a materialist view of the world, one that is accepted without criticism and must never be questioned, I hope that this socially-entrenched attitude can finally be freed from its dogmatic shackles through our scientific work.

Meanwhile, research into near-death experiences (NDEs), which has gained enormous acceptance in the last 20-30 years, enjoys a significantly different and more positive public treatment. Especially due to the frequent involvement of medical personnel and doctors, who are naturally considered to have a high degree of credibility, such reports and studies have increasingly found their way into the public domain through established and reputable information channels. The cornerstone for this was certainly the book by the psychiatrist Dr Raymond Moody *Life after Death*[6] published in 1975, followed by many other authors, especially Evelyn Elsaesser's *Was wir aus Nahtod-Erfahrungen für das Leben gewinnen (What We Gain for Life from Near-Death Experiences)*[7] and Pim van Lommel's *Consciousness Beyond Life*[8] were further milestones in this field. But also the death researcher Dr Elisabeth Kübler-Ross has done true pioneering work in this field. In her work *On Life after Death*[9] she describes the experiences of dying people with out-of-body experiences. She reports, for example, the cases of blind people who left their bodies in the face of death and were suddenly able to see.

'And these blind people who have had an out-of-body experience and have come back can tell them in detail what colours and what jewellery they were wearing at the time they were present, what pattern their jumper or tie had and so on. You understand that this is not something that can be fantasised.'[10]

Psychologist and physician Dr Brian L. Weiss reports a similar case. Among other things, he was head of the psychological-pharmacological department at the University Hospital Miami and chief physician of the psychiatric department. With over 4,000 reincarnation patients, he is one of the best-known and most successful reincarnation therapists in the world. He tells of an incident during resuscitation of an elderly lady who suffered cardiac arrest at Mount Sinai Medical Center in Miami. Her cardiologist and other medical staff were on the scene in the intensive care unit. They tried to bring the lady back to life with resuscitation measures. The cardiologist dropped his gold ball pen on the floor and it rolled under a window. During a short pause, he picked it up again. The lady could finally be revived, and she told her cardiologist a little later that she had floated out of her body and watched everything. The cardiologist only said that this could not be, after all she had been unconscious and in a coma. Then the lady said that she had seen him drop his golden pen and pick it up again a little later. The doctor was dumbfounded and surprised that the lady had seen this, not only that she was unconscious, but also that she was blind.[11]

Sceptics often regard these phenomena as a result of a lack of oxygen in the brain. I take exactly the position of Dr Kübler-Ross on this: why not simply prescribe oxygen deprivation to all blind people in the world? Besides, oxygen deficiency always leads to confusion and unconsciousness, but never to increased consciousness. Sceptics also like to refer to another pseudo-argument, namely that it is all just hallucinations caused by the body's own dimethyltryptamine (DMT), a naturally occurring serotonin antagonist from the pineal gland. Dr Eben Alexander had a neocortex that was completely damaged by bacteria when he had his near-death experience which could not possibly have been stimulated by DMT[12], yet such arguments are stubbornly held on to. One of the biggest criticisms of near-death experiences, however, is that the patients did not really die. This could make the statements and reports of experiences not really meaningful. But that is why we have gone a step further with our EREAMS study: the deceased in our study are actually and irretrievably dead. Attempts by doubters and critics to explain a lack of oxygen in the brain, DMT, or that they are not really dead therefore come to nothing with us. Critics then say that in such afterlife contact studies the participants' own emotional state and their longing for the deceased could produce these phenomena. In order to exclude this as a cause the most important evidence is the production of unequivocal proof that, for example, the bereaved person has received a message with information that is still unknown to him or her and which can only come from the deceased. If this is later found to be accurate, or if a medium relays private secrets and facts that he or she could not possibly have known, we have our solid evidence.

7.1 The EREAMS-Study on the effectiveness and authenticity of messages from the spiritual world

Original version in German

Ich bin ...

Ich bin die Liebe, die uns ewig vereint.
Ein Leben, das euch nun so sinnlos erscheint.
Ich lass euch nicht los und ihr auch mich nicht.
Ein Gedanke an mich erhellt stets mein Licht.
Ich bin nicht fort, ich bin nur nebenan,
auch wenn man mich nicht mehr anfassen kann.
Ein Streicheln, das zu 'ner Gänsehaut führt,
das ist meine Seele, die euch sanft berührt.
Mein Bett, meine Kleidung, mein Zimmer, mein Duft,
ich bin euch so nah, doch es herrscht eine Kluft.

Berühren, Umarmen, das geht leider nicht.
Ein Schmerz, der brutal mein Herzlein zersticht.
Freunde werden kommen, ob neu oder alt,
ihr werdet verstanden, sie geben euch Halt.
Ich kann euch fühlen und sehn, was ihr macht.
Es gibt mir viel Kraft, wenn ihr lebt und auch lacht.

Oliver Lazar
Für alle Eltern, die ein Kind haben vorausgehen lassen müssen

---

English translation by analogy

I am ...

I am the love that unites us eternally.
A life that now seems so meaningless to you.
I will not let go of you and you will not let go of me.
A thought of me always brightens my light.
I am not gone, I am only next door,
even if you can no longer touch me.
A caress that gives you goose bumps,
that's my soul gently touching you.
My bed, my clothes, my room, my scent,
I'm so close to you, but there's a gulf.
Touch, embrace, alas, it is not possible.
A pain that brutally crushes my little heart.
Friends will come, new or old
You will be understood, they will give you hold.
I can feel you and see what you are doing.
It gives me a lot of strength when you live and laugh.

Oliver Lazar
For all parents who have had to let a child go before them.

The name of our study is EREAMS which stands for *Empirical Research into the Effectiveness and Authenticity of Messages from Spirit*. I deliberately chose not to publish this study in a scientific journal because the danger is too great that our work would then come to a dead end, just like the Cardeña study. After publication in a scientific journal we would have had to buy back the rights to our own study for publication in any other channel, and this didn't seem like the right way to go. Most interested people would probably not even know how and where to get a specialist journal anyway and the reach of such publications is also far too small. I am not interested in scientific reputation, I would rather reach the people who can really use our results in their lives. How many people could I have reached through a parapsychological journal, apart from a few other scientists from this exotic niche, which is controversial in the scientific world anyway? In my view, a peer review is therefore not appropriate here and hardly possible because there are no proven, scientifically recognised experts on afterlife contacts. In my opinion, peer review is only necessary if the topic can be understood exclusively by experts in the field. If, for example, you publish something in the field of quantum mechanical processes you need specialists to be able to assess the content. But the EREAMS study is so simply structured that anyone can understand it without prior or specialist knowledge. Very simple questions are asked, for example about clear evidence or perceived comfort. There is nothing really complicated about it. So I cordially invite every single person in this world to be their own expert and just make up their own mind. I fully disclose our study design and methodology so that everyone can freely decide for themselves whether our procedures and conclusions are comprehensible and coherent. I see my assessment has been absolutely confirmed by Prof. Dr James Tour whom I introduced in Chapter 4: *Origin and evolution of life*. He is one of the top 50 scientists in the world and he has over 750 publications in peer-reviewed journals. During his talk in the *Socrates in the city* series he said the following:

> *'By YouTube I'm hitting the masses, I don't need to hit my colleagues anymore because they are not interested in this. ... It really is the best*

medium, it gets out and you get thousands and thousands of views so quickly and it's an amazing medium and you hit large numbers of people all over the world. It has a real impact! You know, I write all the articles in the journals but nobody ever reads them.'[13]

In our study 500 afterlife contacts were examined ('contacts' are people – the events they participate in are 'sittings') The examining was done by two renowned mediums, each known throughout Europe. A sitting is understood as the establishment of a connection for the purpose of communication between the soul of a deceased person (or animal) directly with the surviving relatives or indirectly through a medium who translates and transmits the messages received. The desire for communication generally exists both in this world from the bereaved and in the spiritual world from the deceased. Previous experience shows that messages from the spiritual world are always full of love and care and they ultimately always serve to heal, comfort and sometimes guide. Such communications can take place without conscious control, as in the After-Death Contacts (ADCs) investigated in the Elsaesser study which can occur mostly during sleep but also in waking consciousness. According to Elsaesser over 90 per cent of the people who had such an experience were convinced of the authenticity of the contact. After their ADC, 92.80 per cent of the participants believed in an afterlife and 94.60 per cent were convinced that the deceased person can contact them. 35.90 per cent sought out an afterlife contact medium after their ADC.[14] It is precisely such afterlife contacts that are the subject of our EREAMS study. A person who makes the conscious decision to get in touch with the soul of the deceased usually does it by consulting a medium.

7.1.1 The current scientific status of afterlife contacts

'Arthur Ford's importance for science lies in the fact that he has provided the most reliable evidence of contact with the beyond to date

(1971, author's note*). His world-wide reputation is based on the validity of his messages from 'over there'. Like myself, thousands of people can confirm that the messages he transmitted contained very personal information, the content of which could not have been agreed upon beforehand and which could only come from the deceased himself.'*[15]

Professor Jerome Ellison, University New Haven, about the medium Arthur Ford

Like Rupert Sheldrake I believe that what many of us call supernatural is rather something quite natural although scientific studies from the controversial field of research on afterlife contacts are sparse. In addition, the public media are usually very reluctant to publish such findings, as they could quickly earn themselves a dubious reputation. Therefore I think it is important that there are courageous scientists who continue to conduct and publish more studies in this field. At some point the findings will no longer be ignored. I hope we can play a part in this with our EREAMS study.

In spite of this, scientific studies on afterlife contacts have been produced for more than 100 years, but the current state of scientific knowledge on this subject can be described as very manageable. Only very few studies have serious scientific claims but all of them only find their way into the public domain via little-noticed parapsychological journals, congresses, popular scientific literature and discussion groups. Sometimes such studies actually end up in recognised medical or psychological journals, but these are all medically-associated and contain, for example, studies of the brain frequency of a medium during a sitting or psychophysiological and psychopathological phenomena and their technical correlations. In this way the investigators run less of a risk of being labelled as cranks in the scientific world. However, a few research projects have actually also dealt with the information content of messages from afterlife contact mediums; I examine these in more detail below.

One of the first serious scientists to conduct such evidence-based research of messages and their information content was the English physicist Sir Prof. Dr Oliver Joseph Lodge (1851 - 1940). He is considered the first discoverer of electromagnetic radiation and was a pioneer of radiotelegraphy. From 1900 to 1920 he was head of the University of Birmingham and served as president of the Society for Psychical Research. His youngest son Raymond Lodge was killed as a soldier at the front in the First World War. Raymond subsequently tried to contact his father from the other side through a medium and was able to prove his continued existence several times. Sir Oliver continued to research these events and messages which were eventually confirmed as completely authentic not only by him but also by many other scientists. He published his studies in his book *Raymond, or Life and Death*[16] published in 1916; it became a sensational bestseller at the time. In the book there is also a photo with which a very special story is connected. The British trance medium Gladys Osbourne Leonard (1882 - 1968) was scientifically studied for over half a century. She transmitted very precise information to Sir Oliver about a photograph. This information apparently came from Raymond and she drew attention to how important this photograph was. It had been transmitted to Gladys spiritually and she had never seen it by normal physical means. She said that in it you could see a group of soldiers with Raymond sitting on the ground in the front row, holding his walking stick. The soldier behind him was leaning on him and almost pushing him aside. Sir Oliver did not know which photo this was supposed to be. A week later he was contacted by the family of another quite different soldier; they had been sent a photo from the front by their son and it also showed the fallen Raymond. They condoled with Sir Oliver and sent him the photo. When he received it he saw that it contained all the details mentioned by Gladys and it corresponded exactly to the description previously given.

After the death of his wife, John F. Thomas wrote his dissertation in 1937 on a study that lasted nine years in collaboration with the medium Gladys Osborne Leonard. This study was conducted under the supervision of Professor McDougall who held the chair of psychology at Duke University in North Carolina. Over the nine years Leonard gave 2,964 specific facts about Thomas's wife. 2,358 of these were correct, 196 were incorrect and the rest were either inconclusive or unverifiable. To date, this is the only doctoral dissertation in the field of research into afterlife contacts; the dissertation is entitled *Beyond normal cognition.*[17]

The American trance medium Leonora E. Piper (1857 - 1950) is one of the most scientifically studied mediums in the world. Parapsychological societies put several professors on her to expose the tricks she was accused of using. Psychological scientist Richard Hodgson was particularly persistent, studying and reviewing it for years. After 15 years, however, his scepticism broke down and he was convinced that she was indeed communicating with deceased people. Among other things, Leonora also passed on messages that neither the sitter nor she herself knew and which had to be researched afterwards and proved to be correct. These kinds of messages also form the core of our EREAMS study. Despite decades of activity in this field, she never asked for money.

Another notable scientist in this field was the famous psychologist Gardner Murphy (1895 -1979) who studied at Yale and Harvard Universities and received his doctorate from Columbia University in 1923. He later served as a professor of psychology there and earned a reputation as one of the world's most influential psychologists. In 1944 he was elected president of the American Psychological Association and in 1949 president of the British Society for Psychical Research, and in 1951 he was appointed director of the Parapsychology Foundation.[18] He was a highly respected scientist and published a carefully designed and executed study of medium-transmitted information. He came to the conclusion that there was no other admissible explanation than that this information must have come from the deceased without any doubt whatsoever. He presented several examples of transmitted messages in his study[19], which can also be found in a similar form in our EREAMS study. As I will show, our study can fully confirm Murphy's findings.

Also worth mentioning is the Brazilian study *Mediumship: review of quantitative studies published in the 21st century* by Bastos Jr. and his team from the Federal University of Mato Grosso do Sul from 2015.[20] The aim of this study was to create an overview of all quantitative studies related to mediumship published since 2000. For this purpose, the researchers searched various electronic catalogues (PubMed, Lilacs, Web of Science and others); in the end, they were only able to identify six studies that dealt with the correctness of mediumistic messages. One of these studies referred to a writing medium who had already died many years ago as part of a retrospective investigation, which will not be looked at in more detail here.

The design of the other studies was relatively the same: different mediums gave sittings to several clients who were not present in a triple-blind study. The clients then had to choose afterwards, from several possible sittings, the one that they felt best suited them or their deceased. In the 2005 study by O'Keefe and Wiseman, there were five professional mediums and five sitters. The sitters had to use a point rating to determine which sitter was the best fit, and there were no significant differences between the ratings. Only one rating showed a correct tendency. This study could therefore not confirm mediumistic skills.[21] The study by Beischel and Schwartz from 2007 showed a similar design but a different result. Eight mediums and eight sitters took part, whereby each sitter received two sittings in absentia that were determined for him. Here, too, the sitters were asked to find out the two sittings designated for them from the various sittings by means of a point evaluation. The results were significant: in 81.00 per cent of the cases (13/16), the sitters correctly selected the sittings intended for them.[22] In 2015, Beischel and her team repeated this study, first with 14 mediums and 28 sitters and then again with 20 mediums and 40 sitters. Here, too, there was a clear positive significance for the correct assignment and thus for actually existing mediumistic abilities.[23] In the same way, Jensen and Cardeña investigated this issue in 2009 with one medium and seven sitters. A rating system was used to find out the most suitable sitting for the sitter. Although none of the seven sitters was able to correctly assign the sitting determined for him, the rating of the sitters was significantly better than expected by chance.[24] Another such experiment was conducted by Kelly and Arcangel in 2011. In a first run with four mediums and twelve sitters, only two out of twelve were able to identify the sitting intended for them. In a second run with nine mediums and 40 sitters, 14 out of 38 were able to do so.[25]

In 2021, the Bigelow Institute for Consciousness Studies (BICS) held a competition in which scientists were invited to submit the best evidence for the continued existence of our soul after death. The founder of the BICS Institute, Robert T. Bigelow, offered prize money of 1.8 million US dollars. Many excellent papers were submitted, all of which can be obtained free of charge from the Institute's homepage[I]. I would like to highlight the work of Dr Julie Beischel entitled *Beyond Reasonable: Scientific Evidence for Survival.* In her study, she also worked with blinding and a subsequent assignment of messages to sitters. 58 sitters participated in the study and 66.00 per cent of the sitters could be correctly assigned. In her paper she writes:

> *'The statistically significant scoring data collected under blinded conditions reflect the accuracy and specificity of the information the mediums reported and are in line with the original hypothesis. Stated more plainly: The mediums in this experiment reported accurate information about deceased people that they had no way of knowing.'*[26]

In 2022, an Italian research group led by Patrizio Tressoldi was able to confirm Dr Beischel's findings in a very similar triple-blind study with 100 participants and 28 mediums. 65.8 % of the sittings were correctly assigned.[27]

All in all, however, these attribution studies show a very diffuse picture; there is a positive tendency, but a doubt-free finding cannot necessarily be derived from it, which is why it is all the more important that further studies be conducted in this area. In the case of the latter studies, the design with the retrospective attribution of sittings, while very impressive, is not really solid in terms of the authenticity of the messages. They do not necessarily prove the existence and presence of a deceased person, because the transmitted information is also known to the bereaved person, so that one could also assume a telepathic connection between medium and sitter

---

[I] https://www.bigelowinstitute.org

and not between medium and deceased person. Furthermore, a sitting is a highly sensitive process between the medium, the deceased and the sitter. The medium goes into resonance with the soul of the deceased and a shared sacred moment of connection is created, filled with love, compassion and respect for the sitter and the soul from beyond. In my opinion, this can only be guaranteed if there is personal contact between the people involved. However, due to the blinding, they cannot perceive each other intensively enough. In this way, necessary conditions for a good sitting in the base are already prevented. Nevertheless, the results of these studies are very impressive, but need to be complemented with other methods which, in my opinion, are better suited to prove the existence of mediumistic abilities, the authenticity of messages and, above all, the existence of souls after physical death, than by subsequently assigning blinded sittings to sitters. There is nothing wrong with a medium having direct contact with the sitter; it ultimately serves the quality of a good connection. The usual accusations of cold-reading, hot-reading and the use of the telepathic abilities of the medium to extract information from the sitter's thoughts and memories can also be conscientiously ruled out in other ways. In our EREAMS study, for example, we are investigating the extent to which messages containing information that neither the client nor the medium could know at the time of the sitting could be verified afterwards. This happened, for example, in my first sitting with Joma when she told the medium about horse riding and showed two number ones. Neither the medium nor I could match this, but a few weeks later Joma's mother told me that her daughter had won first place twice in an equestrian tournament just before her accident. This information could not have been invented by the medium or have come telepathically from me - it could only have come from Joma. This is also the reason why blinding could not be used in our EREAMS study: a subsequent assignment of messages would not have been possible as long as the content was not known to the bereaved person. For example, I would not have been able to recognise the message with the two number ones as information relevant to me, so blinding did not fit our study design. However, the combination of the studies with blinding and our EREAMS study provides great synergies and high evidence for life after death.

In addition to these scientific publications, there are also occasional reports of investigations and smaller studies. For example, one of the most accurate mediums in the world at the moment, Gordon Smith from Scotland, told on the online congress Flow Summit 2020 that he was examined by Prof. Dr Archie Roy of the University of Glasgow during afterlife contacts while he was passing on messages from the deceased. His brain was in sleep mode and his heart rate was only a third of normal, but he appeared to be fully awake. He reported that during one of these sessions he was given the name of the murderer of the client's murdered daughter, the murderer was eventually caught and brought to justice.[28]

In 2013, the well-known medium Theresa Caputo (the 'Long Island Medium') had herself examined in front of running cameras by the US-American psychiatrist and specialist for brain diseases Dr Daniel Amen. While she was giving an afterlife contact session, the quantitative EEG showed significant changes in her brain waves. The activity of alpha waves, which represent a state between wake and sleeping (also called the gateway to meditation), significantly decreased throughout the brain. The state of a medium during an afterlife contact can therefore not be equated with meditation. At the same time, there was a significant increase in delta waves throughout the brain and particularly strong in the lateral temporal lobes.[29] Delta waves represent the unconscious realm, dreamless deep sleep, trance and an intuitive awareness with an increase in empathy. The same research was done in 2019 with Tyler Henry (*Hollywood Medium*), known from his TV show, while giving actor Steve-O an afterlife contact with his mother.[30] It showed very similar results. During an afterlife contact, mediums' brains are clearly no longer working in normal mode but have the wonderful ability to connect with the soul on a spiritual level. The EEGs clearly show that the telepathically transmitted impressions are visualised and recognised in the brain so that the messages can finally be translated from them. A medium who would work with psychological tricks and cold reading would have to be highly focused in daytime consciousness and think analytically. Delta waves would never be found in the EEG to the same extent as in the measured mediums. Rather, beta waves would dominate the picture.

> *'In more than forty years I have held about eight thousand séances, and the most capable and tenacious scientists of three generations have scrutinised my work and myself countless times. They have used electron apparatus and detectives, they have not only put me through my paces, but have hardly disregarded any organ of my body as often as it was necessary to determine the physiological changes in the trance and during communication with other beings. They have tested and analysed everything there was to test and analyse, and at the end of the investigation they have confirmed the fact of the phenomena that occurred - they have not yet clarified it and included it as a real fact in our catalogue of knowledge. I do not know how many manifestations over what periods of time still have to be examined before such processes are accepted ad hoc as any physical phenomenon. I fear I will not live to see that day.'*[31]
>
> *Probably the most studied medium in the world, Arthur Ford*

Arthur Ford was to be proved right, he died in 1971, and today, more than 50 years later, the situation has still not changed. Nevertheless, it seems to me that our society is increasingly undergoing a change and is becoming more and more open to these spiritual truths. Not least through the work of courageous scientists and the publication of serious studies from this field of research in spiritual science, the basis is being constructed for a world that can no longer deny the immortality of souls. This does not require a religion, a faith or an ideology, it simply resorts to the tried and tested ways of empiricism and established methods of science. I grew up with a materialist world view and lived it with conviction for many years. But if there are good arguments and even clear scientific findings that make a materialist view increasingly unlikely, then one cannot simply ignore precisely because *ignoring* is the opposite of science. The German philosopher and educator Stefan Ahmann describes it very aptly in his book *Eine neue Aufklärung* (*A New Enlightenment*):

'The sentence "I believe" in the sense of "I have a spiritual world view, I believe in transcendence" makes less and less sense semantically, simply because in view of the massive, irrefutable evidence we have at our disposal today, this so-called belief has long since become knowledge. On the other hand, the sentence "I do not believe" in the sense of "I believe only in the material world I see and not in a transcendent spiritual world" should actually be replaced by the formulation "I refuse to take note of..." or "I do not want to know about...". In other words, if one wants to use the word "faith" to describe a world view that cannot be rationally justified, then this word only fits for materialistic "faith", but not for "faith" in transcendence, because, to repeat: We know about transcendence. A dimension beyond the world we perceive as material is the only possible explanation for numerous well-documented phenomena.'[32]

I sometimes dream of a world in which every human being was aware that they are always accompanied and loved, that there is no separation, that every action and decision not only have an influence on the current life but that one may and must be responsible for one's actions, both positive and negative, beyond death. When heads of state who order airstrikes on helpless children, schools and hospitals or ruthless and violent soldiers who torture their opponents to death and rape and kill women become aware through scientific evidence that they will one day meet again every single soul whose death they are responsible for and must feel the suffering of each one as if it were their own, then I am sure that our world can develop into a respectful and peaceful coexistence in large and small ways. Afterlife research therefore holds the potential not only for individual healing but also for global healing.

7.1.2 How does a serious medium work?

In terms of labour law there is no official job title for a medium. There is neither a state-recognised training nor the granting of a status equivalent to that of other kinds of non-medical practitioner. The designation 'medium' is therefore not protected and in principle anyone can call themselves such. This poses a great danger for those bereaved who, in their grief, go in search of a suitable medium because there are undoubtedly shady characters in this area. Sometimes they are simply frauds but sometimes they are completely overstretched would-be mediums who vastly overestimate their own competence and abilities. In both cases, this ultimately means an emotional catastrophe for the bereaved, and the already great suffering is usually intensified by such a blunder. However, there are some criteria by which, in my opinion, a good and serious medium can be recognised. (I am describing my personal view here.) In principle a medium should always work with evidence, that is he or she must provide clear evidence so that the authenticity of the deceased is also ensured. Searchable information has no value here, it must be highly specific information.

Reputable mediums always offer a money-back guarantee and they do not ask for any information from the client in advance. In fact I always recommend that clients register with a false name. A medium should always have a sound training and be able to communicate openly and to prove that they can do this. The training should definitely be more extensive than two weekend seminars. A good medium usually reports about training on his or her homepage and proves competence through many years of training with renowned mediums and organisations that are mentioned by name. The medium should definitely have been trained according to British Spiritualism and also work according to it. I sometimes receive letters criticising me for citing a good training as an important prerequisite, because there are enough good mediums who do good work through their talent and experience alone. That is true, but a medium works with the most important thing we possess, the soul. Only with a good training will you be made aware of all the pitfalls and possible mistakes, only there will you benefit from the experience of others. When I have an open-heart operation I want a well-trained surgeon to do it and not just anyone even if they have a lot of talent. At this point I would like to briefly discuss the distinction between the terms *British Spiritualism* and the *Spiritualist church*. The latter is to be considered as a religion. In the UK there are spiritual thinkers and practitioners who have nothing to do with the Spiritualist church but they respect that church and work with it and might in other countries call themselves *Spiritists*, but they don't ever do that and this gives rises to some confusion. In this book when I use *British Spiritualism* I mean the whole range of ideas from the actual Spiritualist church at one end to a totally free spirituality such as my own. I view any form of religion very sceptically. It often imposes rigid rules and is the source of dogmatism. I prefer to see spiritualism detached from religious dogma as part of science, which allows it to undergo constant change according to the latest findings.

British Spiritualism always uses the evidence method in its afterlife contacts. This ultimately means that the medium, before transmitting a message, must first prove the deceased. Without adequate proof, the message is worth nothing.

Imagine the following situation, a relative sits with a medium who gives the following message: 'I have your grandma here and she says that she will always accompany you and love you'. Would you believe the medium? Probably not. Such a message is not worth a penny. But what if the medium were to use somewhat more precise descriptions? 'I have your grandma here, she walks a little crooked and shows me that she has pain in her back. She likes drinking coffee and says she accompanies you and loves you.' How about that? The description of the granny probably fits 95.00 per cent of all grannies and is therefore also not useful. The evidence must be of a much higher quality and very specific. The most impressive evidence is that which is so individual and specific that only the deceased and the survivor alone can know it, or when the message that came through can only be verified afterwards through research. I can cite several such examples from the sittings we have examined, examples which completely fulfil the required criteria and are of a quality beyond all doubt. For only when specific evidence is obtained can one be sure that it is an authentic message, and only then can healing and comfort result.

In British Spiritualism great emphasis is placed on the distinction between sensitivity and mediumship. Sensitivity is the intuitive perception of space or of people through the six psychic senses:

- **Clairsentience**: This is understood as the perception of physical and emotional states.
- **Clairvoyance**: This has nothing to do with 'looking into the future'. Objective clairvoyance means genuinely seeing objects, people, scenarios etc. with one's own eyes or, more often, subjective clairvoyance in the mind's eye.
- **Clairaudience**: This is the hearing of individual words or even entire sentences. Here, too, a distinction is made between subjective hearing of an inner voice and objective, real hearing, which is usually perceived as very high-frequency and fast.
- **Claircognizance**: The medium suddenly knows certain things.
- **Clairsalience**: This is the perception of a certain smell such as a scent or cigarette smoke.
- **Clairgustance**: This is the perception of a taste; for example the medium suddenly has the taste of strawberry cake or vanilla in his mouth.

Through sensitivity, you can read energies in your environment and from people. But this has nothing to do with the spiritual world. There are different levels here. However, someone who is sensitive usually also has very good mediumistic abilities because communication from the spiritual world also takes place via the psychic senses. A good medium can therefore differentiate between energies that come from the local space or from living people and the energies of souls and spiritual beings from the spiritual world. This distinction is one of the most important aspects of British Spiritualism.

Even if highly specific information is passed on in a sitting that can be attributed exclusively to the deceased some people will still have doubts about its authenticity. The doubt is then often based on the fact that, according to some sceptics, this information does not necessarily have to come from the deceased but could possibly come from some kind of energetic database or information field such as the morphic field or the Akashic Chronicle. But this is not a useful approach because there is a serious difference between reading information (from whatever source) and a soul contact from the spiritual world. From the point of view of a computer scientist, I can testify without any doubt that no database in the world is capable of storing love. But love is the key to the bond between souls and no information in the world could ever replace that. Love is not information. in the following I will describe what a soul contact generally feels like so that you can get an impression of this kind of communication which goes far beyond the mere acquisition of information. I will go into this aspect in more detail later in this chapter.

Now that I have completed my own basic mediumistic training, I am not only describing things that have been brought to me by other mediums but for the most part things that come from my own perception. Even though there are individual differences in perception there are also certain basic patterns that seem to be felt by every medium in the same or at least very similar way. Often a soul contact is noticeable at the beginning by goose bumps. These goose bumps can be limited to one side of the body, move up and down from the head to the lower leg, but can also be limited and occur locally in individual places. Often a medium feels an inner vibration during a soul contact and is surrounded by a feeling of a presence coupled with an indescribable love. This love is the bond with the bereaved. Once this bond is established, perception and telepathic communication can begin. Depending on the talent and the psychic experience of the medium the psychic senses are then addressed by the soul so it is also possible, for example, that the soul transmits its cause of death by letting the medium feel its physical suffering at that time.

Every medium has differently developed senses; one must not think of communication as an actual conversation, but rather as symbolic language with an emotional underpinning. Images and symbols appear to a medium like a memory; here it is important to silence one's own thoughts so that one's own topics and images do not get mixed up with the transmitted images. Some mediums can also see with their physical eyes, noticing how a deceased person appears for instance as he or she looked when alive. I find it particularly valuable when a medium can hear words or even sentences. In this way, names, places and even phrases typical of the deceased can be communicated precisely. A good medium has a routine in this kind of communication and can really get into a flow of speech and receive a lot of information through the various psychic senses.

A good medium can also be recognised by the fact that he or she wants to know as little as possible about you in advance. The less a medium knows about you, the easier it will be to provide authentic and convincing evidence. You should also always pay attention to a money-back guarantee, because a medium is also only a human being, and there can always be bad days, or the soul does not feel comfortable with this medium and does not want to go into contact, or the time is simply not yet ripe for it. Of course, it can also happen that the messages are mistranslated by the medium; we must not forget that the medium does not have a telephone conversation with the deceased but has to interpret and translate a symbolic language via the psychic senses. Of course, this can also lead to misinterpretations, although a good medium has a lot of helpful routines that can be used in translating. But then there are also sceptics who, after ten clear and correct pieces of proof, receive one single piece of wrong information and suddenly question everything again. Sometimes sitters put themselves and their deceased under too much pressure. They meticulously agree in advance on signs of recognition and sentences that must be mentioned word for word. If you build up too much expectation in advance and only fixate on very specific things this can also have a bad effect on the outcome of the sitting. One should go into a sitting completely open, without pressure and full of love and trust that the spirit world will transmit exactly the right thing. The most important criteria for a good medium, however, are certainly recommendations and reputation. Good mediums are usually in great demand and are often already booked up for longer periods of time. Long waiting times and a well-structured registration procedure for an appointment are further indications of a serious medium.

7.1.3 Project design

The EREAMS project is a questionnaire-based study aimed at researching messages from the spiritual world in the so-called mixed-methods approach. This combines and integrates qualitative and quantitative research strategies and should ultimately lead to an increase in knowledge. Thanks to the sitters' statements the study sheds light on what experiences they had in an afterlife contact, whether in their opinion an authentic soul contact took place and how it was perceived. Thus, the following two main research questions crystallise:

(1) Authenticity of the messages transmitted by the medium

The most important question in our study is whether the afterlife contact was authentic, that is, whether there was actually a genuine and verifiable contact with the soul of the deceased. The focus of the study is therefore on the examination and verification of the evidence brought through; this is the most important prerequisite for the messages brought through by the medium to be believed and accepted at all.

(2) Effects of the sitting on faith and consolation

The second research question deals with the extent to which an afterlife contact can change one's own belief in a spiritual world and how this can affect healing and comforting.

To collect the data, we developed a compact questionnaire with thirteen simple questions. We deliberately decided, also for ethical reasons, not to ask too many questions so as not to overburden or demotivate the participants, most of whom were still grieving. Depending on how extensively the client commented on his experiences in the free text fields the processing could be completed in a period of about five to ten minutes. These are the questions of the questionnaire:

Personal data

- How old are you?
- Your sex?

Motivation

- What motivated you to go to an afterlife contact?

Before – After

- How much did you believe in the further existence of the souls after the physical death BEFORE you have met the medium?
- How much did you believe in the further existence of the souls after the physical death AFTER you have met the medium?

Evidence

- What percentage of the messages given were correct or coherent according to your opinion?
- Was the medium able to provide clear evidence, i.e. report events or facts that it could not possibly have known?
- If you answered the last question with 'clearly yes' or with 'rather yes', we would like to know more details about this evidence and ask you to share them with us.

Verification

- Were there any statements during the sitting that neither you nor the medium could immediately verify? (e.g. statements about the future or about circumstances that were unknown to you at the time.)
- if you answered 'yes' to the last question, have these not-immediately-verifiable statements made in the sitting come true in retrospect (e.g. by personal research)?
- if you answered 'yes' to the last question, we would like to know details about the statements that were not immediately verifiable.

Conviction

- After the sitting, to what extent are you convinced that the deceased person is still part of your life, accompanies you, knows your feelings and thoughts and receives everything that is important?

Comfort

- Please indicate to what extent the afterlife contact was comforting for you.

A reunion with the deceased

- How much are you convinced by the sitting that you will meet the deceased again in the spiritual world?

Questions about the afterlife contact

- Here you can address further points about your sitting and we are looking forward to your feedback.

The participants in our study booked their appointment for an afterlife contact via the homepage set up by the two mediums. The two mediums received a message only one day before the respective appointment, informing them of the name of the sitter and time of the appointment. At their own request they did not receive any other information about the sitter or about any possible deceased persons in advance. The sittings took place on the premises of the mediums, where personal contact also took place. I will explain later why, from our point of view, personal contact is very important and how we free ourselves from the accusation of hot and cold reading.

Since we had to implement this study on our own without research funds it was also necessary to integrate all the processes for this into our usual daily business. A sitting lasted an average of 45 minutes. Because we also wanted to find out whether information from the sitting, which could not be known to either the sitter or the medium, was later verified, the survey did not take place immediately after the respective afterlife contact, but only about three to four weeks after the appointment. We then sent each participant an individualised email with the link to the online questionnaire. It was ensured that each client could only participate once. The time between the sitting and the questionnaire also allowed the clients to reflect calmly on the experience and to be able to evaluate it with a certain distance in a completely unbiased way. In this way a possible false positive answer to the questionnaire, triggered by a possible initial euphoria directly after the sitting, could also be excluded. The response rate was about 69 per cent, meaning that more than two out of three clients actually took part in the survey. This is a very good result and can certainly be explained by the emotional depth of the event. The impression that male participants find it somewhat more difficult to open up to this topic and then to tell others about it (even if anonymously) in a questionnaire is confirmed by the somewhat lower response rate of 60.00 per cent; the women for themselves had a response rate of 71.00 per cent. In total, we received 500 questionnaires in this international study from Germany, Austria, the USA, Denmark, Switzerland, Spain, Luxembourg, France and India. The survey started in March 2019 and ended in September 2022.

7.1.4 Project team

The project team consists of the following persons:

- Bettina-Suvi Rode
  Spiritual book author, teacher, coach and medium, Dortmund, Germany
- Tanja Schlömer
  Spiritual teacher, coach and medium, Bottrop, Germany
- Kathrin Stephan
  Psychotherapist, Tübingen, Germany
- Prof. Dr. rer. medic. Oliver Lazar
  Scientific Project Management, Essen, Germany

The two mediums together have given a total of over 12,000 sittings so far and Kathrin Stephan has been treating grieving people in her own practice for over 20 years. We have brought an enormous amount of experience and expertise from this field to the study.

7.1.5 Demographic data

There is a clear difference between the sexes: out of 500 questionnaires, 439 were completed by women (87.80 per cent) and only 61 by men (12.20 per cent). The topic of afterlife contacts is very emotionally charged. Women are obviously better able to open up to it and are much more likely to admit that there must be more to it. Due to the lack of social and scientific acceptance many men, influenced by a materialistic world view, seem unable and unwilling to get really involved. In my opinion the low percentage of men is also directly due to the influence of the natural and technical sciences. The so called STEM[I] field is extremely male-heavy. The proportion of female first-year students in STEM fields was 31.50 per cent in the winter semester 2017/18. In the professional world, only 15.20 per cent of 7.7 million employees in the STEM field in Germany are female so far.[33] Men are increasingly educated in the natural sciences and if schools and universities teach nothing but a materialistic world view then it is no surprise if few men can open up to the spiritual world, for that would involve questioning their own world view. Women apparently rather stand by their feelings and also dare to admit and express this publicly. The average age of the participants was 49.4 years, the youngest participant was 17, the oldest 86 years old. 302 sessions were conducted in person, 198 online via zoom (due to the pandemic situation).

[I] STEM = Science, Technology, Engineering and Mathematics

7.1.6 Results

When examining the motivations for booking an afterlife contact (see Figure 7-1), grief processing was by far the biggest main motivation, although clients could give several reasons at the same time. 74.80 per cent of all clients gave this reason, followed by love with 38.20 per cent, unanswered questions with 37.00 per cent and curiosity with 26.20 per cent.

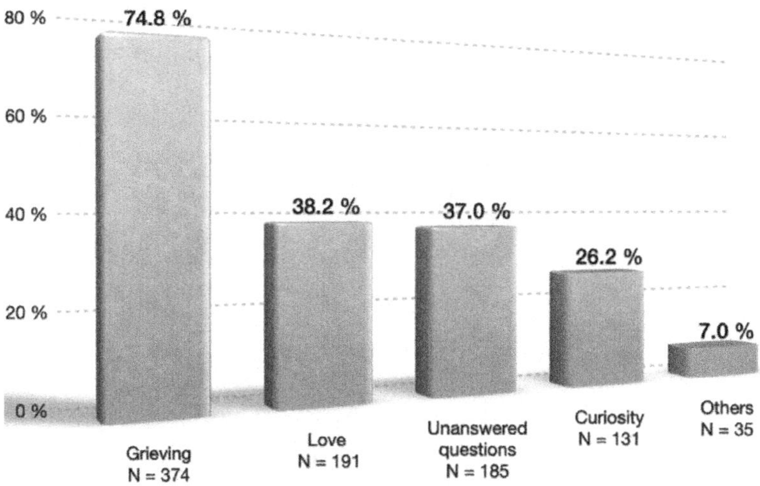

Figure 7-1: *What motivated you to book an afterlife contact?*

Among the other motivations, longing, feelings of guilt and 'experiencing knowledge from the beyond' were mentioned. A sharp separation of motivations is not always possible because the processing of grief overlaps with love and longing, for example. After all, grieving only takes place because one loves the deceased. Longing is ultimately a natural aspect of it. One questionnaire in particular caught my eye during the analysis. In it a man stated that he had to promise his deceased wife while she was still alive that he would go to a medium after her death. This man had stated that before the visit to the medium he had no belief in the survival of souls. After the visit, he stated that he received clear evidence; 90.00 per cent of the statements were correct and coherent. He found the sitting very comforting and was now completely convinced that his wife would accompany him in his daily life and that he would see her again one day. He commented on the sitting as follows:

> *'I didn't believe it until the sitting, but things came up that only we within the family could know, no one else.'*

I find this story so wonderful, almost romantic, because the man got over his own prejudices out of love for his wife and went to a medium anyway, against his convictions. His wife and the medium gave him a wonderful gift in return.

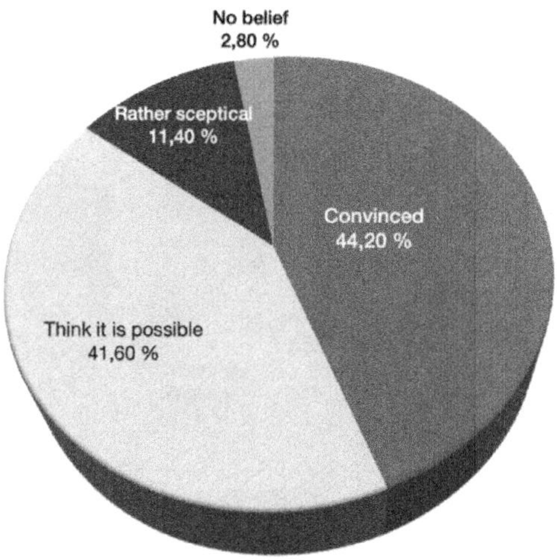

***Figure** 7-2: Belief in a continuation of the soul after physical death – before the Sitting (N = 500)*

Figure 7-2 shows the distribution of the sitters' belief in the survival of souls after physical death before their visit to the medium. 44.20 per cent were already convinced of this beforehand, 41.60 per cent thought it was possible, 11.40 per cent were rather sceptical and 2.80 per cent did not believe in it. In the first survey with 243 participants the difference between men and women was striking. Proportionally, men were almost twice as sceptical and non-believing as women. After the second survey with 500 participants 18.03 per cent of the men and 13.67 per cent of the women were sceptical respectively non-believing. Thus, a total of 71 sceptics participated in the study.

233 out of 279 (83.50 per cent) of the sitters who were not already fully convinced showed an increase in their belief. Only one of the already completely-convinced was downgraded in his conviction by one level. 262 sitters remained at the same level with their opinion (220 of them were already fully convinced beforehand). Only five sitters found that their belief decreased after the sitting. 14 sitters stated that they had absolutely no belief in the survival of the soul after death beforehand, eight of them were fully convinced afterwards, and four still consider it possible. 13 of them said that they had received clear evidence and one person said that the quality of the evidence was still quite high. Their messages had an average coherence and correctness of over 75.00 per cent in relation to the whole sitting. A very frequent criticism voiced by many sceptics is that the client would believe in the authenticity of an afterlife contact anyway, otherwise he would not go there in the first place. Their own wishes and hopes would then influence their perception in such a way that the sitting would always be experienced as a positive experience. But this way of looking at things does not correspond to reality, as our very experienced psychotherapist Kathrin Stephan can also confirm from countless sessions with bereaved people. For there is hardly anyone more critical than a grieving bereaved person who is really exclusively concerned with the absolute truth. So the longing for an authentic contact does not make one blind, it rather sharpens the critical eye, because a bereaved person would not allow himself to be lied to. Bettina looks back on years of experience with several thousand afterlife contacts. She describes the situation as follows:

> *'No one is as critical as a mother or a father who has lost a child. It is always said that they believe everything. No. Exactly those, exactly those people who are in the deepest grief, they no longer believe in anything, and by no longer believing in anything, they very often also let the person die a second time, because they often cannot allow the soul to continue to exist, and the soul must be terribly sad about that.'*[34]

However, the example with the man who went to the sitting for his deceased wife and the data of the other 13 participants who had absolutely no belief in it show quite clearly that one's own views are absolutely not a prerequisite for the success of a sitting. In addition to these 14 hardline sceptics, 57 other rather sceptical clients took part in the study. In this group of 71 sceptics, the same results were shown as in the other subgroups who had previously believed that soul survival was possible. So it does not matter whether someone believes in it beforehand or not.

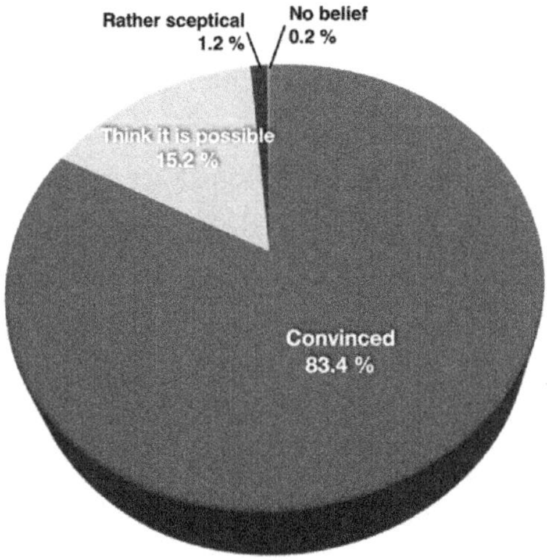

Figure 7-3: *Belief in a continuation of the soul after physical death – after the Sitting (N=500)*

Figure 7-3 shows the distribution after the visit to the medium for the belief in the survival of souls after physical death. Only one participant chose the option 'no belief' and six further chose 'rather sceptical'. This results in the following percentages: 0.20 per cent have no belief, 1.20 per cent are rather sceptical, 15.20 per cent think it is possible and an impressive 83.40 per cent are convinced. I think that is a remarkable change. Basically, almost all the scepticism has been eradicated.

The main research question in this study investigates the authenticity of a soul contact. Why is authenticity so important? Authenticity gives certainty to the bereaved and the only way to get certainty from the spiritual world is through clear evidence from the deceased. This is at the heart of British spiritualism. The medium must prove the deceased is really there, for only clear evidence has the potential to give credibility to the other messages from the sitting as well as to give true comfort and healing. The correlation between good evidence and the degree of comfort seems obvious, but we will nevertheless test this correlation in a correlation analysis. The first parameter from this area of evidence relates to the correctness and coherence of the messages. This should be about the overall impression of the sitting. It can happen that the medium can name one really good proof, but the rest of the sitting does not really fit or other messages are not correct.

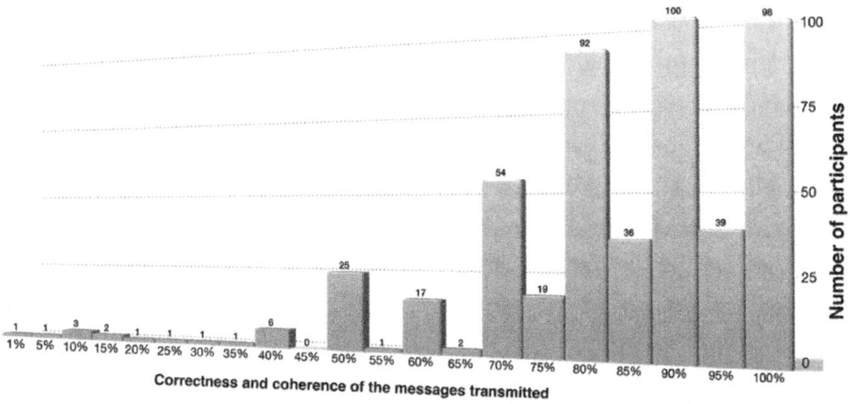

Figure 7-4: The correctness and coherence of the entire sitting

Sometimes one single wrong or bad piece of information can destroy all the good evidence that the medium has already presented. For coherence and correctness, the mean score is 81.90 per cent. 98 participants even gave the maximum value of 100.00 per cent, while only 17 gave less than 50.00 per cent. 365 people (almost three quarters of all participants) scored between 80.00 and 100.00 per cent (see Figure 7-4). These values show that a large part of the sitters found the entire sitting to be coherent and correct.

The objection often raised by sceptics that a medium would make use of the Barnum effect is ruled out from the outset by our study design. The Barnum effect means that sitters refer vague and *generally* valid statements to themselves and are then convinced that they are true for themselves. But we focussed exclusively on highly *specific* statements. Furthermore, one has to ask oneself how one can actually be sure that the medium is passing on messages from the deceased and not guessing, researching or trying to analyse the client through cold reading? In order to shed more light on this issue, let us consider what results we might expect under this assumption of fraud. So, if one looks at a typical sitting conversation from a purely materialist world view, all supernatural explanations must be ruled out. That a medium relies on crude, random guesswork of evidence in transmitting the messages is something we cannot completely rule out, but we can with a clear conscience leave it aside. For the probability of randomly naming highly specific evidence that only the client, his family or the deceased can know approaches zero given the vast number of possibilities. A medium who worked exclusively in this way is likely to be out of a job very quickly. We focus on a more realistic scenario. If we assume that a suspected fraudulent medium is clever and has done research on the client in advance - still this would hardly be able to produce details, but some information might still be found. As a rule, however, a reputable medium does not have a great deal of information to hand before the appointment. He or she would of their own accord refrain from providing any advance information. For example, Bettina and Tanja, the two mediums from our EREAMS study, only received the name of the client and the time of the appointment from their management one day before the appointment, nothing else. Often, however, the client's name given is not even the real one, or the client has registered using a friend's name, and we even recommend this. Sometimes Tanja and Bettina each have up to sixteen clients on a weekend, and to research them in just one day would be almost impossible. But let's return to our constructed scenario with a fictitious cheating medium. We might assume that such a medium could use cold reading to read his or her sitter and therefore determine appropriate information. However, all cold reading strategies (the Barnum effect, the Rainbow Ruse, Shotgunning and so on) usually only work in group events and they only provide general statements and no specific detailed information.

The heart of our investigation is therefore the question from the questionnaire on the clarity of the evidence and the events and facts that the medium could not possibly have known. The emphasis here is on impossible knowledge through unmistakable evidence. Vague statements and commonplace things (see the Barnum effect) in the evidence, such as 'The deceased liked to go for walks', 'The deceased liked to travel' or 'You have a box of old unsorted photographs in your house' cannot be considered as evidence in the impossible knowledge category. Such pseudo-evidence, moreover, is not found particularly convincing by sitters either. One must not forget that just because someone is in mourning and ardently desires an afterlife contact he does not suddenly become naïve and stupid; on the contrary, he becomes more critical than ever before. Even in mourning, scepticism, common sense and the ability to critically question something are not only retained. As a rule, these qualities are even strengthened. A sitter is looking for real comfort and healing, he does not want to lie to himself. So anyone who claims that the Barnum effect is the reason for the positive experience of an afterlife contact has probably never really talked to grieving people. Never would a mum or dad who has lost their child be fooled by the Barnum effect - it just doesn't happen! Anyone who still claims this can't really have dealt with this issue at the front line. We distinguish between two categories of highly specific evidence in our study:

(1) The highly specific proof that can be verified immediately by the bereaved person.
(2) The highly specific proof that can NOT be verified immediately by the bereaved person. It requires further research e.g. by checking documents, interviewing relatives or the event is yet to occur.

Let's deal with the first category first. To give you a sense of what good evidence looks like and how it can work, I have selected some examples of evidence from the sitters' reports because I think it is very important not only to include the evidence in the statistics as mere numbers but also to give it a human face:

'The medium used the same phrases [as the deceased], and besides this form of expression, the gestures were also the same.'

'Not only was the deceased reported, but the medium also knew that I lost two babies during pregnancy, that too was correct. She even saw the pets (a rabbit and a fish) of the deceased. After all, what girl has a single fish as a pet? Surely you can't just guess that.'

'Being rather sceptical about the whole thing, I was very surprised how it was possible! There were statements that only the deceased and I knew! Actually, it is still incomprehensible to me, but in a way also comforting! It's nice to know that it's not quite over after that!'

'The medium described my father so well, as if she had seen a photo of him. She mentioned specifics of his life. She also knew facts about the cause of death, the funeral and our house that the woman, who was unknown to me until then, could not have known. She described my relationship with my father and knew that I was an only child.'

'She even listed the foods that my father liked the most.'

'The sitting was very impressive and I received much more information than I would have thought possible. Likewise, the medium made contact with my grandpa. She was able to reproduce exactly what I said to him at his deathbed.'

'In the sitting, some realities were mentioned that only my husband and I knew.'

'The medium had no prior knowledge about me and described my father as well as other deceased people with expressions, phrases and interests that were unique.'

'The medium knew specific physical characteristics of my partner that she could not have known because I never mentioned them. She described in great detail the circumstances in which it happened. She knew that I perform certain rituals daily to feel closer to his soul. She described certain events and described his character very well, as if she knew him. She described other souls who were present, although the medium did not know that I lost not only my partner but also my grandmother and my dog, even the breed was correct. These are all proofs to me that there must be more to this world than what we perceive with our eyes. How else would she know all this very private information about me, which is also impossible to find out through third parties or through publicly available or social media; above all she didn't want any prior information from me either, she just put her hands on mine for a moment and immediately the medium knew everything.'

'I was told the exact cause of death (suicide by carbon monoxide).'

'Several clear pieces of evidence were provided. The medium knew who had died, knew names, knew what people had died from and described the manner of the deceased perfectly, as they acted when they were alive too.'

'The medium told me things about the deceased as if she had known them personally when they were alive, and quite well, even knowing their tics when speaking and imitating it. In addition, she knew in detail what I had done a few days before the sitting, for example. I didn't tell anyone about these things, and the activities were so special that the medium simply couldn't know. Besides that, she knew a lot about my desires, or more specifically, goals that I have set for myself this year, which are also quite specific.'

'The medium told of family things that no one but me could know because I had those thoughts in my head only for me. According to the medium, my grandma knew in minute detail what I was worrying about. There were so many things that were personally proven to me one hundred per cent. It was a very special experience which I will never forget.'

'It was very impressive how many details and even names were right. Also my husband transmitted through the medium, that we were going to live in France later.'

'The proof related to something I had only thought about but no one else knew about.'

'The medium was very precise in relaying things and evidence that it had no way of knowing, such as what was in the coffin with them.'

'The medium mentioned a cousin's name, my father's severe disability, things he liked to do at my sister's house, previous ownership of a kiosk, our grandmother's clothes and pocket contents, our father's dialect, our mother's typical dress request when she was buried. My nephew was addressed by his pet name, which he asked our mother to prove before the sitting, as he is very sceptical.'

When asked about the specific evidence in the questionnaire, especially whether the medium could report facts or events that he or she could not possibly have known, the participants had four answer options to choose from:

- Definitely yes, I got at least one clear proof.
- Rather yes, some of the evidence was not very clear.
- Rather no, there was too little evidence or the proof was too imprecise.
- Definitely no, there was no evidence or the statements were wrong.

The questions about specific evidence are the most important part in our study because we are leaving the realm of subjectivity. One criticism put forward by many sceptics is that spiritual studies are merely subjectively verifiable and thus elude scientifically recognised methodology. But now we are reaching a whole new level of quality in our study. When a medium reports highly specific incidents, as I have quoted from the sitters above, then in most cases this can be clearly verified. Referring to the example of the single fish, we can see that the bereaved can be completely as to whether the deceased girl had a single fish as a pet or not. The same applies to objects that were placed in the coffin, last words at the deathbed or the reproduction of typical phrases and speech impediments of the deceased. So we are no longer talking about a personal feeling or one's own subjective perception. We are talking about verifiable facts.

What result could be expected from this question on the specific evidence under the assumption of a fraudulent medium? It can be assumed that the two extreme values, that there was at least one clear proof and that there was no evidence at all, would be chosen rather rarely. The chance that clear, highly specific evidence that the medium could not possibly have known would actually be mentioned would have to be estimated as very low, because this phenomenon could definitely not be explained with coincidence, research or cold reading. For the reverse case, that the medium could not say anything correct at all, the chances would also be low, because the medium would have about 45 minutes to produce some kind of pseudo-evidence. It is quite within the realm of possibility, whether by chance or skilful conversation management, that at least something halfway fitting would be forthcoming. It is therefore to be expected that the participants will choose one of the two middle options, 'rather yes' or 'rather no'. However, the actual answers from the questionnaires showed a completely different picture than the expected values.

Figure 7-5 shows the values determined in the questionnaire. The answers show an absolutely clear result. The option 'definitely no' was chosen by only 1.20 per cent, 'rather no' by 2.20 per cent. The option 'rather yes' was chosen by 10.40 per cent, and an overwhelming majority of 86.20 per cent stated that they had received clear evidence. So 431 (!) out of 500 people said: 'Yes, I got clear, highly specific evidence that the medium could not possibly have known!' The amazing thing about this result is that it came to approximately the same results in all participant groups. That is, it does not matter whether the participant was previously convinced of the survival of the soul after physical death or whether he was a sceptic, the percentages remained almost the same.

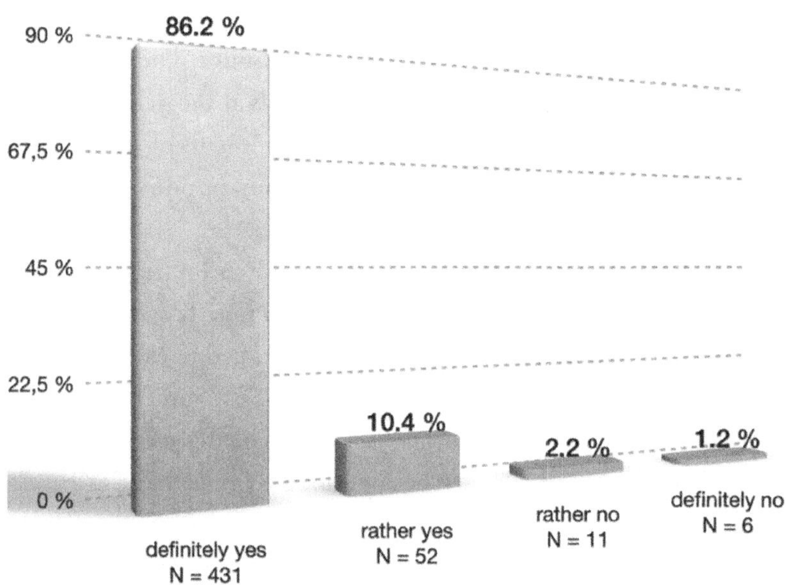

Figure 7-5: ***Was the medium able to provide clear evidence, i.e. report events or facts that she could not possibly have known?*** *The result on the specific evidence is highly statistically significant.*

Figure 7-6 shows the results on the highly specific messages broken down into the four groups of those already convinced in advance, those who thought it was possible, those who were rather sceptical and those with absolutely no belief. Surprisingly, 92.90 per cent of the most sceptical participants from the no-belief group said: 'Yes, I definitely received a highly specific message, that the medium could not possibly have known.' This is even 5.00 per cent better than in the group of those who were already convinced in advance.

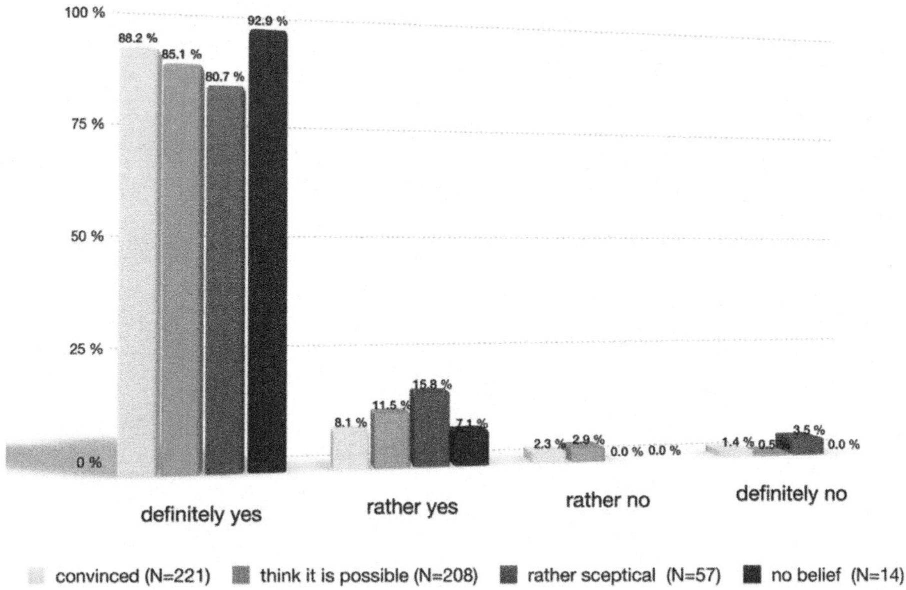

Figure 7-6: *Was the medium able to provide clear evidence, i.e. report events or facts that she could not possibly have known? The results on the highly specific messages broken down into the four groups.*

A typical objection of the sceptics is that only the mourners went to an afterlife contact anyway, because only they had a reason. In their grief and longing they only want to experience confirmation, therefore they accept all messages uncritically and within the scope of their allegedly selective perception and a confirmation bias, that is the tendency to accept only information in such a way that one's own expectations are fulfilled, the occurrence of the positive study results could be explained. This assessment can be considered refuted. In our study, 126 people participated who were not in mourning. Also in this subgroup the positive results on the highly specific messages were confirmed (see Figure 7-7). Thus it becomes apparent that both persons who are not in mourning and the greatest sceptics experience and evaluate an afterlife contact in the same way as those who are in mourning and believed in a survival. Selective perception and confirmation bias are therefore not legitimate explanations.

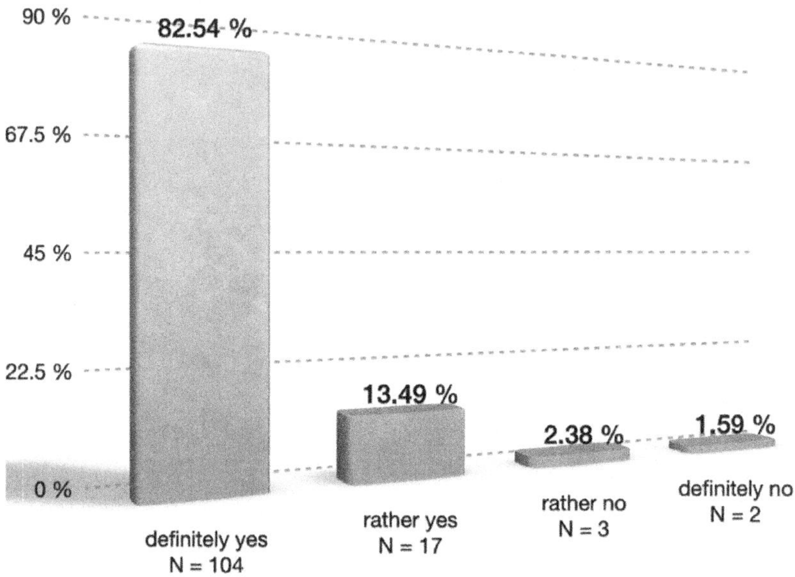

***Figure 7-7:** Was the medium able to provide clear evidence, i.e. report events or facts that she could not possibly have known? The results on the highly specific messages for the participants who are not in mourning (N=126).*

With the start of the second survey wave, 198 sittings took place online via video chat due to the pandemic situation. The evaluation of the data showed that there was a discrepancy between the online sessions and the face-to-face sessions in terms of the quality of the highly specific messages. For this question, 90.70 per cent of the participants in face-to-face gave the answer: 'Definitely yes, I received information that the medium could not possibly have known.' In the online sessions it was only 79.30 per cent, which is still a very good result overall (see Figure 7-8). One explanation for this decline is that the energy between the medium and the sitter can always flow better in direct contact than virtually via the internet. The mutual feeling and the connection are much more intense in a direct contact.

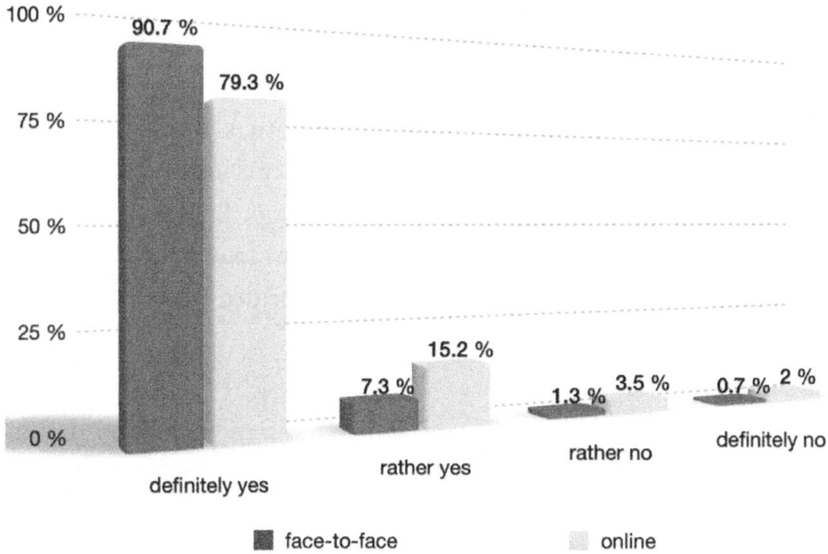

Figure 7-8: *Was the medium able to provide clear evidence, i.e. report events or facts that it could not possibly have known? The results on the highly specific messages online vs. face-to-face.*

From this clear result on the highly-specific messages question it is conscientious and logical to draw the conclusion that there was obviously a real telepathic communication. Whether this communication really took place between the medium and the deceased from the spiritual world, however, we cannot completely confirm with this value alone. It would be quite conceivable that there might also have been a telepathic connection between the medium and the sitter and that the medium had ultimately received the information from the sitter himself. Thus, the test could have proved telepathy but not necessarily that the soul of a deceased person was present and that the messages actually came from him or her. However, this differentiation was very important to us in our study. In order to check whether the messages and evidence actually came from the deceased, we asked the sitters whether there were details in the afterlife contact that neither the sitter nor the medium could have known during the sitting. This includes, for example, information about events that lie in the future or that required more precise verification. In order to be able to record this we did not interview the sitters immediately after the sitting but only some three to four weeks later, thus leaving time for them to check whether there was an opportunity for verification in the meantime. This time span was not sufficient in all cases for sitters to really check the information. Some participants said in the comments section of the questionnaire that they had not yet come to a verification. Therefore our study contains a first suggestion about this after three to four weeks and it can be assumed that the number of subsequently verified proofs would increase after a somewhat longer period.

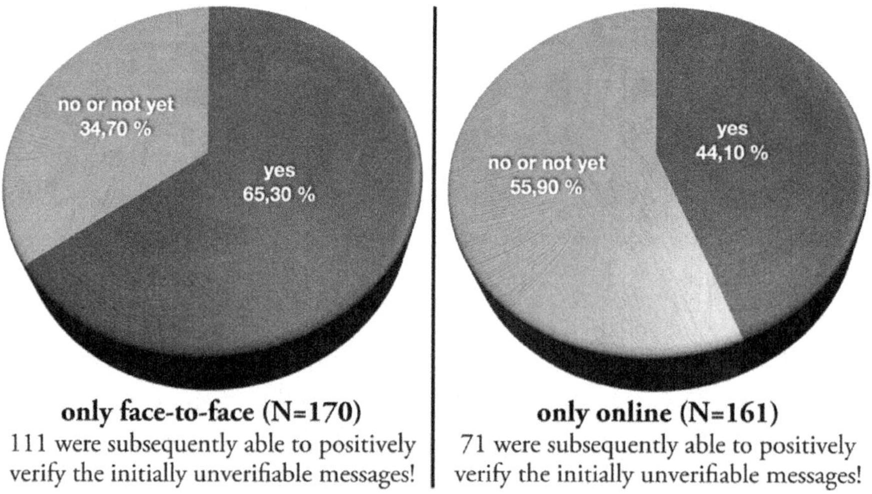

***Figure** 7-9: Could the message with unknown facts be verified within three to four weeks after the sitting? (online vs. face-to-face)*

The verification of such messages is immensely valuable because the information cannot originate from the medium or the sitter. The best and most obvious explanation based on the available data is that the source of this information is indeed the deceased. So let's look at the results on this question (see Figure 7-9).

331 people stated that there were such initially-unverifiable messages in their sitting. On this point there was a big difference in the results between the face-to-face and the online sessions. Face-to-face, 111 out of

170 people (65.30 per cent) were subsequently able to verify positively their initially unknown information from the message. That is almost two thirds of the participants concerned. In the group of online sessions it was 71 out of 161 (44.10 per cent), about 20 per cent less. However, one must not mistakenly get the impression that 44.10 per cent is a bad value, because even if it had only been one per cent this would have been highly astonishing and could not be explained rationally in materialist terms. For a cold reader, or a presumably fraudulent medium, the probability of being wrong would be immensely greater than being right in the case of messages with unknown and initially unverifiable information. Thus, a 'yes' can be considered a sensation because in a purely materialistic world view it is extremely much less likely than a 'no or not yet'. Again, I attribute the discrepancy between face-to-face and online sessions to the lack of direct contact and thus poorer energy and connection between medium and sitter in a virtual-only online session. In the group of the 71 sceptics, this value was at 48.00 per cent. This result can definitely not be explained by chance. We have already been able to show clearly that there is a very high level of evidence for telepathic communication via the psychic senses with the medium. If personal messages are then also given in the process, messages containing information which is known neither to the sitter nor to the medium, but which proves to be true afterwards, then it must necessarily be impossible for the sitter to be the source of this information.

Sceptics repeatedly say that the highly specific messages transmitted by the medium do not necessarily have to come from the consciousness of the deceased. All this information could also have been stored in a spiritual database, a morphic field or the Akashic Chronicle and the medium has only elicited it. From my point of view, other sources than the soul of the deceased are not very plausible although I am confronted with this objection again and again. The afterlife researcher Thomas Campbell for instance speaks of a kind of spiritual database, but anyone who has ever been in contact with the soul of a deceased person, as I have, will never consider a dead database as a source of information. A sitting is not only characterised by the quality of the information in the messages, the greatest and most important thing in such a contact is the love between the bereaved and the deceased. No database in the world is capable of storing such love and why would a database do such a thing? And if a database were able to store love and feelings, then it would be alive, and a database is not alive.

Nevertheless, let's just assume that Joma's soul really disappeared for good after her death and only the experiences of her entire life ended up in a spiritual database. How should we imagine this in practice when a medium transmits messages? A database itself is completely stupid, it has neither intellect nor its own desires, it can only be used by an intelligent being. In computer science there is a special language for querying databases, the so-called Structured Query Language (SQL). Using SQL one could search the database for the desired information. But what search criteria would a medium be able to use? A soul database would have to contain an unimaginable number of data records and how could one find just the right records from the almost infinite quantity? Assuming the survivor brings some kind of soul ID of the deceased, the medium could make a suitable query. In SQL, it would then look like this: 'select * from soul-database where soul-ID=Joma' This command means that all records should be found from the soul database where the soul ID belongs to Joma. Even for a 13-year-old girl we would get millions of records as a result because the database contains Joma's entire life with all its events. Which of these millions of data sets should a medium choose? How does the medium know which data set is so good that it would be accepted as valid evidence by the surviving relatives? Without the intervention of an intelligence that controls this selection process it is not possible. Databases or information fields cannot do this on their own, nor can they simply filter out exactly THE suitable events and facts from the hypothetical millions of data records of the entire life of the deceased and transmit them by a push message which a survivor would then find to be evident proof. This requires awareness and intelligence. The only permissible and logical conclusion is that this information must quite obviously come from the deceased, from the spiritual world, because no one other than the deceased himself or herself can know these facts, and no one else can filter out and name exactly THE decisive information, and no one else can have such a great interest in presenting this evidence.

The deceased still have their own wishes and needs which they communicate to the medium; it is not only data from the past and the life of the deceased that is reproduced, but also current and future things from the life of the bereaved. Why should a database be interested in continuing to accompany a bereaved person? What sense would love have if it ends up in a database? An afterlife contact is not only characterised by the pure transmission of information, it also contains the indescribably deep love that accompanies such a contact. Many clients have even reported actually feeling the presence of their deceased one themselves during the session, experiencing goose bumps or touches. Why should there be an infinite love between souls if all that remains in the end is information? From my point of view, it definitely cannot be a database, because love is not information!

To give an impression of the quality of this evidence which can only be verified afterwards I have selected some descriptions from the participants' comments:

> *'My grandfather pointed out a damp wall in the house. This had gone unnoticed through the wallpaper. The exact corner described by grandpa was damp.'*
>
> *'The medium stated that the deceased showed her a photo of me as proof. I knew which photo it must be but I could not remember the details described. At home I looked closely at the photo with a magnifying glass. The details are as described by the medium in the picture.'*
>
> *'We found the papers and pictures to which we were referred.'*
>
> *'I had no contact with the deceased for over six years. There were some things I did not know. I discussed these points with the sister of the deceased. She confirmed all these things. They really happened in exactly the same way."*

'My mother had lost a child. I didn't know this, but she had told my sister-in-law, who confirmed it to me.'

'"Work in a new country!", my husband was told. Now we know, in October we are really going to a new country again.'

'The plaque was found that no one knew about.'

'A statement about a family event was subsequently clarified by a family member.'

'For example, a peach tree garden from childhood days with the family was described in detail, of which I knew nothing until then. This then proved true through research.'

'The medium told me that the deceased had used drugs during his lifetime. I had not known that until then, [...] I asked relatives about it, who confirmed it. It had been deliberately kept from me when I was a child to spare me.'

'The medium saw a bridge and there my [deceased] son left a jacket. I didn't know that and a policewoman confirmed it to me in a conversation afterwards.'

'The deceased knew I was pregnant BEFORE I did.'

'The second thing that came through was a message from a so-called sister, older than me, ordering me greetings. I was confused, I was an only child and my parents had no other children, before me or after me. Sometime after a few weeks I spoke to my mother about it, because this thought wouldn't let me go. She immediately started crying and tearfully confessed to me that she had had a miscarriage before me, a girl who was not viable due to her illness at the time. So I would have an older sister now.'

'He showed her an ice rink and that he had skates in his hand. Well, I couldn't do anything with that. A few hours later I found out that my granddaughter was going to learn to skate in a club.'

'Grandma Klara was supposed to have had an abortion in the 1930s. Luckily her daughter (my father's sister) was still alive to confirm this to me. No one in the family - except Hannelore - knew this incident!'

'The medium said that someone from our family wanted to get a tattoo on his shoulder. "It can only be our son", I said, but I don't know anything about it. I shouldn't say anything and wait and see, but the thought was already there, the medium replied. On 23 December, three weeks after the sitting, he came and said he wanted to get a tattoo. He then pointed to his upper arm and shoulder. He already showed me motifs and was already thinking about which studio it should be in. I really had no idea and I didn't believe it either because he's totally stressed out in his studies right now.'

'She said a relative worked in a mine. Later it turned out to be my grandpa. This I did not know.'

'She told about a piece of jewellery or a necklace with a dolphin as a pendant, which I was not aware of. Afterwards, I found out from my sister that my mother did indeed have such a necklace.'

'The medium mentioned the diagnosis of borderline, which I didn't know but was later confirmed to me by my [deceased] daughter's boyfriend. She died in her second suicide attempt, I didn't know about the first one but her friend confirmed it.'

'The medium told me that my son would show her his funeral. His favourite teacher was also there and he was wearing an orange jacket.'

The last example with the favourite teacher and his orange jacket is particularly fascinating because the parents contacted me and told me that on the day of the funeral they were stuck in a kind of tunnel and did not notice who was actually there. There were about 500 people at the funeral. They said they didn't know who their son's favourite teacher actually was. So they questioned their son's classmates. When they finally found out who the favourite teacher was, they contacted him and asked him what clothes he wore to the funeral. He replied, 'I was wearing an orange jacket.' I think this case is very valuable because there are several strangers involved in the process of unravelling the message. It is a chain of questioning across different groups of people and in the end the information from the message was confirmed so impressively.

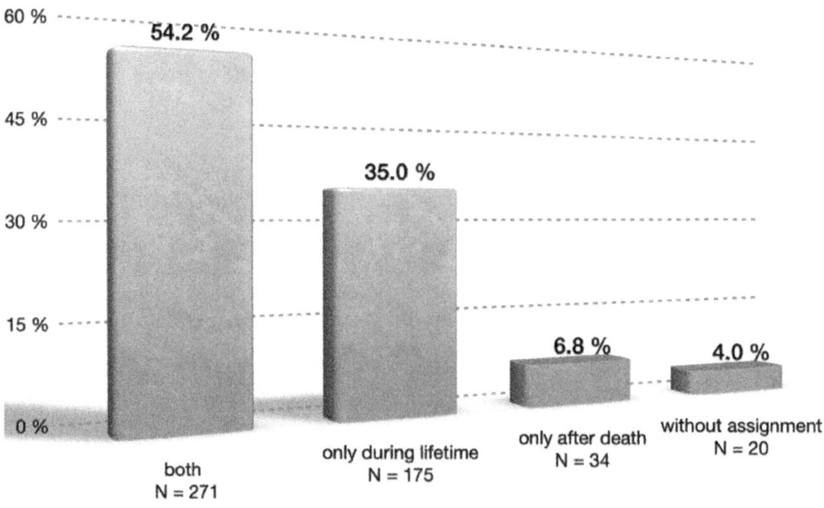

Figure 7-10: *Did the evidence relate to events that took place during the deceased's lifetime or after his death?*

89.20 per cent of the participants stated that their received messages related to events that took place while the deceased was alive. 61.00 per cent stated that the messages related to things that happened after the deceased's death. A differentiated presentation of these results is shown in Figure 7-10. These values indicate that it is first of all important for a deceased person to prove himself and so evidence relating to events that took place during his lifetime dominates. Only 6.80 per cent of all participants failed to receive any evidence from the deceased's life and only received evidence relating to events after his death. More than half of the participants (54.20 per cent) received both types of evidence. This is very important for the effectiveness of the sitting as the deceased not only wants to prove himself but also his still existing participation in the life of the bereaved person, thus showing that he continues to accompany them.

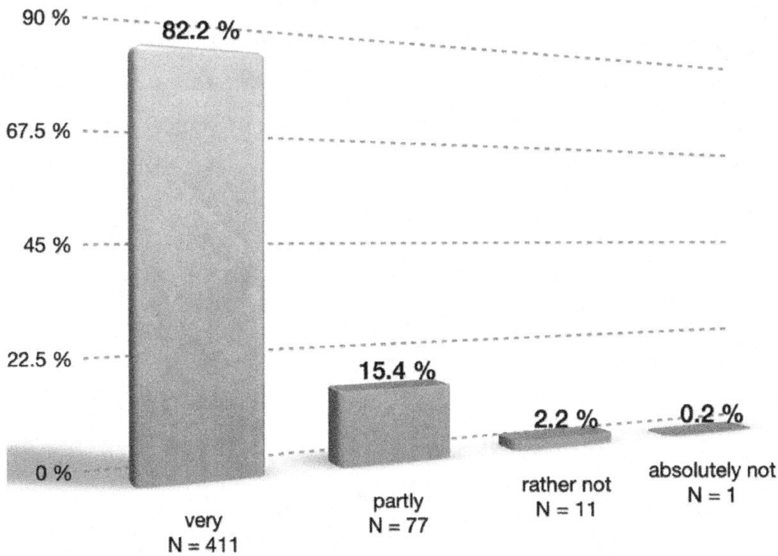

Figure 7-11: *After the afterlife contact, how much are you convinced that the deceased person is still part of your life, accompanies you, knows your feelings and thoughts, and witnesses everything important?*

This is also shown in the evaluation of the question as to how much the sitter is convinced after the afterlife contact that the deceased person continues to be part of his life, accompanies him, knows his feelings and thoughts and notices everything important. An impressive 90.04 per cent of participants who received evidence of events that took place both during the lifetime and after the death of the deceased said they were very convinced. If there was no evidence from the sitter's current life after the deceased's passing, then this belief dropped to 73.33 per cent. Lack of evidence from the current life thus does not lead to a serious drop in the conviction that they continue to be accompanied by the deceased, but the proportion of the very convinced drops noticeably by almost 17.00 per cent. Overall, there was only one single participant (0.20 per cent) who felt after the sitting that he is no longer accompanied by his deceased, only 11 participants (2.20 per cent) said they were rather not convinced. 77 participants (15.40 per cent) were at least partly convinced and 411 (82.20 per cent) were very convinced (see Figure 7-11).

The question about the comfort of a sitting is for me, after the questions about evidence, the most important aspect of this study. After the loss of a loved one, a person goes through different stages of grief. Elisabeth Kübler-Ross has defined five stages of grief for this purpose:

- Phase 1 – Denial
- Phase 2 – Anger
- Phase 3 – Negotiation
- Phase 4 – Depression
- Phase 5 – Acceptance[35]

These phases are not all experienced with the same intensity by every bereaved person - the processing is very individual. The course of these phases is also not necessarily always linear, they can be gone through again and again without a rigid pattern. At the end of this process, however, there is usually acceptance. For most people it is an acceptance of an infinite pain, of a torn heart, of letting go and of an ultimate and final loss in eternal separation. In a material world view one must then be content and come to terms with this for there is nothing in the physical, gross world that can comfort or even give healing. I find the concept of letting go the worst, because letting go is about the last thing a bereaved person wants to do. On the contrary, a bereaved person wants to hold on to the deceased forever, to have them with them and never have to let go, and that is a good thing. But no one needs to let go, neither the deceased nor the bereaved. Those who have been united in love can never be separated. What must not happen, of course, is that a bereaved person loses a sense of reality by holding on to the deceased and can no longer lead an independent life worth living. You can let go of the pain, but you can always have your deceased with you.

Psychological treatments and psychotropic drugs are certainly also a good way to help people get back on their feet, but this will never lead to healing, at best it can lead to acceptance. I am firmly convinced that a sitting with authentic evidence has a positive influence on grief processing and that this is the only way to be able to experience comfort and thus also healing. At the same time one should realise that true consolation can never arise only from one's own wishful thinking. One can neither lie to oneself about comfort nor talk oneself into it. Comfort must always be induced from the outside, by receiving knowledge that was previously unknown. Critics will certainly want to argue that the bereaved long for consolation after all and therefore accept everything said, even worn-out platitudes, benevolently. But in evaluating the consolation one must not make the mistake of basing its effectiveness on the expectations and hopes of the sitters. The belief in the survival of souls after physical death is not at all related to the perceived comfort. 11 of the 14 participants who had no belief in soul survival at all nevertheless stated that they found the sitting very comforting, the remaining three still found it somewhat comforting. It is not the faith that influences the degree of comfort, but the quality of the evidence in the medium's messages. As mentioned at the beginning, a grieving person does not suddenly become gullible and naïve out of grief and believe every message said by a medium. The argument of confirmation bias is very popular among sceptics as an explanation for a positively perceived afterlife contact but it does not correspond to reality. Anyone who puts forward such arguments cannot really have dealt with grieving people in the front line. As Kathrin Stephan reports from her work as a psychological psychotherapist, in her experience grieving people are even more sceptical and critical in their suffering than before, because they really want to know what happened to their loved one. Real consolation can only come through a genuine afterlife contact with convincing evidence, only then do the bereaved realise that death is not a final end and that they are not separated. Only then hope for a reunion arises, only then can the messages be accepted as true and be effective. Therefore a high degree of consolation is an excellent indicator of the authenticity of an afterlife contact. Figure 7-12 shows the rating of the question about the comfort experienced. 80.60 per cent of all participants found the sitting very comforting and 15.60 per cent found it a little comforting. 2.60 per cent found it rather not comforting and 1.20 per cent not comforting at all.

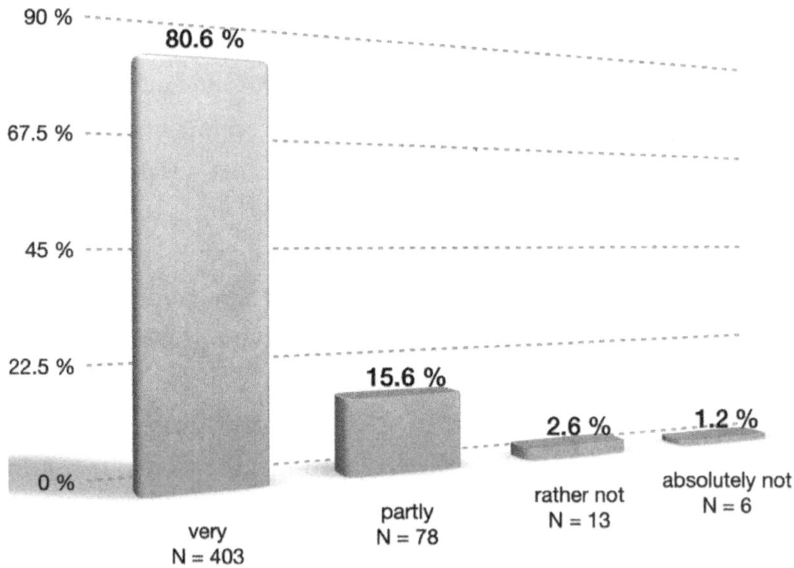

***Figure** 7-12: How much was the afterlife contact comforting for you?*

Only very occasionally were even good sittings felt to be too upsetting and thus not very comforting. Basically, a clear positive correlation is confirmed between clear evidence with comfort. A sitting with clear evidence thus definitely also leads to great comfort. Among participants who received clear evidence 88.17 per cent said that the sitting was very comforting, and 11.14 per cent still found it somewhat comforting, for a total of an impressive 99.31 per cent! For participants who selected 'rather yes' for the clear evidence, the comfort is already much weaker, only 42.31 per cent still found the sitting very comforting, 46.15 per cent still rather comforting and 11.54 per cent rather not comforting. From the group of participants who received 'rather no' clear evidence, only one person (9.09 per cent) still chose very comforting, 45.45 per cent still found it a little comforting.

Even in the sceptic group (rather sceptical + no belief), the level of comfort was still very high. 66.20 per cent of them found the sitting very and another 28.17 per cent still partly comforting. That's a total of 92.37 per cent of the sceptics. In Figure 7-13 you can find the results on this question broken down into the four groups in relation to the original belief on the subject of survival of the soul.

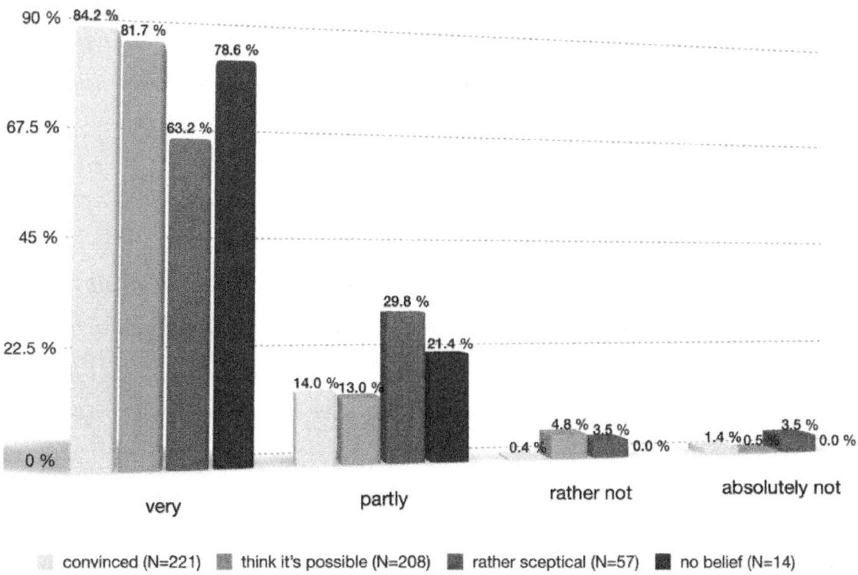

Figure 7-13: *How much was the afterlife contact comforting for you? The results on the experienced comfort broken down into the four groups*

This enormous degree of comfort is very impressive. It underpins the huge potential and positive effect of an afterlife contact in the processing of grief. Neither medication nor psychological treatment procedures have anywhere near such a powerful effect. It would be almost negligent, in view of these clear study results, not to recommend an afterlife contact to mourners in therapy. I believe that a synergetic collaboration between conventional medicine, psychology and afterlife contacts by mediumship is the best possible form for the processing. I would like to quote some participants from our study. They confirm, in part very touchingly, how comforting and healing such an afterlife contact can be:

> *'I lost my beloved three-year-old son in a tragic accident and had strong suicidal thoughts for the first six months. Psychotherapy was not nearly as helpful in helping me to come to terms with my grief as the three sessions I have had so far with the medium. For me, this experience was my salvation, otherwise I would have given in to my suicidal thoughts at that time. All this knowledge about the afterlife and the messages from my son through the medium have changed my whole thinking and life. I can only recommend a session with the medium to every person who experiences such a blow of fate.'*

> *'Only through the sitting it was possible for me to move on!'*

> *'The medium's way of dealing with me was unique! Not only was the sitting one hundred per cent right, which was fabulous!!! Also her kindness and being so compassionate and supportive helped me immensely to get through this difficult time. The Sitting has really helped me immensely!!!'*

> *'The sitting has completely changed my life (in a positive way). It has given me back my quality of life. It helped me through a very bad time and gave my life meaning again. I would always seek the help of a medium again. Thank you so much for having people like this.'*

> *'Through this sitting I started to live. My faith deepened a thousandfold. (...) I am deeply grateful that there are such loving people.'*

'After the death of my son, I was very distressed. Even today it is the case that a piece of my soul has travelled with him to the Otherworld. The medium was the first who could give me peace and comfort. I was fascinated by the gravestone for my son that she had described. (...) In winter I love to go to Essen [city in Germany, author's note*] to the butterfly seminar to celebrate a bit of Christmas with my children. The butterfly seminar with the medium gives me strength and courage every year to continue and not give up. With her empathetic and loving way she gives us comfort, love and the conviction that our children, parents, siblings, friends, all those we love and who have passed away, are always with us, love us and protect us. And for that I am immensely grateful.'*

'For me, this sitting has been very healing. It gave me courage to look forward.'

'Making this appointment with the medium was the best decision I could have made in my grief. I finally felt like I could breathe again. And a short time after my sitting, my pain and sadness turned into love and safety. I finally felt like I was no longer alone.'

'Attending a sitting is the only help I have found in coping with grief. Thank you so much for this.'

'The sitting brought me personally something like healing in the grieving process. Knowing that my dearly departed are still with me gives me a lot of strength to carry on.'

'I left the sitting with great inner satisfaction, confidence and a beautiful feeling of affirmation and worth and for the first time in a long time I am looking forward to what may come in my life. From the bottom of my heart, thank you for everything!'

'His death was the worst event in my life (and I certainly have not had an easy life). The after death and afterlife contacts meant and still mean survival to me.'

'I am a psychological and educational counsellor myself. The unexpected passing of our baby was a shock to us. I and my husband were on the verge of madness. (...) The feeling of inconsolability is not describable. Psychological grief processing seemed too little for us. Medication or rational explanations and statements such as that this is just life and we should practise patience and acceptance would not have helped us at all. (...) If I hadn't seen Oliver Lazar, I wouldn't have met Bettina Suvi Rode, and if I hadn't met Bettina, I would have ended up in a psychiatric ward and my husband would have taken his own life. No grief counselling could have done that.'

One of the most beautiful thoughts of a bereaved person is to be able to see and embrace their deceased again one day. Therefore, our last question aims at the extent to which the participant is convinced by the sitting that he will meet the deceased person again in the spiritual world. Figure 7-14 shows the results on this. Only three participants (0.60 per cent) completely rule out a reunion, 1.40 per cent rather do not believe in it, 15.00 per cent are partly convinced and 83.00 per cent are completely convinced. This result is related to the clear evidence in the same way as the comfort. The clearer the evidence was, the greater the conviction of meeting again in the spiritual world. Of the participants who originally did not believe or rather did not believe in the survival of souls after physical death, 57.75 per cent said they were very convinced that they would meet again in the spiritual world, 35.21 per cent were at least partly convinced, making a total of 92.96 per cent of the original sceptics. This point also shows that the original beliefs had no influence on the answer to this question. Ultimately, it is the evidence and the coherence of the sitting that decide on effectiveness.

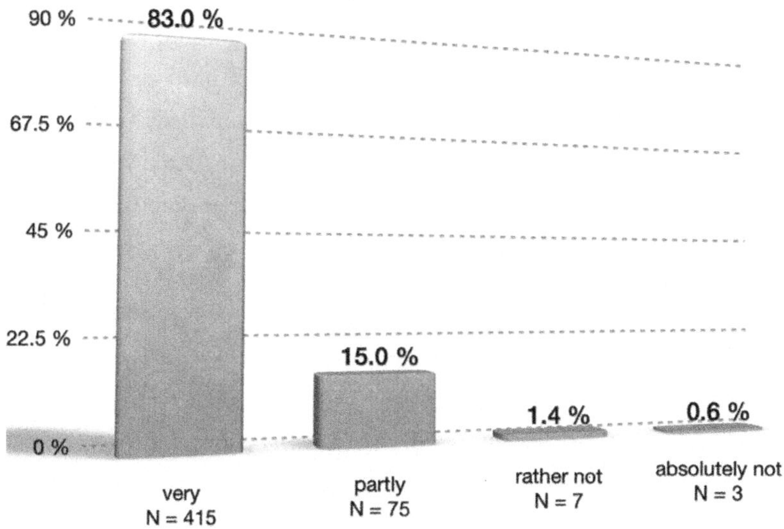

Figure 7-14: *How convinced are you by the sitting that you will meet the deceased person again in the spiritual world?*

7.1.7 Content of the messages

Only when the deceased has been able to prove himself, it makes sense to transmit messages. Only then do they gain authenticity. The proof in a message is in itself usually enough and, in my opinion, the most healing thing about a sitting. The evidence presented is usually not earth-shattering events, but very simple things that are highly specific and can only be mentioned by the deceased himself. This is the most important thing to the deceased at first, because he wants to be recognised. But what else would a deceased person like to say to his surviving relatives? The spectrum of messages is very broad. It depends primarily on the relationship the deceased had with the sitter, the circumstances under which the dying process took place and which topics, e.g. illness, addiction, quarrels, etc., were important. By the way, not every deceased was a loving and lovable person who will be infinitely missed after his passing. Sometimes the situation is difficult. For example, a deceased person may have been a cruel and brutal husband or father during his lifetime who mistreated the bereaved, or someone who had no time for his family, gave no love or simply made life difficult for them all the time. Such deceased people usually come into an afterlife contact very humbly, almost purified, as if they had come to terms with their life and their behaviour in some form of empathic way, also from the point of view of the others involved. Two participants reported the following about this:

> *'Our ancestors are always present in my eyes, even if they live in another world that is not visible to us, and they see their lives and their mistakes in full depth. They are, in a way, a purified version of the people they were here on planet Earth. Knowing that our beloved ancestors and family are still there for us and will come forward in a sitting and openly regret what they have done to you or simply explain things about themselves or encourage us in our path is a comfort and encouragement to me to go through life despite all the adversity and terrible things that happen on this planet. Through the sittings and the information they convey, I am sure of their love and convinced that we will meet again.'*

> *'The reason for my sitting was a difficult relationship with my father that was never resolved while he was alive. After his death, this made me feel bad and plagued by guilt. I hoped that through an afterlife contact with him things could be clarified. It was a great relief to me that my father actually came and immediately apologised to me for everything that strained our relationship. He assured me that he was never aware of what he was triggering in me with his behaviour and that he never wanted me to feel bad and that he had always loved me. He just couldn't show it. In retrospect, I can feel a decades-old wound gently beginning to heal and I am beginning to make peace with the situation. This is so much more than I had dared to hope for and priceless to me.'*

Open questions remain, however, especially in the case of deceased persons who have died by suicide. Especially when it concerns teenagers or young adults, the bereaved parents not infrequently feel great reproach for not having been able to help their child. In such cases, too, the main focus is on consolation and healing; unanswered questions about *why* are answered. But sometimes there are also very funny messages. The spiritual world has a lot of humour, and it is also allowed to laugh during a sitting. Two of our participants explicitly referred in their comments to laughing together in a sitting. Dr Joachim Nikolay gave a wonderful and refreshingly funny lecture on this topic at the conference *Near-Death Experiences - Deathbed Visions - After-Death Contacts 2019* in Bregenz/ Germany entitled *Humour in Near-Death Experiences - Humour in the Afterlife*[36], which was also published as part of the Thanatos.TV format.

A deceased person always comes in love and understanding. He still has his own typical character, but he is never aggressive, angry, frightened or reproachful. As a rule, the deceased shows that he is doing very well where he is now, that he is happy, no longer ill and no longer in pain. Often the deceased shows himself to the medium as he looked when he was at his best. He also lets his bereaved know that he is well aware of their emotional states and circumstances, to show that he continues to be part of their lives and to accompany them. In summary, the messages are about forgiveness, understanding, clarification, love, care, connection, comfort and healing.

7.1.8 Evaluation and discussion

After Joma's accident, I asked myself how and where she could be now. It seemed unimaginable to me that all the love that this girl had with her parents, her smile, her joy of life and everything that made her who she was, were simply no longer there. Deep inside me there was a feeling that had long since given me the answer to Joma's continued existence, because she knew exactly how to reach my heart and soul. But my mind demanded clear and distinct answers. So I began the search and embarked on a spiritually scientific journey of discovery. At the beginning of the book I wrote that I was following this scientific path in complete freedom, no matter where it might lead me. That is exactly what I did, and the path led me to impressive and sometimes surprising insights. I thought that if I wanted to know whether and possibly how things would continue after death, it would be a good idea to start with the human body and its formation. A body is made of matter, and we have seen that matter is really just a lot of nothing and binding energy. There is nothing really material. At the smallest level, we ultimately consist of energetic vibrations, and quantum mechanics has shown us, moreover, that neither space nor time exist at this level. Even the best horse in the stable of natural scientists, chemical and biological evolution for the origin of life and the species, is in the end neither proven nor remotely probable. There are no natural processes that ever created information, let alone complex information like in DNA or RNA. Our materialistic science is in dire straits when it comes to critically questioning many of the universally accepted models and theories. As I studied the countless literature sources for this book and searched for answers, it became increasingly clear to me that the world as science had tried to explain it to me all my life did not have the stability I had attributed to it. Our world or our existence cannot be justified in this purely materialistic form, and this realisation has nothing to do with religion, esoteric delusion or ignorance, but is the result of a critical, objective and scientific debate, without regard to prevailing paradigms and world views. On my liberal path to knowledge, the paving stones of materialism began to crumble and a radiant spiritual path revealed itself to me that was much more plausible, logical and probable. In particular, this path culminated in our EREAMS study, which by its impressive results can basically only lead to one conclusion. I myself am a critical person. I also question my own findings and do not allow myself to be convinced prematurely, but if one looks quite honestly and neutrally at the clear results of the EREAMS study, then from my point of view there is simply no room left for any doubt. Our study results show very impressive evidence for the spiritual world and the survival of the souls of our deceased in every respect. I have disclosed the procedure in our study using standard scientific methods and have documented our work in a comprehensible way. Our findings have not been created or manipulated out of esoteric wishful thinking, they are solely the result of empirical research and the obvious and logically derived consequence of the available data base. Our study presents very convincingly that we are embedded in a spiritual world. Our deceased continue to be part of our lives, they accompany us and are eternally linked to us in love. Each and every one of us exists completely independent of matter and a body. When the physical body dies, the soul is free again and returns to its spiritual home on another level of consciousness. This level is not or only with difficulty accessible for most of us humans. However, our study was able to show in a very impressive way that good mediums have this access to the spiritual world and can receive authentic messages. My original motivation to write this book and to start the EREAMS study was the question of what happened to Joma after her accident. Although I was not allowed to meet her in this life, she came into my life like a whirlwind of light without my intervention. She touched my soul in such a wonderful way and gave me the strength and courage to embark on this fascinating journey with all its ups and downs. After my feeling had made it clear to me from the beginning that she was still there, I now see myself one hundred per cent confirmed in this. She was able to clearly prove herself to me and I perceive her without a doubt inside and outside. She took my hand and with all her love showed me the door to a much larger world. In the end, I found not only her, but also myself. Death leads solely to the death of the physical body. Just because you can no longer physically see and touch your deceased doesn't mean that all other levels of being have disappeared. We do not need a body to love and be. We are all eternal souls, pure consciousness and infinite love.

Original version in German

Helles Dunkel

Wie kann es nur so dunkel sein,
wo Liebe hell erstrahlt?
Es sticht mir in mein Herz hinein,
die Zukunft schwarz gemalt.
Was bleibt für mich von dir besteh'n,
wenn Spuren bald verschwinden?
Ich lass dich niemals von mir geh'n,
ich werd' dich wiederfinden.
Und wenn die Sehnsucht mich ereilt,
beklag' ich nicht mein Leid.
Mit Liebe hast du mich geheilt,
uns trennt ja nur die Zeit.
Um mich herum wird alles still,
die Trauer darf nun geh'n.
Denn wer die Sterne sehen will,
muss selbst im Dunkel steh'n.

Oliver Lazar

English translation by analogy

Bright darkness

How can it be so dark,
where love shines bright?
It stings my heart,
the future painted black.
What will remain for me of you,
when traces soon disappear?
I'll never let you go from me,
I'll find you again.
And when longing comes to me,
I won't mourn my sorrow.
With love you have healed me,
only time separates us.
All around me will be quiet,
grief may now go.
For he who wants to see the stars,
must stand in the darkness himself.

Oliver Lazar

Annotations

1 And suddenly everything was different

1 Moorjani, Anita: *Dying to be me: My journey from cancer, to near death, to true healing*, Hay House, 2022.

2 Moorjani, Anita: *Contribution to the Online Congress Spirit Summit 2019*, 2019, https://www.spiritsummit.net [URL inactive], TS 8:00, visited on 18 January 2019.

3 Demarmels, Ursula: *Spiritual regression for peace & healing: discover your life mission through past life exploration*, Llewellyn Publications, 2015.

4 Weiss, Brian: *Many lives, many masters: The true story of a prominent psychiatrist, his young patient, and the past-life therapy that changed both their lives,* Simon & Schuster, 1988.

5 Kean, Leslie: *Surviving death: a journalist investigates evidence for an afterlife,* Three Rivers Press, an imprint of the Crown Publishing Group, a division of Penguin Random House LLC, 2018.

6 Leininger, Bruce: *Soul survivor: The reincarnation of a World War II fighter pilot,* Grand Central Publishing, 2010.

7 Risi, Armin: *Ihr seid Lichtwesen, Ursprung und Geschichte des Menschen,* Govinda, Zürich, 2013, p. 112.

8 Weiss, Brian: *Seelenwege. Reinkarnation und zukünftige Lebenswege,* Ullstein Buchverlag, Berlin, 2018, p. 20. (English version: *Same soul, many bodies: Discover the healing power of future lives through progression therapy,* Free Press, 2005.)

9 Lommel, Pim van: *Endloses Bewusstsein, Neue medizinische Fakten zur Nahtoderfahrung,* MensSana Verlag, Munich, 2013, p. 98. (English version: *Consciousness beyond life: The science of the near-death experience,* HarperCollins, 2011.)

10 Ibid., p. 99.

11 Herzberg, Nina: *Fragen rund um die geistige Welt, August 2020,* https://youtu.be/l5lr5VJjy0s, TS: 8:03-10:08, visited on 6 August 2020.

12 Kübler-Ross, Elisabeth: *Über den Tod und das Leben danach,* Silberschnur Verlag, Güllesheim, 2013, p. 28. (English version: *On Life after Death,* Celestial Arts, 2004.)

13 Weiss, Brian: *Die zahlreichen Leben der Seele. Die Chronik einer Reinkarnationstherapie,* Goldmann Verlag, Munich, 2005, p. 112. (English version: *Many lives, many masters: The true story of a prominent psychiatrist, his young patient, and the past-life therapy that changed both their lives,* Simon & Schuster, 1988.)

14 Hawley, Jack: *Bhagavad Gita: Der Gesang Gottes,* Goldmann Verlag, Munich, 2002, p. 112. (English version: *The Bhagavad Gita: A walkthrough for westerners,* New World Library, 2011.)

15 Radecke, Hans-Dieter/Teufel, Lorenz: *Was zu bezweifeln war, Die Lüge von der objektiven Wissenschaft,* Droemer Verlag, Munich, 2010, p. 39.

2 Science and spirituality

1 Kübler-Ross, Elisabeth: *Über den Tod und das Leben danach,* Silberschnur Verlag, Güllesheim, 2013, p. 4. (English version: *On Life after Death,* Celestial Arts, 2004.)

2 Maischberger, Sandra: *Übersinnliche Kräfte. Mysterium oder Mumpitz?* Das Erste, November 2010, https://youtu.be/Huk5IJnwnPI, visited on 22 November 2020.

3 Ibid., TS: 6:54-7:06.

4 Maischberger Sandra: *Übersinnliche Kräfte. Mysterium oder Mumpitz? III,* Das Erste, November 2010,

https://youtu.be/slll4SJJK9Y, TS: 0:20-2:30, visited on 22 November 2020.

5 Sheldrake, Rupert: *Der Wissenschaftswahn. Warum der Materialismus ausgedient hat,* Droemer Verlag, Munich, 2015, pp. 26-27. (English version: *The science delusion: Feeling the spirit of enquiry*, Coronet, 2020.)

6 Fara, Patricia: *Science, A four thousand year history,* Oxford University Press, Oxford New York, 2009, p. 132.

7 Radecke, Hans-Dieter/Teufel, Lorenz: *Was zu bezweifeln war, Die Lüge von der objektiven Wissenschaft,* Droemer *Verlag,* Munich, 2010, p. 134.

8 Kant, Immanuel: *Kritik der reinen Vernunft,* Meiner Verlag, Hamburg, 1998.

9 Dürr, Hans-Peter: *Geist, Kosmos und Physik, Gedanken über die Einheit des Lebens,* Crotona Verlag, Amerang, 2010, p. 23.

10 Jaspers, Karl: *Kleine Schule des philosophischen Denkens,* Piper Verlag, Munich/Zürich 2012, p. 20.

11 Alexander, Eben: *Blick in die Ewigkeit, Die faszinierende Nahtoderfahrung eines Neurochirurgen,* Heyne Verlag, Munich, 2016, pp. 206f. (English version: *Proof of heaven: A neurosurgeon's journey into the afterlife*, Simon & Schuster, 2012.)

12 Jaeger, Lars: *Wissenschaft und Spiritualität, Universum, Leben, Geist, Zwei Wege zu den großen Geheimnissen,* Springer Verlag, Berlin/Heidelberg, 2016, p. 270.

13 Gentner, Ingo: *Nahtoderfahrungen, Gibt es Himmel und Hölle wirklich?* https://www.bild.de/bild-plus/news/2019/news/nahtod-erfahrung-nach-kopfschuss-ich-war-tot-und-landete-in-der-hoelle-60397024.bild.html, visited on 21 May 2019.

14 Kuhn, Thomas: *Die Struktur wissenschaftlicher Revolutionen,* Suhrkamp Verlag, Frankfurt/Main, 1976.

15 Lommel, Pim van: *Endloses Bewusstsein, Neue medizinische Fakten zur Nahtoderfahrung,* MensSana Verlag, Munich, 2013, p. 293. (English version: *Consciousness beyond life: The science of the near-*

death experience, HarperCollins, 2011.)

16 Kruse, Eckhard: *Der Geist in der Materie, Die Begegnung von Wissenschaft und Spiritualität,* Crotona Verlag, Amerang, 2013, p. 53.

17 Dschulnigg, Franz: *Thesen zur Jenseitsforschung,* Internet, Empirische Jenseitsforschung, 2019, https://youtu.be/NTg4pMzI9UM, TS: 2:40-2:53, visited on 13 June 2019.

18 Precht, Richard David: *Sei du selbst, Von der Philosophie nach Hegel bis zur Philosophie der Jahrhundertwende,* Goldmann Verlag, Munich, 2019, p. 91.

19 Sheldrake, Rupert: *Der Wissenschaftswahn. Warum der Materialismus ausgedient hat,* Droemer Verlag, Munich, 2015, p. 16. (English version: *The science delusion: Feeling the spirit of enquiry,* Coronet, 2020.)

20 Dawkins, Richard: *Der Gotteswahn,* Ullstein Buchverlag, Berlin, 2008. (English version: *The god delusion*, Random House, 2016.)

21 Behe, Michael: *Darwins Black Box, Biochemische Einwände gegen die Evolutionstheorie,* Resch Verlag, Gräfelfing, 2007. (English version: *Darwin's black box: The biochemical challenge to evolution,* Free Press, 2006.)

22 Dawkins, Richard: *Der Gotteswahn,* Ullstein Buchverlag, Berlin, 2008, pp. 185-187. (English version: *The god delusion*, Random House, 2016.)

23 Radecke, Hans-Dieter/Teufel, Lorenz: *Was zu bezweifeln war, Die Lüge von der objektiven Wissenschaft,* Droemer Verlag, Munich, 2010, pp. 26-27.

24 Sheldrake, Rupert: *How widely is blind assessment used in scientific research?* Alternative Therapies 5, 1999, pp. 88-91.

25 Watt, Caroline/Nagtegaal, Marleen: *Reporting of blind methods, An interdisciplinary survey,* Journal of the Society of Psychical Research 68, 2004, pp. 105–114.

26 Sheldrake, Rupert: *Der Wissenschaftswahn. Warum der Materialismus ausgedient hat,* Droemer Verlag, Munich, 2015, p. 397. (Eng-

lish version: *The science delusion: Feeling the spirit of enquiry*, Coronet, 2020.)

27 Dawkins, Richard: *Der Gotteswahn,* Ullstein Buchverlag, Berlin, 2008, p. 178. (English version: *The god delusion*, Random House, 2016.)

28 Ibid., p. 187.

29 Kübler-Ross, Elisabeth: *Über den Tod und das Leben danach,* Silberschnur Verlag, Güllesheim, 2013, p. 11. (English version: *On Life after Death,* Celestial Arts, 2004.)

30 von Goethe, Johann Wolfgang: *Maximen und Reflexionen, Aphorismen und Aufzeichnungen,* Verlag der Goethe-Gesellschaft, Weimar, 1907, n. pag.

31 Risi, Armin: *Der radikale Mittelweg. Überwindung von Atheismus und Monotheismus, Das Buch zum aktuellen Paradigmenwechsel,* Kopp Verlag, Rottenburg, 2016, 2nd edition.

32 Risi, Armin: *Ihr seid Lichtwesen, Ursprung und Geschichte des Menschen*, Govinda Verlag, Zürich, 2013, pp. 22-23.

33 Stein, Ben/Miller, Kevin: *Expelled, No intelligence allowed*, Rampant Films, 2008.

34 Schumacher, Jörn: *Vom atheistischen Wissenschaftler zum gläubigen Evolutionskritiker,* https://www.promedienmagazin.de/gesellschaft/menschen/2017/09/27/vom-atheistischen-wissenschaftler-zum-glaeubigen-evolutionskritiker/ [URL inactive], 2017, visited on 20 May 2019.

35 Stein, Ben/Miller, Kevin: *Expelled, No intelligence allowed*, Rampant Films, 2008, TS: 7:14 - 7:30.

36 Röthlein, Brigitte: *Der Nobelpreisträger als Parapsychologe,* Bild der Wissenschaft, October 1997, p. 66.

37 Myers, David G.: *Kritisch denken mit wissenschaftlicher Psychologie,* Springer Verlag, Berlin/Heidelberg, 2014, p. 22.

38 Cardeña, Etzel: *The Experimental Evidence for Parapsychological Phenomena, A Review,* American Psychologist 73, July 2018, pp. 663-677.

39 Hofstadter, Douglas: *A Cutoff for Craziness,* New York Times, January 2011, https://www.nytimes.com/roomfordebate/2011/01/06/the-esp-study-when-science-goes-psychic/a-cutoff-for-craziness, visited on 10 January 2023.

40 Alexander, Eben: *Blick in die Ewigkeit, Die faszinierende Nahtoderfahrung eines Neurochirurgen,* Heyne Verlag, Munich, 2016. (English version: *Proof of heaven: A neurosurgeon's journey into the afterlife,* Simon & Schuster, 2012.)

41 Steinhardt, Paul: *Endless universe, Beyond the Big Bang,* Weidenfeld & Nicolson, London 2007, pp. 169f.

42 Risi, Armin: Wie lange dauert das Kali-Yuga? n.d., https://armin-risi.ch/Artikel/Vedisc h/Wie-lange-dauert-das-Kali-Yuga.php, visited on 14 January 2020.

43 Kübler-Ross, Elisabeth: *Über den Tod und das Leben danach,* Silberschnur Verlag, Güllesheim, 2013, pp. 43f. (English version: *On Life after Death,* Celestial Arts, 2004.)

44 EVS: *European Values Study 2017, Integrated Dataset,* EVS 2017, Data file 2018, http://dx.doi.org/10.4232/1.13090, visited on 26 May 2019.

45 Schreiber, Mathias: Die Reise ins Licht, SPIEGEL, April 2007, https://www.spiegel.de/spiegel/print/d-51132266.html, visited on 24 July 2020.

3 Matter

1 Rubbia, Carlo: *Neue Zürcher Zeitung,* March 1993, n. pag.

2 Sheldrake, Rupert: *Der Wissenschaftswahn. Warum der Materialismus ausgedient hat,* Droemer Verlag, Munich, 2015, pp. 149-151. (English version: *The science delusion: Feeling the spirit of enquiry,* Coronet, 2020.)

3 Kennedy, Donald/Norman, Colin: *What Don't We Know?,* Science 309, Nr. 5731, 2005, p. 75.

4 Lommel, Pim van: *Endloses Bewusstsein, Neue medizinische Fakten*

zur Nahtoderfahrung, MensSana Verlag, Munich, 2013, p. 16. (English version: *Consciousness beyond life: The science of the near-death experience,* HarperCollins, 2011.)

5 Radecke, Hans-Dieter/ Teufel, Lorenz: *Was zu bezweifeln war. Die Lüge von der objektiven Wissenschaft,* Droemer Verlag, Munich, 2010, p. 287.

6 Vaas, Rüdiger: *Der Urknall,* Bild der Wissenschaft, November 2009, p. 40.

7 Zaun, Harald: *Was vor dem Urknall war,* Telepolis, Special Kosmologie, February 2007, p. 90.

8 Lesch, Harald: *α-Centauri. Was ist der Urknall?,* BR-alpha mit Sterne und Weltraum, Co-Produktion, TV, 2000, TS: 0:55-1:09.

9 Helmenstine, Anne Marie: *Chemical Composition of the Human Body,* May 2019, https://www.thoughtco.com/chemical-composition-of-the-human-body-603995, visited on 10 January 2023.

10 Lesch, Harald: *α-Centauri. Was geschah in den ersten drei Minuten?,* BR-alpha mit Sterne und Weltraum, Co-Produktion, TV, 2000.

11 Lesch, Harald/Gaßner, Josef M.: *Urknall, Weltall und das Leben. Vom Nichts bis heute Morgen,* Komplett-Media Verlag, Grünwald/Munich, 2014, pp. 148-152.

12 Lesch, Harald: *α-Centauri. Woher kommt unser Gold?,* BR-alpha mit Sterne und Weltraum, Co-Produktion, TV, 2000.

13 Crick, Francis: *Memory and molecular turnover,* Nature Nr. 312, 1984, p. 101.

14 Lommel, Pim van: *Endloses Bewusstsein, Neue medizinische Fakten zur Nahtoderfahrung,* MensSana Verlag, Munich, 2013, p. 312. (English version: *Consciousness beyond life: The science of the near-death experience,* HarperCollins, 2011.)

15 Dijksterhuis, Eduard J.: *The Mechanization of the World Picture,* Oxford, 1961, p. 9.

16 Sheldrake, Rupert: *Der Wissenschaftswahn. Warum der Materialis-*

mus ausgedient hat, Droemer Verlag, Munich, 2015, p. 84. (English version: *The science delusion: Feeling the spirit of enquiry*, Coronet, 2020.)

17 Lesch, Harald/Gaßner, Josef M.: *Urknall, Weltall und das Leben. Vom Nichts bis heute Morgen*, Komplett-Media Verlag, Grünwald/Munich, 2014, p. 62.

18 M. Gaßner, Josef/ Lesch, Harald: *Spins, Nichts und das Higgsfeld,* Internet, Urknall, Weltall und das Leben, 2014, https://youtu.be/7TUIvg-1VuE, TS: 4:12-4:35, visited on 10 August 2019.

19 Dürr, Hans-Peter: *Geist, Kosmos und Physik. Gedanken über die Einheit des Lebens,* Crotona Verlag, Amerang, 2010, p. 62.

20 Sheldrake, Rupert: *Der Wissenschaftswahn. Warum der Materialismus ausgedient hat,* Droemer Verlag, Munich, 2015, pp. 153f. (English version: *The science delusion: Feeling the spirit of enquiry*, Coronet, 2020.)

21 Humphrey, Nicholas: *Soul dust. The magic of consciousness,* Quercus, London, 2012.

22 Sheldrake, Rupert: *Der Wissenschaftswahn. Warum der Materialismus ausgedient hat,* Droemer Verlag, Munich, 2015, p. 155. (English version: *The science delusion: Feeling the spirit of enquiry*, Coronet, 2020.)

23 Nagel, Thomas: *Mind and cosmos. Why the materialist neo-Darwinian conception of nature is almost certainly false,* Oxford University Press, New York, 2012.

24 Strawson, Galen: *Realistic Monism. Why Physicalism Entails Panpsychism,* Journal of Consciousness Studies 13, Nrn. 10-11, 2006, pp. 3– 31.

25 Jaeger, Lars: *Wissenschaft und Spiritualität. Universum, Leben, Geist. Zwei Wege zu den großen Geheimnissen,* Springer Verlag, Berlin/Heidelberg, 2016, pp. 190-191.

26 Lesch, Harald: *Das Higgs-Boson. Gottes Teilchen?* Internet, Terra X Lesch & Co, 2019, https://youtu.be/ACD_qndPwws, TS: 9:38-

9:55, visited on 16 August 2019.

27 Risi, Armin: *Ihr seid Lichtwesen. Ursprung und Geschichte des Menschen,* Govinda Verlag, Zürich, 2013, p. 41.

4 Origin and evolution of life

1 Lesch, Harald/Gaßner, Josef M.: *Urknall, Weltall und das Leben. Vom Nichts bis heute Morgen*, Komplett-Media Verlag, Grünwald/Munich, 2014, p. 232.

2 Hirsch-Kauffmann, Monica/Schweiger, Manfred: *Biologie für Mediziner, Pharmazeuten und Chemiker,* Georg Thieme Verlag, Stuttgart/New York, 1987, p. 224.

3 Discovery-Institute: *A Scientific Dissent from Darwinism,* May 2023, http://discovery.org/f/660, visited on 2 June 2023.

4 Risi, Armin: *Evolution. Stammt der Mensch von den Tieren ab?,* Govinda Verlag, Zürich, 2014, p. 12.

5 Jaeger, Lars: *Wissenschaft und Spiritualität. Universum, Leben, Geist. Zwei Wege zu den großen Geheimnissen,* Springer Verlag, Berlin/Heidelberg, 2016, pp. 279-280.

6 Brierley, Justin: *Daniel Dennett vs Keith Ward. Are we more than matter? Mind, consciousness and free will,* Unbelievable?, October 2018, https://youtu.be/mongL_ 2KMGg, TS: 2:20-2:25, visited on 31 July 2020.

7 Tour, James: *Molecules Don't Care About Life,* Dr. James Tour, September 2020, https://youtu.be/hAga9GDUXl4, TS: 1:15-1:23, visited on 11 January 2023.

8 Graf, Philipp: *Leben ist Definitionssache,* Max Planck Gesellschaft, n.d., https://www.synthetische-biologie.mpg.de/17480/was-ist-leben, visited on 2 September 2019.

9 Varela, Francisco G./Maturana, Humberto R./Uribe, R.: *Autopoiesis. The organization of living systems, its characterization and a model,* BioSystems 5, May 1974, pp. 187–196.

10 Graf, Philipp: *Leben ist Definitionssache,* Max Planck Gesellschaft,

n.d., https://www.synthetische-biologie.mpg.de/17480/was-ist-leben, visited on 2 September 2019.

11 Matthiesen, Rune: *Bioinformatics Methods in Clinical Research,* Bd. 593, January 2012, p. 49.

12 Nguyen-Kim, Dr. Mai Thi: *Entstand so das Leben? Die RNA-Welt,* Terra X Lesch & Co, 2019, https://youtu.be/b8CNQOe-Rbs, TS: 3:50-5:07, visited on 12 September 2019.

13 Wagner, Kerstin: *Neuartiger Regulationsmechanismus steuert Differenzierung embryonaler Stammzellen,* idw-Informationsdienst Wissenschaft, April 2015, https://idw-online.de/de/news628574, visited on 16 Dezember 2019.

14 Knirr, Thomas: *Darwins Black Box. Was Charles Darwin übersehen hat,* Der laute Ruf, April 2011, https://youtu.be/3419E8mP7PU, TS: 53:19, visited on 25 January 2021.

15 Grävemeyer, Arne: *DNA speichert TV-Serie fehlerfrei,* c't, Heise Verlag, 20 September 2020, p. 58.

16 Grävemeyer Arne: *DNA speichert das Menschheitswissen,* c't, Heise Verlag, 26 December 2020, p. 47.

17 Finkel, Simone: *Massenhaft Speicherplatz. Das ist die größte SSD der Welt,* Chip, November 2020, https://www.chip.de/news/Groesste-SSD-der-Welt_182741150.html, visited on 25 January 2021.

18 Tour, James: *Episode 2/13. Primordial Soup. A Course on Abiogenesis by Dr. James Tour,* https://youtu.be/tNbl-g8QoAg, TS: 8: 48-11:39, visited on 15 March 2021.

19 Ibid., TS: 9:31.

20 Ibid., TS: 10:45.

21 Brierley, Jason: *Unbelievable? Can chemistry solve the origin of life?,* https://youtu.be/Njuso5A2jts, visited on 16 March 2021.

22 Ibid., TS : 9:55 - 10:49.

23 Ibid., TS: 10:50 - 10:55.

24 Jaeger, Lars: *Wissenschaft und Spiritualität. Universum, Leben, Geist. Zwei Wege zu den großen Geheimnissen,* Springer Verlag,

Berlin/Heidelberg, 2016, p. 275.

25 Gaßner, Josef M./Lesch, Harald: *Lesch & Gaßner. Die Entstehung des Lebens,* Urknall, Weltall und das Leben, 2014, https://youtu.be/u4LL_3zoEBQ, TS: 5:18-6:15, visited on 12 September 2019.

26 Ibid., TS: 6:43-7:00.

27 Nguyen-Kim, Dr. Mai Thi: *Entstand so das Leben? Die RNA-Welt,* Terra X Lesch & Co, 2019, https://youtu.be/b8CNQOe-Rbs, TS: 2:30-2:48, visited on 12 September 2019.

28 Miller, Stanley L.: *A Production of Amino Acids Under Possible Primitive Earth Conditions,* Science 117, Nr. 3046, 1953, pp. 528–529, https://science.sciencemag.org/content/117/3046/528, visited 5 February 2023.

29 Lesch, Harald/Gaßner, Josef M.: *Urknall, Weltall und das Leben. Vom Nichts bis heute Morgen*, Komplett-Media Verlag, Grünwald/Munich, 2014, p. 229.

30 Junker, Reinhard: *Evolution. Ein kritisches Lehrbuch,* Weyel Verlag, Giessen, 1998, p. 138.

31 Ibid., p. 140.

32 Grävemeyer, Arne: *AlphaFold kann Protein-Origami,* c't, Heise Verlag, 1 December 2020, p. 50.

33 Axe, Douglas: *Estimating the Prevalence of Protein Sequences Adopting Functional Enzyme Folds,* Journal of molecular biology, 341, September 2004, pp. 1295-315.

34 Tour, James: *Episode 5/13. Carbohydrates. A Course on Abiogenesis by Dr. James Tour*, https://youtu.be/rdqd_EvpsZM, TS: 25:58-34:20, visited on 16 March 2021.

35 Barclay, Derek: *Die Wahrheit aufgedeckt. Band 6,* Ebozon Verlag, Traunreut, 2017.

36 Nguyen-Kim, Dr. Mai Thi: *Entstand so das Leben? Die RNA-Welt,* Terra X Lesch & Co, 2019, https://youtu.be/b8CNQOe-Rbs, TS: 6:10-7:00, visited on 12 September 2019.

37 Behe, Michael: *Darwins Black Box, Biochemische Einwände gegen*

die Evolutionstheorie, Resch Verlag, Gräfelfing, 2007 p. 268. (English version: *Darwin's black box: The biochemical challenge to evolution*, Free Press, 2006.)

38 Tour, James: *Episode 8/13. Nucleotides. A Course on Abiogenesis by Dr. James Tour,* https://youtu.be/CYiguQYCSio, TS: 43:14, visited on 17 March 2021.

39 Stein, Ben/Miller, Kevin: *Expelled. No intelligence allowed,* Rampant Films, 2008, TS: 1:27:08-1:28:06.

40 Lesch, Harald/Gaßner, Josef M.: *Urknall, Weltall und das Leben. Vom Nichts bis heute Morgen*, Komplett-Media Verlag, Grünwald/Munich, 2014, p. 235.

41 Tompa, Peter/Rose, George: *The Levinthal paradox of the interactome,* Protein Science, December 2011, 20 (12), pp. 2074-9.

42 Meyer, Stephen: *Darwin's doubt. The explosive origin of animal life and the case for intelligent design,* HarperOne, An imprint of HarperCollinsPublishers, New York, 2013.

43 Meyer, Stephen: *Signature in the Cell. Stephen Meyer Faces his Critics. pt. 1. The Presentatio*n, 2014, https://youtu.be/eW6egHV6jAw, TS: 53:15 - 53:49, visited on 11 January 2023.

44 Lesch, Harald: *Entstehung des Lebens aus toter Materie,* Urknall, Weltall und das Leben, 2019, https://youtu.be/qv_t77LS0t0, visited on 12 October 2019.

45 Liu, Luping, Zou, Yike, Bhattacharya, Ahanjit et al.: *Enzyme-free synthesis of natural phospholipids in water,* Nat. Chem. 12, 2020, pp. 1029–1034.

46 Lesch, Harald: *Entstehung des Lebens aus toter Materie,* Urknall, Weltall und das Leben, 2019, https://youtu.be/qv_t77LS0t0, TS: 6:48-7:04, visited on 12 October 2019.

47 Eigen, Manfred: *Selforganization of matter and the evolution of biological macromolecules,* Naturwissenschaften 58, Nr. 10, October 1971, pp. 465–523.

48 Greuling, Heinz: *So entstand die Erdatmosphäre und das erste Leben,* Quarks, 2014, https://youtu.be/tthNNLyVBUs, TS: 3:24-3:55, visited on 4 October 2019.

49 Trinks, Hauke: *Auf den Spuren des Lebens. Bericht zur Expedition in das Eis von Spitzbergen vom 17. Mai 1999 bis 14. September 2000,* Technical University Hamburg-Harburg, January 2001, https://tore.tuhh.de/bitstream/11420/200/1/Auf_den_Spuren_des_Lebens.pdf, visited on 13. October 2019.

50 Mainzer, Klaus: *Materie. Von der Urmaterie zum Leben,* C. H. Beck Verlag. Munich, 1996, p. 82.

51 Pennisi, Elizabeth: *Synthetic Genome Brings New Life to Bacterium,* Science 328, Nr. 5981, 2010, pp. 958–959.

52 SpiegelOnline: *Forscher erschaffen erstmals künstliches Leben,* Spiegel online, May 2010, https://www.spiegel.de/wissenschaft/natur/durchbruch-forscher-erschaffen-erstmals-kuenstliches-leben-a-696016.html, visited on 15 December 2019.

53 Posener, Alan: *Wir sind Gott!,* Die Welt, May 2010, https://www.welt.de/welt_print/kultur/literatur/article7750885/WIR-SIND-GOTT.html, visited on 15 December 2019.

54 Rüegg, Peter: *Kein künstliches Leben,* ETH Life, May 2010, http://www.ethlife.ethz.ch/archive_articles/100526_venter_kuenstl_genom_per/, visited on 15 December 2019.

55 Henn, Volker: *Das synthetische Genom. Ein Schritt zum Minimalorganismus,* Telepolis-Heise online, January 2014, https://www.heise.de/tp/features/Das-synthetische-Genom- ein-Schritt-zum-Minimalorganismus-3362986.html [URL inactive], visited on 15 December 2019.

56 Ibid.

57 Könau, Janek: *Steckt in diesem Laborkolben der Ursprung des Le-*

bens?, Bild, 4 September 2022, https://www.bild.de/regional/thueringen/thueringen-aktuell/forschung-steckt-in-diesem-laborkolben-der-ursprung-des-lebens-81222194.bild.html, visited on 12 January 2023.

58 Behe, Michael: *Darwins Black Box, Biochemische Einwände gegen die Evolutionstheorie,* Resch Verlag, Gräfelfing, 2007, p. 276. (English version: *Darwin's black box: The biochemical challenge to evolution*, Free Press, 2006.)

59 Dose, Klaus: *The Origin of Life. More Questions Than Answers,* Interdisciplinary Science Reviews 13, Nr. 4, 1988, p. 348.

60 Shirai, Yasuhiro et al.: *Directional Control in Thermally Driven Single-Molecule Nanocars,* Nano letters 5, December 2005, pp. 2330-4.

61 TheBestSchools.org: *The 50 Most Influential Scientists in the World Today,* TheBestSchools.org, 2020, https://thebestschools.org/features/50-influential-scientists-world -today/ [URL inactive], visited on 23 February 2020.

62 Tour, James: *Das Geheimnis der Entstehung des Lebens,* Dr. James Tour, March 2019, https://youtu.be/zU7Lww-sBPg, visited on 12 January 2023.

63 Jaeger, Lars: *Wissenschaft und Spiritualität. Universum, Leben, Geist. Zwei Wege zu den großen Geheimnissen,* Springer Verlag, Berlin/Heidelberg, 2016, pp. 275f.

64 Brierley, Justin: *Are we close to discovering the Origin Of Life? James Tour vs. Lee Cronin,* Unbelievable?, February 2020, https://youtu.be/3DHvNRK452c, visited on 23 September 2020.

65 Tour, James: *The Origin of Life Has Not Been Explained,* Internet, Discovery Science, 2019, https://youtu.be/r4sP1E1Jd_Y, visited on 22 February 2020.

66 Strobel, Lee: *The case for faith. A journalist investigates the toughest objections to Christianity,* Grand Rapids, Zondervan, Michigan, 2000, p. 111.

67 Risi, Armin: *Ihr seid Lichtwesen. Ursprung und Geschichte des Menschen,* Govinda Verlag, Zürich, 2013, p. 121.

68 Cronin, Lee: *Lee Cronin will Materie zum Leben erwecken,* TED, 2011, https://youtu.be/unNRCSj0igI, visited on 12 January 2023.

69 Lerch, Harold A.: *Die Bibel. Wahrheit oder Fabel. Ist die Bibel wörtlich?,* Harold A. Lerch. Sr., 2018, p. 38, https://books.google.de/books?id=RBx5DwAAQBAJ, visited on 17 December 2019.

70 Junker, Reinhard: *Evolution. Ein kritisches Lehrbuch,* Weyel Verlag, Giessen, 1998, p. 19.

71 Darwin, Charles: *Die Entstehung der Arten,* Nikol Verlag, Hamburg, 2008.

72 Max-Planck Society: *Zellorganellen. Die Endosymbiontentheorie,* Max-Planck Society, 2015, https://youtu.be/9LTMDLDsL98, visited on 4 October 2019.

73 Junker, Reinhard: *Evolution. Ein kritisches Lehrbuch,* Weyel Verlag, Giessen, 1998, pp. 168-169.

74 Lesch, Harald/Gaßner, Josef M.: *Urknall, Weltall und das Leben. Vom Nichts bis heute Morgen*, Komplett-Media Verlag, Grünwald/Munich, 2014, p. 256.

75 Ibid., p. 255.

76 Behe, Michael: *Revolutionär. Michael Behe und das Geheimnis molekularer Maschinen,* Discovery Institute, Drei Linden Filmproduktion, 2016, TS: 45:27-47:43.

77 Behe, Michael: *Richard Lenski and Citrate Hype. Now Deflated,* Evolution News & Science Today, May 2016, https://evolutionnews.org/2016/05/richard_lenski/, visited on 4 October 2019.

78 Ebert, Vince: *Was wäre, wenn es einen intelligenten Designer gäbe?,* Spektrum.de, November 2017, https://www.spektrum.de/kolumne/was-waere-wenn-es-einen-intelligenten-designer-gaebe/1517199, visited on 28 January 2020.

79 Ibid.

80 Ibid.

81 Nilsson, Dan-E./Pelger, Susanne: *A Pessimistic Estimate of the Time Required for an Eye to Evolve,* Proceedings, Biological sciences, The Royal Society 256, May 1994, pp. 53–8.

82 Ebert, Vince: *Was wäre, wenn es einen intelligenten Designer gäbe?,* Spektrum.de, November 2017, https://www.spektrum.de/kolumne/was-waere-wenn-es-einen-intelligenten-designer-gaebe/1517199, visited on 28 January 2020.

83 Hirsch-Kauffmann, Monica/Schweiger, Manfred: *Biologie für Mediziner, Pharmazeuten und Chemiker,* Georg Thieme Verlag, Stuttgart/New York, 1987, p. 224.

84 Junker, Reinhard: *Evolution. Ein kritisches Lehrbuch,* Weyel Verlag, Giessen, 1998, p. 49.

85 Dürr, Hans-Peter: *Es gibt keine Materie,* Crotona Verlag, Amerang, 2012, p. 58.

86 Miersch, Michael: *Der Rabenversteher,* Welt 2009, https://www.welt.de/welt_print/vermischtes/article5208366/Der-Rabenversteher.html, visited on 30 October 2019.

87 Dawkins, Richard: *Der Gotteswahn,* Ullstein Buchverlag, Berlin, 2008, p. 296. (English version: *The god delusion*, Random House, 2016.)

88 Junker, Reinhard: *Evolution. Ein kritisches Lehrbuch,* Weyel Verlag, Giessen, 1998, p. 53.

89 Max-Planck Society: *Warum erforschen Wissenschaftler Fliegen?,* Max Planck Society, n.d., https://www.mpg.de/10885922/warum-erforschen-wissenschaftler-fruchtfliegen, visited on 25 October 2019.

90 Risi, Armin: *Evolution. Stammt der Mensch von den Tieren ab?,* Govinda Verlag, Zürich, 2014, p. 48.

91 Jones, Steve: *Wie der Wal zur Flosse kam. Ein neuer Blick auf den Ursprung der Arten,* dtv-Verlag, Munich, 2002, p. 278.

92 Gish, Duane: *Fossilien. Stumme Zeugen der Vergangenheit,* Christliche Literatur-Verbreitung, Bielefeld, 1992, p. 279.

93 Risi, Armin: *Evolution. War alles ganz anders?,* NuoViso.TV, 2017, https://www.youtube.com/watch?v=5FEeoEmOXwc, TS:24:18-29:31, visited on 26 October 2019.

94 Gerhard Neuweiler: *Evolutionary aspects of bat echolocation*, Journal of Comparative Physiology A 189, 2003, pp. 245-256.

95 Junker, Reinhard: *Der Ursprung der Fledermäuse,* Studium Integrale Journal 18, 2011, pp. 17–25 and 78–88.

96 Risi, Armin: *Evolution. War alles ganz anders?,* NuoViso.TV, 2017, https://www.youtube.com/watch?v=5FEeoEmOXwc, TS: 25:24-25:33, visited on 26 October 2019.

97 Dawkins, Richard: *Der Gotteswahn,* Ullstein Buchverlag, Berlin, 2008, p. 171. (English version: *The god delusion,* Random House, 2016.)

98 Ott, Clara: *Warum der Specht keine Gehirnerschütterung bekommt,* Welt.de, April 2011, https://www.welt.de/wissenschaft/umwelt/article13183573/Warum-der-Specht-keine-Gehirnerschuetterung-bekommt.html, visited on 17 January 2020.

99 Lesch, Harald: *α-Centauri. Was geschah im Kambrium?,* BR-alpha mit Sterne und Weltraum, Co-Produktion, 2006, TS: 2:48-3:53.

100 Meyer, Stephen: *Charles Darwin. A Myth for the Post-Christian Mind,* Ligonier Ministries, 2016, https://www.youtube.com/watch?v=PbcY9iya40o, TS: 19:42-25:50, visited on 8 December 2019.

101 Ibid., TS: 34:18-34:51.

102 Planck, Max: *Vorträge und Erinnerungen,* S. Hirzel-Verlag, Stuttgart, 1949, p. 13.

103 Ellison, Arthur: *Wandlungen,* SWF 3, 1992.

104 Dawkins, Richard: *Der Gotteswahn,* Ullstein Buchverlag, Berlin, 2008, pp. 391f. (English version: *The god delusion*, Random House, 2016.)

105 Woollacott, Marjorie/ Lorimer, David: *Spiritual awakenings: Scientists and academics describe their experiences*, Academy for the Advancement of Postmaterialist Sciences, 2022.

106 Kripal, Jeffrey J.: *The Flip: Epiphanies of mind and the future of knowledge*, Bellevue Literary Press, 2019.

107 Precht, Richard David: *Wer bin ich, und wenn ja, wie viele? Eine philosophische Reise,* Goldmann Verlag, Munich, 2012, pp. 133 and 230.

108 Precht, Richard David: *Sei du selbst. Von der Philosophie nach Hegel bis zur Philosophie der Jahrhundertwende,* Goldmann Verlag, Munich, 2019, p. 99.

109 Geisler, Norman L./Turek, Frank: *Um Atheist zu sein, fehlt mir der Glaube,* CMV, Bielefeld, 2018, p. 183f. (English version: *I don't have enough faith to be an atheist,* Crossway Books, 2021.)

110 Dawkins, Richard: *Der Gotteswahn,* Ullstein Buchverlag, Berlin, 2008, pp. 177f. (English version: *The god delusion*, Random House, 2016.)

111 Bajpai, Sunil/ Thewissen, Johannes G. M./ Sahni, Ashok: *The origin and early evolution of whales. Macroevolution documented on the Indian Subcontinent,* Journal of biosciences 34, November 2009, pp. 673-86.

112 Park, Travis: *Fossil of ancient four-legged whale found in Peru,* April 2019, https://www.bbc.com/news/ science-environment-47822228, visited on 11 November 2019.

113 Voss, M. u. a.: *Stomach contents of the archaeocete Basilosaurus isis. Apex predator in oceans of the late Eocene,* PLoS ONE 14, Nr. 1, 2005.

114 Sea Museum: *Basilosaurus. Dorudon and strange evolutionary experiments,* October 2014, https://www.sea.museum/2014/10/29/whale-evolution-and-adaptation/evolutionary-experiments, visited on 14 November 2019.

115 Ibid.

116 Vieweg, Martin: *Evolution der Wale. Ur-Sieb-Gebiss entdeckt,*

Wissenschaft.de, 2017, https://www.wissenschaft.de/erde-klima/evolution-der-wale-ur-sieb-gebiss-entdeckt/, visited on 27 November 2019.

117 Peredo, Carlos et al.: *Tooth Loss Precedes the Origin of Baleen in Whales,* Current Biology 28, November 2018.

118 Spaulding, Michelle/Maureen O'Leary/John Gatesy: *Relationships of Cetacea. Artiodactyla. Among Mammals. Increased Taxon Sampling Alters Interpretations of Key Fossils and Character Evolution,* PloS one 4, September 2009, e7062.

119 Diehl, Manfred: *Abstammungslehre,* Quelle & Meyer Verlag, Heidelberg, 1980, p. 12.

120 Lesch, Harald: *Hat Gott die Welt erschaffen?,* Terra X Lesch & Co, 2017, https://www.youtube.com/watch?v=D3dT44jH0iE, TS: 3:48-4:20, visited on 29 November 2019.

121 Ibid., TS: 4:25-4:42.

122 Ibid., TS: 5:00-5:10.

123 bild der wissenschaft: *Der Weg ins Meer. Wie Moby Dick schwimmen lernte,* Bild der Wissenschaft, December 1995, p. 93.

124 Risi, Armin: *Evolution. Stammt der Mensch von den Tieren ab?,* Govinda Verlag, Zürich, 2014, p. 80.

125 König, Timo/Bechly, Günter: *Glaube an Schöpfung fand ich primitiv,* September 2018, https://www.erf.de/themen/glaube/glaube-an-schoepfung-fand-ich-primitiv/2803-542-6173, visited on 29 November 2019.

126 Ibid.

127 Roach, John: *Oldest Antarctic Whale Found. Shows Fast Evolution,* National Geographic, November 2011, https://www.nationalgeographic.com/news/2011/11/111116-antarctica-whales-oldest-evolution-animals-science/, visited on 17 December 2019.

128 Wells, Jonathan: *Killer Whales Zombie Science Author Explains a Fatal Challenge to Evolution,* Broken Biscuit, July 2019, https://www.youtube.com/watch?v= dH5SqUeIkAI, TS: 4:30-4:50, visited on 17 December 2019.

129 Falkner, Markus: *Erbgut. Der Mensch ist zur Hälfte eine Banane,* Berliner Morgenpost, April 2013, https://www.morgenpost.de/kultur/berlin-kultur/article115517396/ Erbgut-der-Mensch-ist-zur-Haelfte-eine-Banane.html, visited on 17 December 2019.

130 Matthiesen, Rune: *Bioinformatics Methods in Clinical Research,* Bd. 593, January 2012, p. 49.

131 Dawkins, Richard: *The blind watchmaker,* Penguin Books, London, 2006, pp. 17-18, 116.

132 Lommel, Pim van: *Endloses Bewusstsein, Neue medizinische Fakten zur Nahtoderfahrung,* MensSana Verlag, Munich, 2013, p. 318. (English version: *Consciousness beyond life: The science of the near-death experience,* HarperCollins, 2011.)

133 Falkner, Markus: *Erbgut. Der Mensch ist zur Hälfte eine Banane,* Berliner Morgenpost, April 2013, https://www.morgenpost.de/kultur/berlin-kultur/article115517396/ Erbgut-der-Mensch-ist-zur-Haelfte-eine-Banane.html, visited on 17 December 2019.

134 Geisler, Norman L./Turek, Frank: *Um Atheist zu sein, fehlt mir der Glaube,* CMV, Bielefeld, 2018, p. 164. (English version: *I don't have enough faith to be an atheist,* Crossway Books, 2021.)

135 Mantegna, R. N. et al.: *Linguistic Features of Noncoding DNA Sequences,* Phys. Rev. Lett. 73, 23, 1994, pp. 3169–3172.

136 Pflanzenforschung.de: *Es geht auch ohne Junk-DNA. Unscheinbare Wasserpflanze bringt wissenschaftliche Theorie ins Wanken,* Pflanzenforschung.de, May 2013, https://www.pflanzenforschung.de/de/journal/journalbeitrage/es-geht-auch-ohne-junk-dna-unscheinbare-wasserpflanze-b-10047, visited on 17 December 2019.

137 Ibarra-Laclette, Enrique u. a.: *Architecture and evolution of a minute plant genome,* Nature 498, May 2013.

138 Pflanzenforschung.de: *Es geht auch ohne Junk-DNA. Unscheinbare*

Wasserpflanze bringt wissenschaftliche Theorie ins Wanken, Pflanzenforschung.de, May 2013, https://www.pflanzenforschung.de/de/journal/journalbeitrage/es-geht-auch-ohne-junk-dna-unscheinbare-wasserpflanze-b-10047, visited on 17 December 2019.

139 Lommel, Pim van: *Endloses Bewusstsein, Neue medizinische Fakten zur Nahtoderfahrung,* MensSana Verlag, Munich, 2013, p. 334. (English version: *Consciousness beyond life: The science of the near-death experience,* HarperCollins, 2011.)

140 Dreien, Bernadette von: *Christina. Band 2. Die Vision des Guten,* Govinda Verlag, Rheinau 2018, p. 34.

141 Risi, Armin: *Ihr seid Lichtwesen. Ursprung und Geschichte des Menschen,* Govinda Verlag, Zürich, 2013, p. 131.

142 Penrose, Roger/Schrödinger, Erwin: *What Is Life? With Mind and Matter and Autobiographical Sketches,* Cambridge University Press, Canto Edition, Cambridge, 2013.

143 Sheldrake, Rupert: *Der Wissenschaftswahn. Warum der Materialismus ausgedient hat,* Droemer Verlag, Munich, 2015, p. 136. (English version: *The science delusion: Feeling the spirit of enquiry,* Coronet, 2020.)

144 Lommel, Pim van: *Endloses Bewusstsein, Neue medizinische Fakten zur Nahtoderfahrung,* MensSana Verlag, Munich, 2013, p. 325. (English version: *Consciousness beyond life: The science of the near-death experience,* HarperCollins, 2011.)

145 Gilliver, Moira A. et al.: *Antibiotic resistance found in wild rodents,* Nature 401, September 1999, p. 233.

146 Sheldrake, Rupert: *Der siebte Sinn der Tiere,* Fischer Taschenbuch Verlag, Frankfurt/Main, 2007, p. 365. (English version: *Dogs that know when their owners are coming home:*, National Geographic Books, 2011.)

147 Ibid., pp. 365-366.

148 Backster, Cleve: *Primary perception. Biocommunication with plants. Living foods and human cells,* White Rose Millennium

Press, Anza, Calif, 2003.

149 Lommel, Pim van: *Endloses Bewusstsein, Neue medizinische Fakten zur Nahtoderfahrung,* MensSana Verlag, Munich, 2013, p. 332. (English version: *Consciousness beyond life: The science of the near-death experience,* HarperCollins, 2011.)

150 Sylvia, Claire: *Herzensfremd,* Bastei-Lübbe Verlag, Bergisch Gladbach, 1999. (English version: *A change of heart: A memoir,* Little, Brown, 1997.)

151 Huemer, Werner: *Phänomen Gedächtnistransplantation,* 2010, https://www.werner-huemer.net/texte/weltanschauliches/organtransplantation [URL inactive], visited on 4 January 2020.

152 Pearsall, Paul/ Schwartz, GE/ Russek, LG: *Changes in heart transplant recipients that parallel the personalities of their donors,* Integrative medicine, Integrating conventional and alternative medicine 2, April 2000, pp. 65-72.

153 Westerhoff, Nikolas: *Mit dem Herzen eines Fischers,* Süddeutsche Zeitung, October 2007.

154 Lauff, Sigrid/Prem, Lata Gupta: *Nach der Transplantation,* ARD, Planet Wissen, February 2018, https://www.planet-wissen.de/gesellschaft/medizin/organverpflanzung/pwiewissensfrage106.html [URL inactive], visited on 4 January 2020.

155 Westerhoff, Nikolas: *Mit dem Herzen eines Fischers,* Süddeutsche Zeitung, October 2007.

156 Frickel, Claudia: *Die Theorie vom Zell-Gedächtnis. Werden bei Organtransplantationen Eigenschaften übertragen?,* web.de, January 2017, https://web.de/magazine/wissen/mystery/theorie-zell-gedaechtnis-organtransplantationen-eigenschaften-uebertragen-32136114, visited on 4 January 2020.

157 Darwin, Charles: *Über die Entstehung der Arten,* Parkland Verlag, Cologne, 2002, p. 206. (English version: *The origin of species,* National Geographic Books, 2003.)

158 Behe, Michael: *Darwins Black Box, Biochemische Einwände gegen die Evolutionstheorie,* Resch Verlag, Gräfelfing, 2007. (English

version: *Darwin's black box: The biochemical challenge to evolution*, Free Press, 2006.)

159 Meyer, Stephen: *Darwin's doubt. The explosive origin of animal life and the case for intelligent design,* HarperOne, An imprint of HarperCollinsPublishers, New York, 2013.

160 Axe, Douglas: *Undeniable. How biology confirms our intuition that life is designed,* HarperOne, New York, 2017.

161 Lesch, Harald: *Hat Gott die Welt erschaffen?,* Terra X Lesch & Co, 2017, https://www.youtube.com/watch?v=D3dT44jH0iE, TS: 0:22-1:15, visited on 29 November 2019.

162 Ebert, Vince: *Was wäre, wenn es einen intelligenten Designer gäbe?,* Spektrum.de, November 2017, https://www.spektrum.de/kolumne/was-waere-wenn-es-einen-intelligenten-designer-gaebe/1517199, visited on 28 January 2020.

163 Behe, Michael: *Revolutionär. Michael Behe und das Geheimnis molekularer Maschinen,* Discovery Institute, Drei Linden Filmproduktion, 2016, TS: 12:46.

164 Scherer, Siegfried: *Die Entstehung des bakteriellen Rotationsmotors ist Unbekannt,* Studiengemeinschaft Wort und Wissen e. V., 2010, 7, http://www.evolutionslehrbuch.info/teil-4/kapitel-09-04-r01.pdf, visited on 31 January 2020.

165 Behe, Michael: *Darwins Black Box, Biochemische Einwände gegen die Evolutionstheorie,* Resch Verlag, Gräfelfing, 2007, p. 121. (English version: *Darwin's black box: The biochemical challenge to evolution*, Free Press, 2006.)

166 Behe, Michael: *Revolutionär. Michael Behe und das Geheimnis molekularer Maschinen,* Discovery Institute, Drei Linden Filmproduktion, 2016, TS: 19:05-19:15.

167 Ibid., TS: 32:07-32:16.

168 Minnich, Scott/ Meyer, Stephen: *Genetic analysis of coordinate flagellar and type III regulatory circuits in pathogenic bacteria,* 180, January 2003.

169 Abby, Sophie/ Rocha, Eduardo: *The Non-Flagellar Type III Secretion System Evolved from the Bacterial Flagellum and Diversified into Host-Cell Adapted Systems,* PLoS genetics 8, September 2012, e1002983.

170 Precht, Richard David: *Wer bin ich, und wenn ja, wie viele? Eine philosophische Reise,* Goldmann Verlag, Munich, 2012, p. 295.

171 Allen, Lad: *Metamorphose. Die geheimnisvolle Schönheit der Schmetterlinge,* Illustra Media, Drei Linden Filmproduktion, 2012, TS: 32:30-33:17.

172 Geisler, Norman L./Turek, Frank: *Um Atheist zu sein, fehlt mir der Glaube,* CMV, Bielefeld, 2018, pp. 170-177. (English version: *I don't have enough faith to be an atheist,* Crossway Books, 2021.)

173 Ibid., p. 174.

174 Discovery-Institute: *A Scientific Dissent from Darwinism,* May 2023, http://discovery.org/f/660, visited on 2 June 2023.

175 Krachten, Christoph: *Evolutionstheorie endgültig bestätigt. Kreationisten auf verlorenem Posten,* Clixoom Science & Fiction, 2017, https://www.youtube.com/watch?v=nQwIc2hXa_A, TS: 6:52-7:52, visited on 10 February 2020.

176 Ibid., TS: 5:35-5:51.

177 Ebert, Vince: *Was wäre, wenn es einen intelligenten Designer gäbe?,* Spektrum.de, November 2017, https://www.spektrum.de/kolumne/was-waere-wenn-es-einen-intelligenten-designer-gaebe/1517199, visited on 28 January 2020.

178 Martin, Loren G.: *What is the function of the human appendix? Did it once have a purpose that has since been lost?,* October 1999, https://www.scientificamerican.com/article/what-is-the-function-of-the-human-appendix-did-it-once-have-a-purpose-that-has-since-been-lost/, visited on 11 February 2020.

179 Behe, Michael: *Darwins Black Box, Biochemische Einwände gegen die Evolutionstheorie,* Resch Verlag, Gräfelfing, 2007, p. 346. (English version: *Darwin's black box: The biochemical challenge to*

evolution, Free Press, 2006.)

180 Geisler, Norman L./Turek, Frank: *Um Atheist zu sein, fehlt mir der Glaube,* CMV, Bielefeld, 2018, p. 173. (English version: *I don't have enough faith to be an atheist,* Crossway Books, 2021.)

181 Ibid., p. 174.

182 Meyer, Stephen: *Signature in the Cell. Stephen Meyer Faces his Critics. pt. 1. The Presentation*, 2014, https://www.youtube.com/watch?v=eW6egHV6jAw, TS: 30:45, visited on 11 January 2023.

183 Johannsen, Wolfgang: *Information und ihre Bedeutung in der Natur. Das Leben erfindet die Welt,* Springer Verlag, Berlin/Heidelberg, 2016, p. 12.

184 Gitt, Werner: *Information. Der Schlüssel zum Leben,* Christliche Literaturverbreitung, Bielefeld, 2016, p. 211.

185 Bulle, Bernard: *Automatisierung komplexer Industrieprozesse : Systeme, Verfahren und Informationsmanagement, Springer Verlag,* Wien, 2004, p. 156.

186 Gitt, Werner: *Information. Der Schlüssel zum Leben,* Christliche Literaturverbreitung, Bielefeld, 2016, pp. 44-88.

187 Ibid., p. 50.

188 Ibid., p. 53.

189 Shannon, Claude: *The mathematical theory of communication*, University of Illinois Press, Urbana, 1964.

190 Gitt, Werner: *Information. Der Schlüssel zum Leben,* Christliche Literaturverbreitung, Bielefeld, 2016, pp. 69f.

191 Ibid., p. 53.

192 Ibid., p. 83.

193 Marks, Robert: *Biological information-new perspectives. Proceedings of a symposium held May 31, 2011 through June 3, 2011 at Cornell University,* World Scientific, Hackensack, New Jersey, 2013.

194 Lesch, Harald: *α-Centauri. Kann die Physik die Welt erklären?,* BR-alpha mit Sterne und Weltraum, Co-Produktion, 2002, TS: 5:00 - 6:19.

195 Ibid., TS: 6:24-13:18.

196 Precht, Richard David: *Wer bin ich, und wenn ja, wie viele? Eine philosophische Reise,* Goldmann Verlag, Munich, 2012, p. 374.

197 Geisler, Norman L./Turek, Frank: *Um Atheist zu sein, fehlt mir der Glaube,* CMV, Bielefeld, 2018, p. 171. (English version: *I don't have enough faith to be an atheist,* Crossway Books, 2021.)

198 Meyer, Stephen/ Axe, Douglas D.: *Information Enigma. Where does information come from?,* Discovery Science, 2015, https://www.youtube.com/watch?v=aA-FcnLsF1g, TS: 17:36-20:23, visited on 28 February 2020.

199 Meyer, Stephen: *Signature in the Cell. Stephen Meyer Faces his Critics. pt. 1. The Presentatio*n, 2014, https://www.youtube.com/watch?v=eW6egHV6jAw, TS: 30:45, visited on 11 January 2023.

200 Eigen, Manfred: *Stufen zum Leben. Die frühe Evolution im Visier der Molekularbiologie,* Piper Verlag, Munich/Zürich, 1987, p. 55.

201 Küppers, Bernd-Olaf: *Der Ursprung biologischer Information. Zur Naturphilosophie der Lebensentstehung*, Piper Verlag, Munich/Zürich, 1990, p. 17.

202 Gitt, Werner: *Information. Der Schlüssel zum Leben,* Christliche Literaturverbreitung, Bielefeld, 2016, p. 171.

203 Ibid., p. 173.

204 Gowlett, John: *Auf Adams Spuren. Die Archäologie des frühen Menschen*, Verlag Herder, Freiburg im Breisgau/Basel/Wien, 1985.

205 Stelzner, Ruben/Schad, Wolfgang: *Der Goldene Schnitt*, University Witten Herdecke, 2003, p. 29, http://www.golden-section.eu/goldener_schnitt.pdf, visited on 29 February 2020.

206 Hemenway, Priya: *Der geheime Code. Die rätselhafte Formel, die Kunst, Natur und Wissenschaft bestimmt*, Evergreen Verlag, Cologne, 2008, p. 140.

207 Stelzner, Ruben/Schad, Wolfgang: *Der Goldene Schnitt*, Uni-

verity Witten Herdecke, 2003, p. 29, http://www.golden-section.eu/goldener_schnitt.pdf, visited on 29 February 2020.

208 Hawley, Jack: *Bhagavad Gita: Der Gesang Gottes,* Goldmann Verlag, Munich, 2002, p. 167. (English version: *The Bhagavad Gita: A walkthrough for westerners,* New World Library, 2011.)

209 Ibid., pp. 110f.

210 Elijah, Bruce: *Aussage eines Indianerhäuptlings*, n.d., https://www.naturheilkunde-wellness.de/weisheit/, visited on 12 January 2023.

211 Hawley, Jack: *Bhagavad Gita: Der Gesang Gottes,* Goldmann Verlag, Munich, 2002, p. 173. (English version: *The Bhagavad Gita: A walkthrough for westerners,* New World Library, 2011.)

212 Ibid., pp. 130f., 145.

213 Risi, Armin: *Ihr seid Lichtwesen. Ursprung und Geschichte des Menschen,* Govinda Verlag, Zürich, 2013, p. 2.

214 Ibid., p. 24.

215 Ibid., p. 25.

216 Kübler-Ross, Elisabeth: *Über den Tod und das Leben danach,* Silberschnur Verlag, Güllesheim, 2013, pp. 38-45. (English version: *On Life after Death,* Celestial Arts, 2004.)

217 Meckelburg, Ernst: *Wir alle sind unsterblich. Der Irrtum mit dem Tod,* Langen Müller Verlag, Munich, 1997, pp. 195f.

218 Risi, Armin: *Ihr seid Lichtwesen. Ursprung und Geschichte des Menschen,* Govinda Verlag, Zürich, 2013, pp. 55-67.

219 Bürgin, Luc: *Das Wunder Mirin Dajo. Der unverletzbare Prophet und seine paranormalen Kräfte*, Kopp Verlag, Rottenburg, 2004.

220 Bürgin, Luc: *Mirin Dajo. Der unverletzbare Prophet,* Mysteries Magazin, 2010, https://youtu.be/GWnkSxFINQQ, TS: 2:50-3:10, visited on 14 June 2020.

221 Bürgin, Luc: *Das Wunder Mirin Dajo. Der unverletzbare Prophet und seine paranormalen Kräfte*, Kopp Verlag, Rottenburg, 2004, p. 30.

222 Bürgin, Luc: *Mirin Dajo. Der unverletzbare Prophet,* Mysteries

Magazin, 2010, https://youtu.be/GWnkSxFINQQ, TS: 1:12-1:21, visited on 14 June 2020.

223 Risi, Armin: *Ihr seid Lichtwesen. Uhenrsprung und Geschichte des Menschen,* Govinda Verlag, Zürich, 2013, p. 65.

224 Ibid., p. 64.

225 Hawley, Jack: *Bhagavad Gita: Der Gesang Gottes,* Goldmann Verlag, Munich, 2002, p. 62. (English version: *The Bhagavad Gita: A walkthrough for westerners,* New World Library, 2011.)

5 Consciousness

1 Allgeier, Kurt: *Niemand stirbt für ewig. Tod, Reinkarnation und Wiedergeburt,* Hey! Publishing Verlag, Munich, 2013, n. pag.

2 Hasler, Felix: *Neuromythologie. Eine Streitschrift gegen die Deutungsmacht der Hirnforschung,* Transcript Verlag, Bielefeld, 2012.

3 Preuk, Monika: *Antidepressiva so häufig verschrieben wie noch nie. Wann sie sinnvoll sind und wann nicht,* Focus online, October 2018, https://www.focus.de/gesundheit/ratgeber/psychologie/depressionen-angststoerungen-borderline-antidepressiva-in-deutschland-so-haeufig-verschrieben-wie-noch-nie-wann-sie-wirklich-sinnvoll-sind-und-wann-nicht_id_ 9740636.html [URL inactive], visited on 20 June 2019.

4 Munkholm, Klaus/Paludan-Müller, Asger Sand/Boesen, Kim: *Considering the methodological limitations in the evidence base of antidepressants for depression. A reanalysis of a network meta-analysis,* BMJ Open 9:e024886, 2019.

5 Hunziker, Gabriella: *Neurowissenschaft. Begrenztheit der Hirnforschung,* Deutsches Ärzteblatt 3/110, Januar 2013, p. 84.

6 Lommel, Pim van: *Endloses Bewusstsein, Neue medizinische Fakten zur Nahtoderfahrung,* MensSana Verlag, Munich, 2013, p. 215. (English version: *Consciousness beyond life: The science of the near-death experience,* HarperCollins, 2011.)

7 Beauregard, Mario: *The spiritual brain. A neuroscientist's case for*

the existence of the soul. HarperOne, New York, 2008, pp. 125-180.

8 Precht, Richard David: *Wer bin ich, und wenn ja, wie viele? Eine philosophische Reise,* Goldmann Verlag, Munich, 2012, pp. 79-83.

9 Lommel, Pim van: *Endloses Bewusstsein, Neue medizinische Fakten zur Nahtoderfahrung,* MensSana Verlag, Munich, 2013, p. 193. (English version: *Consciousness beyond life: The science of the near-death experience,* HarperCollins, 2011.)

10 Lewin, Roger: *Is Your Brain Really Necessary?,* Science 210, Nr. 4475, Dezember 1980, pp. 1232-1234.

11 Meckelburg, Ernst: *Wir alle sind unsterblich. Der Irrtum mit dem Tod,* Langen Müller Verlag, Munich, 1997, p. 60.

12 Sheldrake, Rupert: *Der Wissenschaftswahn. Warum der Materialismus ausgedient hat,* Droemer Verlag, Munich, 2015, p. 253. (English version: *The science delusion: Feeling the spirit of enquiry,* Coronet, 2020.)

13 Meckelburg, Ernst: *Wir alle sind unsterblich. Der Irrtum mit dem Tod,* Langen Müller Verlag, Munich, 1997, p. 60.

14 Alexander, Eben: *Blick in die Ewigkeit, Die faszinierende Nahtoderfahrung eines Neurochirurgen,* Heyne Verlag, Munich, 2016, p. 253. (English version: *Proof of heaven: A neurosurgeon's journey into the afterlife,* Simon & Schuster, 2012.)

15 Smith, Gordon: *Beitrag auf dem Online-Kongress Spirit Summit 2019,* 2019, https://www.spiritsummit.net, TS:27:20-27:40, visited on 18 January 2019.

16 Dürr, Hans-Peter: *Es gibt keine Materie,* Crotona Verlag, Amerang, 2012, p. 14.

17 Berbalk, Heinrich: *Liebesforschung. Eine Wissenschaft für sich,* Junge Karriere, Nr. 001, January 2005, p. 82.

18 Nawalny, Alexej: *Nawalnys bewegende Worte über das Koma und die Liebe,* September 2020, https://www.bz-berlin.de/berlin/nawalnys-bewegende-worte-ueber-das-koma-und-die-liebe, visited on 21 September 2020.

19 Fisher, Helen: *Warum wir lieben. Die Chemie der Leidenschaft,* Walter Verlag, Düsseldorf/Zürich, 2005, pp. 7 f.

20 dpa Deutsche Presse-Agentur: *Eifersucht aufs Haustier. Wenn der Hund an erster Stelle steht,* Frankfurter Rundschau, March 2014, https://www.fr.de/ratgeber/gesundheit/wenn-hund-erster-stelle-steht-11225886.html, visited on 12 January 2021.

21 Kruse, Eckhard: *Der Geist in der Materie. Die Begegnung von Wissenschaft und Spiritualität,* Crotona Verlag, Amerang, 2013, p. 243.

22 Mertens, Margit: *Wo die Liebe wohnt,* June 2009, https://www.fr.de/wissen/liebe-wohnt-11483093.html, visited on 2 July 2020.

23 Schneider, Bettina: *Wie wahre Liebe unser Gehirn verändert,* December 2016, https://www.welt.de/kmpkt/article160096039/Wie-wahre-Liebe-unser-Gehirn-veraendert.html, visited on 2 July 2020.

24 Mertens, Margit: *Wo die Liebe wohnt,* June 2009, https://www.fr.de/wissen/liebe-wohnt-11483093.html, visited on 2 July 2020.

25 Barwanietz, Ulrike/Kölbel, Ralf: *Was bedeutet Liebe?,* SWR2 Wissen, 2018, https://docplayer.org/81302521-Was-bedeutet-liebe-gegenueber-verliebtheit-liebe-ein-gefaehrlicher-zustand.html, visited on 18 December 2020.

26 Hähnel, Martin: *Was ist Liebe? Philosophische Texte von der Antike bis zur Gegenwart,* Reclam Verlag, Stuttgart, 2015, p. 82.

27 Hawley, Jack: *Bhagavad Gita: Der Gesang Gottes,* Goldmann Verlag, Munich, 2002, p. 126. (English version: *The Bhagavad Gita: A walkthrough for westerners,* New World Library, 2011.)

6 Quantum mechanics and spirituality

1 Hümmler, Holm: *Relativer Quantenquark. Kann die moderne Physik die Esoterik belegen,* Springer *Verlag,* Berlin, 2017.

2 Jaeger, Lars: *Die zweite Quantenrevolution. Vom Spuk im Mikrokosmos zu neuen Supertechnologien,* Springer Verlag, Berlin, 2018, p. 378.

3 Planck, Max: *Archiv zur Geschichte der Max-Planck-Gesellschaft,* Abt. Va. Rep. 11 Planck, Nr. 1797, 1944.

4 Mann, Frido/Mann, Christine: *Es werde Licht. Die Einheit von Geist und Materie in der Quantenphysik,* S. Fischer Verlag, Frankfurt/Main, 2017.

5 Warnke, Ulrich: *Quantenphilosophie und Spiritualität, Wie unser Wille Gesundheit und Wohlbefinden steuert,* Goldmann Verlag, Munich, 2017.

6 Hey, Anthony: *The new quantum universe,* Cambridge University Press, Cambridge U.K., New York, 2003, p. 2.

7 Lesch, Harald: *Der Weg zur Quantenmechanik.* uni auditorium, wissen online, 2015, https://youtu.be/Z2EGx32HaNc, TS: 2:05-2:23, visited on 27 February 2019.

8 Tegmark, Max/Wheeler, John Archibald: *100 Jahre Quantentheorie,* Spektrum der Wissenschaft, 2003, p. 7.

9 Al-Khalili, Jim: *Quantum. Moderne Physik zum Staunen,* Elsevier, Spektrum Akademischer Verlag, Heidelberg, 2005, p. 33.

10 Jaeger, Lars: *Die zweite Quantenrevolution. Vom Spuk im Mikrokosmos zu neuen Supertechnologien,* Springer Verlag, Berlin, 2018, p. 111.

11 Al-Khalili, Jim: *Quantum. Moderne Physik zum Staunen,* Elsevier, Spektrum Akademischer Verlag, Heidelberg, 2005, p. 25.

12 Jaeger, Lars: *Die zweite Quantenrevolution. Vom Spuk im Mikrokosmos zu neuen Supertechnologien,* Springer Verlag, Berlin, 2018, pp. 145f.

13 Gaßner, Josef M.: *Schrödingergleichung Tunneleffekt. Aristoteles. Stringtheorie (29). Josef M. Gaßner,* Urknall, Weltall und das Leben, 2018, https://www.youtube.com/watch?v=pcOdX6y-LIg, TS: 3:20-3:25, visited on 4 June 2019.

14 Warnke, Ulrich: *Quantenphilosophie und Spiritualität, Wie unser*

Wille Gesundheit und Wohlbefinden steuert, Goldmann Verlag, Munich, 2017, p.136.

15 Ibid.

16 Jaeger, Lars: *Die zweite Quantenrevolution. Vom Spuk im Mikrokosmos zu neuen Supertechnologien,* Springer Verlag, Berlin, 2018, pp. 506-518.

17 Tegmark, Max/Wheeler, John Archibald: *100 Jahre Quantentheorie,* Spektrum der Wissenschaft, 2003, pp. 10f.

18 Kargl, Gerald: *Quantenmechanik. Doppelspalt, Verschränkung und Nichtlokalität. Doku,* Urknall, Weltall und das Leben, 2014, https://www.youtube.com/watch?v=7BV0Fs4eM0I, TS: 21:16-21:33, visited on 9 June 2019.

19 Grävemeyer, Arne: *Quantensicher verschlüsseln,* c't 17, Heise, August 2018, pp. 66-69.

20 Gaßner, Josef M.: *Quantenradierer (zeitliche Verschränkung). Von Aristoteles zur Stringtheorie (35). Josef M. Gaßner*, Urknall, Weltall und das Leben, 2018, https://youtu.be/-eHY2yX2gX4, TS: 0:15-0:22, visited on 25 November 2020.

21 Ibid., TS: 7:59.

22 Ibid., TS: 15:37.

23 Ibid.

24 Libet, Benjamin u. a.: *Subjective referral of the timing for a conscious sensory experience,* Brain 102, 1979, pp. 193-224.

25 Jahn, Robert: *An den Rändern des Realen. Über die Rolle des Bewusstseins in der physikalischen Welt,* Zweitausendeins Buch, 2000, Frankfurt/Main, 1999.

26 Radecke, Hans-Dieter/Teufel, Lorenz: *Was zu bezweifeln war. Die Lüge von der objektiven Wissenschaft,* Droemer Verlag, Munich, 2010, p. 30.

27 Nelson, Roger D.: *Princeton Engineering Anomalies Research (PEAR),* Psi Encyclopedia, London, The Society for Psychical Research, October 2017, https://psi-encyclopedia. spr.ac.uk/articles/princeton-engineering-anomalies-research-pear, visited on 24

January 2021.

28 Radecke, Hans-Dieter/Teufel, Lorenz: *Was zu bezweifeln war. Die Lüge von der objektiven Wissenschaft,* Droemer Verlag, Munich, 2010, pp. 32f.

29 Gitt, Werner: *Herkunft des Lebens aus Sicht der Information,* 2007, https://www.youtube.com/watch?v=2kuJLYiRai8, TS: 56:32-59:40, visited on 27 January 2020.

30 Weiss, Brian: *Die zahlreichen Leben der Seele. Die Chronik einer Reinkarnationstherapie,* Goldmann Verlag, Munich, 2005, p. 148. (English version: *Many lives, many masters: The true story of a prominent psychiatrist, his young patient, and the past-life therapy that changed both their lives,* Simon & Schuster, 1988.)

31 Meckelburg, Ernst: *Wir alle sind unsterblich. Der Irrtum mit dem Tod,* Langen Müller Verlag, Munich, 1997, p. 185.

32 Voggenhuber, Pascal: *Botschafter der unsichtbaren Welt. Wie der Dialog mit dem Jenseits unser Leben bereichert und heilt,* Heyne Verlag, Munich, 2012, p. 69.

33 Dreien, Bernadette von: *Christina. Band 1. Zwillinge als Licht geboren,* Govinda Verlag, Zürich, 2017, p. 149.

7 Is there evidence for a spiritual world?

1 Alexander, Eben: *Blick in die Ewigkeit, Die faszinierende Nahtoderfahrung eines Neurochirurgen,* Heyne Verlag, Munich, 2016, p. 176. (English version: *Proof of heaven: A neurosurgeon's journey into the afterlife,* Simon & Schuster, 2012.)

2 Döring, Nicola/Bortz, Jürgen: *Forschungsmethoden und Evaluation in den Sozial- und Humanwissenschaften,* Springer Verlag, Berlin, 2016, pp. 4-6.

3 Ibid., p. 13.

4 Elsaesser, Evelyn/Roe, Chris A./Cooper, Callum E.: *Investigation of the phenomenology and impact of spontaneous and direct After-Death Communications.ADCs. Research Findings,* Geneva, Salvia,

2020, https://www.evelyn-elsaesser.com/wp-content/uploads/2020/02/Booklet_Web_English_Research.pdf, visited on 13 April 2020.

5 Ibid., p. 1.

6 Moody, Raymond: *Leben nach dem Tod. Die Erforschung einer unerklärlichen Erfahrung,* Rowohlt Taschenbuch Verlag, Reinbek bei Hamburg, 2001. (English version: *Life after life*, HarperOne, 2015.)

7 Elsaesser, Evelyn: *Was wir aus Nahtoderfahrungen für das Leben gewinnen,* Crotona Verlag, Amerang, 2020.

8 Lommel, Pim van: *Endloses Bewusstsein, Neue medizinische Fakten zur Nahtoderfahrung,* MensSana Verlag, Munich, 2013. (English version: *Consciousness beyond life: The science of the near-death experience,* HarperCollins, 2011.)

9 Kübler-Ross, Elisabeth: *Über den Tod und das Leben danach,* Silberschnur Verlag, Güllesheim, 2013. (English version: *On Life after Death,* Celestial Arts, 2004.)

10 Ibid., p. 14.

11 Weiss, Brian: *Seelenwege. Reinkarnation und zukünftige Lebenswege,* Ullstein Buchverlag, Berlin, 2018, p. 21-22. (English version: *Same soul, many bodies: Discover the healing power of future lives through progression therapy,* Free Press, 2005.)

12 Alexander, Eben: *Blick in die Ewigkeit, Die faszinierende Nahtoderfahrung eines Neurochirurgen,* Heyne Verlag, Munich, 2016, pp. 252f. (English version: *Proof of heaven: A neurosurgeon's journey into the afterlife*, Simon & Schuster, 2012.)

13 Tour, James: *How Did Life Come into Being?*, Socrates in the city, January 2023, https://youtu.be/9qxoH7u3FXw, TS: 1:12:53-1:13:01 and 1:24:16–1:24:39, visited on 27 January 2023.

14 Elsaesser, Evelyn/Roe, Chris A./Cooper, Callum E.: *Investigation of the phenomenology and impact of spontaneous and direct After-Death Communications.ADCs. Research Findings,* Geneva, Salvia,

2020, pp. 17-20, https://www.evelyn-elsaesser.com/wp-content/uploads/2020/02/Booklet_Web_English_Research.pdf, visited on 13 April 2020.

15 Ford, Arthur: *Bericht vom Leben nach dem Tode,* cover text, Scherz Verlag, Bern, 1971. (English version: *The Life Beyond Death,* G. P. Putnam's Sons, 1971.)

16 Lodge, Oliver J.: *Raymond or Life and Death. With Examples of the Evidence for Survival of Memory and Affection After Death,* Classic Reprint, Forgotten Books, London, 2012.

17 Thomas, John F., McDougall, William: *Beyond Normal Cognition: An Evaluative and Methodological Study of the Mental Content of Certain Trance Phenomena,* Literary Licensing, LLC, 27 October 2013.

18 Smith, Martin: *World authors. 1900-1950,* H.W. Wilson, New York, 1996, p. 1876.

19 Ford, Arthur: *Bericht vom Leben nach dem Tode,* Scherz Verlag, Bern, 1971, pp. 41f. (English version: *The Life Beyond Death,* G. P. Putnam's Sons, 1971.)

20 Bastos, Marco Aurélio Vinhosa Jr. u. a.: *Mediumship. Review of quantitatives studies published in the 21st century,* Archives of Clinical Psychiatry, São Paulo, October 2015, pp. 129-138.

21 O'Keeffe, Ciarán/Wiseman, Richard: *Testing alleged mediumship. Methods and results,* British Journal of Psychology 96, Nr. 2, 2005, pp. 165-179.

22 Beischel, Julie/Schwartz, Gary: *Anomalous Information Reception by Research Mediums Demonstrated Using a Novel Triple-Blind Protocol,* Explore.,New York, 3 January 2007, pp. 23-7.

23 Beischel, Julie u.a.: *Anomalous Information Reception by Research Mediums Under Blinded Conditions II. Replication and Extension,* Explore, The Journal of Science and Healing, 11 January 2015.

24 Jensen, Christian Gaden/Cardeña, Etzel: *A controlled long-distance test of a professional medium,* European Journal of Parapsychology 24, Nr. 1, 2009, pp. 53-67.

25 Kelly, Emily/Arcangel, Dianne: *An Investigation of Mediums Who Claim to Give Information About Deceased Persons,* The Journal of nervous and mental disease 199, January 2011, pp. 11-7.

26 Beischel, Julie: *Beyond Reasonable: Scientific Evidence for Survival,* https://www.bigelowinstitute.org/wp-content/uploads/2022/10/beischel-scientific-evidence-survival.pdf, visited on 21 April 2022, p. 32.

27 Tressoldi, Patrizio/Liberale, Laura/Sinesio, Fernando: *Is there someone in the hereafter? Mediumship accuracy of 100 readings obtained with a triple level of blinding protocol,* Omega-Journal of Death and Dying, 2022, http://www.patriziotressoldi.it/cmssimpled/uploads/images/IsThereSomeoneInTheHereafter_22.pdf, visited on 12 April 2023.

28 Smith, Gordon: *Contribution at the Online-Congress Flow Summit 2020,* Video, 2020, https://www.flowsummit.net/flow-summit-2020-tag-2/, TS: 19:05-23:10, visited on 2 March 2020.

29 Öz, Mehmet Cengiz/Amen, Daniel/Caputo, Theresa: *Long Island Medium. Inside a Psychic's Brain,* 2013, https://www.doctoroz.com/episode/long-island-medium-inside-psychics-brain/particle-5 [URL inactive], TS: 2:20, visited on 18 March 2021.

30 Tyler, Henry: *Hollywood Medium with Tyler Henry,* Season 4, Episode 9, 2019.

31 Ford, Arthur: *Bericht vom Leben nach dem Tode,* Scherz Verlag, Bern, 1971, pp. 217f. (English version: *The Life Beyond Death,* G. P. Putnam's Sons, 1971.)

32 Ahmann, Stefan: *Eine Neue Aufklärung. Langfassung. Antworten auf die wichtigen Fragen,* tredition Verlag, Hamburg, 2019, p. 14.

33 Maier, Petra: *Warum es immer noch so wenige Frauen im MINT-Bereich gibt,* Spiegel.de, August 2019, https://www.spiegel.de/karriere/mint-faecher-warum-frauen-so-oft-allein-unter-maennern-bleiben-a-1281877.html, visited on 19 April 2020.

34 Rode, Bettina Suvi: *Jenseitskontakt. Was Sie beachten sollten, wenn*

Sie ein Medium aussuchen, July 2020, https://youtu.be/gOH1l-6hS1M, TS: 7:58-8:35, visited on 25 August 2020.

35 Oelmann, Doreen: *Das Fünf-Phasen-Modell zum Sterbeprozess nach Kübler-Ross,* Grin Verlag, Munich, 2008, pp. 7-9.

36 Nikolay, Joachim: *Humor in Nahtoderfahrungen. Humor im Jenseits,* October 2019, https://youtu.be/y_vL8_jk9FY, visited on 6 February 2021.

Picture credits

P. 107: (Figure 4-1) 'Chirality with hands' (22.10.2011), creator: Unknown on Wikimedia Commons under Public Domain Licence.

P. 130: (Figure 4-2) 'Darwin's finches by Gould' (before 1882), creator: John Gould on Wikimedia Commons under Public Domain Licence.

P. 138: (Figure 4-3) 'Biological classification S Pengo' (24.03.2007), creator: Pengo on Wikimedia Commons under Public Domain Licence, edited by Oliver Lazar.

P. 144: (Figure 4-4) Oliver Lazar (2020).

P. 153: (Figure 4-5) 'Dunning-Kruger-Effect' (20.01.2020), Labels edited by Oliver Lazar, creator: Sciencia58 on Wikimedia Commons under Public Domain Licence.

P. 158: (Figure 4-6) 'Indohyus BW' (23.12.2007), creator: Nobu Tamura on Wikimedia Commons under Creative Commons Attribution 3.0 Unported Licence: https://creativecommons.org/licenses/by/3.0.

P. 158: (Figure 4-7) 'Pakicetus BW' (29.11.2007), creator: Nobu Tamura on Wikimedia Commons under Creative Commons Attribution 3.0 Unported Licence: https://creativecommons.org/licenses/by/3.0.

P. 159: (Figure 4-8) 'Ambulocetus BW' (29.10.2007), creator: Nobu Tamura on Wikimedia Commons under Creative Commons Attribution 3.0 Unported Licence: https://creativecommons.org/licenses/by/3.0.

P. 159: (Figure 4-9) 'Basilosaurus BW' (cropped and removed the second basilosaurus, 26.01.2008) and 'Dorudon cropped' (19.02.2012), creator: Nobu Tamura on Wikimedia Commons under Creative Commons Attribution 3.0 Unported Licence: https://creativecommons.org/licenses/by/3.0.

P. 160: (Figure 4-10) 'Blue whale size' (removed the diver, 29.07.2013), creator: Kurzon on Wikimedia Commons under Creative Commons Attribution 3.0 Unported Licence: https://creativecommons.org/licenses/by/3.0.

P. 161: (Figure 4-11) Compiled and edited by Oliver Lazar; 'Blue whale size' (29.07.2013), creator: Kurzon; 'Sperm whale size' (19.05.2007), creator: Kurzon; 'Dorudon cropped' (19.02.2012), creator: Nobu Tamura; 'Ambulocetus BW' (29.10.2007), creator: Nobu Tamura; 'Pakicetus BW' (29.11.2007), creator: Nobu Tamura; 'Indohyus BW' (23.12.2007), creator: Nobu Tamura; Wikimedia Commons under Creative Commons Attribution 3.0 Unported Licence: https://creativecommons.org/licenses/by/3.0.

P. 162: (Figure 4-12) Grundzüge der vergleichenden Anatomie. 2. umgearb. Auflage. Mit 319 Holzschnitten. Leipzig, Verl. von Wilhelm Engelmann, 1870. 892 pp. fig. 223. p. 692, creator: Carl Gegenbaur, Wikimedia Commons under Public Domain Licence.

P. 164: (Figure 4-13) 'Whale skeleton', from Meyers Konversionlexikon (1888), Wikimedia Commons under Public Domain Licence.

P. 185: (Figure 4-14) 'Flagellum base diagram' (17.08.2011), creator: Mariana Ruiz Villareal on Wikimedia Commons, Public Domain.

P. 203: (Figure 4-15) 'Egyptian hieroglyphs Detail' (01.11.2014), section of the image, creator: Gtoffoletto on Wikimedia Commons under Creative Commons Attribution-Share Alike 4.0 International Licence: https://creativecommons.org/licenses/by-sa/4.0/deed.en.

P. 205: (Figure 4-16) 'Die fünf Ebenen der Universellen Information' (2016), creator: Werner Gitt, 'Information - Der Schlüssel zum Leben', Christliche Literaturverbreitung, Bielefeld, p. 53.

P. 209: (Figure 4-17) Graphic revised by Oliver Lazar following 'Die fünf Ebenen der Universellen Information' (2016), creator: Werner Gitt, 'Information - Der Schlüssel zum Leben', Christliche Literaturverbreitung, Bielefeld, p. 53.

P. 216: (Figure 4-18) Oliver Lazar (2020).

P. 218: (Figure 4-19) 'Fibonacci spiral' (16.07.2015), creator: Anna Benczur on Wikimedia Commons under Creative Commons Attribution-Share Alike 4.0 International Licence: https://creativecommons.org/licenses/by-sa/4.0/deed.en.

P. 218: (Figure 4-20) 'Fibonacci spiral' (03.05.2017), creator: Jahobr on Wikimedia Commons under Creative Commons CC0 1.0 Universal Public Domain Dedication.

P. 219: (Figure 4-21) 'NautilusCutawayLogarithmicSpiral' (05.05.2004), creator: Chris_73 on Wikimedia Commons under Creative Commons Attribution 3.0 Unported Licence: https://creativecommons.org/licenses/by/3.0 und 'Spiral Galaxy NGC 3147' (10/2017-03/2018), creator: NASA on Wikimedia Commons - Public Domain.

P. 257: (Figure 6-1) Oliver Lazar (2023).

P. 257: (Figure 6-2) 'white-dust-spray-isolated-on-transparent-background-realistic-set-of-smoke-or-powder-with-particles-splash-from-aerosol-stream-of-spraying-cosmetic-fragrance-or-deodorant', Urheber: upklyak on Freepik under

Freepik-Licence and Oliver Lazar (2023).

P. 258: (Figure 6-3) Oliver Lazar (2023).

P. 259: (Figure 6-4) Oliver Lazar (2023).

P. 261: (Figure 6-5) Oliver Lazar (2023).

P. 262: (Figure 6-6) Oliver Lazar (2023).

P. 265: (Figure 6-7) Oliver Lazar (2023).

P. 267: (Figure 6-8) Oliver Lazar (2023) following Josef M. Gaßner, Quantenradierer (zeitliche Verschränkung) - von Aristoteles zur Stringtheorie (35) — Josef M. Gaßner, Urknall, Weltall und das Leben, 2018, https://youtu.be/-eHY2yX2gX4, TS: 7:59, visited on 25 November 2020.

P. 268: (Figure 6-9) Oliver Lazar (2023) in Anlehnung Josef M. Gaßner, Quantenradierer (zeitliche Verschränkung) - von Aristoteles zur Stringtheorie (35) — Josef M. Gaßner, Urknall, Weltall und das Leben, 2018, https://youtu.be/-eHY2yX2gX4, TS: 15:37, visited on 25 November 2020.

P. 269: (Figure 6-10) 'The REG experiment at PEAR' (31.10.2017), creator: Roger D. Nelson, Princeton Engineering Anomalies Research (PEAR), Psi Encyclopedia, London, The Society for Psychical Research, https://psi-encyclopedia.spr.ac.uk/articles/princeton-engineering-anomalies-research-pear, visited on 24 January 2021.

P. 305: (Figure 7-1) Oliver Lazar (2023).

P. 306: (Figure 7-2) Oliver Lazar (2023).

P. 308: (Figure 7-3) Oliver Lazar (2023).

P. 309: (Figure 7-4) Oliver Lazar (2023).

P. 316: (Figure 7-5) Oliver Lazar (2023).

P. 317: (Figure 7-6) Oliver Lazar (2023).

P. 318: (Figure 7-7) Oliver Lazar (2023).

P. 319: (Figure 7-8) Oliver Lazar (2023).

P. 320: (Figure 7-9) Oliver Lazar (2023).

P. 326: (Figure 7-10) Oliver Lazar (2023).

P. 327: (Figure 7-11) Oliver Lazar (2023).

P. 330: (Figure 7-12) Oliver Lazar (2023).
P. 331: (Figure 7-13) Oliver Lazar (2023).
P. 335: (Figure 7-14) Oliver Lazar (2023).

Printed in Dunstable, United Kingdom

68592916R00221